Understanding Art

Custom Edition for Troy University

Lois Fichner-Rathus

CENGAGE
Learning™

Australia • Brazil • Japan • Korea • Mexico • Singapore • Spain • United Kingdom • United States

Understanding Art: Custom Edition for Troy University

Lois Fichner-Rathus

Executive Editors:
Michele Baird
Maureen Staudt
Michael Stranz

Project Development Manager:
Linda deStefano

Senior Marketing Coordinators:
Sara Mercurio
Lindsay Shapiro

Production/Manufacturing Manager:
Donna M. Brown

PreMedia Services Supervisor:
Rebecca A. Walker

Rights & Permissions Specialist:
Kalina Hintz

Cover Image:
Getty Images*

© 2008, 2007 Cengage Learning

For product information and technology assistance, contact us at
Cengage Learning Customer & Sales Support, 1-800-354-9706

For permission to use material from this text or product,
submit all requests online at **cengage.com/permissions**
Further permissions questions can be emailed to
permissionrequest@cengage.com

ISBN-13: 978-0-495-45776-3

ISBN-10: 0-495-45776-0

Cengage Learning
5191 Natorp Boulevard
Mason, Ohio 45040
USA

Cengage Learning is a leading provider of customized learning solutions with office locations around the globe, including Singapore, the United Kingdom, Australia, Mexico, Brazil, and Japan. Locate your local office at:
international.cengage.com/region

Cengage Learning products are represented in Canada by Nelson Education, Ltd.

For your lifelong learning solutions, visit **custom.cengage.com**

Visit our corporate website at **cengage.com**

Printed in the United States of America

UNDERSTANDING THE OBJECTS, THE IMAGES, THE SPACES and all else that can be perceived by human senses is a daunting challenge. However, to closely observe and experience these things made by humans throughout the ages is the pathway to understanding art—understanding humanity.

Troy University recognizes the intrinsic value that visual art has on not only interpreting antiquity, but for designing and sustaining the future. Whether you are a scientist, a writer, a mathematician, an entrepreneur or other, you cannot escape the necessity of critical thinking and imagination, which are at the core of art and humanity. Whatever your background; whatever your future; *Understanding Art* will guide you through a well-paved discovery of visual passion for telling the human narrative. This narrative will enhance your perspective of life no matter what your profession or discipline is.

Jerry R. Johnson, Chairman
TROY Department of Art and Design

TROY
UNIVERSITY

DEPARTMENT OF ART AND DESIGN
WWW.TROY.EDU
HTTP://TROY.TROY.EDU/ARTDESIGN
(334) 670-3391

Bronze sculpture by Larry Strickland. This Trojan Warrior stands tall on the quadrangle of the TROY campus in Troy, Alabama.

ABOUT THE COVER

The graphical premise of the cover montage is the Golden Rectangle. The Golden Rectangle has been known since antiquity as one having a pleasing shape, and is frequently found in art and architecture as a rectangular shape that seems 'right' to the eye. Integrated into the cover design by TROY Professor—Greg Skaggs, are works of art from various art instructors at TROY.

A. Larry Percy, ceramics, *Holy Ghost Canyon Series*

B. Gayle Nelson, engraving/hand-coloured, *Bird Boat*

C. Greg Skaggs, mixed-media, *Shooting Gallery*

D. Pamela Allen, encaustic, *Target*

E. Russell Everett, soapstone/empress wood, *Canebreak*

F. Sara Dismukes, polymer clay, *untitled*

THESE SAMPLE WORKS were created by just a few of the many active artists teaching for TROY worldwide.

Known for piney woods, boiled peanuts, and more importantly—the forefront of the historic civil rights movement... south Alabama offers a public university with artistic and design ambitions that literally touch the world.

Nestled in the piney wood setting of lower Alabama (known as L.A. around these parts) lies a jewel that literally shines world-wide—TROY University. TROY has been serving a broad range of students on four different campuses in Alabama and on more than 60 campuses in 17 states and also in 11 nations.

Sure, TROY main campus offers all the amenities that you would expect from a traditional college experience such as social organizations, Division I athletics, strong fine arts programs in art, music and theatre plus many opportunities for students to assume campus leadership roles. Students from 60 nations study at TROY. It is fair to say that "the world is coming to TROY" and due to the

multi-national presence of TROY's academic programs and its 110,000 graduates—it is safe to say that "TROY is going to the world." Although the main campus is attended by only 6000 full-time students, TROY boasts a full-time enrollment of 30,000 students through its multicampus and distance learning programs both undergraduate and graduate.

TROY and its Department of Art and Design have made an audacious commitment to international education through inter-cultural collaboration and transdisciplinary instruction. Additionally, emphasis is placed on the instructional experience to the benefit of the individual learner. One indicator of this is blatantly revealed in the exponentially growing art and design program at TROY as it has seen a 500% increase in majors in just five short years.

The TROY Department of Art and Design is constantly incubating programs of study for a new breed of artist/ designer. In this age of hybrid disciplines, virtual realms, intercultural communications and new technologies, it has become increasingly imperative that higher education birth innovative and relevant methods, experiences and strategies for preparing the artists, designers, and educators of tomorrow. Currently, there are 8 full-time and 4 part-time professors that service the instructional needs of the nearly 200 majors in the art and design programs on site. Approximately 90% of these instructors hold terminal degrees (MFA or Ph.D.) in their area of instruction. Many are well known nationally for their professional expertise in not only education but in their respective medium or discipline.

PHILOSOPHY

There is an underlying philosophy at TROY Art and Design. Transdisciplinary approaches and hybrid media are the rule rather than the exception. From foundational courses to Senior Thesis, students are required to explore hybrid media as well as collaborative problem-solving. Additionally, students are inundated with technology early on in their academic careers. The results have been phenomenal as students take risks and experience new genres and processes. It would not be atypical of TROY students to blend photography with sculpture or to synthesize painting with music or to merge digital design with ecology. By design, traditional boundaries and margins are not greatly respected in the learning culture at TROY Art and Design. It is in the converging of these disciplines, media and practices that new ideas—new solutions begin to emerge.

In the traditional sense, TROY Art and Design offers liberal arts and professional baccalaureate degrees in various studio areas (2D, 3D, Digital and Photo). TROY also offers special degrees in art education and graphic design (known as <<dti>> which stands for Design, Technology and Industry). <<dti>> is certainly at the helm of the growth phenomenon as it is positioning itself as an economic factor through its partnerships with businesses and industries in the region through the Center for Design, Technology and Industry. Since <<dti>>'s formal inception in 2002, graphic design students have won nearly 100 design, advertising and photography awards. Some of these awards came from noted professional competitions typically exclusive of student entries. TROY students have had work selected to compete in the highly juried American Advertising Federation's National Student ADDY® Awards.

PLACEMENT

TROY provides a highly active job placement supplement for its students and alumni. Through the department's web site, students can quickly find internship and employment opportunities as well as a master list of job links for quick access. Additionally, students can find helpful hints for writing effective letters of application and resumes, for building strong portfolios, and for confidently handling the job interview—all of this is one click away at http://troy.troy.edu/artdesign/jobportal. A quick glance at the alumni postings on the department's main page will corroborate the effectiveness of this process and the sincerity of the department's resolve to place its graduates into the marketplace of ideas and business.

VISITING ARTISTS/LECTURERS

TROY sponsors a visiting lecturer and artist series each year. Due to TROY Art and Design's transdisciplinary approach to learning, it is common for guests to be brought in for many reasons other than fine art work. Entrepreneurs, marketing experts, architects, propagandists, scientists, as well as fine artists and designers are brought in to engage with TROY students. Segmented learning has been pervasive for far too long in the view of this department. Making connections throughout the whole of learning is the best approach to education in these times.

TROY TO THE WORLD

Internationalism is more than a mere buzz word within the Department of Art and Design. In fact, due to TROY's long-standing leadership role of providing educational opportunities for men and women of the U.S. armed forces, TROY is now taking that successful model to the rest of the world through its multicampus sites and its plethora of industrial and academic partners in many nations. TROY Art and Design is actively engaged in international initiatives from South America to as far away as to the People's Republic of China. TROY has partnered with several Chinese universities to provide cooperative education for Chinese students. TROY students regularly participate in a TROY sponsored African Photo Safari in Kenya, Africa. TROY participated in the World's Largest International Online Student Design Project called Creative Waves© where students and faculty from 22 countries and 6 continents studied and produced work—collaboratively and online—in a six week project. TROY faculty and students have partnered with a university in Sweden to establish an exciting degree program for those interested in educational and entertainment software design—known as multimedia design. New relationships are now being fostered with our neighbors in Central and South America through faculty and student exchanges.

Ah yes, locally though, it is still quaint ol' Alabama. However, among the fragrances of sweet Magnolia blossoms and pecan pie there is a growing mix of curry and sushi. iPods® around here are now playing more than bluegrass, rap and southern rock. Ear buds are beginning to pump with sounds of world music and hand-held devices are streaming with an eclectic mix of imagery from virtually every corner of the earth.

ART AND DESIGN PROGRAMS AT TROY

TROY offers an array of relevant and timely **programs of study in the disciplines** of art and design. Below is a list of those **programs available as of August 2007:**

Bachelor of Science:
- 2D Studio Art
- 3D Studio Art
- Photo Studio Art
- <<dti>> (graphic design)*

Bachelor of Fine Arts (professional degree)
- 2D Studio Art
- 3D Studio Art
- Photo Studio Art
- Digital Studio Art

Bachelor of Science in Education:
- Art Education (P-12)

Master of Education:
- Art Specialization

*The <<dti>> degree (Design, Technology and Industry) is an innovative graphic design program unique to TROY. <<dti>> students are **required to hybridize their design studies with** another discipline such as marketing, mass communications, intercultural communications, multimedia design**, music industry, technical theatre, information systems, advertising, foreign languages, and many more. Programs of study can be customized to address the students' career interests while still meeting all **accreditation standards.**

The multimedia design program is offered through Halmstad University in Sweden as a partnership between TROY and Halmstad. A one-semester residency in Halmstad is required. For more information about this program or others, **contact TROY Art and Design at 334-670-3391 or email Jerry Johnson at jjohnson@troy.edu.

CONTENTS

PREFACE

Everyone wants to understand art. Why not try to understand the song of a bird?
Why does one love the night, flowers, everything around one without trying
to understand them? But in the case of a painting, people have to understand.

—Pablo Picasso

There is a note of frustration in Picasso's statement, reflecting perhaps the burden of having to explain his paintings to viewers who were trying desperately to understand them. Perhaps he was concerned that some of the "indescribable" in art, that which mesmerizes, enchants, frightens, and delights, would be, quite literally, lost in translation. Maybe he was guarding against affixing meaning to his work that he as the artist never intended. Picasso seems to suggest, in this quote, that mystery enhances experience and that too much knowledge will compromise the authenticity of the relationship between art and the viewer. Do you think Picasso was right?

Here we are, together, embarking on the study of art and art history between the covers of a book called *Understanding Art*. Maybe we can declare Picasso's view half right, and it can serve as our cue for how to confront what we are about to see. A textbook on art is not like a textbook in other academic disciplines. Yes, there is a special vocabulary of art. Yes, this vocabulary is woven into a language that, once learned, enables us to better verbalize the visual. But the most important aspect of an art book is its images, because a student's journey toward understanding art ought to always begin with looking.

Think of this art appreciation textbook as your "*i*-book"—it begins with looking at *i*mages. Having said that, *learning to look* is equally important for art appreciation, and that's where some other "*i*-words" play an important role: *i*nformation, *i*nsight, and *i*nterpretation. We gather information about how a work of art is conceived and constructed using visual elements, design principles, composition, content, style, symbolism. We explore the motives of artists and the historical, social, political, even personal contexts in which a work of art came into existence. These investigations will lend insight into the complex factors contributing to the creation of works of art. And as we gather confidence in our knowledge and insights, we will turn more comfortably to the dimension of interpretation, your dimension. It is here where the "I" really counts, for we all bring the weight of our own experience to our interpretations, our unique perceptions to our likes or dislikes of a work of art.

Picasso said, in the same interview, "People who try to explain pictures are usually barking up the wrong tree." The words *explain* and *understand,* though, have very different meanings. One can argue that only artists can *explain* their work, can make intelligible something that is not known or not understood. But *understanding* is defined as full awareness or knowledge that is arrived at through an intellectual or emotional process—including the ability to extract meaning or to interpret. The ability to *appreciate,* or to perceive the value or worth of something from a discriminating perspective, then, is the consummate reward of understanding.

The Approach of *Understanding Art*

The eighth edition of *Understanding Art,* like earlier editions, remains a textbook that is intended to work both for students and professors. *Understanding Art* continues to serve as a tool to help organize and enlighten this demanding, often whirlwindlike course. My goal has been to write a book that would do it all: edify and inform students and, at the same time, keep them engaged, animated, and inspired while meeting the desire of instructors for comprehensive exposition. All in all, *Understanding Art* contains a fully balanced approach to appreciating art. The understanding and appreciation of art are enhanced by familiarity with three areas of art: the language of art (visual elements, principles of design, and style), the nature of the media used in art, and the history of art.

Features

The eighth edition of *Understanding Art* contains unique features that stimulate student interest, emphasize key points in art fundamentals and art history, highlight contemporary events in art, and reflect the ways in which professors teach.

Compare and Contrast™ These features show two or more works of art side by side and phrase questions that help students focus on stylistic and technical similarities and differ-

ences. They parallel the time-honored pedagogical technique of presenting slides in class for comparison and contrast. For example, "Compare and Contrast Wood's *American Gothic* with Rosenthal's *He Said . . . She Said*" in Chapter 4 shows how artists may use different styles to illustrate themes about similar subjects.

Among the additions to the eighth edition, we compare and contrast the *Piano Lesson* by Henri Matisse with that of Romare Bearden (Chapter 1) and the *Susannah and the Elders* of Tintoretto with that of Gentileschi (Chapter 16). The feature on the *Piano Lesson*(s) shows how artists use various methods of composition to impose order on the elements in a work of art. Tintoretto and Gentileschi tell more or less the same biblical story about Susannah, but we see that in Tintoretto's version, Susannah could be viewed as something of a temptress, whereas Artemisia Gentileschi portrays Susannah as a victim of prying eyes and lies.

Exercises on both the CD-ROM and ThomsonNOW include interactive exercises directly linked to all the Compare and Contrast features.

A Closer Look These features offer insights into artists' personalities and delve into various topics in greater depth. In chapter 5, "Life, Death, and Dwelling in the Deep South" highlights an African American artist's portrayal of the organic relationship between a woman and her home in South Carolina. "Paper Dolls for a Post-Columbian World," also in Chapter 5, shows how a Native American artist uses biting humor to display some of the "gifts" of European Americans to Native Americans. In Chapter 18, "Why Did van Gogh Cut Off His Ear?" offers a number of explanations, including psychodynamic hypotheses, for why the Postimpressionist mutilated himself.

Among the new A Closer Look features in the eighth edition we find "Christo and Jeanne-Claude: *The Gates, Central Park, New York City, 1979–2005*" (Chapter 9) and "King Tut: The Face That Launched a Thousand High-Res Images" (Chapter 12). These features, like several others, highlight important events in art. In the case of *The Gates,* we have a monumental installation that transformed the winter heart of the city of New York. With the feature on King Tut, we describe how contemporary scanning techniques have helped us form a picture of the face of a ruler who lived some 3,300 years ago.

A Closer Look is also expanded upon further through the CD-ROM and ThomsonNOW.

ArtTour™ The eighth edition includes eight ArtTours on the cities of New York, Chicago, Washington D.C., Jerusalem, Rome, Dallas/Fort Worth, London, and Paris. Each ArtTour is rich in photographs and works of art. The

ArtTours are no mere lists of works and sites and museums in these cities. Instead, the tours literally walk students through the cities, providing them with routes they can take to benefit from the cultural riches that are available.

The new ArtTours on Chicago and Dallas/Fort Worth, in the north-central and south-central parts of the United States, will help many students appreciate the art and architecture that are situated close to home.

The companion CD-ROM and ThomsonNOW expand on the ArtTours with helpful "travel-guide" information, such as additional photos, maps, restaurant guides, and links to useful web pages. The tours are meant to encourage students to travel as well as to guide them once they have reached their destinations.

Quotations Quotations at the top of pages by artists, critics, and others allow students to "get into the minds" of artists and others in the art world. For example, Chapter 20, "Contemporary Art," includes quotations by Joseph Kosuth, Adolph Gottlieb, Lee Krasner, Willem de Kooning, Agnes Martin, Henry Moore, Jean Tinguely, Daniel Libeskind, http://www.designboom.com/portrait/beecroft.html (on the performance art of Vanessa Beecroft), Ken Feingold, Sarah Lucas, William Pope.L, and Kara Walker.

Glossary Key terms are boldface in the text and defined in a glossary at the end of the textbook. A "Talking Glossary" also appears on the companion website.

The Contents of the Eighth Edition of *Understanding Art*

The eighth edition of *Understanding Art* contains many new images ranging from ancient times to the present day, such as new views of the Egyptian pharaoh Tutankhamen, the grand chambers and halls of the Vatican captured by the news media when Pope Benedict XVI was elected, and new buildings by Santiago Calatrava and David Childs/Daniel Liebeskind under development for "Ground Zero" in Manhattan.

The book is organized into the following parts:

I. Introduction The first chapter of the text, "What Is Art?" helps the student arrive at a definition of art by discussing the things that art does, from enhancing our environment to protesting injustice and raising social consciousness.

II. The Language of Art Chapters 2–4 provide comprehensive discussion of the visual elements of art, principles of design, and style, form, and content. The language of art is then applied throughout the remainder of the text in discussions of media and surveys of art through the ages and throughout the world.

III. Two-Dimensional Media Chapters 5–8—on drawing, painting, printmaking, and imaging—explain how artists combine the visual elements of art to create two-dimensional compositions. The media discussed are as traditional as drawing a pencil across a sheet of paper and as innovative as spray painting color fields and clicking a mouse to access a menu of electronic techniques and design elements.

IV. Three-Dimensional Media Chapters 9–11 discuss the opportunities and issues provided by three-dimensional art forms, including sculpture, architecture, and craft and design.

V. Art through the Ages Chapters 12–17 contain a solid core of art history on the development of art from ancient times to the dawn of the modern era. Chapter 17, "Art beyond the West," introduces students to art forms beyond the Western tradition, for example, the art of Africa, the South Pacific, and the Americas; the Islamic art of the Near, Middle, and Far East; Indian art; and the art of China and Japan. The chapter offers a broadening experience, as students learn that much of this art cannot be appreciated by means of the same concepts and standards that are applied to Western Art.

VI. Art in Modern and Postmodern Times Chapters 18–20 examine the great changes that have occurred in the world of art since the late eighteenth century. These chapters attempt to answer the question, "Just what is modern about modern art?" Whereas some artists have rejected the flatness of the canvas and moved art into innumerable new directions, some have maintained traditional paths. Controversy and conflict are part of the modern history of art. But movements such as Postmodern art and Deconstructivist architecture also make it possible to speak of the "modern world and beyond." Although nobody can say exactly where art is going, these chapters discuss the various movements and works that appear to be most vital at the current moment.

Student Resources

ArtExperience 2.0 **CD-ROM** This book-specific CD-ROM, which may be packaged with every new copy of the book, gives students interactive, hands-on experience and access to a host of technology resources in six modules to help them understand art (see page viii for a chapter-by-chapter list).

Foundations. Divided into three subtopics—Visual Elements, Principles of Design, and Style, Form, and Content—this section includes interactive exercises using line art and fine art images to demonstrate the points of the text.

In the Studio. This section features video footage of actual studio art classes so that students can get a peek at the art-making process. Each clip includes interviews of both students and instructors. Classes include drawing, painting, lithography, wheelworking, sculpture-plastercasting, architecture, and glassblowing.

Compare and Contrast. This section expands on the text features with quizzes that allow students to check their understanding.

Flashcards. This section allows students to make flashcards to create study sets using the images from within the text. Students can hide or show the caption information for review purposes. Most of the images in the text are available as digital flashcards.

A Closer Look. Expanding on A Closer Look features in the book, this section offers students web links to further resources on the topic discussed.

ArtTours. Additional photos, maps, restaurant guides, and links to helpful web pages are supplied for further touring.

ThomsonNOW for Fichner-Rathus's *Understanding Art,* Eighth Edition ThomsonNOW is a web-based study system that saves time for students and instructors by providing a complete package of diagnostic quizzes (pretests and posttests, a personalized study plan, the contents of the CD-ROM, and a grade book for instructors). Thomson-NOW utilizes an intelligent and pedagogically accurate system to help students formulate a personalized study plan based on their current understanding of course material. Professors can track their students' progress via a grade book, which is compatible with WebCT and Blackboard course management systems.

On the ThomsonNOW product, students will also find the following features: ArtTours to supplement the ArtTours from the text; brief "Field Trips," which include photos of Monet's garden at Giverny, the Piazza della Signoria in Florence, and Olmsted's Central Park in New York City; Art Projects; and Study Notes offering brief outlines of the central concepts.

Companion Website Students and professors using *Understanding Art* will also benefit from the book's dynamic interactive website. The website will help students grasp the material of the text and also link them to the world of art. The following features are found on the website: tutorial quizzing; InfoTrac® College Edition exercises; Internet activities; artist flashcards and glossary flashcards with pronunciations; and more (see page viii for a chapter-by-chapter list).

Study Guide The *Study Guide* by Ruth Pettigrew (Colorado State University) helps students learn the terms, works of art, and concepts in each chapter. The assignments and projects foster an understanding of art in different media, time periods, and styles. Sections of the *Study Guide* include "Understanding Concepts," "Making Connections," "Enhancing Your Observational Powers," and "Preparing for Tests."

Thinking and Writing about Art *Thinking and Writing about Art,* written by Lois Fichner-Rathus, enhances students' critical thinking and interpretive skills.

SlideGuide with Student Test Packet The *SlideGuide with Student Test Packet* helps students learn and study more effectively inside and outside the classroom. The *SlideGuide* allows students to take notes alongside representations of the art images shown in class, and the *Student Test Packet* offers a practice test with complete answers for each chapter of the book.

InfoTrac College Edition InfoTrac College Edition may be packaged for free with every new copy of this book. Upon instructors' request, students receive a four-month subscription to this extensive online library, opening the door to the full text (not just abstracts) of countless articles from thousands of publications, going back more than 20 years.

Instructor Resources

Multimedia Manager with Instructor's Resources and JoinIn™ on Turning Point® This CD-ROM set contains everything instructors need to prepare for class, present innovative lectures, and create quizzes and tests. The Multimedia Manager CD-ROM set includes the following resources for instructors:

High-quality digital images show the maps, diagrams, and fine art images presented in the text.

Microsoft® PowerPoint® lecture outlines include maps and images and can be used as they are or adapted by instructors.

The *Instructor's Manual* features summaries and methods for approaching each chapter.

The *Test Bank* includes multiple-choice, matching, short answer, and essay questions formatted for use with ExamView® Computerized Testing. ExamView offers a Quick Test Wizard and an Online Test Wizard—step-by-step guides through the process of creating tests. The software's unique capability shows instructors the test on-screen exactly as it will print or display online. Tests can include up to 250 questions with as many as 12 question types. ExamView's complete word-processing capabilities allow entry of an unlimited number of new questions and editing of existing questions.

Image-specific questions for use with JoinIn on Turning Point software enable professors to pose questions in their lectures that students can respond to with personal response systems, or "clickers." Questions specifically created for use with this software are provided alongside images from *Understanding Art* on Microsoft PowerPoint slides.

The *Resource Integration Guide* offers instructors a chapter-by-chapter breakdown of all the supplementary resources for *Understanding Art.*

Slide Set A set of slides contains 150 select, high-quality images from the text.

WebTutor™ on Blackboard and WebCT WebTutor on WebCT and Blackboard provides text-specific, preformatted content and total flexibility for easily creating and managing a personal website. WebTutor's course management tool gives instructors the ability to provide virtual office hours, post syllabi, set up threaded discussions, track student progress with the quizzing material, and much more. For students, WebTutor offers real-time access to a full array of study tools also found on the book companion website.

Acknowledgments

I consider myself fortunate to have studied with a fine group of artists, art historians, and art professionals who helped shape my love of art and my thinking about art throughout my career. *Understanding Art* would not have taken its present form and might not have come into being without the broad knowledge, skills, and dedication of James S. Ackerman, Stanford Anderson, Wayne V. Anderson, Whitney Chadwick, Michael Graves, George Heard Hamilton, Ann Sutherland Harris, Julius S. Held, Sam Hunter, Henry A. Millon, Konrad Oberhuber, John C. Overbeck, Michael Rinehart, Andrew C. Ritchie, Mark W. Roskill, Theodore Roszak, Miriam Schapiro, Bernice Steinbaum, and Jack Tworkov.

I'd like to thank the following people for contributing to the ancillary package for the eighth edition, William Allen, Arkansas State University; Cynthia Andreas, Lynn University; Patricia Belleville, Eastern Illinois University; Joy Bertinuson, American River College; Lynn Metcalf, St. Cloud State University; Kate Plowden, Piedmont Technical College; Ruth Pettigrew, Colorado State University; and Gay Sweely, Eastern Kentucky University.

I also wish to thank those reviewers who helped in revising this edition: Patricia Belleville, Eastern Illinois University; Phyllis Evans, South Texas College; Rosemary Goodell, Baton Rouge Community College; Jennifer

Hecker, SUNY College at Brockport; Lee Stanton, Columbia College of Missouri; and Gay Sweely, Eastern Kentucky University.

The eighth edition of *Understanding Art* is also indebted to the support and expertise of a fine group of Thomson Wadsworth publishing professionals. Let me begin by acknowledging the support of Susan Badger, CEO; Sean Wakely, President; Marcus Boggs, Editor-in-Chief, Humanities; Clark Baxter, Publisher; John R. Swanson, Acquisitions Editor; Sharon Adams Poore, Senior Development Editor; Anne Gittinger, Assistant Editor; Allison Roper, Editorial Assistant; Kim Adams, Senior Production Project Manager; Mark Orr, Senior Marketing Manager; and David Lionetti, Technology Project Manager. I must also acknowledge the tireless professionalism of Gretchen Otto of G & S Book Services who, with her colleagues, has provided the resources to make the eighth edition the finest edition.

Lois Fichner-Rathus
UnderstandingArt@aol.com

About the Author

Lois Fichner-Rathus is Professor of Art in the Art Department of The College of New Jersey. She holds a combined undergraduate degree in fine arts and art history, an M.A. from the Williams College Graduate Program in the History of Art, and a Ph.D. in the History, Theory, and Criticism of Art from the Massachusetts Institute of Technology. Her areas of specialization include contemporary art, feminist art history and criticism, and modern art and architecture. She has authored grants, contributed to books, curated exhibitions, published articles in professional journals, and exhibited her large-format photographic prints. She resides in New York.

The eighth edition of Understanding Art *is dedicated to my daughters—seen here with me on a college field trip to Paris. (From left to right: Jordan, Taylor, the author, Allyn)*

WHAT IS ART?

Everyone wants to understand art. Why not try to understand the song of a bird? Why does one love the night, flowers, everything around one without trying to understand them? But in the case of a painting, people have to understand.

—Pablo Picasso

Beauty, truth, immortality, order, harmony—these concepts and ideals have occupied us since the dawn of history. They enrich our lives and encourage us to extend ourselves beyond the limits of flesh and blood. Without them, life would be but a mean struggle for survival, and the value of survival itself would be unclear.

It is in the sciences and the arts that we strive to weave our experiences into coherent bodies of knowledge and to communicate them. Many of us are more comfortable with the sciences than with the arts. Science teaches us that the universe is not ruled purely by chance. The sciences provide ways of observing the world and experimenting so that we can learn what forces determine the courses of atoms and galaxies. Even those of us who do not consider ourselves "scientific" recognize that the scientific method permits us to predict and control many important events on a grand scale.

The beautiful is in nature, and it is encountered in the most diverse forms of reality. Once it is found, it belongs to art, or, rather, to the artist who discovers it.

— Gustave Courbet

The arts are more elusive to define, more difficult to gather into a conceptual net. We would probably all agree that the arts enhance daily experience; some of us would contend that they are linked to the very quality of life. Art has touched everyone, and art is all around us. Crayon drawings, paper cutouts, and the like are part of the daily lives of our children—an integral function of both magnet and refrigerator door. We all look for art to brighten our dormitory rooms, enhance our interior decor, beautify our cities, and embellish our places of worship. We are certain that we do not want to be without the arts, yet we are hard pressed to define them and sometimes even to understand them. In fact, the very word *art* encompasses many meanings, including ability, process, and product. As ability, art is the human capacity to make things of beauty and things that stir us; it is creativity. As process, art encompasses acts such as drawing, painting, sculpting, designing buildings, and using the camera to create memorable works. This definition is ever expanding, as materials and methods are employed in innovative ways to bring forth a creative product. As product, art is the completed work—an etching, a sculpture, a structure, a tapestry. If as individuals we do not understand science, we are at least comforted by the thought that others do. With art, however, the experience of a work is unique. Reactions to a work will vary according to the nature of the individual, time period, place, and culture. And although we may find ourselves before a work of art that has us befuddled, saying, "I hate it! I don't understand it!" we suspect that there is something about the very nature of art that transcends understanding.

This book is about the visual arts. Despite their often enigmatic nature, we shall try to share something of what is known about them so that understanding may begin. We do not aim to force our aesthetic preferences on you; if in the end you dislike a work as much as you did to start, that is completely acceptable. But we will aim to heighten awareness of what we respond to in a work of art and try to communicate why what an artist has done is important. In this way, you can counter with, "I hate it, but at least I understand it."

As in many areas of study—languages, computers, the sciences—amassing a basic vocabulary is intrinsic to understanding the material. You will want to be able to describe the attributes of a work of art and be able to express your reactions to it. The language or vocabulary of art includes the visual elements, principles of design, style, form, and content. We shall see how the visual elements of art, such as line, shape, and color, are composed according to principles of design into works of art with certain styles and content. We shall examine many media, including drawing, painting, printmaking, the camera and computer arts, sculpture, architecture, ceramics, and fiber arts.

When asked why we should study history, the historian answers that we must know about the past in order to have a sense of where we are and where we may be going. This argument also holds true for the arts; there is more to art history than memorizing dates! Examining a work in its historical, social, and political context will enable you to have a more meaningful dialogue with that work. You will be amazed and entertained by the ways in which the creative process has been intertwined with world events and individual personalities. We shall follow the journey of art, therefore, from the wall paintings of our Stone Age ancestors through the graffiti art of today's subway station. The media, the forms, the styles, and the subjects may evolve and change from millennium to millennium, from day to day, but uniting threads lie in the persistent quest for beauty or for truth or for self-expression.

Many philosophers have argued that art serves no function, that it exists for its own sake. Some have asserted that there is something about the essence of art that transcends the human occupation with usefulness. Others have held that in trying to analyze art too closely, one loses sight of its beauty and wonderment.

These may be valid points of view. Nevertheless, our understanding and appreciation of art often can be enhanced by asking the questions "Why was this created?" "What is its purpose?" In this section we shall see that works of art come into existence for a host of reasons that are as varied as the human condition. Perhaps we will not arrive at a single definition of art, but we can come to understand art by knowing what art does.

ART CREATES BEAUTY

Art has always added beauty to our lives. At times, the artist has looked to nature as the standard of beauty and has thus imitated it. At other times, the artist has aimed to improve

1-1 LEONARDO DA VINCI.
Mona Lisa (c. 1503–1505).
Oil on wood panel. 30¼″ × 21″.
Louvre Museum, Paris/Réunion des Musées Nationaux/Art Resource, New York.

1-2 Kenyan woman, Masai tribe.
Standards for beauty can differ from culture to culture.
Copyright Jim Zuckerman/CORBIS.

upon nature, developing an alternative standard—an idealized form. Standards of beauty in and of themselves are by no means universal. The Classical Greeks were obsessed with their idea of beauty and fashioned mathematical formulas for rendering the human body in sculpture so that it would achieve a majesty and perfection unknown in nature. The sixteenth-century artist Leonardo da Vinci, in what is perhaps the most famous painting in the history of Western art, enchants generations of viewers with the eternal beauty and mysteriousness of the smiling *Mona Lisa* (Fig. 1-1). But appreciation of the stately repose and refined features of this Italian woman is tied to an affinity to a Western standard of beauty. Elsewhere in the world, these very features might seem alien, unattractive, or undesirable. On the other hand, the standard of beauty in some non-Western societies that hold scarification, body painting, tattooing, and adornment (Fig. 1-2) both beautiful and sacred may seem odd and un-

attractive to someone from the Western world. One art form need not be seen as intrinsically superior to the other; in these works, quite simply, beauty is in the eye of the society's beholder.

ART ENHANCES OUR ENVIRONMENT

We have all decided at one time or another to change the color of our bedrooms. We have hung a poster or painting here rather than there, and we have arranged a vase of flowers or placed a potted plant in just the right spot in the room. We may not have created works of art, but we did accomplish one thing: We managed to delight our senses and turn our otherwise ordinary environments into pleasurable havens.

A Portrait in the Flesh

For centuries, artists have devoted their full resources, their lives, to their work. Orlan has also offered her pound of flesh—to the surgeon's scalpel.

Orlan (Fig. 1-3) is a French multimedia performance artist who has been undergoing a series of cosmetic operations to create, in herself, a composite sketch of what Western art has long set forth as the pinnacle of human beauty: the facial features that we find in classic works such as Botticelli's *The Birth of Venus* (Fig. 1-4), Leonardo's *Mona Lisa* (Fig. 1-1), and Boucher's *Europa,* or, more specifically, Venus's chin, the Mona Lisa's forehead, and Europa's mouth.

Most people undergo cosmetic surgery in private, but not Orlan. Several of her operations have been performances or media events. Her first series of operations were carried out in France and Belgium. The operating rooms were filled with symbols of flowering womanhood in a form compatible with medicine: sterilized plastic fruit. There were huge photos of Orlan, and the surgeons and their assistants were decked out not in surgical greens but in costumes created by celebrated couturiers. A recent operation was performed in the New York office of a cosmetic surgeon and transmitted via satellite to the Sandra Gering Gallery in the city's famed SoHo district. Orlan did not lie unconscious in a hospital gown. Rather, she lay awake in a long black dress and read from a work on psychoanalysis while the surgeon implanted silicone in her face to imitate the protruding forehead of *Mona Lisa*.

When will it all end? Orlan says that "I will stop my work when it is as close as possible to the computer composite,"* as the lips of Europa split into a smile. ∎

---

*Margalit Fox, "A Portrait in Skin and Bone," *New York Times,* November 21, 1993, V8.

1-3 French performance artist Orlan, who has dedicated herself to embodying Western classic beauty as found in the works of Leonardo, Botticelli, and Boucher through multiple plastic surgeries. Here Orlan is being "prepped" for one in a series of operations.

Copyright 2003 Orlan/Artists Rights Society (ARS), New York/ADAGP, Paris.

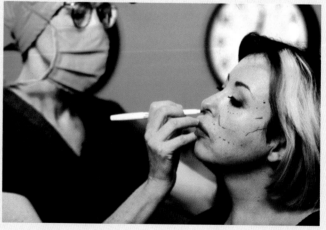

1-4   SANDRO BOTTICELLI.
The Birth of Venus (1486). Detail.
Tempera on canvas. 5'8⅞" × 9'1⅐".
Uffizi Gallery, Florence/Scala/Art Resource, New York.

1-5 JOYCE KOZLOFF.
Galla Placidia in Philadelphia
(1985).
Mosaic installation.
13′ × 16′.
Penn Center Suburban Station,
Philadelphia. Courtesy of Henri
Gross, Penn Associates, Philadelphia.

Works of art have been used to create pleasing environments for centuries. Paintings are not merely objects of beauty in themselves; they also hang on walls and can be painted directly on them. Sculptures find their way into rooms, courts, and gardens; photographs are found in books; and fiber arts are seen on walls and floors. Whatever other functions they may serve, many works of art are also decorative. Joyce Kozloff's *Galla Placidia in Philadelphia* (Fig. 1-5), a mosaic for the Penn Center Suburban Station in that city, elevates decorative patterns to the level of fine art and raises the art-historical consciousness of the casual commuter. The original Mausoleum of Galla Placidia is the fifth-century chapel and burial place of a Byzantine empress, a landmark monument known for its complex and colorful mosaics. Kozloff's own intricate and diverse designs dazzle the eye and stimulate the intellect, providing an oasis of color in an otherwise humdrum city scene.

Glass sculptor Dale Chihuly's *Fioridi Como* (Fig. 1-6) is a 70-foot-long ceiling piece that is suspended above the reception area of the Bellagio Hotel in Las Vegas. The visitor must pass under the work—or astutely determine to avoid it—to register at the hotel or stroll into the casino. Chihuly has also "decorated" public spaces with his many chandeliers in places ranging from Venice to the countryside of Washington State. Their common message seems to be "You are now in another place." You can click your heels beneath *Fioridi Como* (the small town of Bellagio, after which the

1-6 DALE CHIHULY.
Fioridi Como (1998).
70′ × 30′ × 12′
Bellagio Hotel, Las Vegas, NV. Courtesy of Dale Chihuly, Seattle, WA.

It is the glory and good of Art,
That Art remains the one way possible
Of speaking truths, to mouths like mine at least.

—Robert Browning

hotel is named, lies on the shore of Italy's spectacular Lake Como), but you will find, like Dorothy in *The Wizard of Oz,* that you aren't in Kansas anymore.

ART REVEALS TRUTH

Art is a powerful tool, and the artist knows this well. It can be used to replicate reality in the finest detail, tricking the eye into perceiving truth in imitation. The ancient Greeks, the Renaissance artist, the contemporary Photorealist painter, all, in their way, pursued truth and attempted to reveal it: truth about how the world looks; truth about how the world works. But artists have also reached outward to describe truths about humanity and have reached inward to describe truths about themselves. Sometimes their pursuit has led them to beauty, at other times to shame and outrage. The "ugly truth," just like the beautiful truth, provides a valid commentary on the human condition.

In her self-portraits, the Mexican painter Frida Kahlo used her tragic life as an emblem for human suffering. At the age of 18, she was injured when a streetcar slammed into a bus on which she was a passenger. The accident left her with many serious wounds, including a fractured pelvis and vertebrae, and chronic pain. Kahlo's marriage to the painter Diego Rivera was also painful. She once told a friend, "I have suffered two serious accidents in my life, one in which a streetcar ran over me. . . . The other accident was Diego."[1] As in *Diego in My Thoughts* (Fig. 1-7), her face is always painted with extreme realism and set within a compressed space, requiring the viewer to confront the "true" Frida. When asked why she painted herself so often, she replied, "Porque estoy muy sola" (Because I am all alone). Those who knew Kahlo conjecture that she painted self-portraits in order to "survive, to endure, to conquer death."

Another haunting portrayal of unvarnished truth can be seen in Robert Mapplethorpe's *Self-Portrait* (Fig. 1-8). The veracity of the photographic medium is

1-7 FRIDA KAHLO.
Diego in My Thoughts (Diego y yo) (1949).
Oil on canvas, mounted on Masonite. 24″ × 36″.
Courtesy of Mary-Anne Martin Fine Art, New York.
Copyright 2005 Banco de Mexico Trust.

[1] Martha Zamora, *Frida Kahlo: The Brush of Anguish* (San Francisco: Chronicle Books, 1990), 37.

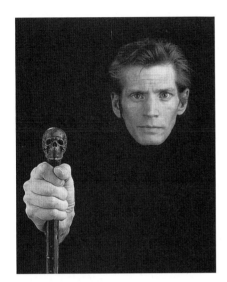

1-8   ROBERT MAPPLETHORPE.
Self-Portrait (1988).
Gelatin silver print.
MAP #1860 copyright 2003 The Robert
Mapplethorpe Foundation. Courtesy of Art &
Commerce Anthology.

In *Four Marilyns* (Fig. 1-9), Pop artist Andy Warhol participated in the cultural immortalization of a film icon of the 1960s by reproducing a well-known photograph of Monroe on canvas. Proclaimed a "sex symbol" of the silver screen, she rapidly rose to fame and shocked her fans by taking her own life at an early age. In the decades since Monroe's death, her image is still found on posters and calendars, books and songs are still written about her, and the public's appetite for information about her early years and romances remains insatiable. In other renderings, Warhol

1-9   ANDY WARHOL.
Four Marilyns (1962).
Synthetic polymer paint and silkscreen ink on canvas.
30″ × 23⅞″.
Copyright 2003 Andy Warhol Foundation for the Visual Arts, Inc./
Artists Rights Society (ARS), New York/Art Resource, New York.

inescapable; the viewer is forced to confront the artist's troublesome gaze. But the portrait also discloses the truth about Mapplethorpe's battle with AIDS, and perhaps suggests an attempt to reconcile his inevitable death. The artist's skeletal head slips into a background haze while his tightly clenched fist grips a cane with a skull and juts forward into sharp focus. The anger and defiance of Mapplethorpe's whitened knuckles contrast with the soft, almost pained expression of the artist's face.

ART IMMORTALIZES

In the face of certain death, an artist such as Robert Mapplethorpe can defy mortality by creating a work that will keep his talents and his tragedy in the public's consciousness for decades. Human beings are the only species conscious of death, and for millennia, they have used art to overleap the limits of this life.

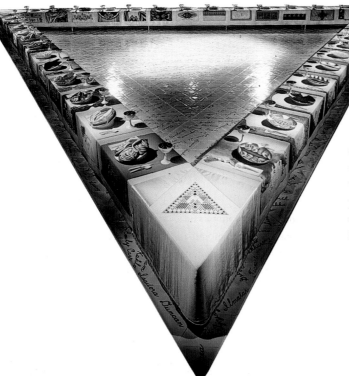

1-10   JUDY CHICAGO.
The Dinner Party (1974–1979).
Painted porcelain and needlework. $48' \times 48' \times 48' \times 3'$.
Copyright 2003 Judy Chicago, ACA Galleries, New York. Copyright 2003
Artists Rights Society (ARS), New York.

Cameroon, human beings across time and cultures have sought answers to the unanswerable and have salved their souls with belief in life after death. It is not surprising that in the absence of physical embodiments for the deities they fashioned, humans developed art forms to visually render the unseen. Often the physical attributes granted to their gods were a reflection of humans themselves. It has been said, for example, that the Greeks made their men into gods and their gods into men. In other societies, deities were often represented as powerful and mysterious animals, or composite men-beasts. Ritual and ceremony grew alongside the establishment of religions and the representation of deities, in actual or symbolic form. Until modern times, one could

arranged multiple images of the star as if lined up on supermarket shelves, commenting, perhaps, on the ways in which contemporary flesh peddlers have packaged and sold her—in death as well as life.

The lines between life and death, between place and time, are temporarily dissolved in the renowned installation *The Dinner Party* (Fig. 1-10) by feminist artist Judy Chicago. The idea for this multimedia work, which is constructed to honor and immortalize history's notable women, revolves around a fantastic dinner party, where the guests of honor meet before place settings designed to reflect their personalities and accomplishments. Chicago and numerous other women artists have invested much energy in alerting the public to the significant role of women in the arts and society.

ART EXPRESSES RELIGIOUS BELIEFS

The quest for immortality is the bedrock of organized religion. From the cradle of civilization to the contemporary era, from Asia to the Americas, and from the Crimea to the

1-11   JESSIE OONARK.
A Shaman's Helping Spirits (1971).
Stonecut and stencil. $37\frac{1}{6}'' \times 25\frac{1}{6}''$.
Art Gallery of Ontario, Toronto, ON. Gift of the Klamer family, 1978.
Copyright 2003 Jessie Oonark.

probably study the history of art in terms of works expressing religious values alone.

Art has been used to express hopes for fertility, to propitiate the gods, to symbolize great religious events and values, and to commend heavenward the souls of the departed. Inuit artist Jessie Oonark, who lived in the Canadian Arctic, created the image *A Shaman's Helping Spirits* (Fig. 1-11) as a symbol of the healing rituals associated with the medicine men of her culture. Shamanism is a religion based on a belief in good and evil spirits that can be controlled and influenced only by the power of the shaman, a kind of priest. The strong, flat shapes and bright colors lend a directness and vitality to her expression.

Another artist of color, Aaron Douglas, translated a biblical story into a work that speaks to the African American sensibility. In his *Noah's Ark* (Fig. 1-12), one of seven paintings based on James Weldon Johnson's book *God's Trombones: Seven Negro Sermons in Verse,* Douglas expressed a powerful vision of the great flood. Animals enter the ark in pairs as lightning flashes about them, and the sky turns a hazy gray purple with the impending storm. African men, rendered in rough-hewn profile, ready the ark and direct the action in a dynamically choreographed composition that takes possession of and personalizes the biblical event for Douglas's race and culture.

The spectacular Hagia Sophia (Fig. 1-13) was built as a Christian church in 532–537 CE. After the Ottoman conquest of 1453, it was converted to an Islamic mosque. In contemporary Istanbul, the building serves as a museum. The dome of the ancient church is a wonder. Although it is made of stone, it seems to float on the light that streams through the windows encircling its base like diamonds in a necklace. Light sparkles in the mosaic tiles and is reflected by glistening marble surfaces and ceremonial objects. Intellectually, the visitor may ponder how that monstrous weight is supported and how the dome can have survived century upon century of earthquakes and human assaults. But emotionally, it seems as if paradise is beckoning outside the dome.

1-12 AARON DOUGLAS.
Noah's Ark (c. 1927).
Oil on masonite. 48″ × 36″.
The Carl Van Vechten Gallery of Fine Arts, Fisk University, Nashville, TN.

1-13 ANTHEMIUS OF TRALLES AND ISIDORUS OF MILETUS.
Hagia Sophia, Constantinople (modern-day Istanbul), Turkey (532–537 CE).
Interior view.
Copyright Lawrence Manning/CORBIS.

ART EXPRESSES FANTASY

Art also serves as a vehicle by which artists can express their inmost fantasies. Whereas some have labored to reconstruct reality and commemorate actual experiences, others have used art to give vent to their imaginary inner lives. There are many types of fantasies, such as those found in dreams and daydreams or simply the objects and landscapes that are conceived in the imagination. The French painter Odilon Redon once said that there is "a kind of drawing which the imagination has liberated from any concern with the details of reality in order to allow it to serve freely for the representation of things conceived" in the mind. In an attempt to capture the inner self, many twentieth-century artists looked to the psychoanalytic writings of Sigmund Freud and Carl Jung, who suggested that primeval forces are at work in the unconscious reaches of the mind. These artists sought to use their art as an outlet for these unconscious forces, as we shall see in Chapters 19 and 20.

Marc Chagall's self-portrait, *I and the Village* (Fig. 1-14), provides a fragmented image of the artist among fantasized objects that seem to float in and out of one another. Fleeting memories of life in his Russian village are assembled like so many pieces of a dreamlike puzzle, reflecting the very frag-

1-15 MAX BECKMANN.
The Dream (1921).
Oil on canvas. 73⅛" × 35".
The Saint Louis Art Museum. Bequest of Morton D. May. Copyright 2003 Artists Rights Society (ARS), New York/VG Bild-Kunst, Bonn.

1-14 MARC CHAGALL.
I and the Village (1911).
Oil on canvas. 6'3⅝" × 4'11⅝".
The Museum of Modern Art, New York. Mrs. Simon Guggenheim Fund. Copyright The Museum of Modern Art, New York. Licensed by SCALA / Art Resource, New York. Copyright 2003 Artists Rights Society (ARS), New York/ADAGP, Paris.

mentary nature of memory itself. Chagall's world is a happy, though private one; the strange juxtaposition of images is reconciled only in the artist's own mind.

A similar process of fragmentation and juxtaposition was employed by German artist Max Beckmann in *The Dream* (Fig. 1-15), but with a very different effect. The suggestion of space and atmosphere in Chagall's painting has given way to a claustrophobic room in which figures are compressed into a zigzag group. The soft, rolling hills and curving lines that gave the village painting its pleasant, dreamy quality have been forfeited for harsh, angular shapes and deformations. Horror hides in every nook and cranny, from the amputated and bandaged hands of the man in red stripes to the blinded street musician and maimed harlequin. Are these marionettes from some dark comedy or human puppets locked in a world of manipulation and hopelessness?

ART STIMULATES THE INTELLECT AND FIRES THE EMOTIONS

Art has the power to make us think profoundly, to make us feel deeply. Beautiful or controversial works of all media can trigger many associations for us. Whether we gaze upon a landscape painting that reminds us of a vacation past, an abstract work that challenges our grasp of geometry, or a quilt that evokes family ties and traditions, it is almost impossible to truly confront a work and remain unaffected. We may think about what the subjects are doing, thinking, and feeling. We may reflect on the purposes of the artist. We may seek to trace the sources of our own emotional response or advance our self-knowledge and our knowledge of the outside world.

Consider Jenny Holzer's installation of **conceptual art** illuminating the interior spiral of New York's Solomon R. Guggenheim Museum (Fig. 1-16). Conceptual art does not necessarily represent only external objects. It also challenges the traditional view of the artist as creative visionary, skilled craftsperson, and master of one's media. The "art" lies in the artist's conception. **Wordworks** such as this seem to comment on the impersonal information systems of modern times, while posing a challenge to the formal premises of art and stirring an intellectual response in the viewer. Holzer's wordworks compel readers to stop and think, sometimes through the presentation of piercing feminist declarations. This particular piece urges readers to reconsider the rules by which they live and warns that sometimes we do not rethink our lives until we are faced with disaster.

At its most extreme, the conceptual art product may exist solely in the mind of the artist, with or without a

1-16   JENNY HOLZER.
Untitled (1989–1990).
Selection from "Truism: Inflammatory Essays, The Living Series, The Survival Series, Under a Rock, Laments, and Mother and Child Text."
LED electronic display signboard installation. 11″ × 162′ × 44″ (27.9 cm × 49.4 m × 111.8 cm).
Installation at the Solomon R. Guggenheim Museum, New York. Copyright 2003 Jenny Holzer/Artists Rights Society (ARS), New York. Courtesy of the Solomon R. Guggenheim Museum, New York.

Art is harmony.

—Georges Seurat

I try not to have things look as if chance had brought them together,
but as if they had a necessary bond between them.

—Jean-François Millet

physical embodiment. Consider these: a wordwork by Robert Barry—

> *ALL THE THINGS I KNOW*
> *BUT OF WHICH I AM NOT*
> *AT THE MOMENT THINKING—*
> *1:36 PM; JUNE 15, 1969*

or a concept by artist Lawrence Weiner, sold to a patron, who installed the work himself: "A two-inch wide, one-inch deep trench, cut across a standard one-car driveway."

ART CREATES ORDER AND HARMONY

Artists and scientists have been intrigued by, and have ventured to discover and describe, the underlying order of nature. The Classical Greeks fine-polished the rough edges of nature by applying mathematical formulas to the human figure to perfect it; the nineteenth-century painter Paul Cézanne once remarked that all of nature could be reduced to the cylinder, the sphere, and the cone.

One of the most perfect expressions of order and harmony is found in the fragile Japanese sand garden (Fig. 1-17). These medieval gardens are frequently part of a pavilion complex and are tended by the practitioners of **Zen,** a Buddhist sect that seeks inner harmony through introspection and meditation. The gentle raked pattern of the sand symbolizes water and rocks, mountains reaching heavenward.

Such gardens do not invite the observer to mill about; their perfection precludes walking. They are microcosms, really—universes unto themselves.

When can order pose a threat to harmony and psychological well-being? Perhaps this is the question that Laurie Simmons set out to answer in her color photograph called

1-17   Ryoanji Zen Temple, Japanese sand garden, Kyoto, Japan.
Copyright 2005 Topfoto/The Image Works.

The *Piano Lesson*(s) by Matisse and Bearden

1-18   HENRI MATISSE.
Piano Lesson (1916).
Oil on canvas. 8'½" × 6'11¾".

Courtesy of Museum of Modern Art New York. Mrs. Simon Guggenheim
Fund. Copyright 2003 Succession H. Matisse, Paris/Artists Rights Society
(ARS), New York/Art Resource, New York.

Frequently an artist will use composition, or the arrangement of elements, to impose order. In Henri Matisse's *Piano Lesson* (Fig. 1-18), every object, every color, every line seems to be placed to lead the eye around the canvas. The pea green wedge of drapery at the window is repeated in the shape of the metronome atop the piano, the wrought-iron grillwork at the window is complemented by the curvilinear lines of the music desk, and the enigmatic figure in the upper right background finds her counterpart in a small sculpture placed diagonally across the canvas. Through contrast and repetition, unity within the diversity is achieved. The painting exudes solitude, resulting from the regularity of the compositional elements more than the atmosphere in the room. The boy's face appears quite tense, in fact, under the watchful eye of the seated woman behind him.

   With Matisse's painting in mind, does Romare Bearden's *Piano Lesson* (Fig. 1-19) appear then to be an example of disharmony, of disorder? Certainly it is a cacophony of shapes, lines, and unpredictable vantage points. But as in Matisse's painting, color repetition draws the composition's dis-

parate parts together—the red of background is balanced by the touches of red in the costumes of the figures up front; an undulating green strip on the piano is echoed in the billowing green drapes beyond. Ironically, there seems to be a more genuine feeling of serenity, in spite of the jumbled atmosphere. Is it because Matisse's seated woman—not touching? not feeling?—has a more flesh-and-blood counterpart in Bearden's work—a teacher? a mother?—who guides the young girl with the loving placement of a hand on her shoulder? When seen side by side, these paintings convey two different experiences. Matisse's piano student seems a product of his surroundings, a child of privilege partaking in an obligatory cultural ritual. Bearden's student, an African American girl in an apartment decorated catch-as-catch-can, seems to be breaking the bonds of her surroundings through the transcendence of music. ■

1-19   ROMARE BEARDEN.
Piano Lesson (1983).
Oil with collage.

Collection of Walter O. Evans. Copyright 2005 The Romare
Bearden Foundation. Licensed by VAGA, New York.

1-20 LAURIE SIMMONS.
Red Library #2 (1983).
Color photograph. 48½″ × 38¼″.
Collection of the artist. Courtesy of Metro Pictures, New York.

Red Library #2 (Fig. 1-20). Here, in a compulsively organized library, where nothing is a hair out of place, a robot-like woman assesses her job well done. She has become one with her task; even her dress, hair, and skin match the decor.

ART EXPRESSES CHAOS

Just as beauty has its dark side and the intellect is balanced by the emotion, so, too, do order and harmony presume the existence of chaos. Artists have portrayed chaos in many

1-21 JAUNE QUICK-TO-SEE SMITH.
Eclipse (1987).
Oil on canvas. 60″ × 60″.
Collection of the artist.

ways throughout the history of art, seeking analogies in apocalyptic events such as war, famine, or natural catastrophe. But chaos can be suggested even in the absence of specific content. In *Eclipse* (Fig. 1-21), without reference to nature or reality, Native American artist Jaune Quick-to-See Smith creates an agitated, chaotic atmosphere of color, line, shape, and movement. The artist grew up on the Flathead Indian reservation in Montana and uses a full vocabulary of Native American geometric motifs and organic images from the rich pictorial culture of her ancestors.

ART RECORDS AND COMMEMORATES EXPERIENCE

From humanity's earliest days, art has served to record and communicate experiences and events. From prehistoric cave paintings, thought to record significant events in the history of Paleolithic societies, to a work such as the Vietnam Memorial in Washington, D.C., installed in honor of

Art is not a handicraft; it is the transmission of feeling the artist has experienced.

—Leo Tolstoy

1-22   LOUISA CHASE.
Storm (1981).
Oil on canvas. 90″ × 120″.
Denver Art Museum. Purchased with funds from National Endowment for the Arts Matching Fund and Alliance for Contemporary Art.

American service personnel who died during this country's involvement in that war, art has been used to inform future generations of what and who have gone before them. Art also serves to convey the personal experiences of an artist in ways that words cannot.

American painter Louisa Chase was inspired to paint nature's unbridled power as revealed in waves, waterfalls, and thunderstorms, though the intensity of her subjects is often tempered by her own presence in the piece. In *Storm* (Fig. 1-22), a cluster of thick, black clouds lets go a torrent of rain, which, in league with the decorative **palette** of pinks and purples, turns an artificial blue. The highly charged im-

ages on the left side of the canvas are balanced on the right by the most delicate of ferns, spiraling upward, nourished by the downpour. Beneath the sprig, the artist's hand cups the raindrops, becoming part of the painting and part of nature's event as well. Chase said of a similar storm painting, "During the [marking] process I do become the storm—lost—yet not lost. An amazing feeling of losing myself yet remaining totally conscious."[2]

[2] Louisa Chase, journal entry for February 20, 1984, in *Louisa Chase* (New York: Robert Miller Gallery, 1984).

[On The Steerage*] I stood spellbound for a while, looking and looking. Could I photograph what I felt, looking and looking and still looking? I saw shapes related to each other. I saw a picture of shapes and underlying that the feeling I had about life. . . . Rembrandt came into my mind and I wondered would he have felt as I was feeling.*

—Alfred Stieglitz (about *The Steerage*)

1-23 ALFRED STIEGLITZ.
The Steerage (1907).
Photograph.

Courtesy of The Royal Photographic Society/Heritage Images Partnership (HIP), heritage-images.com.

The photographer Alfred Stieglitz, who recognized the medium as a fine art as well as a tool for recording events, happened upon the striking composition of *The Steerage* (Fig. 1-23) on an Atlantic crossing aboard the *Kaiser Wilhelm II.* He rushed to his cabin for his camera, hoping that the upper and lower masses of humanity would maintain their balanced relationships to one another, to the drawbridge that divides the scene, to the stairway, the funnel, and the horizontal beam of the mast. The "steerage" of a ship was the least expensive accommodation. Here the "huddled masses" seem suspended in limbo by machinery and by

1-24 FAITH RINGGOLD.
Tar Beach (1988).
Acrylic paint on canvas and pieced fabric.
74″ × 68½″.

Collection of the Solomon R. Guggenheim Museum, New York.

Works of art all through the ages show us in the clearest fashion how mankind has changed,
how a stage that has once appeared never reappears.

—Philipp Otto Runge

symbolic as well as actual bridges. Yet the tenacious human spirit may best be symbolized by the jaunty patch of light that strikes the straw hat of one passenger on the upper deck. Stieglitz was utterly fascinated and moved by what he saw.

More than 80 years after Stieglitz captured the great hope of immigrants entering New York harbor, African American artist Faith Ringgold tells the story of life and dreams on a tar-covered rooftop. *Tar Beach* (Fig. 1-24) is a painted patchwork quilt that stitches together the artist's memories of family, friends, and feelings while growing up in Harlem. Ringgold is noted for her use of materials and techniques associated with women's traditions as well as her use of narrative or storytelling, a strong tradition in African American families. A large, painted square with images of Faith, her brother, her parents, and neighbors dominates the quilt and is framed with brightly patterned pieces of fabric. Along the top and bottom are inserts crowded with Ringgold's written description of her experiences. This wonderfully innocent and joyful monologue begins:

> I will always remember when the stars fell down around me and lifted me up above the George Washington Bridge . . .

ART REFLECTS THE SOCIAL AND CULTURAL CONTEXT

Faith Ringgold's *Tar Beach* tells us the story of a young girl growing up in Harlem. Her experiences take place within a specific social and cultural context. In recording experience, artists frequently record the activities and objects of their times and places, reflecting contemporary fashions and beliefs as well as the states of the crafts and sciences.

The architecture, the hairstyles, hats, and shoulder pads, even the price of cigars (only five cents) all set Edward Hopper's *Nighthawks* (Fig. 1-25) unmistakably in an American city during the late 1930s or 1940s. The subject is commonplace and uneventful, though somewhat eerie. There is a tension between the desolate spaces of the vacant street and the corner diner. Familiar objects become distant. The warm patch of artificial light seems precious, even precarious, as if night and all its troubled symbols are threatening to break in on disordered lives. Hopper uses a specific sociocultural context to communicate an unsettling, introspective mood of aloneness, of being outside the mainstream of experience.

1-25 EDWARD HOPPER. *Nighthawks* (1942). Oil on canvas. 30″ × 60″.
Courtesy of the Art Institute of Chicago, Friends of American Art Collection.

In Richard Hamilton's *Just What Is It That Makes Today's Homes So Different, So Appealing?* (Fig. 1-26), the aims are identical, but the result is self-mocking, upbeat, and altogether fun. This little collage functions as a veritable time capsule for the 1950s, a decade during which the speedy advance of technology finds everyone buying pieces of the American dream. What is that dream? Comic books, TV, movies, and tape recorders; canned hams and TV dinners; enviable physiques, Tootsie Pops, vacuum cleaners that finally let the "lady of the house" clean all the stairs at once. Hamilton's piece serves as a memento of the time and the place and the values of the decade for future generations.

1-26   RICHARD HAMILTON.
Just What Is It That Makes Today's Homes So Different, So Appealing? (1956). Collage. 10¼″ × 9¾″.
Kunsthalle Tübingen, Germany. Collection of G. F. Zundel.

1-27   ZAHA HADID.
Sheikh Zayed Bridge, Abu Dhabi, to be completed in 2006. Designed by Zaha Hadid
Zaha Hadid/ESTO.

We more commonly think of visual art (painting and sculpture, for example) when we consider the connection between art and social or cultural context, but art history is full of examples of architecture that reflect or embody the ideas or beliefs of a people at a point in time. Think of the Parthenon in Classical Athens or Chartres Cathedral in the Middle Ages. Symbolism is often disguised in architecture, but sometimes it is the very essence of its design. Zaha Hadid's Sheik Zayed Bridge (Fig. 1-27), connecting Abu Dhabi island to the mainland, is composed of sweeping, irregular rhythms of arches. Hadid has acknowledged the influence of Arabic calligraphy on the flowing forms of her structures, but in this work, the arches—each different from one another in height and span—reflect the dunes of the nearby topography, thus connecting it (metaphorically and literally) to a specific place and time.

ART PROTESTS INJUSTICE AND RAISES SOCIAL CONSCIOUSNESS

As other people have, artists have taken on bitter struggles against the injustices of their times and have tried to persuade others to join them in their causes, and it has been natural for them to use their creative skills to do so.

The nineteenth-century Spanish painter Francisco Goya used his art to satirize the political foibles of his day and to condemn the horrors of war (see Fig. 18-8). In the twentieth century another Spanish painter, Pablo Picasso, would condemn war in his masterpiece *Guernica* (see Fig. 19-10).

Goya's French contemporary Eugène Delacroix painted the familiar image of *Liberty Leading the People* (Fig. 1-28)

1-28 EUGÈNE DELACROIX.
Liberty Leading the People (1830).
Oil on canvas. 8′6″ × 10′10″.
Louvre Museum, Paris / Réunion des Musées Nationaux / Art Resource, New York.

Art has always been employed by the different social classes who hold the balance of power as one instrument of domination—hence, a political instrument. One can analyze epoch after epoch—from the Stone Age to our own day—and see that there is no form of art which does not also play an essential political role.

—Diego Rivera

1-29 SUZANNE LACY AND LESLIE LABOWITZ.
In Mourning and in Rage (1977).
Performance at Los Angeles City Hall.
Photograph courtesy of Suzanne Lacy and
Leslie Labowitz.

in order to keep the spirit of the French Revolution alive in 1830. In this painting, people of all classes are united in rising up against injustice, led onward by an allegorical figure of liberty. Rifles, swords, a flag—even pistols—join in an upward rhythm, underscoring the pyramid shape of the composition.

Suzanne Lacy and Leslie Labowitz's performance *In Mourning and in Rage* (Fig. 1-29), was a carefully orchestrated media event reminiscent of ancient public rituals. Members of feminist groups donned black robes to commemorate women who had been victims of rape-murders and to protest the shoddy media coverage usually given such tragedies.

Millions of us have grown up with a benevolent, maternal Aunt Jemima. She has graced packages of pancake mix and bottles of maple syrup for generations. How many of us have really thought about what she symbolizes? Artists such as African American artist Betye Saar have been doubly offended by Aunt Jemima's state of servitude, which harks

1-30 BETYE SAAR.
The Liberation of Aunt Jemima (1972).
Mixed media. 11¾″ × 8″ × 2¾″.
University of California, Berkeley Art Museum, purchased with the aid of funds from the National Endowment for the Arts (selected by the Committee for the Acquisition of Afro-American Art).

not only to the days of slavery but also to the suffocating traditional domestic role of the female. Sharon F. Patton notes:

> The Liberation of Aunt Jemima subverts the black mammy stereotype of the black American woman: a heavy, dark-skinned maternal figure, of smiling demeanor. This stereotype, started in the nineteenth century, was still popular culture's favorite representation of the African-American woman. She features in Hollywood films and notably as the advertising and packaging image for Pillsbury's "Aunt Jemima's Pancake Mix."[3]

The Aunt Jemima in Betye Saar's *The Liberation of Aunt Jemima* (Fig. 1-30) is revised to reflect the quest for libera-

tion from servitude and the stereotype. She holds a broomstick in one hand but a rifle in the other. Before her stands a portrait with a small white child violated by a clenched black fist representing the symbol of Black Power. The image of the liberated Aunt Jemima confronts viewers and compels them to cast off the stereotypes that lead to intolerance.

ART ELEVATES THE COMMONPLACE

Have you come across embroidered dish towels or aprons with the words *God Bless Our Happy Home* or *I Hate Housework*? Miriam Schapiro's *Wonderland* (Fig. 1-31) is a collage

---

[3] Sharon F. Patton, *African-American Art* (New York: Oxford University Press, 1998), 201.

1-31   MIRIAM SCHAPIRO.
Wonderland (1983).
Acrylic and fabric collage on canvas. 90″ × 144″ (framed).
Smithsonian American Art Museum, Washington, D.C./Art Resource, New York.

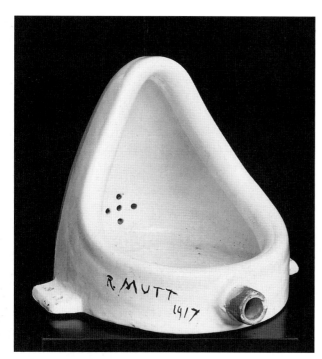

1-32   MARCEL DUCHAMP.
Fountain (1917).
1951 version after lost original. Porcelain urinal. H: 24".
Courtesy Sidney Janis Gallery, New York. Copyright 2003 Artists Rights
Society (ARS), New York/ADAGP, Paris/Succession Marcel Duchamp.

ART MEETS THE NEEDS OF THE ARTIST

Artists may have special talents and perceptive qualities, but they are also people with needs and the motivation to meet those needs. Psychologists speak of the need for "self-actualization"—that is, the need to fulfill one's unique potential. Self-actualizing people have needs for novelty, exploration, and understanding; and they have aesthetic needs for art, beauty, and order. Under perfect circumstances, art permits the individual to meet needs for achievement or self-actualization and, at the same time, to earn a living.

Murals such as José Clemente Orozco's *Epic of American Civilization: Hispano-America* (Fig. 1-33) were created for a branch of the Works Progress Administration (WPA), a federal work–relief program intended to help people in the United States, including artists, survive the Great Depression. The WPA made it possible for many artists to meet basic survival needs while continuing to work, and be paid, as artists. Scores of public buildings were decorated with murals or canvas paintings by artists in the Fine Arts Program (FAP) of the WPA. Some of them were among the best known of their generation. Orozco's epic also met another, personal need—the need to call attention to and express his outrage at what he believed to be financial and military injustices imposed upon the Mexican peasant.

Creating works of art that are accepted by one's audience can lead to an artist's social acceptance and recognition. But sometimes art really is created only to meet the needs of the artist and nothing beyond—with no thought to a sale, or exhibition, or review, or recognition. Such is the story of *outsider art,* a catch-all category that has been used for works by untrained artists; self-taught artists who have been incarcerated for committing crimes and who use the circumstances of their isolation as a motive for creating; people who are psychologically compromised and sometimes institutionalized for conditions ranging from autism (Fig. 1-34) to schizophrenia. Works of art by these individuals and others like them are almost always *not* intended to be seen. Thus, in the purest sense, they come into existence to meet some essential emotional or psychological need of the artist and the artist alone.

As we noted at the outset, the question "What is art?" has no single answer and raises many other questions. Our discussion of the meanings and purposes of art is meant to facilitate the individual endeavor to understand art but is not intended to be exhaustive. Some people will feel that we have omitted several important meanings and purposes of

that reflects her "femmage" aesthetic—her interest in depicting women's domestic culture. The work contains ordinary doilies, needlework, crocheted aprons, handkerchiefs, and quilt blocks, all anchored to a geometric patterned background that is augmented with brushstrokes of paint. In the center is the most commonplace of the commonplace: an embroidered image of a housewife who curtsies beneath the legend "Welcome to Our Home."

Some of the more interesting elevations of the commonplace to the realm of art are found in the **readymades** and **assemblages** of twentieth-century artists. Marcel Duchamp's *Fountain* (Fig. 1-32) is a urinal, turned upside down and labeled. Pablo Picasso's *Bull's Head* (see Fig. 9-20) is fashioned from the seat and handlebars of an old bicycle. In **Pop art,** the dependence on commonplace objects and visual clichés reaches a peak. Prepared foods, soup and beer cans, media images of beautiful women and automobile accidents—these became the subject matter of Pop art. As we saw in Figures 1-9 and 1-26, Pop art impels us to cast a more critical eye on the symbols and objects with which we surround ourselves.

1-33 JOSÉ CLEMENTE
OROZCO.
*Epic of American
Civilization: Hispano-
America* (c. 1932–1934).
Fresco. 10′ × 9′11″.

Commissioned by the Trustees
of Dartmouth College, Hanover,
NH. Hood Museum of Art.
Copyright 2005 Clemente
Orozco Valladares, Artists Rights
Society (ARS), New York.

1-34 MATTHEW I. SMITH.
Untitled (n.d.).
Graphite on paper. 8½″ × 11″.
Courtesy Frank Maresca.

art; others will think we have included too many. But these considerations hint at the richness and elusiveness of the concept of art.

In Chapters 2, 3, and 4 we expand our discussion of the meanings and purposes of art to include the "language" of art. These chapters will not provide us with a precise definition of art either, but they will afford us insight into the ways in which artists use elements of art such as line, shape, and color to create compositions of a certain style and content. Even though art has always been with us, the understanding of art is in its infancy.

2

VISUAL ELEMENTS OF ART

*I found I could say things with color and shapes that I couldn't say
in any other way—things I had no words for.*

—Georgia O'Keeffe

Color and shape are but two of the visual elements of art. The language of art is the very language of our visual and tactile experiences in the world, and the words or vocabulary of this language consist of the visual elements of *line, shape, light, value, color, texture, space, time,* and *motion.* Line can define shape; light can reveal it. Color can describe the world around us and reveal the worlds within us; we are blue with sorrow, red with rage. Texture is linked with all the emotion of touching, with the cold sharpness of rock or the warm, yielding sensations of flesh. We exist in space; we occupy space and space envelops us. Time allows us to develop into what we are capable of being; time ultimately takes from us what we have been. We are all in motion through space, in a solar system that is traversing the rim of our galaxy at thousands of miles per second, or rotating on the surface of our own globe at a thousand miles per hour. Yet it is the smaller motion—the motion of lifting an arm or of riding through a field—that we are more likely to sense and hence to represent in art.

This vocabulary—*line, shape, light, value, color, texture, space, time,* and *motion*—makes up what we call the **visual elements** or **plastic elements** of art. Artists select from a variety of media, including, but by no means limited to, drawing, painting, sculpture, architecture, photography, textiles, and ceramics. They then employ the visual elements of art to express themselves in the chosen medium. In their self-expression, they use these elements to design compositions of a certain style, form, and content.

Visual elements, design, style, form, and content—these make up the language of art. A language is a means of communicating thoughts and feelings. In spoken and written languages we communicate by means of sounds and symbols; in the visual arts we communicate through the visual media we find in this book—although by the time this book is in print, there may well be new ones.

Languages such as English and French have symbols—words—that are combined according to rules of grammar to create a message. The visual arts have a "vocabulary" of visual elements that are combined according to the "grammar" of art, or principles of design. These principles include unity, balance, rhythm, scale, and proportion, among others. The composition of the elements creates the style, form, and content of the work—even if this content is an abstract image and not a natural subject such as a human figure or a landscape.

In this chapter we explore the basic vocabulary or visual elements in the language of art. In Chapter 3 we see how artists use principles of design. In Chapter 4 we learn about the style, form, and content of works of art.

LINE

Line is at once the simplest and most complex of the elements of art. It serves as a basic building block around which an art form is constructed and, by itself, has the capacity to evoke forests of thought and emotion. In geometry, we learn that line is made up of an infinite number of points and that the shortest distance between two points is a straight line. In art, a line is more commonly defined as a moving dot.

Characteristics of Line

Measure of Line

The **measure** of a line is its length and its width. If we conceptualize line as a moving dot, the dots that compose it can be of any size, creating a line of lesser or greater width, and of any number, creating a shorter or a longer line.

Some works of art, such as Sol LeWitt's *Lines from Four Corners to Points on a Grid* (Fig. 2-1), have lines whose measures are carefully devised. LeWitt's lines are so precise and mathematical that he was acutely conscious of their measure. The act of measuring to create exact mathematical relationships seems to be intrinsic to the work—or *is* the work. LeWitt's installations are temporary; their "ownership" means possession of a set of instructions for reproducing them. The Whitney Museum of American Art owns the work (the instructions), but once placed it (the instructions) "on loan" to the Museum of Modern Art.

By contrast, the very notion of measuring the lengths of line that are both the subject and the process of Jackson Pollock's *Number 14: Gray* (Fig. 2-2) seems ludicrous and incomprehensible. Pollock's lines weave and overlap and swell and pinch, creating a sense of infinite flow and freedom from constraint (where constraint is defined as logical and mathematical measurement). LeWitt's lines are precise; Pollock's are gestural, fluid, and loose. The effects of the LeWitt and the Pollock are very different. The LeWitt is static; the Pollock grows and recedes. The LeWitt encourages us to think; the Pollock encourages us to dream.

Expressive Qualities of Line

The works by LeWitt and Pollock also reveal the expressive characteristics of line. Lines may be perceived as delicate, tentative, elegant, assertive, forceful, or even brutal. The lines in the LeWitt installation are assertive but cold. The emotional human element is missing. The work seems to express the human capacity to detach the intellect from emotional response, and perhaps to program computers (and other people) to carry out precise instructions. The lines in the Pollock work combine the apparently incongruous expressive qualities of delicacy and force. They are well rounded and human, combining intellect with passion. The LeWitt suggests the presence of a plan. The Pollock suggests the presence of a human being weaving elegantly through the complexities of thought and life.

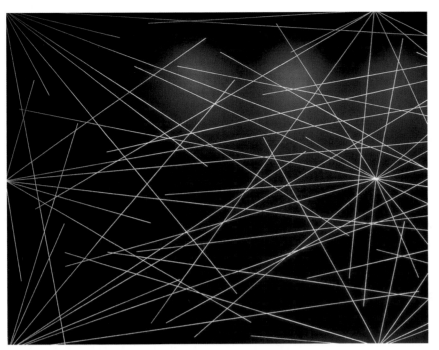

2-1 SOL LEWITT.
Lines from Four Corners to Points on a Grid (1976). Detail.
A 6″ (15 cm) grid covering each of four black walls. White lines to points on grids. 1st wall: 24 lines from the center; 2nd wall: 12 lines from the midpoint of each of the sides; 3rd wall: 12 lines from each corner; 4th wall: 24 lines from the center; 12 lines from the midpoint of each of the sides, 12 lines from each corner. White crayon lines and black crayon grid on black walls. Dimensions variable.

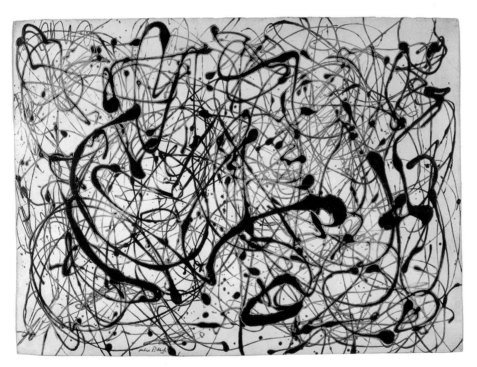

2-2 JACKSON POLLOCK.
Number 14: Gray (1948).
Enamel and gesso on paper. 22¾″ × 31″.

Types of Line

The variety of line would seem to be as infinite as the number of points that, we are told, determine it. Lines can be straight or curved. They can be vertical, horizontal, or diagonal. A curved line can be circular or oval. It can run full circle to join itself where it began, thereby creating a complete shape. Curved lines can also be segments or arcs—parts of circles or ovals. As a line proceeds, it can change direction abruptly: A straight line that stops and changes course becomes a zigzag. A curved line that forms an arc and then reverses direction becomes wavy. Circular and oval lines that turn ever inward on themselves create vertiginous spirals. Art's most basic element is a tool of infinite variety.

Contour lines are created by the edges of things. They are perceived when three-dimensional shapes curve back into space. Edges are perceived because the objects differ from the backgrounds in value (lighter versus darker), texture, or color. If you hold up your arm so that you perceive it against the wall (or, if you are outside, the sky), you will discriminate its edge—its contour line—because the wall is

2-3   EDWARD WESTON.
Knees (1927).
Gelatin silver print. $6\frac{1}{4}'' \times 9\frac{3}{16}''$.
San Francisco Museum of Art, San Francisco, CA. Alan M. Bender Collection. Alan M. Bender Fund Purchase.

lighter or darker, because it differs from the wall in color, and because the texture of flesh differs from the wallboard or plaster or wood or brick—whatever—of the wall.

Edward Weston's photograph *Knees* (Fig. 2-3) highlights the aesthetic possibilities in contour lines. Weston was drawn to the sculptural forms of the human figure, plant life, and natural inanimate objects such as rocks. In *Knees,* the contour lines (edges) of the legs are created by the subtle differences in value (light and dark) and texture between the legs and the wall and the floor. The legs take on the abstract quality of an exercise to demonstrate how contour lines define the human form and how shading creates or *models* roundness.

Actual line can be distinguished from *implied line*. The points in **actual line** are connected and continuous. The Le-Witt (Fig. 2-1) and Pollock (Fig. 2-2) are examples of works

with actual line. Works with **implied line** are completed by the viewer. An implied line can be a discontinuous line that the viewer reads as continuous because of the overall context of the image. Implied lines can be suggested by series of points or dots, as in Part B of Figure 2-4. They can be suggested by the nearby endpoints of series of parallel or nearly parallel lines of different lengths, as in Part C of Figure 2-4. The movements and glances of the figures in a composition also imply lines.

One of the hallmarks of Renaissance paintings is the use of implied lines to create or echo the structure of the composition. Geometric shapes such as triangles and circles are suggested through the use of linear patterns created by the position and physical gestures of the participants and, often, glances between them. These shapes often serve as the central focus and the main organizational device of the com-

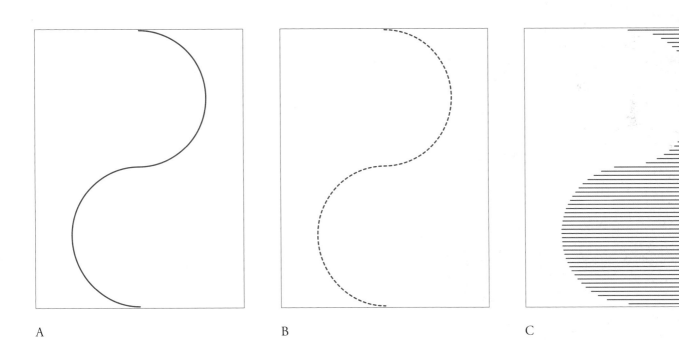

A   B   C

2-4 A, B, and C Actual line (A) versus two kinds of implied lines, one formed by dots (B) and the other formed by psychologically connecting the edges of a series of straight lines (C).

2-5   LEONARDO DA VINCI.
Madonna of the Rocks (c. 1483).
Oil on panel, transferred to canvas. 78½″ × 48″.
Louvre Museum, Paris / Réunion des Musées Nationaux / Art Resource,
New York.

2-6   The pyramidal structure of the *Madonna of the Rocks*.

positions. In the *Madonna of the Rocks* (Fig. 2-5), Leonardo da Vinci places the head of the Virgin Mary in the apex of a rather broad, stable pyramid formed not by actual lines but by the extension of her arms and the direction of her glance. The base of the pyramid is suggested by an implied line that joins the "endpoints" of the baby Jesus and the infant John the Baptist. Figure 2-6 highlights the pyramidal structure of the composition.

Implied line also refers to the gaps that exist in an otherwise continuous outline, as we find in Larry Rivers's *Dutch Masters and Cigars* (Fig. 2-7). As a twentieth-century Pop

artist, Rivers reworked many images that had become hackneyed, such as Rembrandt's masterpiece *The Syndics of the Drapers' Guild* (see Fig. 16-19), which was painted in the 1660s and achieved a wider audience—one might say—through its placement on the inside cover of Dutch Masters cigar boxes in the 1900s. Some of Rivers's lines are forceful and complete, but many of them stop short. He leaves it to us, for example, to complete the implied outlines of some of the figures and the cigars. The image is with us, but not entirely. The use of implied line seems to compel us to confront the question as to where the image really "belongs"—

2-7 LARRY RIVERS.
Dutch Masters and Cigars (1963).
Oil on canvas.
96" × 67¾".
Copyright Estate of Larry Rivers. Licensed by VAGA, New York.

on the wall of a museum in Amsterdam or on millions of cigar boxes? Perhaps Rivers's answer is that the image rightly resides in our collective cultural consciousness, emerging then receding, emerging then receding.

Functions of Line

The line, as an element of art, is alive with possibilities. Artists use line to outline shapes, to evoke forms and movement, to imply solid mass, or for its own sake. In groupings, lines can create shadows and even visual illusions.

To Outline and Shape

When you make or observe an outline, you are describing or suggesting the edge of a form or a shape. It is line that defines a shape or form as separate from its surrounding space; it is line that gives birth to shape or form. It is line that grants them substance.

Lines made of brass wire separate the figures in Alexander Calder's whimsical *The Brass Family* (Fig. 2-8) from their surrounding space. Yet space also flows through because these are not contour lines; these are outlines. Calder gave birth to many such playful figures and groupings. Given the openness of the figures, it is easy for them to maintain their balancing act. The wire outline of genitals and breasts makes them toylike rather than evocative or erotic. Note the intersection of implied triangles in the overall shape (Fig. 2-9).

In addition to defining shape, line can also function as form itself. *Madonna and Child* (Fig. 2-10) by Rimma Gerlovina and Valeriy Gerlovin is a revision of one of the most popular religious themes of the Renaissance. Taking their cue from works by artists such as Raphael, the Gerlovins use their signature combination of the body and braided hair to embroider a contemporary image of the Virgin Mary and the infant Jesus. The Gerlovins are the principal subjects of their work, and in this piece Gerlovina serves as the model for the Virgin. Braid extensions of her own

2-8   ALEXANDER CALDER.
The Brass Family (1927).
Brass wire and painted wood. 66³⁄₈″ × 40″ × 8″.

Collection of the Whitney Museum of American Art, New York. Gift of the artist. Copyright 2003 Estate of Alexander Calder/Artists Rights Society (ARS), New York.

2-9   The intersecting triangles that define the structure of the overall composition of *The Brass Family*.

sandy brown hair cascade from a sculptural head
whose three-dimensionality stands in marked contrast to the flatness of the rippling braids. These
braids flow into the contours of the Christ-child's
body, nested in the palm of a sculpted hand.

To Create Depth and Texture

The face of Elizabeth Catlett's sturdy *Sharecropper*
(Fig. 2-11) is etched by series of short, vigorous
lines that are echoed in the atmosphere that surrounds her. The lines give the woman's features a
gaunt, hollowed-out look and are also used to create a harsh texture in a turbulent environment. The
textures of her garment, hair, and hat are also represented by series of lines.

2-12 Illusion of three-dimensionality.
Dots and lines can be used to create the illusion of three-dimensionality through shading. Part A shows the method of stippling, in which shading is represented by a pattern of dots that thickens and thins. Part B represents shading by means of hatching—that is, using a series of closely spaced parallel lines. Part C shows the method of cross-hatching, in which the series of lines intersects another series of lines. Part D shows how directional changes in hatching can define contours.

A. Stippling

B. Hatching

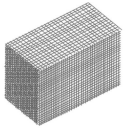

C. Cross-hatching

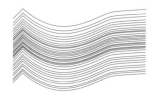

D. Contour hatching

Modeling on a two-dimensional surface is the creation of the illusion of roundness or three dimensions through the use of light and shadow. As shown in Figure 2-12, shadows can be created by the use of dots and lines. Part A shows the method of **stippling,** of using a pattern of dots that thickens and thins. Areas where the dots are thicker are darker and create the illusion of being more shaded. Part B shows the technique of **hatching,** or using series of closely spaced parallel lines to achieve a similar effect. Areas in which lines are closer together appear to be more shaded. **Cross-hatching,** shown in Part C, is similar to hatching, but as the name implies, series of lines run in different directions and cross one another.

Contours can be created when hatching changes direction, as in Part D. Notice how the sharecropper's face is carved by hatching that alters direction to give shape to the wells of the eyes, the nose, the lips, and the chin. Directional changes in hatching also define the prominent anatomic features of the sharecropper's neck.

To Suggest Direction and Movement

Renaissance artist Sandro Botticelli's *The Birth of Venus* (Fig. 2-13) shows how line can be used to outline forms and evoke movement. In this painting, firm lines carve out the figures from the rigid horizontal of the horizon and the ver-

2-13 SANDRO BOTTICELLI.
The Birth of Venus
(c. 1482).
Oil on canvas.
5'8⅞" × 9'1⅞".
Uffizi Gallery, Florence/Scala/
Art Resource, New York.

2-14 JACOB LAWRENCE.
Harriet Tubman Series, No. 4 (1939–1940).
Casein tempera on gessoed hardboard. 12″ × 17⅞″.
Hampton University Museum, Hampton, VA. Copyright 2005 Artists
Rights Society (ARS), New York.

ticals of the trees. Straight lines carry the breath of the Zephyr from the left, and the curved lines of the drapery imply the movement of the Zephyrs and of the nymph to the right. Implied compositional lines give this work an overall triangular structure.

Horizontal lines, like horizon lines, suggest stability. Vertical lines, like the sweeping verticals in skyscrapers, defy gravity and suggest assertiveness. Diagonal lines are often used to imply movement and directionality, as in the directionality and movement of the breath of the Zephyr in *The Birth of Venus*. African American artist Jacob Lawrence used assertive sticklike diagonals to give the slave children in his painting (Fig. 2-14) a powerful sense of movement and directionality. While the horizon line provides a somewhat stable world, the brightly clad children perform acrobatic leaps, their branchlike limbs akin to the wood above. The enduring world implied by the horizon is shattered by the agitated back and forth of the brushed lines that define ground and sky. Such turmoil presumably awaits the children once they mature and realize their lot in life.

SHAPE, VOLUME, AND MASS

The word *shape* has many meanings. Parents or teachers may tell you to "shape up" when they are concerned about your behavior. When you started arranging things in your dorm room or apartment, you may have thoughts as things begin to "take shape." Such expressions suggest "definition"—that is, pulling things together within defined boundaries to distinguish them from what surrounds them. We say our bodies are "out of shape" when they violate our preferred physical contours. In works of art, **shapes** are defined as the areas within a composition that have boundaries that separate them from what surrounds them; shapes make these areas distinct.

Shapes are formed when intersecting or connected lines enclose space. In Botticelli's *The Birth of Venus* and in the Lawrence painting, for example, shape is clearly communicated by lines that enclose specific areas of the painting. Shape can also be communicated through patches of color or texture. In three-dimensional works, such as sculpture

The more basic the color, the more inward: the more pure.

—Piet Mondrian

2-15   PIET MONDRIAN.
*Composition with Red, Blue,
and Yellow* (1930).
Oil on canvas. 28½″ × 21¼″.

2-16   HELENE BRANDT.
*Mondrian Variations, Construction No. 3B with Four Red
Squares and Two Planes* (1996).
Welded steel, wood, paint. 22″ × 19″ × 17″.

and architecture, shape is discerned when the work is viewed against its environment. The edges, colors, and textures of the work give it shape against the background. Piet Mondrian's *Composition with Red, Blue, and Yellow* (Fig. 2-15) features colorful geometric shapes—rectangles of various dimensions—that are created when vertical and horizontal black lines slice through the canvas space and intersect to define areas distinct from the rest of the surface.

The word **form** is often used to speak about shape in sculpture or architecture—three-dimensional works of art. Helene Brandt's *Mondrian Variations, Construction No. 3B with Four Red Squares and Two Planes* (Fig. 2-16) is a translation of Mondrian's composition into three dimensions. Therefore, some artists and people who write about art

might prefer to speak of the *form* of the Brandt sculpture rather than its *shape*. Others use the word *shape* to apply to both two-dimensional and three-dimensional works of art. We will use the terms interchangeably.

The word **volume** refers to the mass or bulk of a three-dimensional work. The volume of a work is the amount of space it contains. In geometry, the volume of a rectangular solid is computed as its length times its width times its height. But one might use the concept more loosely to say that a structure has a great *volume* as a way of generally describing its enormity. Gerrit Rietveldt's Schroeder House in Utrecht (Fig. 2-17) seems to be a volumetric translation of Mondrian's geometric shapes. Here is an example of the usefulness of the term *volume* as it conveys a sense of containment.

2-17 GERRIT RIETVELDT.
Schroeder House, Utrecht (1924).

Copyright Jannes Linders. Copyright 2003 Artists
Rights Society (ARS), New York/Beeldrect,
Amsterdam.

Mass

Like volume, the term *mass* also has a specific meaning in science. In physics, the mass of an object reflects the amount of force it would require to move it. Objects that have more mass are harder to budge. In three-dimensional art, the **mass** of an object refers to its bulk. A solid work made of steel with the same dimensions as Helene Brandt's sculpture would have more mass.

We would be hard pressed to conjure a better exemplar of mass than Rachel Whiteread's Holocaust Memorial in Vienna (Fig. 2-18). It possesses the gravity of a stone pyramid (see Fig. 12-14) and evokes the simplicity and serenity of a mausoleum. Built of concrete and weighing 250 tons, the memorial is designed as an inverted library—the "books" protrude on the outside—in recognition of the significance of study to the

2-18 RACHEL WHITEREAD.
Holocaust Memorial, Vienna (2000).

Copyright Reuters NewMedia Inc./CORBIS.

2-19 ELIHU VEDDER.
The Questioner of the Sphinx (1863).
Oil on canvas. 36¼″ × 42¼″.
Museum of Fine Arts, Boston. Bequest of Mrs. Martin Brimmer (06.2430).

Jewish people, "the people of the book." But the doors to this "library" are bolted, making the books inaccessible. In the wake of the destruction of the Austrian Jewish community, there is no longer any use for them. The names of the places to which the country's Jews were deported for annihilation are inscribed in alphabetical order around the exterior. There is murder, death, and loss here, and the massiveness of the memorial shapes a sense of gloom that cannot be lifted.

Actual Mass versus Implied Mass

The Whiteread Memorial has **actual mass.** It occupies three-dimensional space and has measurable volume and weight.

Objects that are depicted as three-dimensional on a two-dimensional surface (such as a drawing or a painting) have what we call **implied mass.** That is, they create the illusion of possessing volume, having weight, and occupying three-dimensional space. Consider a two-dimensional work of art that features massive shapes found, along with the Pyramids, in Egypt's Valley of the Kings. In *The Questioner of the Sphinx* (Fig. 2-19), Elihu Vedder meticulously portrays the remnants of a colossal sculpture amidst the

ruins of temples and the unending sands of the desert. His realistic style helps create the illusion of three dimensions on the two-dimensional canvas surface. The extraordinary mass of the oversized stone head is implied, whereas the archeological remains that it intends to invoke have actual mass.

Types of Shape

Shapes that are found in geometric figures such as rectangles and circles are called **geometric shapes.** Geometric shapes are regular and precise. They may be made up of straight (rectilinear) or curved (curvilinear) lines, but they have an unnatural, mathematical appearance. Shapes that resemble organisms found in nature—the forms of animals and plant life—are called **organic shapes** and have a natural appearance. Most of the organic shapes found in art are soft, curvilinear, and irregular, although some natural shapes, such as those found in the structure of crystals, are harsh and angular. Artists also work with *biomorphic* and *amorphous* shapes.

Geometric shapes can be **rectilinear** when straight lines intersect to form them. Geometric shapes can also be **curvilinear** when curving lines intersect to form them or when they circle back to join themselves and make up closed geometric figures. Geometric shapes frequently look crisp, or hard edged. David Smith explored the relationships among diverse geometric shapes such as cylinders, cubes, and disks in works such as *Cubi XVIII* (Fig. 2-20). His *Cubi* series represent nothing found in nature. Rather, they are abstract geometric concepts rendered in steel.

Frank Gehry, the architect of the Guggenheim Museum in Bilbao, Spain (Fig. 2-21), refers to his work as a "metallic flower." Others have found the billowing, curvilinear shapes to be reminiscent of ships, linking the machine-tooled structure that is perched on the water's edge to the history of Bilbao as an international seaport. It is as if free-floating geometric shapes have collided on this site, and on another day, they might have assumed a different configuration.

2-20   DAVID SMITH. *Cubi XVIII* (1964).
Polished stainless steel. 9'7¾" × 5' × 1'9¾".

Museum of Fine Arts, Boston. Gift of Susan W. and Stephen B. Paine.
Copyright Estate of David Smith. Licensed by VAGA, New York.

2-21   FRANK GEHRY.
Guggenheim Museum, Bilbao, Spain (1997).

Copyright E. Streichan/ZEFA/CORBIS.

Picasso's *Les Demoiselles d'Avignon* with Colescott's *Les Demoiselles d'Alabama: Vestidas*

In the year 1907, a young Pablo Picasso unveiled a painting that he had been secretly working on for a couple of years. A culmination of what was known as his Rose Period, this new work—*Les Demoiselles d'Avignon* (Fig. 2-22)—would turn the tide of modern painting. Picasso had studied the work of African and Iberian artists in Parisian museums and galleries. He was struck by the universality of the masks, believing that their rough-hewn, simplified, and angular features crossed time and culture. This was the painting that launched the movement called Cubism, which geometricizes organic forms. The contours of the body in *Demoiselles* are harsh and rectilinear, forming straighter lines than are found in nature. The women in the painting are expressionless and lack identity; some of them even have rectilinear masks in lieu of faces. The intellectual exercise of transforming the hu-

man form into geometric shapes takes precedence over any interest in expressing the plight of these women, who are prostitutes in the French underworld. The "figures" in the work transcend the period and culture in which the women lived and worked.

2-22   PABLO PICASSO.
Les Demoiselles d'Avignon (1907).
Oil on canvas. 8′ × 7′8″.

You have heard the expression "Clothing makes the man." In Robert Colescott's *Les Demoiselles d'Alabama: Vestidas* (Fig. 2-23), it could be argued that clothing makes the woman. The women in Picasso's painting are dehumanized in part by their nudity. The subjects of Colescott's painting, executed some 80 years later, are given strong individuality by their choice of costume. Colescott's painting is one of the thousands of instances in which one artist transforms the work of another in a certain way to make a certain point. Picasso's nudes have a harsh and jagged quality that gives an overall splintered quality to his work; the movement of the women seems to be abrupt and choppy. By contrast, Colescott's women are well rounded (in the literal sense) and fleshy—they are natural, organic, "real" counterparts to Picasso's geometry. The flowing, curvilinear lines of the women cause them to undulate across the canvas with fluid movement.

Whereas Picasso's rectilinear women are timeless (and "placeless"), the curvilinear, clothed women of Colescott are very much tied to their time and place—an American South full of life and spontaneity and emotional expression. Whereas Picasso seemed to relish the intellectual transformation of the prostitutes into timeless figures, Colescott seems to revel in the tangibility and sensuality of his sexy subjects.

■

2-23   ROBERT COLESCOTT.
Les Demoiselles d'Alabama: Vestidas (1985).
Acrylic on canvas. 96″ × 92″.
Collection of Hanford Yang, New York.

Elizabeth Murray's *Careless Love* (Fig. 2-24) is reminiscent of any number of bodily organs or underwater life—although no medical student or botanist could ever quite place it according to kingdom, phylum, and so on. The shape looks rawly excised from some creature. The interlacing tubes are reminiscent of veins and capillaries carrying who knows what (or who wants to know what). Such imagery is said to have a **biomorphic** shape—that is, it has the form (the Greek *morphē*) of biological entities. Rather than have strictly defined shapes, whose boundaries are unyielding, biomorphic shapes seem to ebb and flow, expand and contract, or metamorphose as directed by some inner life force.

Shapes need not be clearly defined or derived from nature or the laws of geometry. Many artists, such as the contemporary painter Helen Frankenthaler, create **amorphous** shapes. In *Bay Side* (Fig. 2-25), Frankenthaler literally poured paint onto her canvas, creating a nebulous work dense in form and rich in texture. The "contents" of the loosely defined shapes spill beyond their boundaries, filling the canvas with irregularly shaped pools of poured paint.

2-24   ELIZABETH MURRAY.
Careless Love (1995–1996).
Oil on shaped canvas with wood.
106½″ × 99½″ × 27″.
Courtesy of PaceWildenstein.

2-25   HELEN FRANKENTHALER.
Bay Side (1967).
Acrylic on canvas.
Copyright Helen Frankenthaler. Courtesy of the
André Emmerich Gallery, New York.

> *Time is not just a mental concept or a mathematical abstraction in the salt desert of Utah's great basin. It can also take on a physical presence.*
>
> —Nancy Holt

Positive and Negative Shapes

Viewers usually focus on the objects or figures represented in works of art. These are referred to as the **positive shapes.** Whatever is left over in the composition, whether empty space or space filled with other imagery, is termed the **negative shape** or shapes of the composition.

Positive and negative shapes in a work of art have a **figure–ground** relationship. The part or parts of the work that are seen as what the artist intended to depict are the figure, and the other parts are seen as the ground, or background. Barbara Kruger's *What Big Muscles You Have!* (Fig. 2-26) illustrates that the figure and ground can be distinct even when the relationship between the two is not so clear-cut. Against a satirical running text of the mindless mantra of a hero-worshiper, Kruger sums up the litany with the proclamation "What big muscles you have!" The viewer identifies the larger type as figure and the smaller type of the running text as ground. Notice the visual tension between

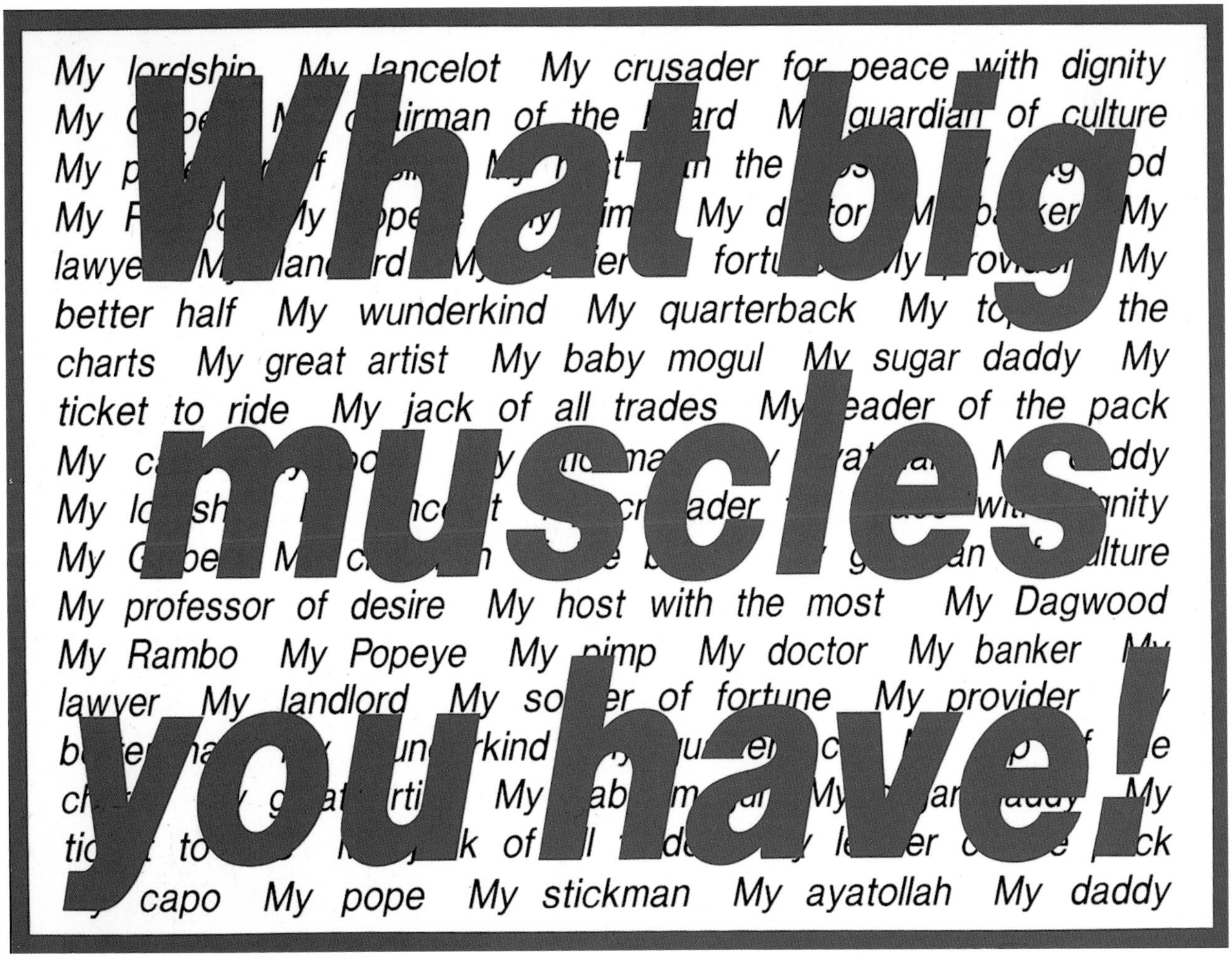

2-26 BARBARA KRUGER.
What Big Muscles You Have! (1985).
Vinyl lettering on Plexiglas. 60″ × 80″.
Centre Georges Pompidou, Paris. Copyright Art Resource, New York.

2-27 NANCY HOLT.
Sun Tunnels (1973–1976).
Concrete. Great Basin Desert, UT.
Copyright Scott T. Smith/CORBIS.

2-28 A Rubin vase.
Gestalt psychologists use this drawing to illustrate the fact that humans tend to perceive objects within their context. When we focus on the vase, it is the figure, and the white shapes to the sides are part of the ground. But when we focus on the "profiles of heads" suggested by the white shapes where they intersect with the sides of the vase, the vase becomes the ground. The drawing is ambiguous; that is, it can be perceived in different ways. As a result, the viewer may experience figure–ground reversals.

the large and small type. As we read the larger type, our eye shifts to the pattern and flow of the words behind, and vice versa. The smaller type serves as a kind of psychological wallpaper, signifying one of the horrors of an age of male supremacy that Kruger hopes we left behind in the last millennium.

For many sculptors, negative shapes, or open spaces, are part and parcel of their compositions. The positive shapes in Nancy Holt's *Sun Tunnels* (Fig. 2-27) consist of the huge concrete pipes she placed in the Utah desert. But the views framed by looking through the interiors of these massive structures—the voids, or negative shapes—have as much or more meaning than the solids. The flow of air and light through the pipes—the "sun tunnels"—lends them a lightness of being that contrasts with their actual mass. The artist has, in effect, enlisted the sun as an element in her composition.

Gestalt psychologists have noted that shapes can be ambiguous, so as to encourage **figure–ground reversals** with

viewers. Figure 2-28 shows a Rubin vase, which is a classic illustration of figure–ground reversals found in psychology textbooks. The central shape is that of a vase, and when the viewer focuses on it, it is the figure. But "carved" into the sides of the vase are the shapes of human profiles; when the viewer focuses on them, they become the figure and the vase becomes the ground. The point of the Gestalt psychologists is that we tend to perceive things *in context*. When we are focusing on the profiles, the vase is relegated to be perceived as ground, not figure.

The visual ambiguity between figure and ground is a key aspect of John Klima's Screenshot from *Earth, Landsat-7 layer* (Fig. 2-29). *Earth* is an electronic work culled from the Internet that consists of multiple layers of data about our planet. All the information is projected onto a spherical map of Earth as shot from weather satellites. The combination of two- and three-dimensional views of the planet and several layers of imagery send the viewer's eye darting back and forth, searching for a resting place. In a sense, the flood of confusing information in the work appears to comment on the perceptual crashes that take place on the information superhighway every day.

Edward Steichen's photograph of the sculptor Auguste Rodin silhouetted against his sculpted portrait of Victor Hugo (Fig. 2-30) creates a visual limbo between figure and ground. The eye readily perceives the contours of the face of Rodin sitting opposite his bronze sculpture of *The Thinker,* also set against the Hugo sculpture. The viewer's sense of what is a positive shape and what is a negative shape undergoes reversals, as the white-clouded image of the background work seems to float toward the viewer. The spectrelike image of Hugo hovers between and above the dark images, filling the space between them and pushing them visually into the background.

2-29 JOHN KLIMA.
Screenshot from *Earth, Landsat-7 layer* (2001).
Courtesy, Postmasters Gallery, New York. Copyright John Klima.

2-30 EDWARD STEICHEN.
Rodin with His Sculptures "Victor Hugo" and "The Thinker" (1902).
Carbon print, toned.
From *Camera Work* 11 (July 1905), 35. Courtesy of The Royal Photographic Society/ Heritage Image Partnership (HIP), heritage-images.com.

LIGHT AND VALUE

Light is fascinating stuff. It radiates. It illuminates. It dazzles. It glows. It beckons like a beacon. We speak of the "light of reason." We speak of genius as "brilliance." **Visible light** is part of the spectrum of electromagnetic energy that also includes radio waves and cosmic rays. It undulates wavelike throughout the universe. It bounces off objects and excites cells in our eyes, enabling us to see. Light is at the very core of the visual arts. Without light there is no art. Without light there is no life.

One of the lobes of the brain contains a theater for light. Somehow it distinguishes light from dark. Somehow it translates wavelengths of energy into colors. We perceive the colors of the visible spectrum, ranging from violet to red. Although red has the longest wavelength of the colors of the visible spectrum, these waves are measured in terms of *bil-lionths* of a meter. And if our eyes were sensitive to light of a slightly longer wavelength, we would perceive infrared light waves. Sources of heat, such as our mates, would then literally glow in the dark. And our perceptions, and our visible arts, would be quite different.

Light makes it possible for us to see points, lines, shapes, and textures. All of these can be perceived as light against dark or in the case of a pencil line on a sheet of paper, as dark against light. Light against dark, dark against light—in the language of art these are said to be differences in *value*.

The **value** of a color of a surface is its lightness or darkness. The value is determined by the amount of light reflected by the surface: the greater the amount of light reflected, the lighter the surface. More light is reflected by a white surface than by a gray surface, and gray reflects more than black. White, therefore, is lighter than gray, and gray is lighter than black.

2-31　A value scale of grays.
Do the circles become darker as they move to the right, or do they only appear to do so? How does this value scale support the view of Gestalt psychologists that people make judgments about the objects they perceive that are based on the context of those objects?

2-32　Value contrast.
Artists and designers know that figures with high value contrast are easier to see. They tend to "pop" out at the viewer. Why is Part A of this figure relatively difficult to read? Why are Parts B and C easier to read?

A

B

2-33　HENRI ROUSSEAU.
The Sleeping Gypsy (1897).
Oil on canvas. 4′3″ × 6′7″.

The Museum of Modern Art, New York. Gift of
Mrs. Simon Guggenheim/Art Resource, New York.

2-34　HENRI ROUSSEAU.
The Sleeping Gypsy, rendered in a palette
of grays.

Infinite shades of gray lie between black and white. Figure 2-31 is a value scale of gray that contains seven shades of gray, varying between a gray that is almost black to the left and one that is slightly off-white to the right. When we describe works of art in terms of value, not only do we distinguish their range of grays but we also characterize their *relative* lightness and darkness, that is, their value contrast. **Value contrast** refers to the degrees of difference between shades of gray. Look again at Figure 2-31. Note that there are circles within the squares. Each of them is exactly of the same value (they are all equally dark). However, their value contrast with the squares that contain them differs. The circle and square in the center are of the same value, and therefore they have no value contrast. The circles at either end of the scale have high value contrast with the squares that contain them.

Drawing objects or figures with high value contrast makes them easy to see, or makes them "pop." Consider Figure 2-32. Part A shows a gray sentence typed on gray paper that is nearly as dark; it is difficult to read. Part B shows nearly black type on off-white paper; it is easy to read. Part C shows light type that is "dropped out" of dark gray—it, too, pops out at the reader because of high value contrast.

We can discuss the relative lightness and darkness in a work regardless of whether it is a black-and-white or full-color composition. Sometimes it is easier to discriminate value contrasts in looking at black-and-white reproductions of color works. Figure 2-33 shows Rousseau's *The Sleeping Gypsy* in its original color. In Figure 2-34 its richly colored palette is transformed into an infinite palette of grays. What is captured in the gray version is the relative lightness or darkness of the hues in the original painting. The nearly white body of the mandolin echoes the value and shape of the moon, and both pop out at the viewer from the surrounding darker grays. The spectrum of hues that compose the tunic of the gypsy is reduced to harmonious variations in gray.

Although the circles in Figure 2-31 are all of the same value, when they are placed within a lighter square, they appear to be darker. Thus, the circles seem to be getting darker as they move to the right, even though they remain the same. The mandolin in Figure 2-34 looks brighter than it would if it were lying in the gypsy's lap. Why?

Chiaroscuro

Artists use many methods to create the illusion of three dimensions in two-dimensional media such as painting, drawing, or printmaking. They frequently rely on a pattern of values termed **chiaroscuro,** or the gradual shifting from light to dark through a successive gradation of tones across a curved surface. By use of many gradations of value, artists can give objects portrayed on a flat surface a rounded, three-dimensional appearance.

In *La Source* (Fig. 2-35), Pierre-Paul Prud'hon creates the illusion of rounded surfaces on blue gray paper by using black and white chalk to portray light gradually dissolving into shade. His subtle modeling of the nude is facilitated by the middle value of the paper and the gradation of tones from light to dark through a series of changing grays. Prud'hon's light source is not raking and harsh, but diffuse and natural. The forms are not sharply outlined; we must work to find outlining anywhere but in the drapery and in the hair. The softly brushed edges of the figure lead your eye to perceive three-dimensional form (continuing around into space) rather than flat, two-dimensional shape.

Picasso used chiaroscuro in his *Self-Portrait* (Fig. 2-36), sketched at the age of 19. Although he restricted himself to

2-35   PIERRE-PAUL PRUD'HON.
La Source (c. 1801).
Black and white chalk on blue gray paper. 21³⁄₁₆″ × 15⁵⁄₁₆″.
Sterling and Francine Clark Art Institute, Williamstown, MA.

2-36   PABLO PICASSO.
Self-Portrait (1900).
Charcoal on paper. 8⁷⁄₈″ × 6½″.
Museu Picasso, Barcelona. Copyright 2003 Estate of Pablo Picasso/Artists Rights Society (ARS), New York.

the use of charcoal, he managed to effect a more subtle gradation of tone through shading that softly delineates his facial features. Sharp contrasts are eliminated by the choice of a buff-colored paper that provides a uniform flesh tone. In effect, the sides of the nose and cheek are built up through the use of soft shadows. The chin and jaw jut out above the neck through the use of sharper shadowing. The eyes achieve their intensity because they are a dark counterpoint to the evenly modeled flesh. There is a tension between the angularity of the lines in the drawing and the modeling. If you focus on the lines, the drawing may seem to be more angular and geometric than organic. But the use of chiaroscuro creates a more subtle and human rounding of the face.

Descriptive and Expressive Properties of Value

Values—black, grays, white—may be used purely to describe objects, or they can be used to evoke emotional responses in the viewer.

Black and white may have expressive properties or symbolic associations. Consider the photograph of a performance piece by Lorraine O'Grady (Fig. 2-37) staged in protest of the opening of an exhibit entitled "Personae," which featured the work of nine white artists and *no* artists of color. Labeling herself "Mlle Bourgeoisie Noire" (or Miss Middle-Class Black), O'Grady appeared in an evening gown constructed of 180 pairs of white gloves and shouted poems that lashed out against the racial politics of the art establishment. Clearly, the white gloves were both evocative and provocative. They were at once a symbol of high society and servitude, of the elegant attire of the exclusive dinner party and the vaudevillian costume of blackface and white-gloved hands.

Even though Robert Ryman's *Winsor 6* (Fig. 2-38) may seem very far removed from the symbolic references of O'Grady's character, his composition nonetheless suggests a certain purity that is associated with white. Indeed, the theory behind his minimalist work was expressed by the art critic Clement Greenberg, who encouraged artists to emphasize the "objecthood" or actuality of their works. The issue to Greenberg and Ryman was not what the painting represented but rather the existence of the painting as an object in its own right.

2-37 LORRAINE O'GRADY. *Mlle Bourgeoise Noire Goes to the New Museum* (1981). Courtesy of the artist.

2-38 ROBERT RYMAN. *Winsor 6* (1965). Oil on linen. 75¾″ × 75¾″. Private Collection. Courtesy Thomas Amman Fine Art, Zürich.

It is only after years of preparation that the young artist should touch color—
not color used descriptively, that is, but as a means of personal expression.

—Henri Matisse

COLOR

Color is a central element in our spoken language as well as in the language of art. The language connects emotion with color: we speak of being blue with sorrow, red with anger, green with envy.

The color in works of art can also trigger strong emotional responses in the observer, working hand in hand with line and shape to enrich the viewing experience. The Postimpressionist Vincent van Gogh often chose color more for its emotive qualities rather than for its fidelity to nature. Likewise in some amorphous abstract works, such as *Bay Side* (Fig. 2-25), color itself seems to be much of the "message" being communicated by the artist.

What is color? You have no doubt seen a rainbow or observed how light sometimes separates into several colors when it is filtered through a window. Sir Isaac Newton discovered that sunlight, or white light, can be broken down into different colors by a triangular glass solid called a **prism** (Fig. 2-39).

Psychological Dimensions of Color: Hue, Value, and Saturation

The wavelength of light determines its color, or **hue.** The visible spectrum consists of the colors red, orange, yellow, green, blue, indigo, and violet. The wavelength for red is longer than that for orange, and so on through violet.

The value of a color, like the value of any light, is its degree of lightness or darkness. If we wrap the colors of the spectrum around into a circle, we create a color wheel such as that shown in Figure 2-40. (We must add some purples not found in the spectrum to complete the circle.) Yellow is the lightest of the colors on the wheel, and violet is the darkest. As we work our way around from yellow to violet, we encounter progressively darker colors. Blue green is about equal in value to red orange, but green is lighter than red.

The colors on the green–blue side of the color wheel are considered **cool** in "temperature," whereas the colors on the yellow–orange–red side are considered **warm.** Perhaps greens and blues suggest the coolness of the ocean or the sky, and hot things tend to burn red or orange. A room decorated in green or blue may appear more appealing on a hot day in July than a room decorated in red or orange. On a canvas, warm colors seem to advance toward the picture plane. Cool colors, on the other hand, seem to recede.

The **saturation** of a color is its pureness. Pure hues have the greatest intensity, or brightness. The saturation, and hence the intensity, decrease when another hue or black, gray, or white is added. Artists produce **shades** of a given hue by adding black, and **tints** by adding white.

2-39   Prism.
A prism breaks down white light into the colors of the visible spectrum.
Courtesy of Bausch & Lomb.

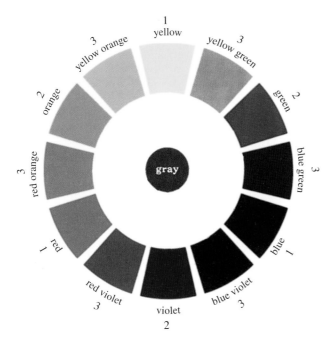

2-40 A color wheel.
The color wheel bends the colors of the visible spectrum into a circle and adds a few missing hues to complete the circle.

Complementary versus Analogous Colors

The colors opposite each other on the color wheel are said to be **complementary.** Red-green and blue-yellow are the major complementary pairs. If we mix complementary colors together, they dissolve into neutral gray.

Wait! You may say that blue and yellow cannot be "complementary" because by mixing **pigments** of blue and yellow, we create green, not gray. That is true, but we are talking about mixing *lights,* not pigments. Light is the source of all color; pigments reflect and absorb different wavelengths of light selectively. The mixture of lights is an *additive* process (Fig. 2-41), whereas the mixture of pigments is *subtractive* (Fig. 2-42).

Pigments attain their colors by absorbing light from certain segments of the spectrum and reflecting the rest. For example, we see most plant life as green because the pigment in chlorophyll absorbs most of the red, blue, and violet wavelengths of light. The remaining green is reflected. A red pigment absorbs most of the spectrum but reflects red. White pigment reflects all colors equally. Black pigment reflects very little light; it absorbs all wavelengths without prejudice. Black and white may be considered colors, but not hues.

Black, white, and their mixture of gray are **achromatic,** or neutral, "colors," also referred to simply as **neutrals.**

The pigments of red, blue, and yellow are the **primary colors,** those that we cannot produce by mixing other hues. Mixing pigments of the primary colors creates **secondary colors.** The three secondary colors are orange (derived from mixing red and yellow), green (blue and yellow), and violet (red and blue), denoted by the number 2 on the color wheel. **Tertiary colors** are created by mixing pigments of primary and adjoining secondary colors and are denoted by a 3 on the color wheel.

Hues that lie next to one another on the color wheel are **analogous.** They form families of color, such as yellow and

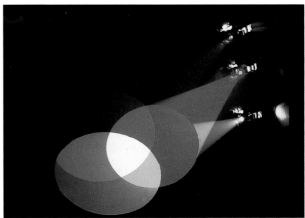

2-41 Additive color mixtures.
One adds colors by mixing lights.
Copyright Fritz Goro, Time & Life Pictures/Getty Images.

2-42 Subtractive color mixtures.
One subtracts colors by mixing pigments.
Copyright Fritz Goro, Time & Life Pictures/Getty Images.

2-43 ROMARE BEARDEN.
J Mood (c. 1985).

Romare Bearden Foundation. Licensed by
VAGA, New York.

2-44 VICTOR VASARELY.
Orion (1956).

Paper on paper mounted on wood.
6′10½″ × 6′6¾″.

Hirshhorn Museum and Sculpture Garden,
Smithsonian Institution, Washington, DC.
Gift of Joseph H. Hirshhorn, 1966.
Copyright 2003 Artists Rights Society (ARS),
New York/ADGAP, Paris.

orange, orange and red, and green and blue. As we work our way around the wheel, the families intermarry, such as blue with violet and violet with red. Works that use closely related families of color seem harmonious, such as Romare Bearden's *J Mood* (Fig. 2-43). Works that juxtapose colors that lie across from one another on the color wheel will have the opposite effect. They will appear jarring and discordant rather than harmonious.

Victor Vasarely's *Orion* (Fig. 2-44) is an assemblage of paper cutouts that take on different intensities depending on their backgrounds. Vasarely, an Op artist, sought to create optical illusions in many of his works. In *Orion,* the shifts from warm to cool hues cause elements of the arrangement to move toward or away from the viewer. The progressions of circles and ellipses within lighter and darker squares contribute to the pulsating sense of the piece.

Many pictures show a balance of hues, although artists do not necessarily think in terms of complementary and analogous colors. Artists may simply experiment with their compositions until they find them pleasing, but our analyzing their use of color and other elements of art helps us appreciate their work.

2-45 CLAUDE MONET.
Haystack at Sunset near Giverny (1891).
Oil on canvas. $28\frac{7}{8}'' \times 36\frac{1}{2}''$.
Museum of Fine Arts, Boston. Juliana Cheney
Edwards Collection. Bequest of Robert J. Edwards in
memory of his mother/The Bridgeman Art Library.

Local versus Optical Color

Have you ever driven at night and wondered
whether vague, wavy lines in the distance
outlined the peaks of hills or the bases of
clouds? Objects may take on different hues as
a function of distance or lighting conditions.
The greenness of the trees on a mountain
may make a strong impression from the base
of the mountain, but from a distant vantage
point the atmospheric scattering of light rays
may dissolve the hue into a blue haze. Light-
colored objects take on a dark appearance
when lit strongly from behind. Hues fade as
late afternoon wends its way to dusk and
dusk to night. **Local color** is defined as the
hue of an object as created by the colors its
surface reflects under normal lighting conditions. **Optical color** is defined as our perceptions of color, which can vary markedly with
lighting conditions.

Consider the *Haystack at Sunset near
Giverny* (Fig. 2-45) by the French Impressionist Claude Monet. Hay is light brown or
straw colored, but Monet's haystack takes on
fiery hues, reflecting the angle of the light
from the departing sun. The upper reach of
the stack, especially, is given a forceful silhouette through flowing swaths of dark color.
Surely the pigments of the surface of the
haystack are no darker than the roofs of the
houses that cling tenuously to an implied
horizontal line across the center left of the
picture. But the sun washes out their pigmen-
tation. Nor can we with certainty interpret
the horizontal above the roofs. Is it the top of
a distant hill or the base of a cloud? Only in
the visual sanctuary to the front of the haystack do a few possibly accurate greens and browns assert
themselves. The amorphous shapes and pulsating color fields
of *Haystack* lend the painting a powerful emotional impact.

In *The Night Café* (Fig. 2-46), Vincent van Gogh used
color expressively rather than realistically. A café is generally

2-46 VINCENT VAN GOGH.
The Night Café (1888).
Oil on canvas. $27\frac{1}{2}'' \times 35''$.
Yale University Art Gallery, New Haven, CT. Bequest of Stephen C. Clark,
B.A. 1903.

2-47 ERWIN REDL.
Matrix IV 30/5/01
Installation view of at Creative Time's "Massless Medium:
Exploration in Sensory Immersion." The Brooklyn Bridge
Anchorage, Brooklyn, NY.
Collection of the artist.

surround the lamps create lights that never were—
a psychological display of brilliance and agitation.

The familiar expression "sensory overload"
reaches new heights (literally) in Erwin Redl's
Matrix IV 30/5/01 (Fig. 2-47), an installation
that immerses the viewer in a cool and highly
saturated "blueness." The LED display is usually
thought of as a medium for carrying information,
but Redl's wall of light—constructed of LED
points, lines, and grids—is used as a medium
for sensory stimulation. Some of his installations
are programmed to change slowly as the viewer
looks on, in sharp contrast to the rapidly changing
electronic displays that usually confront viewers
today.

Texture is another element of art that can
evoke a strong emotional response.

TEXTURE

The softness of skin and silk, the coarseness of
rawhide and homespun cloth, the coolness of stone
and tile, the warmth of wood—these are but a few
of the **textures** that artists capture in their works.
The word *texture* derives from the Latin for "weaving," and it is used to describe the surface character
of woven fabrics and other materials as experienced
primarily through the sense of touch.

The element of texture adds a significant dimension to art beyond representation. An artist
may emphasize or even distort the textures of objects to evoke a powerful emotional response in the
viewer. Consider the contrasting use of texture—
and the differing emotional impact—of Leon Kossoff's
Portrait of Father, No. 2 (Fig. 2-48) and Marie Laurencin's
Mother and Child (Fig. 2-49). The first contains the harsh,
gouged textures of **impasto**—that is, the thick buildup of
paint on the surface of the canvas. The textures formed by
the technique give rise to an overall aggressive, confronta-
tional feeling. If you try to imagine the image rendered
with smoother, flatter strokes, some of the dysphoria might
well be diminished. As it is, the texture might suggest to
some the type of father/authority figure that the psychoana-
lyst Sigmund Freud believed young boys fear. In Freud's
theory, fathers are dangerous rivals for the affections of their
mothers.

Laurencin's *Mother and Child,* like Kossoff's *Portrait of
Father, No. 2,* is an oil painting. But here the brushstrokes

seen as a place to unwind and relax in the company of
friends, yet the artist chose this harsh palette to tell the
world that this is a place where one "can ruin oneself." The
red of the walls and the green of the ceiling clash, yet the
billiard table and the floor, which both contain reds and
greens, marry the two. The agitated swirls of local color that

2-48 LEON KOSSOFF.
Portrait of Father, No. 2 (1972).
Oil on board. 60″ × 36″.
Courtesy of L. A. Louver, Venice, CA.

2-49 MARIE LAURENCIN.
Mother and Child (1928).
Oil on canvas. 32″ × 25½″ (81.3 cm × 63.8 cm).
Photo copyright The Detroit Institute of Arts. City of Detroit Purchase.
Copyright 2003 Artists Rights Society (ARS), New York/ADAGP, Paris.

are shorter and flatter, and they gradually build up the imagery rather than "carve" it. The overall texture of *Mother and Child* is soft and seems comforting, reinforcing the feeling of tenderness between mother and child.

In these contrasting portraits, the role of texture surpasses the literal content of the works—that is, they are both portraits of people—to add an emotional dimension for the viewer. The father becomes an oppressive figure by virtue of the tension in the texture, and the mother becomes a symbol of nurturance by virtue of the tranquility in the texture. In both portraits, texture augments the meaning of the work.

Types of Texture

In three-dimensional media such as sculpture, crafts, and architecture, the materials themselves have definable textures or *actual texture*. In a two-dimensional medium such as painting, we discuss texture in other terms. For example, the surface of a painting has an *actual* texture—it can be rough, smooth, or something in between. But we typically discuss the surface only when the texture is palpable or unusual, as when thick impasto is used or when an unusual material is added to the surface.

2-50 VINCENT VAN GOGH.
Irises (1889).
Oil on canvas. 28″ × 36¾″.
Collection of the J. Paul Getty Museum, Los Angeles.

2-51 RACHEL RUYSCH.
Flower Still Life (after 1700).
Oil on canvas. 29¾″ × 23⅞″.
The Toledo Museum of Art, OH.
Purchased with funds from the Libbey Endowment,
gift of Edward Drummond Libbey.

Actual Texture

Actual texture is *tactile*. When you touch an object, your fingertips register sensations of its actual texture—rough, smooth, sharp, hard, soft. Any work of art has actual texture—whether it is the hard, cold texture of marble or the rough texture of pigment on canvas. Vincent van Gogh's *Irises* (Fig. 2-50) is rendered with a great deal of surface texture. Van Gogh used impasto—the most common painting technique that yields actual texture—to define his forms, and he often deviated from realistic colors and textures to heighten the emotional impact of his work. The surface texture of the painting goes beyond the real texture of the blossom to communicate an emotional intensity and passion for painting that is independent of the subject matter and more linked to the artistic process—that is, to the artist's method of using gestural brushstrokes to express his sensibilities.

Visual Texture

Simulated texture in a work of art is referred to as **visual texture.** Artists use line, color, and other elements of art to create the illusion of various textures in flat drawings and paintings. The surface of Rachel Ruysch's *Flower Still Life* (Fig. 2-51) is smooth and glasslike; however, an abundance of textures is *simulated* by the painstaking detail of the flowers and leaves.

2-52 DAVID GILHOOLY.
Bowl of Chocolate Moose (1989).
Ceramic. 10″ × 6″ × 7″ (25.4 cm × 15.2 cm × 17.8 cm).
Courtesy of the artist.

2-53 JAMES ROSENQUIST.
Gift Wrapped Doll #19 (1992).
Oil on canvas. 60″ × 60″ (152 cm × 152 cm).
Copyright 2003 James Rosenquist. Licensed by VAGA, New York.

Artists employ a variety of materials to create visual texture, or the illusion of surfaces or textures far removed from their actual texture. Touch Gilhooly's *Bowl of Chocolate Moose* (Fig. 2-52), and, your eyes will tell you, your hand will come away covered with that sticky confection. The surface may appear to be warm and pliable, as if this chocolate moose were panting and melting away into an edible dessert. In fact, it is hard and cool to the touch. The actual texture of the ceramic from which it is made is completely contrary to the illusion that the artist has achieved. *Chocolate Moose* is an artistic pun of virtuoso technique that demonstrates how the visual texture of a work of art affects our response to it. What memories does it conjure up for you? Eating a chocolate bar on a warm summer day?

The success of the visual pun in Gilhooly's *Chocolate Moose* is wholly dependent on the artist's ability to fool the eye. Artists call this **trompe l'oeil**—the French phrase that literally means "trick the eye." Trompe l'oeil has made its appearance throughout the history of art, from first century BCE Roman wall painting to contemporary Photorealism.

In *Gift-Wrapped Doll #19* (Fig. 2-53), Pop artist James Rosenquist uses a common medium—oil on canvas—to simulate the texture of cellophane wrapped around the head of a wide-eyed porcelain doll. The folds of the transparent wrap reflect light, tearing across the innocent face like white-hot rods. We feel, as observers, that were we to poke at the cellophane, we would hear a crackling sound and the pattern of lightning-like stripes would change direction. The image of a doll is usually that of a cuddly companion, but Rosenquist's specimen is haunting and sinister. Perhaps it is a commentary on the ways in which the Western ideal of beauty—blue eyes, blond hair, and a "Cupid's bow" mouth—can suffocate the little girls who grow into women.

Subversive Texture

Textures are sometimes chosen or created by the artist to subvert or undermine our ideas about the objects that they depict. **Subversive texture** compels the viewer to look again at an object and to think about it more deeply.

2-54   MERET OPPENHEIM.
Object (1936).
Fur-covered cup, saucer, and spoon. Overall height: 2⅞″.

You may take objects such as a cup, saucer, and spoon for granted, but not after viewing Meret Oppenheim's *Object* (Fig. 2-54). Oppenheim uses subversive texture in lining a cup, saucer, and spoon with fur. Teacups are usually connected with civilized and refined settings and occasions. The coarse primal fur completely subverts these associations, rendering the thought of drinking from this particular cup repugnant. *Object* also shows how textures can simultaneously attract and repel us. Does Oppenheim want the viewer to ponder the violence that has enabled civilization to grow and endure?

SPACE

"No man is an island, entire of itself," wrote the poet John Donne. If Donne had been speaking of art, he might have written, "No subject exists in and of itself." A building has a site, a sculpture is surrounded by space, and even artists who work in two-dimensional media such as drawing and painting create figures that bear relationships to one another and to their grounds. Objects exist in three-dimensional space. Artists either carve out or model their works within three-dimensional space, or else somehow come to terms with three-dimensional space through two-dimensional art forms.

In Chapters 9 and 10, which discuss the three-dimensional art forms of sculpture and architecture, we explore ways in which artists situate their objects in space and envelop space. In Chapter 10 we chronicle the age-old attempt to enclose vast reaches of space that began with massive support systems and currently focuses on lightweight steel-cage and shell-like structures. In this section we will examine ways in which artists who work in two dimensions create the illusion of depth—that is, the third dimension.

Overlapping

When nearby objects are placed in front of more distant objects, they obscure part or all of the distant objects. Figure 2-55 shows two circles and two arcs, but our perceptual experiences encourage us to interpret the drawing as showing four circles, two in the foreground and two in back. Likewise, it is this perceptual phenomenon that allows an artist to create the illusion of depth by overlapping objects, or apparently placing one in front of another. There are any number of works in your textbook that illustrate the technique of overlapping and its effect in suggesting space—whether deep, as in Church's *Heart of the Andes* (Fig. 2-65), or shallow, as in Beckmann's *The Dream* (see Fig. 1-15).

We decided to make grand history paintings of a small local history.

—Destroy All Monsters Collective

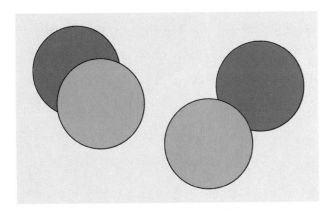

2-55 Overlapping circles and arcs.

In *The Heart of Detroit by Moonlight* (Fig. 2-56), part of an installation by the Destroy All Monsters Collective that appeared in the 2002 Whitney Biennial Exhibition, the overlapping of images of popular (and not-so-popular) Detroit personages—local TV hosts, rock singers, and musical legends—reads like so much pushing and shoving as the personalities joust for position and the attention and money of the viewer-listener. The backdrop of the city on which the figures are superimposed—a seemingly random collection of skyscrapers—recedes from the picture plane, a safe haven that seems impossible to reach. What we are left with is what is literally "in our faces." One of the messages of the piece, according to a participating artist, is that mass media can obliterate any local scene, yet it can also popularize nearly random local "stars" around the globe—transforming them into cultural phenomena, even in the most unlikely far-off places.

Relative Size and Linear Perspective

The farther objects are from us, the smaller they appear to the eye. To re-create this visual phenomenon and to create the illusion of three-dimensionality on a two-dimensional surface, such as a canvas, artists employ a variety of techniques, among them **relative size** and **linear perspective.** For example, in the Church painting (Fig. 2-65), objects in the foreground are smaller in size and scale relative to the mountains in the distance, making them look even more imperious.

2-56 DESTROY ALL MONSTERS COLLECTIVE. *The Heart of Detroit by Moonlight* (2000). From the installation *Strange Früt: Rock Apocrypha,* 2000–2001. Acrylic on canvas. 120″ × 204″.

Collection of the artists. Courtesy, Patrick Painter, Inc., Santa Monica, CA.

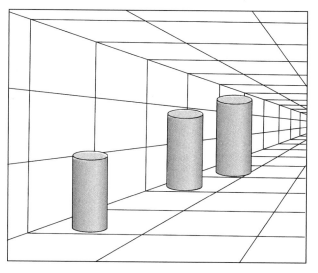

2-58   A visual illusion.

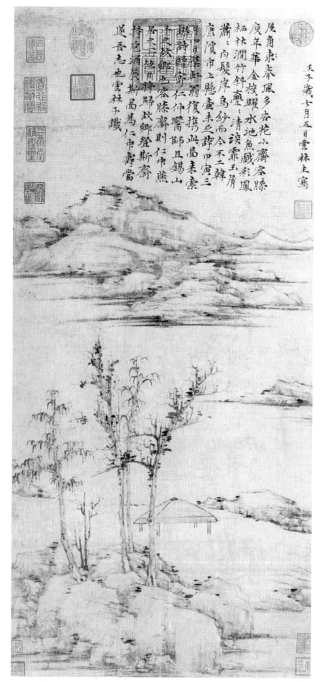

2-57   NI ZAN.
Rongxi Studio (Late Yuan/Early Ming dynasty, 1372 CE).
Hanging scroll; ink on paper. H: 29¼″.
National Palace Museum, Taipei, Taiwan, Republic of China.

In the Chinese ink drawing shown in Figure 2-57, the natural elements at the top and bottom of the scroll are shown at the same size, as if they were seen from the same distance. Yet the viewer—particularly the schooled viewer—tends to perceive the hills at the top as being far-ther away. Again, objects depicted at the bottom of a work tend to be perceived as closer to the viewer.

Note how the cylinders in Figure 2-58 appear to grow larger toward the top of the composition. Why? For at least two reasons: (1) Objects at the bottom of a composition are usually perceived as being closer to the picture plane, and (2) the converging lines are perceived as being parallel, even when they are not. However, if they were parallel, then space would have to recede toward the center right of the composition, and the cylinder in that region would have to be farthest from the viewer. According to rules of perspec-tive, a distant object that appears to be equal in size to a nearby object would have to be larger, so we perceive the cylinder to the right as the largest, although it is equal in size to the others.

Figures 2-59 through 2-62 show that the illusion of depth can be created in art by making parallel lines come to-gether, or converge, at one or more **vanishing points** on an actual or implied horizon. The height of the **horizon** in the composition corresponds to the apparent location of the viewer's eyes, that is, the **vantage point** of the viewer. As we shall see in later chapters, the Greeks and Romans had some notion of linear perspective, but Renaissance artists such as Leonardo da Vinci refined perspective.

In **one-point perspective** (Fig. 2-59), parallel lines converge at a single vanishing point on the horizon. Photo-realist Richard Estes's *Williamsburg Bridge* (Fig. 2-63) offers the consummate exercise in one-point perspective. One can locate the vanishing point by following converging parallel lines (Fig. 2-64) to where they intersect near the center of the composition. By placing the vanishing point at the eye

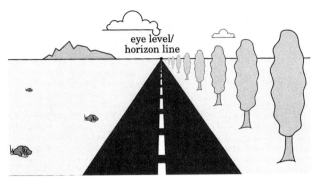

2-59   One-point perspective.

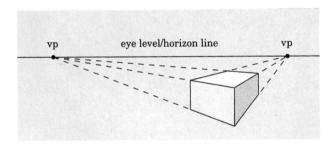

2-60   Two-point perspective.

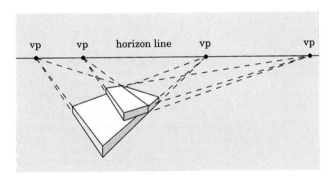

2-61   Perspective drawing of objects set at different angles.

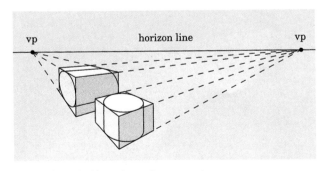

2-62   Curved objects drawn in perspective.

2-63   RICHARD ESTES.
Williamsburg Bridge (1995).
Oil on canvas. 32″ × 32″.
Copyright Richard Estes. Courtesy, Marlborough Gallery, New York.

2-64   Converging parallel lines intersect at the vanishing point.

*First study science, and then follow with practice based on science. . . . The painter who draws by practice
and judgment of the eye without the use of reason is like the mirror that reproduces within itself
all the objects which are set opposite to it without knowledge of the same. . . .
The youth ought first to learn perspective, then the proportions of everything,
then he should learn from the hand of a good master.*

—Leonardo da Vinci

2-65 FREDERIC EDWIN CHURCH.
Heart of the Andes (1859).
Oil on canvas. 66⅛″ × 119¼″ (168 cm × 302.9 cm).

Courtesy of The Metropolitan Museum of Art. Bequest of Margaret E.
Dows, 1909 (09.95). Photograph copyright 1979 The Metropolitan
Museum of Art, New York.

level of a person walking across the bridge, Estes heightens
the impression of "being there."

In **two-point perspective** (Fig. 2-60), two sets of parallel lines converge at separate vanishing points on the horizon. Two-point perspective is appropriate for representing the recession of objects that are seen from an angle, or obliquely.

We can use additional sets of parallel lines to depict objects that are set at different angles, as shown in Figure 2-61. Figure 2-62 shows how curved objects may be "carved out" of rectangular solids.

2-66   SYLVIA PLIMACK MANGOLD.
Schunnemunk Mountain (1979).
Oil on canvas. $60'' \times 80\frac{1}{8}''$.
Courtesy of Dallas Museum of Art, Dallas, TX.

Atmospheric Perspective

In **atmospheric perspective** (also called *aerial perspective*), the illusion of depth is created by techniques such as texture gradients, brightness gradients, color saturation, and the manipulation of warm and cool colors.

A gradient is a progressive change. The effect of a **texture gradient** relies on the fact that closer objects are perceived as having rougher or more detailed surfaces. In the Estes painting, the metal girders in the foreground are more detailed than those in the distance, facilitating the perception of depth. The effect of a **brightness gradient** is due to the lesser intensity of distant objects.

Frederic Edwin Church's masterpiece, *The Heart of the Andes* (Fig. 2-65), relies in part on atmospheric perspective to create the illusion of deep vistas. The foreground of the picture contains such botanical detail that the painting could serve as a scientific record of the species indigenous to the region. As the vista recedes into the distance, the plants and hills become less textured and the colors become less saturated. Church belonged to the Hudson River School of nineteenth-century American painting. The group's members used landscape as a vehicle for communicating the feeling of awe they experienced when they encountered the romantic, scientific, and religious ideas of the era—a world without limits. Vasarely's *Orion* (Fig. 2-44) uses some principles of atmospheric perspective to help create the illusion of movement through a vibrating effect. The brightest, most intense circles are perceived as being closest to the viewer, although, of course, all the mounted scraps of paper are right on the picture plane.

The haunting painting *Schunnemunk Mountain* (Fig. 2-66) reveals Sylvia Plimack Mangold's fascination with the transitional moments of the day. Here in the evening of the Hudson River Valley, brightness gradients employing purple, navy, and cobalt set the hills beneath the sky. The dark foreground is rendered more vacant by twinkling lights that suggest habitation in the valley beyond.

I paint with shapes.

—Alexander Calder

TIME AND MOTION

Objects and figures exist and move not only through space but also through the dimension of time. In its inexorable forward flow, time provides us with the chance to develop and grasp the visions of our dreams. Time also creates the stark limits beyond which none of us may extend.

Artists through the ages have sought to represent three-dimensional space in two-dimensional art forms as well as to represent, or imply, movement and the passage of time. Only in modern times have art forms such as cinematography and video been developed that involve *actual* movement and *actual* time.

Actual Motion

Artists create or capture **actual motion** in various ways. **Kinetic art** (from the Greek *kinesis,* meaning "movement") and photography are two of them. Most works of art sit quietly on the wall or, perhaps, on a pedestal, but kinetic art is designed to move.

The **mobiles** of Alexander Calder are some of the most popular examples of kinetic art in the twentieth century. The colossal mobile that hangs in the interior of the East Building of the National Gallery of Art (Fig. 2-67) is composed of winglike dashes and disks of different sizes that are cantilevered from metal rods such that they can rotate horizontally—in orbits—as currents of air press against them. However, the center of gravity remains stable, so the entire sculpture is hung from a single point. Unlike a painting, the mobile changes according to the movement of air above and the movement of the observer below, who might shift vantage points to create new compositions, new relationships among the shapes and lines.

Philippe Halsman's photograph *Dali Atomicus* (Fig. 2-68) **stopped time** to capture motion. The man in the photograph is the Surrealist artist Salvador Dalí. To make this photo, the photographer counted to four, at which time Dalí leapt into the air. The photographer's assistants tossed a bucket of water and three cats across the room. The photographer's wife held the chair in the air. The result you see represents the twenty-sixth effort to juggle the elements of the photograph to catch a fascinating image.

2-67   ALEXANDER CALDER.
Untitled (1972).
East Building mobile.

National Gallery of Art, Washington, DC. Gift of the Collectors Committee. Copyright 2003 Board of Trustees, National Gallery of Art, Washington, DC, 1976. Copyright 2003 Estate of Alexander Calder/Artists Rights Society (ARS), New York.

2-68 PHILIPPE HALSMAN.
Dali Atomicus (1948).
Gelatin silver print.
Courtesy of the Halsman Estate.

2-69 GIANLORENZO BERNINI.
Apollo and Daphne (1622–1624).
Marble. 7'6".
Galleria Borghese, Rome.

Implied Motion and Time

Dali Atomicus captured motion by stopping time. Other works of art *imply* motion; that is, the viewer infers that motion is occurring or has occurred. **Implied motion** and **implied time** are found in Baroque sculptor Gianlorenzo Bernini's *Apollo and Daphne* (Fig. 2-69) through the use of diagonal lines of force that help simulate movement from left to right. In the Greek myth, the wood nymph Daphne beseeches the gods to help her escape the overtures of Apollo. As Apollo gains on her, her prayer is answered in a most ironic manner because the gods choose to facilitate her "escape" by transforming her into a tree. In Bernini's sculpture we see Daphne just at the point when bark begins to enfold her body, her toes begin to take root, and her fingertips are transformed into the branches of a laurel. The passage of time is implied as she is caught in the midst of her transformation.

In *Apollo and Daphne,* motion is implied in the fluid strides and seamless transfiguration of Daphne. Motion can also be implied through repetitive imagery. We are all familiar with the way in which comic strips suggest the motion of the characters by repetition of imagery that changes slightly from frame to frame. This technique spans time and culture.

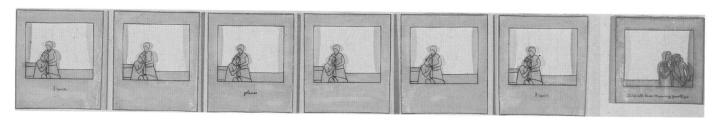

2-70   IDA APPLEBROOG.
I Can't (1981).
Ink and Rhoplex on vellum. Seven parts: 10½″ × 9½″ (6); 9 × 9½″ (1).

The multiple panels of Ida Applebroog's *I Can't* (Fig. 2-70) imply the passage of time in the same way that frames are used to advance a narrative in comic books or film storyboards. A barren scene with two women, their relationship unknown, is repeated six times. Only the words *I can't* and *Please,* randomly assigned to some panels, break up the cloying repetitive rhythm of the work. In the end one of the women is taken away at gunpoint. This panel is set apart from the others in size and color, although it still has the same, bland, uneventful quality as the others. When we read the words *Let's all kiss Mommy goodbye,* on the other hand, the last panel acts like a disturbing period at the end of a sentence.

The Illusion of Motion

There is a difference between implied motion and the illusion of motion. Works such as *Apollo and Daphne* imply that motion has occurred or that time has passed. In other works, artists use techniques to suggest that motion is *in the process of occurring* rather than having occurred. We say that these works contain the illusion of motion.

Early experiments with photography provided an illusion of the figure in motion through the method of rapid multiple exposures. In his *Man Pole Vaulting* (Fig. 2-71), Thomas Eakins—better known for his paintings—used photo sequences to study the movement of the human body.

2-71   THOMAS EAKINS.
Man Pole Vaulting
(c. 1884).
Photograph.

In the wake of these experiments, a number of artists created the illusion of motion by applying the visual results of multiple-exposure photography to their paintings.

Marcel Duchamp's *Nude Descending a Staircase #2* (Fig. 2-72) in effect creates multiple exposures of a machine-tooled figure walking down a flight of stairs. The overlapping of shapes and the repetition of linear patterns blur the contours of the figure. Even though an unkind critic labeled the Duchamp painting "an explosion in a shingle factory," it symbolized the dynamism of the modern machine era.

Umberto Boccioni's *Dynamism of a Soccer Player* (Fig. 2-73) reveals the obsession with the dynamism of the modern machine era of a school of artists called Futurists, who worked in the Italy of 100 years ago. On approaching the painting, one is struck by the sensation of motion long before it becomes possible to decipher the limbs of a running athlete. Spirals, arcs, and what seem to be flame-licked shapes swirl around a core of energy and fan outward, leaving traces of themselves in the surrounding environment. Wedges of sky fall on the figure like so many spotlights, breaking the solids into bits of prismatic color. The soccer player courses, pulsates, and hurtles ahead, cutting through space and time as the viewer is visually drawn into the work by lines and shapes that appear to encircle and ensnare.

2-72 MARCEL DUCHAMP.
Nude Descending a Staircase #2 (1912).
Oil on canvas. 58″ × 35″.
Philadelphia Museum of Art, Louise and Walter Arensberg Collection. Copyright 2005 Artist Rights Society (ARS), New York/ADAGP, Paris/Succession Marcel Duchamp/Art Resource, New York.

2-73 UMBERTO BOCCIONI.
Dynamism of a Soccer Player (1913).
Oil on canvas. 6′4⅛″ × 6′7⅛″.
Museum of Modern Art, New York. The Sidney and Harriet Janis Collection. Copyright Art Resource, New York.

When objects move rapidly, it can be difficult to perceive their shapes. They can be "lost in a blur." Blurring outlines is therefore another way to create the illusion of motion. In the photo-piece *Kitchen Tantrums* (Figs. 2-74 and 2-75), rather than stop time, the photographers used slow shutter speeds so that the objects would have the time to visibly move during the time that the film was exposed to light. In one photo, the woman throwing the tantrum tosses potatoes into the air. Her agitation as well as movement is suggested by the blurred outlines of her head and arms. The movement of the bowl and potatoes is suggested by the blurring of their outlines. In other photos, the potatoes take on a life of their own, apparently having gone from a random airborne pattern to a self-controlled juggling act of some sort. Increased speed is indicated by greater blurring of their shapes.

The movement of the 1960s and 1970s known as **Op Art** was based on creating optical sensations of movement through the repetition and manipulation of color, shape, and line. In kinetic sculpture, movement is real, whether activated by currents of air or motors. In Op Art, bold and apparently vibrating lines and colors create the illusion of movement. Bridget Riley's *Cataract 3* (Fig. 2-76) is composed of a series of curved lines that change in thickness and proximity to one another. These changes seem to suggest waves, but they also create a powerful illusion of rippling movement. Complementary red and green colors also contribute to the illusion of vibration. When we look at a color for an extended period of time, we tend to perceive its **afterimage.** Red is the afterimage of green, and vice versa. Therefore, there seems to be a pulsating in Riley's selection of

2-74 and 2-75
BERNHARD JOHANNES AND ANNA BLUME.
Kitchen Tantrums (1986–1987).
Photo-piece. 51⅛" × 35⅞".
Courtesy of the artist.

2-76 BRIDGET RILEY.
Cataract 3 (1967).
Emulsion on canvas.
5'10½" × 5'10½"
British Council, London.
Copyright Bridget Riley.

color as well as in the tendency of the eye to perceive the lines as rippling.

There are many other ways of creating the illusion of motion, including contemporary cinematography and video. Motion pictures create an illusion of movement so real that it cannot be distinguished from real movement by the naked eye. Motion pictures do not move in the way that they seem to move.[1] Rather, they create the illusion of movement through **stroboscopic motion.** In this method, the viewer is shown from 16 to 24 still pictures per second. Each picture or frame differs slightly from the one that preceded it. The individual who views the frames in rapid succession has the psychological experience—the *illusion*—of seeing moving objects rather than a series of still pictures. It does not matter whether viewers know that they are watching a progression of still images; the illusion of movement is so powerful that it is experienced as real movement. Motion pictures may *capture* real movement, but the way in which they *depict* movement involves illusion.

If the visual elements are considered the basic vocabulary of art, principles of design might be viewed as the grammar of art. Artists use principles of design to combine the visual elements into compositions. In art, as in life, this "language" is idiosyncratic to the individual.

---

[1] Certainly the film moves through the projector so that the frames are projected onto the screen in rapid succession. But each frame contains a still (unmoving) image.

3

PRINCIPLES OF DESIGN

He searched disorder for its unifying principle.

—Brian O'Doherty on Stuart Davis

Unity is one of the principles of design, and principles of design, like visual elements, are also part of the basic language of art. Just as people use principles of grammar to combine words into sentences, artists use principles of design to combine the visual elements of art into compositions that have a certain style, form, and content.

Design or **composition** is a process—the act of organizing the visual elements to effect a desired aesthetic in a work of art. Designs can occur at random, as exemplified by the old mathematical saw that an infinite number of monkeys pecking away at an infinite number of typewriters would eventually (though mindlessly) produce *Hamlet.* But when artists create compositions, they consciously draw upon design principles such as unity and variety, balance, emphasis and focal point, rhythm, scale, and proportion. This is not to say that all artists necessarily apply these principles, or even always recognize the extent of their presence in their work. Indeed, some artists prefer to purposefully violate them.

American Museum of Natural History, New York.

Irritation is made possible in the first place by formal clarity and precise scale.

—Katharina Fritsch

UNITY AND VARIETY

Unity is oneness or wholeness. A work of art achieves unity when its parts seem necessary to the composition as a whole. It is the exaggerated unity, the **extreme unity,** of Katharina Fritsch's *Rattenkönig* (Rat-King) (Fig. 3-1) that impacts the

3-1   KATHARINA FRITSCH.
Rattenkönig (Rat-King) (1993).
Polyester resin. H: 2.8 m.

From the installation at Dia Center for the Arts, 548 West 22nd Street, New York, NY, April 1993–June 1994. Photo by Bill Jacobson. Courtesy, Dia Center for the Arts. Copyright 2003 Artists Rights Society (ARS), New York.

viewer—that, and the fact that the rats are nine feet tall and seem to be poised for attack like so many troops from the legendary Roman infantry. Although the composition was inspired by the artist's encounter with a rat hole behind an unnamed New York art institution, the title of the work harks back to the battle between the nutcracker-turned-prince and the evil Rat King in Tchaikovsky's beloved (albeit scary) ballet. The work achieves extreme unity through its repetition of shapes, the exactitude of the "copies," and their placement in a precise circular configuration. Artists generally prefer to place some variety within a unified composition to add visual interest, but the principle of variety is most often subservient to the sense of oneness or overall unity in a work. The more you look at works of art, the better you will become at sensing the unity of compositions and at pinpointing the ways that artists achieve it. Sometimes the techniques will be obvious, and at other times they will be subtler.

Variety seems to rule the day—or night as the case may be—in Archibald Motley Jr.'s *Saturday Night* (Fig. 3-2), with a captivating array of characters—from the dining and drinking patrons and the waiters balancing their orders on tottering trays to one particularly flamboyant woman in a flame red costume who seems lost in the expressive rhythms of her solo dance. Yet this cacophony of sights and sounds and movements achieves a sense of oneness through a unified color field. To be sure, there is also some variety in the color scheme: The eye leaps from patches of black to black and from white to white, mimicking the riot of movement in the nightclub. However, the overall composition is unified by the pulsating reds that seem to emanate from the center of the dance floor and bathe the atmosphere with emotion, energy, and an almost mystical glow.

3-2   ARCHIBALD J. MOTLEY JR.
Saturday Night (1935).
Oil on canvas. 81.3 cm × 101.6 cm.

The Howard University Gallery of Art, Washington, DC.

3-3 THOMAS HART BENTON.
Palisades, from the American Historical Epic series
(1919–1924).
Oil on cotton duck on aluminum honeycomb panel.
66⅛″ × 72″.

The Nelson-Atkins Museum of Art, Kansas City, MO. Bequest
of the artist (F75-21/2). Copyright 2003 T. H. Benton and
Rita P. Benton Testamentary Trusts. Licensed by VAGA, New York.

Although color harmonies also contribute to a sense of oneness in Thomas Hart Benton's *Palisades* (Fig. 3-3), the curvilinear rhythms of shape and line are the strongest purveyors of unity in this work. Here the diversity of the players in this mythologized narrative of American history—the Spanish conquistador, the European colonizer, the Native American—are joined symbolically and pictorially by the echoing shapes and lines and rhythms that define and distinguish the figures and landscape elements. The emergence of a visual pattern of similar elements dominates the individual parts.

When working with the principles of variety and unity, an artist will often keep one or more aspects of the work constant so that in spite of the multiplicity of images or elements, the composition's overall unity will not be compromised. In Renée Green's witty installation (Fig. 3-4), unrelenting patterns of rose-and-white chintz unify the diverse objects of the interior setting—from chairs and hassocks to drapes and wall coverings. In her presentation of a mock showroom in which one might find groupings of furniture collections that mimic a homelike setting, Green educates the "shopper" in the fine art of creating (or at least buying) "ambience"—that intangible certain something, that distinct atmosphere that makes a house a home.

3-4 RENÉE GREEN.
Installation view (1993).

Galerie Metropol, Vienna, Austria. Christian Nagel Photography, Cologne.

3-5 BEVERLY PEPPER.
Thel (1976–1977).
Cor-Ten steel and ground covering.
H: 1′3″ × W: 1′6″ × L: 11′3″.

As installed at Dartmouth College, Hanover, NH.
Copyright Beverly Pepper. Courtesy, Marlborough Gallery,
New York.

3-6 EMMA AMOS.
Measuring Measuring (1995).
Acrylic on linen canvas, African fabric,
laser-transfer photographs. 84″ × 70″.

Courtesy of the artist. Marlborough Gallery, New York.

Beverly Pepper also achieves unity in *Thel* (Fig. 3-5) by maintaining a constant element. *Thel* is a sculpture that is at once anomalous and yet completely integrated with its site. Set before a traditional "Ivy" building on the Dartmouth College campus, the ribbonlike configuration of steel is unified with its surroundings through the inclusion of a triangular patch of turf that continues from the lawn up the sloping side of the metal pyramid. *Thel* alters the regularity of the environment and yet seems a logical part of the whole.

All of the works we have discussed have **visual unity;** most embrace the principle of variety within unity. There is, however, a way to achieve unity in a composition that does not rely on the consistency or repetition of the elements of art. Sometimes artists pursue, instead, a unity of ideas and impose a **conceptual unity** on their work. They will recognize that the strength of a composition lies in the diversity of elements and their juxtaposition. They reject visual harmonies in favor of discordant punctuations and focus on the relationships between the meaning and functions of the images. Emma Amos's *Measuring Measuring* (Fig. 3-6) offers an example of conceptual unity. The "ideal" human form is represented by works of art from the Western canon flanking the seminude figure of an African woman. "Measuring" has at least a double meaning—the measure of the African standard of beauty against that of the Western tradition and the measure of black against white. The images are physically incongruous, and the elements of the composition do not encourage visual unity. What unites this composition is the concept behind the work—the challenge to address the standard and the canon.

BALANCE

Most people prefer to have some stability in their lives, to have their lives on a "firm footing." In the same way, most people respond positively to some degree of balance in the visual arts. When we walk, run, or perform an athletic feat, balance refers to the way in which our weight is distributed, or shifts, so that we remain in control of our movements. **Balance** in art also refers to the distribution of the weight—of the actual or apparent weight of the elements of a composition. As the athlete uses balance to control movement, so might the artist choose to use balance to control the distribution or emphasis of elements such as line or shape or color in a composition.

The Classical Greek artist Polykleitos was perhaps the first artist to observe the body's shifting of weight in order to achieve balance and to develop a set of rules to apply this observation to representations of the figure. In his *Doryphoros* (Fig. 3-7), or Spear Bearer, Polykleitos featured his weight-shift principle. He observed that when the body is at rest, one leg bears the weight of the body and the other is relaxed. Further, in order for the body to balance itself, the upper torso shifts, as if corresponding to an S curve, so that the arm opposite the tensed leg is tensed, and the one opposite the relaxed leg is relaxed. Thus, with the weight-shift principle, tension and tension and relaxation and relaxation are read diagonally across the body. Overall figural balance is achieved.

Actual Balance and Pictorial Balance

Sculptures such as *Doryphoros* have *actual weight* and may thus also have **actual balance.** Even though actual weight and actual balance are not typically at issue in two-dimensional works such as drawings, paintings, and prints, we nonetheless do speak of balance in these compositions. **Pictorial balance** refers to the distribution of the apparent or *visual weight* of the elements in works that are basically two-dimensional, and there are many ways to achieve it. Brazilian artist Lygia Clark's photograph of her performance piece *Cabeça Coletiva* (Collective Head) (Fig. 3-8) possesses

3-7 POLYKLEITOS.
Doryphoros (c. 450–440 BCE).
Roman copy after bronze Greek
original. Marble. 6′6″.
National Museum, Naples.
Copyright Scala/Art Resource, New York.

3-8 LYGIA CLARK.
Cabeça Coletiva (Collective Head) (1975).
Courtesy, Cultural Association, "The World of Lygia Clark" and "Family
Clark's Collection." Copyright 2003 Artists Rights Society (ARS),
New York/ADAGP, Paris.

both actual and pictorial balance. She and her students filled a large hatlike object with fruit, shoes, love letters—even money—and walked amidst the public, distributing the offerings. The photo reveals that the bearer of gifts is literally engaged in a balancing act while the visual weight of his figure is balanced to the left and right by the companions who guide him.

Symmetrical Balance

You can divide the human body in half vertically, and in the ideal, as in Leonardo da Vinci's most famous drawing, *Proportion of the Human Figure* (Fig. 3-9), there will be an exact correspondence between the left and right sides. **Symmetry** refers to similarity of form or arrangement on either side of a dividing line or plane, or to correspondence of parts in size, shape, and position. When the correspondence is exact, as in Leonardo's drawing, we refer to it as *pure* or *formal symmetry*. In reality, of course, nature is not as perfect as Leonardo would have had it.

Examples of pure or formal symmetry appear no more frequently in art than in nature. More typically, **symmetrical balance** is created through *approximate* symmetry, in which the whole of the work has a symmetrical feeling, but slight variations provide more visual interest than would a mirror image. When the variations to the right and left side of the composition are *more* than slight, yet there remains an overall sense of balance, there is said to be **asymmetrical balance.**

In *pure* or *formal symmetry,* also known as **bilateral symmetry,** everything in a composition to either side of an actual or imaginary line is the same. The regularity and predictability of symmetry cannot help but conjure a sense of peace, calm, comfort, and order. The effect of repetition can be mesmerizing. In architectural works like the United States Capitol Building (Fig. 3-10)—the house in which the laws of the land are created—repetition and symmetry can imply rationality and decorum, tying the structure of the building to a certain symbolic ideal. The design of the Capitol consists of a solid rectangular structure flanked by identical wings that extend from the central part of the building, project forward at right angles, and culminate in "temple fronts" that echo the main entrance beneath a hemispherical dome. An ordinary citizen of the republic takes pride in the architectural grandeur, feels secure in the balance of all of the parts, and—with the obvious references to Greek architecture of the Golden Age—feels a part of the

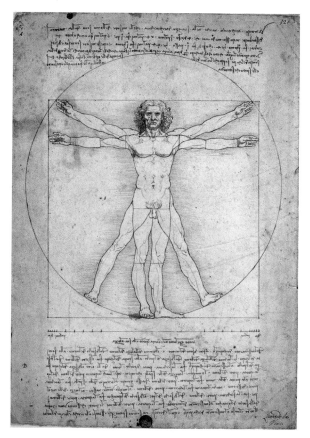

3-9 LEONARDO DA VINCI.
Proportion of the Human Figure (after Vitruvius)
(c. 1485–1490).
Pen and ink. 13½″ × 9¾″.
Academia, Venice, Italy. Copyright Art Resource, New York.

history of democracy. It is no coincidence that for the nation's Capitol, our founders adapted structures such as the Parthenon of Athens in the hope of associating the new republic with the ancient birthplace of democracy.

In many works of art, the symmetry is *approximate* rather than exact. For example, the overall impression of Korean-born video installation artist Nam June Paik's *Fin de Siècle II* (Fig. 3-11) is one of symmetry, attributable to the repetition of the video monitors on the left and right sides of the composition. However, the actual array of monitors is not precisely repeated, and the images being displayed at any given moment also differ. Paik is fascinated by the intersections of video and music, and the visual images change in sync with or in counterpoint to a pulsating electronic rock score. The approximate symmetry provides variety within

3-10　The United States Capitol Building, Washington, DC.
Copyright Kenneth Garrett/Woodfin Camp Associates.

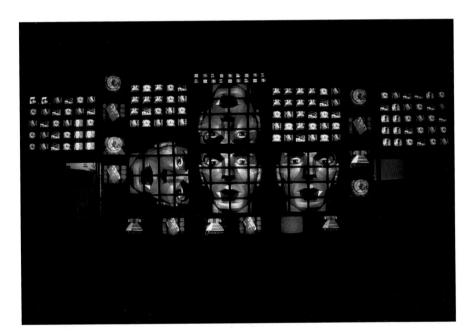

3-11　NAM JUNE PAIK.
Fin de Siècle II (1989).
201 television sets and four laser discs.
480″ × 168″ × 60″.
(1,219.2 cm × 426.7
cm × 152.5 cm) overall.
Whitney Museum of American Art, New York.
Gift of Lalia and Thurston Twigg-Smith.
Copyright Whitney Museum, New York/
Electronic Arts Intermix (EAI), New York.

the overall unified work. If both sides of the composition were exactly the same, consisting of the same monitors displaying the same images, would the bilateral symmetry strengthen or weaken the composition? Would it add or subtract visual interest?

Asymmetrical Balance

When your eyes are telling you that the elements of a composition are skewed but your brain is registering overall balance, chances are you are witnessing asymmetrical balance.

3-12 VINCENT LAFORET (2004).
A pedestrian on Eighth Avenue across from the Port Authority Bus Terminal braved the conditions on Monday evening, December 6, 2004.
Vincent Laforet/ The New York Times.

3-13 HELEN M. TURNER.
Morning News (1915).
Oil on canvas. 16″ × 14″.
Jersey City Museum, Jersey City, NJ.
Gift of Helen M. Turner.

There is probably a human tendency to effect balance at any cost. Sometimes the right and left sides of a composition bear visibly different shapes, colors, textures, or other elements, yet they are arranged or "weighted" in such a way that the impression, in total, is one of balance. In such cases, the artist has employed the design principle of *asymmetrical* or *informal balance.*

Vincent Laforet's photograph (Fig. 3-12) is both asymmetrical and balanced. Against a blurred backdrop of cars and trucks stopped at a traffic light, a black silhouette sporting a large red umbrella on the left is balanced by glowing spheres of city lights that seem to hover in the fog like UFOs. Once again, the viewer can engage in a compositional exercise to ascertain the value of placement and of color in achieving the sense of overall balance: cover the red umbrella, or change its color to black or white, and the result will be one of imbalance.

A high contrast of values can be used to establish asymmetrical balance, as the potency of black against white provides a certain visual weight. In Helen M. Turner's *Morning News* (Fig. 3-13), well-placed touches of color in an asym-

3-14 DEBORAH BUTTERFIELD.
Verde (1990).
Found steel. 79″ × 108″ × 31″.
Courtesy Edward Thorp Gallery, New York.

metrical composition are responsible for the overall visual balance. The artist has placed the figure well to the right, and the newspaper she holds forms a distinct diagonal that leads our eye in this direction. Along an imaginary opposing diagonal, however, patches and swaths of red paint balance the more prominent shapes of the woman and her gazette. The eye bounces from one bright area of saturated color to another against the field of blacks, whites, and grays, pulling the opposing sides together—bringing them into balance. *Morning News* is also an example of how vibrant color will command the viewer's attention, diminishing the effect of other compositional elements. Cover up the red and your eyes will begin to linger on the painting's shapes, lines, and textures.

In Deborah Butterfield's *Verde* (Fig. 3-14), the mane and head of the horse are defined by greenish strips of steel that enframe void space. (The title *Verde* calls our attention to the finish of the steel, a greenish coating referred to as *verdigris*.) The *actual weight* of this upper part of the horse

is negligible. The body, on the other hand, is composed of heavy molded sheets of steel, approximating the volume of the animal's torso. Overall visual balance is achieved in this work because the outlines of the head and neck, silhouetted against the white wall, pop out at the viewer. They become so prominent that they carry enough *visual weight* to balance the more densely compacted sheet metal of the animal's body.

Horizontal, Vertical, and Radial Balance

In works of art with **horizontal balance,** the elements at the left and right sides of the composition seem to be about equal in number or visual emphasis. The United States Capitol Building (Fig. 3-10) and *Fin de Siècle II* (Fig. 3-11) have horizontal balance. So, too, does Gertrude Käsebier's delicately textured photograph *Blessed Art Thou among*

3-16 Bella Coola mask, British Columbia
(before 1897).
Wood. D: 24¾″.
American Museum of Natural History, New York.

3-15 GERTRUDE KÄSEBIER.
Blessed Art Thou among Women (c. 1898).
Photograph.
Courtesy of The Royal Photographic Society/Heritage Image Partnership
(HIP), heritage-images.com.

Women (Fig. 3-15). Notice how the dark value of the girl's dress is balanced both by the dark wall to the left and by the woman's hair. Similarly, the stark light value of the vertical shaft of the doorway to the left and the light values of the right side of the composition are in equilibrium.

In **vertical balance,** the elements at the top and bottom of the composition are in balance. In the case of **radial balance,** the design elements radiate from a center point. Radial balance is familiar to us because nature offers us so many examples. From the petals of a daisy and the filaments of a spider's web to the sun's powerful rays, lines or shapes radiate from a central point and lead the viewer's eye in a circular pattern around the source.

Radial balance is frequently a major principle of design in art forms such as ceramics, jewelry, basketry, stained glass, and other crafts. The Native American Bella Coola mask (Fig. 3-16) consists of a stylized face of a sun god surrounded by an alternating pattern of masks and outstretched hands. The fingertips radiate from the stylized palms toward the circumference of the mask, mimicking the rays of the celestial body that grants warmth and sustenance.

Even if the circular pattern is visually incomplete, it is possible to create centrifugal forces within a composition that accord radial balance. The viewer's eye will take the cue

3-18 ROBERT CAPA.
Death of a Loyalist Soldier
(September 5, 1936).
Gelatin silver print.
Copyright Magnum Photos, Inc./Robert Capa.

3-17 BARBARA MORGAN.
Martha Graham: Letter to the World (Kick) (1940).
Gelatin silver print.
Copyright 1941 by Barbara Morgan.

of the composition, the forces create an overall visual balance as the viewer completes the circular rhythm.

Imbalance

Balance affords a certain level of comfort. The viewer will usually try to impose balance on a work, even when there is asymmetry. But not all art is about comfort; not all art aims to be aesthetically pleasing. Some artists aim to shock the viewer or to play into a viewer's discomfort by creating works with **imbalance.**

Consider Robert Capa's photograph *Death of a Loyalist Soldier* (Fig. 3-18), which was taken during the Spanish Civil War. The photographer has captured the soldier just as an enemy rifleman shot him. By allowing the composition to remain unbalanced, or weighted on the left, the drama of the moment is intensified. The long black shadow behind the soldier seems to pull the figure toward the ground, as he stumbles from the impact of the bullet. The photographer no doubt maintained the visual imbalance in the composition to correspond with the physical imbalance of the victim.

In Capa's photograph, there is a clear sense of movement. The soldier has been running down a grassy hill and suddenly falls backward. Imbalance in a work of art can be used to capture a sense of movement—the fourth dimension—in a two-dimensional or a three-dimensional work.

from what is present and will then "complete" the circular pattern. In Barbara Morgan's photograph of Martha Graham (Fig. 3-17), the folds of the pioneer dancer's costume emanate from the central point of her torso and are set into pinwheel-like motion by the radial extension of her leg. Although the radial pattern is contained within the right side

Niki de Saint-Phalle's *Black Venus* (Fig. 3-19) is a larger-than-life figure of a woman in a psychedelic bathing suit who is catching a beach ball. The placement of the legs and feet at the very least suggests a precariously balanced body. She seems to leap into the air to catch the ball, defying gravity and her own ponderousness. In spite of, or because of, her mountainous appearance, the unbalanced position of her lower body gives the figure a contradictory sense of weightlessness. Niki de Saint-Phalle challenges the ideal of feminine beauty in the Western tradition with figures such as *Black Venus.* How does this spirited form stand apart from traditional Western nudes such as the *Venus of Urbino* (see Fig. 15-28)?

EMPHASIS AND FOCAL POINT

For the most part, we do not view a work of art as we read a page of text. The eye does not start in the upper left corner and then systematically work its way to the right in rows. Rather, some feature of the work usually commands our attention. Artists use the design principle of **emphasis** to focus the viewer's attention on one or more parts of a composition by accentuating certain shapes, intensifying value

3-19 NIKI DE SAINT-PHALLE.
Black Venus (1967).
Painted polyester. 110″ × 35″ × 24″.
Whitney Museum of American Art, New York.
Gift of Howard and Jean Lipman Foundation.
Copyright 2003 Artists Rights Society (ARS),
New York/ADAGP, Paris.

3-20 RICHARD HAMILTON.
My Marilyn (1966).
Silkscreen, printed in color.
20¼″ × 25″.
Copyright The Museum of Modern Art,
New York. Joseph G. Mayer Foundation Fund.
Licensed by Scala/Art Resource, New York.
Copyright Artists Rights Society (ARS),
New York/DACS, London.

3-21   CHUCK CLOSE.
        Lucas II (1987).
        Oil on canvas. 36″ × 30″.
        The Museum of Modern Art, New York. Photo courtesy of
        PaceWildenstein. Copyright Chuck Close.

3-22   JASPER JOHNS.
        Between the Clock and the Bed (1981).
        Encaustic on canvas (three panels). 6′⅛″ × 10′6⅜″.
        Copyright The Museum of Modern Art, New York. Gift of Agnes Gund.
        Licensed by Scala/Art Resource, New York. Copyright Jasper Johns.
        Licensed by VAGA, New York.

or color, featuring directional lines, or strategically placing the objects and images. Emphasis can be used to create **focal points** or specific parts of the work that seize and hold the viewer's interest.

Consider Richard Hamilton's screen print *My Marilyn* (Fig. 3-20). The composition has a unifying regularity of color—a limited palette—and a repetition of the shapes and images that lead the viewer's eye to crisscross the surface. At first glance the work seems completely devoid of emphasis and focal point. Only after the eye picks up the large *X*'s that cancel out the figures does one see the degree to which the artist has directed the viewer's gaze: He causes the eye to move around and then land on the image of Marilyn in the lower right corner, which—because there is no *X* through it—becomes the focal point of the composition. In so many works of art, the artist—by using various forms of emphasis—seems to be saying to the viewer, "Look here. Look here!" In Hamilton's *My Marilyn,* the focal point emerges by virtue of the artist saying, "Don't look here."

As if the overwhelming presence of the face—that is, the *content*—in Chuck Close's *Lucas II* (Fig. 3-21) is not enough to focus the viewer's attention on the center of the composition, the artist emphasizes or draws our eye to a single point—the focal point—between the subject's eyes by creating a targetlike pattern of concentric circles around it. The circles are intersected by broken lines of color that radiate from the center, causing a sense of simultaneous movement outward from the center point and back inward.

Color contributes to the focal point of *Lucas II* in a very dramatic way, but more subtle distributions of value and color can direct the viewer's gaze, as in Jasper Johns's *Between the Clock and the Bed* (Fig. 3-22). The rhythmic interplay of line across the entirety of the three-paneled painting has a degree of uniformity that is altered by a concentration of warmer yellowish hues in the center. In a work that would otherwise seem to have no focal point, this patch of color concentrates the viewer's attention. Whereas the work is given unity by the allover pattern of lines, shifts in color create variety throughout the piece.

If today's arts love the machine, technology and organization, if they aspire to precision and reject anything vague and dreamy, this implies an instinctive repudiation of Chaos and a longing to find the form appropriate to our times.

— Oskar Schlemmer

3-23 PABLO PICASSO.
Family of Saltimbanques
(1905).
Oil on canvas.
83¾″ × 90⅜″.

National Gallery of Art, Washington, DC. Chester Dale Collection. Copyright 2003 Estate of Pablo Picasso/Artists Rights Society (ARS), New York.

In Pablo Picasso's *Family of Saltimbanques* (Fig. 3-23), we see that artists sometimes use the method of emphasis by isolation, in which they separate one object or figure from the many. Amidst a rather desolate landscape, figures of circus performers stand silent, seemingly frozen in their sculptural poses. The patterns, colors, and costume variety of the main figural group are, interestingly, less visually significant than the more delicately rendered figure of the woman seated apart from them in the lower right. Picasso has emphasized her aloneness by pulling her from the group. Her solitude draws us into her private musings; her inner world becomes the focus of our attention.

Oskar Schlemmer's *Bauhaus Stairway* (Fig. 3-24) uses directional lines and color to give his composition a focal point. The painting has an overall bluish tonality, against which the bright red orange of a woman's sweater leaps out toward the viewer. The diagonal thrusts of the staircase converge at her torso and are echoed in repetitive triangles to her right.

Areas of emphasis are created by Varnette Honeywood in *The Caregiver* (Fig. 3-25) in the deep black silhouettes that stand in sharp contrast to a composition that is otherwise a kaleidoscope of color and pattern. The repetition of outstretched hands draws the viewer's attention to a tabletop strewn with first-aid supplies and a Holy Bible, while the strong profile of the African American woman—the caregiver—leads us to a cross-stitched wall hanging bearing the

words *Prayer Is the Answer.* The strong black shapes capture our attention and spotlight the images in the composition that convey its meaning. Honeywood leaves us with the message that there are some things that modern medicine cannot heal, that healing sometimes comes from within.

The power of content can sometimes overwhelm the power of shape, texture, and other elements of art to the point that in spite of other devices used to create focal points, the image will have the tendency to negate or override them. In Edgar Degas's *Woman Leaning near a Vase of*

3-24   OSKAR SCHLEMMER.
Bauhaus Stairway (1932).
Oil on canvas. 63⅞″ × 45″.
Museum of Modern Art, New York. Gift of Philip Johnson. Copyright Art Resource, New York.

3-25   VARNETTE P. HONEYWOOD.
The Caregiver (1995).
Acrylic on canvas. 37″ × 52″.
Copyright Varnette P. Honeywood, 1995.

I like repetition because it includes an endless sequence of substitutes and missed encounters.

—Sherrie Levine

3-26 EDGAR DEGAS.
Woman Leaning near a Vase of Flowers (Mme Paul Valpinçon; erroneously called *Woman with Chrysanthemums*) (1865). Oil on canvas. 29″ × 36½″.

The Metropolitan Museum of Art, New York. H. O. Havemeyer Collection. Bequest of Mrs. H. O. Havemeyer, 1929 (29.100.128). Copyright The Metropolitan Museum of Art, New York.

Flowers (Fig. 3-26), the centerpiece—quite literally—of the composition is an enormous bouquet of chrysanthemums. It has almost everything one could ask of a focal point—central position, brilliant color, dominant texture. And yet our eyes are drawn to the woman who sits off to the side of the vase, daydreaming, gazing beyond the borders of the canvas. A viewer's gaze is seduced by the sight of a human face.

RHYTHM

The world would be a meaningless jumble of sights and sounds were it not for the regular repetition of sensory impressions. Natural **rhythms,** or orderly progressions, regulate

events ranging from the orbits of the planets to the unfolding of the genetic code into flesh and blood. Artists can enhance or exaggerate individual elements in their compositions through minor and major variations in rhythm. And rhythm can move a viewer visually as well as emotionally. Repetitive patterns can be used to lead the eye over the landscape of the work and to evoke a psychological response in the viewer.

Regular repetition is the easiest and most precise way to create rhythm. In fact, it is a dominant design principle in Fritsch's *Rattenkönig* (Fig. 3-1), which we have already discussed in the context of unity.

Rhythm can be present in a work of art even if there is a slight variation in repetition. Magdalena Abakanowicz's

Backs (Fig. 3-27), from a series of body works called *Alterations,* consists of 80 fiber sculptures representing human backs. Although the individual forms look like hunched-over figures, they are without heads, legs, or arms. Even the fronts of the torsos have been hollowed out, leaving an actual and symbolic human shell. In this work, the artist, whose mother was mutilated by the Nazis in World War II, seems to bring to her work the memory of the dehumanization she witnessed. The potency of this message is in large part due to the repetition of forms that have lost their individuality.

Rhythms are found also in architecture. The ceiling of the mosque at Córdoba, Spain (Fig. 3-28), is supported by a rhythmic progression of arches that span the distances between the columns. Mosques constructed with this design could be expanded in any direction by adding columns and arches as the congregation grew.

3-27   MAGDALENA ABAKANOWICZ.
Backs (1976–1982).
Burlap and glue. 80 pieces, 3 sizes: 61 cm × 50 cm × 55 cm; 69 cm × 56 cm × 66 cm; 72 cm × 59 cm × 69 cm.
Copyright Magdalena Abakanowicz. Courtesy of the Marlborough Gallery, New York. Licensed by VAGA, New York.

3-28   Sanctuary of the Mosque at Córdoba, Spain (Islamic) (786–987 CE). Interior view.
Adam Woofitt/Corbis.

Making art is about objectifying your experience of the world, transforming the flow of moments into something visual, or textual, or musical. Art creates a kind of commentary.

—Barbara Kruger

SCALE

Scale refers to size—small, big, or in between. **Scale** is the relative size of an object compared with others of its kind, its setting, or human dimensions. The Great Pyramids at Giza (see Fig. 12-14) and the skyscrapers of New York are imposing because of their scale, that is, their size compared with the size of other buildings, their sites, and people. Their overall size is essential to their impact.

Barbara Kruger's multimedia installation *Power Pleasure Desire Disgust* (Fig. 3-29) combines steadily changing video images of talking heads and projections of the artist's signature phrases and text all over the gallery floors and walls. The overwhelming scale of the work envelops us so completely and the slogans bombard us so relentlessly that it may seem as though the thoughts expressed in the environment have somehow originated in our own minds—phrases we may have once used to hurt others or they us, comments that may have cut to the quick. But interspersed with the bitter are flashes of wit, even flirtatiousness, as the work touches on communication across boundaries of gender and social definition. Thoughts are compelling and haunting

things, made all the more inescapable by the sheer size of their verbal and written articulation.

In the Count de Montizon's photograph *The Hippopotamus at the Zoological Gardens, Regent's Park* (Fig. 3-30), we see how artists communicate the scale of objects in their works by comparing them with other objects. In this photograph, a specimen record of the zoo's prized tenant, the photographer used *relative* size to communicate size. We see that it takes nine people standing shoulder to shoulder to match the length of one animal lazing in the sun. The photographer used the relationship between the familiar (the observers) and the unfamiliar (the hippopotamus) to communicate the size of the hippo to those who weren't there to witness it firsthand. At the time the picture was taken, 1852, the hippopotamus was not yet a familiar denizen of zoos in Europe and the United States. A gift from the pasha of Egypt to Queen Victoria, this hippo was the main attraction at the London Zoo.

Nineteenth-century London's hippopotamus was exotic, its size dramatic. In relation to the scale of ordinary human beings, it was extraordinary. In viewing the photograph, a person could pretty much grasp the magnitude of

3-29 BARBARA KRUGER. *Power Pleasure Desire Disgust* (1997). Multimedia installation.
Courtesy of Deitch Projects, New York.

My painting is not revolutionary. Why should I delude myself that it is informed by a fighting spirit?

—Frida Kahlo

3-30 COUNT DE MONTIZON.
The Hippopotamus at the Zoological Gardens, Regent's Park (1852).
Salted-paper print.
From the *Photographic Album of the Year*, 1855. The Royal Photographic Society, Bath, England.

the animal. By contrast, in Magritte's *Personal Values* (Fig. 3-31) it is impossible for the viewer to comprehend the dimensions of any of the objects within the work because their familiar size relationships are subverted. We don't know whether the objects—the comb and matchstick and glass—are blown out of proportion or whether the bed has shrunk. We cannot rely on our experience of actual dimension to make sense of the content of the work, so our tendency to understand size in relation to other things fails us.

Hierarchical Scaling

Standing "ten feet tall" is a familiar idiom. We use it to describe heroes or to communicate a certain pride we feel in our own accomplishments. It describes our feelings about a deed that sets others or ourselves above the rest, even if for one fleeting moment. In the visual arts, this metaphor, this idiom, finds its analogy in **hierarchical scaling,** or the use of relative size to indicate the relative importance of the objects or people being depicted. The method has been used for literally thousands of years. In ancient Egyptian art, members of royalty and nobility are sized consistently larger than the underlings surrounding them, making very clear their social positions. In medieval manuscript illumination, artists often had their celes-

3-31 RENÉ MAGRITTE.
Personal Values (1952).
Oil on canvas. 31⅝″ × 39½″ (80 cm × 100 cm).
Copyright 2003 C. Herscovici, Brussels/Artists Rights Society (ARS), New York/Art Resources, New York.

tial figures, such as angels and saints, tower over humans. Closer to home, the Mexican artist Frida Kahlo used hierarchical scaling in a modern work to reveal an old-fashioned relationship between husband and wife (Fig. 3-32). Even though both she and her husband, Diego Rivera, were renowned artists in their own right, he loomed as the dominant personality—domestically and artistically. Even the ambiguous title of the painting, *Frida y Diego Rivera o Frida Kahlo y Diego Rivera* (Frida and Diego Rivera or Frida Kahlo and Diego Rivera), reveals her struggle with identity. Under each moniker and in each role—wife and artist—Kahlo portrays herself as quite literally less of a figure. History, it turns out, was kinder to Frida than she was to herself.

Distortion of Scale

Some artists distort or even subvert the realistic scale of objects to challenge the viewer to look at the familiar in a new way. Sometimes they are interested in providing a new perspective on the forms of things; sometimes on the relationships between things.

It is in part the play on the viewer's sense of scale that creates the visual shock and sheer humor of Marisol's *Baby Girl* (Fig. 3-33). A wooden doll with adjustable limbs and

Claes Oldenburg: On Clothespins, Baseball Bats, and Other Monuments

When one drives around Philadelphia's Center Square, one is impressed by the broadness of the avenues, the classical columns and arches of City Hall, the steel and glass curtain walls of the new office buildings, and . . . by a 45-foot-tall clothespin (Fig. 3-34).

Why a clothespin? "I like everything about clothespins," reported Pop artist Claes Oldenburg, "even the name." The clothespin sculpture, aptly called *Clothespin* by its creator, was erected as a tribute to the 1976 Bicentennial. The line down the center of the pin suggests an updating of the cracked Liberty Bell, and the spring could be viewed as spelling out '76. More-

over, the clothespin consists of two structures clasped together, by a spring, in an embrace—an appropriate symbol for Philadelphia, the City of Brotherly Love. One might think that this symbolism was incidental, but Oldenburg had earlier made a silkscreen comparing his clothespin to Brancusi's *The Kiss* (see Fig. 4-6), which also depicts an embrace.

Clothespin is just one of the ordinary objects to which Oldenburg has lent monumentality by upgrading their scale. His 24-foot-high *Lipstick* rises serenely on a Yale University quadrangle, and the Houston Public Library sports an 18-foot-high mouse. The plaza of the Social Security Administration building in Chicago, a city that supports two major league baseball franchises, is punctuated by a 100-foot-tall baseball bat. Oldenburg has drawings of typewriter erasers and upside-down ice-cream cones whose waffle patterns rival the faces of the Egyptian pyramids.

It could be argued that the subjects of Oldenburg's monuments are trivial, but we must also admit that they have a certain symbolic meaning and depth for Americans. In centuries to come, they may say more about twentieth-century America than would a few more bronze riders on horseback. ∎

3-34 CLAES OLDENBURG.
Clothespin (1976).
Cor-Ten steel with stainless steel base. H: 45'.
Courtesy PaceWildenstein.

I find it important to draw attention to thinking and doing as well as to what happens in between, to lightness and heaviness, to the energy that oscillates between.

—Magdalena Jetelová

3-35   MAGDALENA JETELOVÁ.
Domestication of a Pyramid (1992).
Red quartz sand. H: 15 m.
Austrian Museum for Applied Art, Vienna, Austria. Courtesy of the artist.

torso—the sort used for drawing exercises in art classes—sports a portrait of Marisol herself. It is perched on the stocky thigh of the baby, who neither looks at nor touches the "toy." The baby girl, by any other definition a subject that suggests delicacy and softness, is transformed into a cumbersome hunk of a figure. Only the shirring of her puffy sleeves and frilly gathers of her white dress soften the harshness of the overall form. Marisol's manipulation of scale and our perception of it are confirmed by the fact that in looking at the illustration of this work in your book (without sneaking a peek at the dimensions), you would have no real sense of how large or small the work actually is.

Czech-German artist Magdalena Jetelová's installation *Domestication of a Pyramid* (Fig. 3-35) is all about scale, space, and power. Many of Jetelová's installations transform spaces by invasions that challenge the viewer to rethink their architecture and history. The colossal Egyptian pyramids are made of blocks of stone and look as though they will occupy their open desert sites until the end of time. Jetelová invaded the Austrian Museum of Applied Art with a "pyramid" of red sand. She brought a much smaller and far more irregular version of the familiar shape indoors, thereby "domesticating" it. But it is far from tame. It is only about one-tenth the height of the pyramids at Giza, and it is made of material that could blow away in the desert wind. Yet its size in relation to the museum interior renders the powder oppressive and the architecture fragile and dollhouselike. The incursion of the timeless shape into the vestibule of the museum compels visitors to view the familiar architectural form of the building, with its colonnades and arcades, from a new perspective. "Look at this space again and consider whether it will endure," declares the installation.

PROPORTION

"Everything is relative." That is, we tend to think of objects or of works of art as large or small according to their relationships to other things—often to ourselves. However, the objects depicted within works of art can also be large or small in relationship to one another and to the work as a whole. **Proportion,** then, is the comparative relationship, or ratio, of things to one another.

Artists through the ages have sought to determine the proper or most appealing ratios of parts of works to one another and the whole. They have used proportion to represent what they believed to be the ideal or the beautiful. They also have disregarded or subverted proportion to achieve special effects—often to compel viewers to take a new look at the familiar.

The Canon of Proportions: "Keeping Things in Proportion"

The ancient Greeks tied their vision of ideal beauty to what they considered the "proper" proportions of the human body. Polykleitos is credited with the derivation of a **canon of proportions**—a set of rules about body parts and their dimensions relative to one another that became the standard for creating the ideal figure. The physical manifestation of his canon was his *Doryphoros* (Fig. 3-7). Every part of the body is either a specific fraction or multiple of every other part. Ideally, for Polykleitos, the head is one-eighth of the

3-36   ALICE NEEL.
The Family (John Gruen, Jane Wilson and Julia) (1970).
Oil on canvas. 4′11⅞″ × 5′.
Copyright Estate of Alice Neel. Courtesy, Robert Miller Gallery, New York.

total height of the body and the width from shoulder to shoulder should not exceed one-fourth of the body's height.

Violating the Canon for Expressive Purposes

If the *Doryphoros* represents ideal form, Alice Neel's *The Family* (Fig. 3-36) leaves the canon behind in what appears to be the pursuit of unidealized form. The enlarged heads, elongated fingers and calves, and outsized feet are glaring obstacles to realistic representation. And yet, somehow, there is an overarching realism in spite of these artistic liberties that emanates from the relationships among the family members.

The Golden Mean

Just as the Greeks developed a canon of proportions for representing the human figure in the ideal, they developed the concept of the **golden mean** or the **golden section** in order to create ideal proportions in architecture. The golden mean requires that a small part of a work should relate to a larger

3-37 The golden mean.

To create the golden mean, a line is divided ("sectioned") so that the ratio of the shorter segment (AB) is to the larger segment (BC) as the larger segment (BC) is to the whole (AC). Line segment BC is 1.618 times the length of segment AB. Segment BC is the "mean" in the sense that its length lies between the smaller segment (AB) and the entire line (AC). The Greeks considered segment BC to be "golden" in that its use created what they considered to be ideal proportions in architecture.

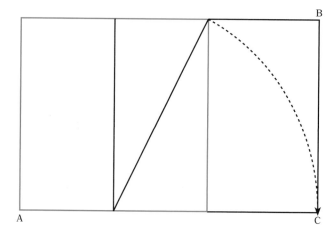

3-38 The golden rectangle.

The width of this rectangle is exactly 1.618 times its height. The triangle can be created by rotating the diagonal of the half square on the left (outlined in red) to the base on the right (point C). This "ideal" rectangle became the basis for the floor plans of Greek temples and represented the artistic embodiment of the Greek maxim "Moderation in all things."

part of the work as the larger part relates to the whole. The line in Figure 3-37 is divided, or *sectioned,* at point B so that the ratio of the shorter segment (AB) is to the larger segment (BC), as the larger segment (BC) is to the whole line (AC). Segment BC is the golden mean.

The rectangle in Figure 3-38 is based on the golden mean and is termed a **golden rectangle.** Its width is 1.618 times its height. The golden rectangle was thought by the Greeks to be the most pleasing rectangle, and it became the basis for many temple designs.

A golden rectangle can be made either by measuring the lengths of the lines or by rotating the diagonal of the half square, as shown in Figure 3-38. We can also rotate the diagonal of the square in both directions, sort of like a windshield wiper. If we add the second smaller rectangle, we obtain a rectangle that is made up of a central square and two smaller rectangles (Fig. 3-39). The entire rectangle is called a **root five rectangle** because its length is 2.236 (the square root of 5) times its width.

The proportions of the root five rectangle have also served as the frame for various works of art and architecture. If you superimpose a diagram of a root five rectangle over a photograph of the east facade of the Parthenon (Fig. 3-40), you can see the almost compulsive adherence to geometric order that the Greeks visited on their places of worship. The facade is constructed of eight columns. The four in the center fit within the central square of the root five rectangle. The portions of the facade occupying the flanking rectangles include the two end columns to either side as well as the outermost points defined by the steps leading to the temple platform.

Most viewers are unaware of the mathematical basis for the Parthenon's design, but they come away with an overall impression of harmony and order. The root five rectangle is

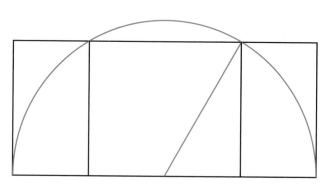

3-39 The root five rectangle.

One obtains a root five rectangle by rotating the diagonal of the square in Fig. 3.38 in both directions. The rectangle obtains its name from the fact that its length is 2.236 (the square root of the number 5) times its width. The root five rectangle has frequently been used to define the frame for works of art, including buildings (see Fig. 3.40) and paintings (see Fig. 3.41).

also the foundation of some paintings that have harmonious compositions. Michelangelo's *The Fall of Man and the Expulsion from the Garden of Eden* (Fig. 3-41), from the Sistine ceiling (see Figs. 15-21 to 15-23), maximizes the components of the root five rectangle. The central square contains

3-40 The east facade of the Parthenon, superimposed with a root five rectangle. When we do not consider the gable (which is absent in this photograph), the facade of the Parthenon is a root five rectangle.

Borromeo/Art Resource, New York.

3-41 MICHELANGELO.
The Fall of Man and the Expulsion from the Garden of Eden
(1508–1512). Portion of the Sistine Chapel ceiling.
Fresco.

The Vatican, Rome/Art Resource, New York.

the Tree of Knowledge from the book of Genesis, that all-important symbol of the temptation and fall of man. The Tree connects the imagery in the outer parts of the root five rectangle—the repetitive figures of Adam and Eve as separated by time and the serpent. The rectangle to the left pulls toward the center, by virtue of the connection between the serpent and Eve, and the rectangle to the right pushes away from center—into the unwritten landscape of humankind's uncertain future—following the sword that is thrust into Adam's neck by the angel who expels them from Paradise.

The Spiral

The Greeks found further meaning in the golden rectangle by relating it to the spiral, which is found in nature on a microscopic scale, a human scale, and even a cosmic scale. As noted in Figure 3-42, a spiral can be created by extending the golden rectangle in an enlarging, circular manner and connecting the corners of the squares with a curve. On the microscopic scale, let us note that DNA, the genetic material that determines the form of the structures of all living things, takes the form of a double spiral, or helix. On the

human scale, we see that the spiral is found in the chambered nautilus and in the pattern of seeds in the head of a sunflower. On the cosmic scale, we find that galaxies such as our own Milky Way spin as vast spirals that light takes millions of years to traverse. No wonder, then, that the spiral has been the source of study and inspiration.

We see the spiral in works as diverse as the Great Mosque at Samarra (see Fig. 17-25) in Iraq to Robert Smithson's *Spiral Jetty* (see Fig. 9-19) in the Great Salt Lake in Utah. Bruce Nauman's neon-lit spiral sculpture *Having Fun / Good Life, Symptoms* (Fig. 3-43) works like a mantra. Two series of words spiral inward through the colors of the spectrum. The spiral on the left contains pairs of antonyms, and the one on the right repeats phrases about having fun. The eye tries to follow the curves to decode the words; however, each spiral requires opposing eye movements, possibly adding to the viewer's visual "symptoms"—and the assorted "fever and chills" of the modern age.

Each age has had its fever and chills, of course, along with its smooth sailing. Artists have strived to capture moments of each of them.

3-42 A spiral.

This spiral is drawn by extending the golden rectangle in a circular manner, increasing its size with each rotation, and then connecting the corners of the squares with a curve. Such spirals found in nature can be small (microscopic) in scale, as is the case with DNA; cosmic in scale, as with spiral-shaped galaxies; and human in scale, as in the cases of the sizes of spiral-shaped snails and flowers.

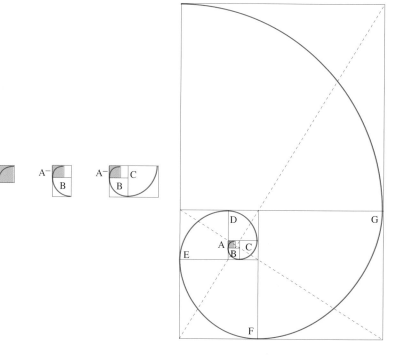

3-43 BRUCE NAUMAN.
Having Fun / Good Life, Symptoms (1985).
Neon and glass tubing. 69″ × 131¼″.

Carnegie Museum of Art. Copyright 2003 Bruce Nauman/Artists Rights
Society (ARS), New York.

4

STYLE, FORM, AND CONTENT

The duty of an artist is to strain against the bonds of the existing style.

—Philip Johnson

Human languages combine words according to rules of grammar to express and communicate emotions and meanings. Artists use the language of art to combine the visual elements of art according to principles of design. The resultant works of art are said to have style and form and to express and communicate a certain content.

Despite individual differences—and despite wholesale revolutions!—through the ages a number of characteristic methods of expression have developed that we refer to as *style*. Works of art can also be said to have a certain *form*, which is the totality of what we see—the product of the composition of the visual elements according to (or in total violation of) principles of design. The *content* of a work includes not only its form but also its subject matter and its underlying meanings or themes. Some works of art can seem to be devoid of content other than the pencil marks or, perhaps, the swaths of paint we find on a sheet of paper or on a canvas.

4-1 *Amorous Couple* (Mayan, Late Classic, 700–900 CE). Polychromed ceramic. H: 9¾″.

Copyright Detroit Institute of the Arts, Detroit, MI. Sounders Society Purchase, Katherine Margaret Kay Bequest Fund and New Endowment Fund.

4-2 ROY LICHTENSTEIN.
Forget It, Forget Me! (1962).
Magna and oil on canvas. 79⅞″ × 68″.

Rose Art Museum, Brandeis University, Waltham, MA. Gevirtz-Minuchin Purchase Fund 1962. Copyright Roy Lichtenstein.

But many are filled with levels of content, more of which are perceived by some viewers than by others. The content of a work varies with the amount of information available to the viewer. For example, viewers who are aware of the symbolism of a particular work of art will find more content in it. Awareness of style, form, and content helps viewers understand and appreciate the visual arts more fully.

STYLE

In the visual arts, **style** refers to a distinctive handling of elements and media associated with the work of an individual artist, a school or movement, or specific culture or time period. Familiar subjects may come and go, but it is in the style of the artist—the unique handling—that creativity, originality, and authenticity dwell.

One of the best ways to illustrate stylistic differences is to choose a group of works with a common theme (such as those illustrated in Figures 4-1 through 4-10) and challenge ourselves to articulate the similarities and differences among them. The first and seemingly obvious connection is that all of the works represent couples. Yet immediately we are struck by the differences among them, both in terms of the stories they imply and the style in which they are rendered. To begin with, the images demand that we get beyond the conventional definition of "couple," for not all couples are composed of a male and a female. What is really striking, however, are the variations in *style,* sometimes linked to the use of different media and sometimes connected to diverse cultural contexts, but always indicative of the characteristic approach of the artist to the subject.

Art, Culture, and Context

The Mayan ceramic couple (Fig. 4-1), for example, is an eighth- to tenth-century pre-Columbian sculpture, whose garments, hairstyles, and facial features link it to the life and times of the Yucatecan people before the onslaught of the Europeans. Similar telltale attributes connect Roy Lichtenstein's *Forget It! Forget Me!* (Fig. 4-2) to the United States in the decade of the 1960s. Henri de Toulouse-Lautrec's *The Two Girlfriends* (Fig. 4-3) transports us to the demimonde

How can you say one style is better than another? You ought to be able to be an Abstract-Expressionist next week, or a Pop artist, or a realist, without feeling you've given up something.

—Andy Warhol

4-3　HENRI DE TOULOUSE-LAUTREC.
The Two Girlfriends (1894).
Oil on cardboard. 48 cm × 34.5 cm.
Musée Toulouse-Lautrec, Albi. Copyright Corbis.

4-4　ROBERT MAPPLETHORPE.
Ken Moody and Robert Sherman (1984).
Photograph.
Copyright The Estate of Robert Mapplethorpe. Courtesy Art and Commerce Anthology.

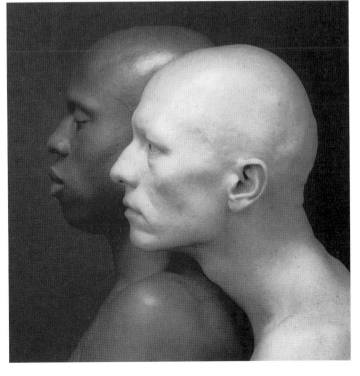

of turn-of-the-century Paris where, as we were told in the film *Moulin Rouge,* the greatest thing is to love and be loved in return. The weather-worn faces and postcard-perfect surroundings in Grant Wood's *American Gothic* (Fig. 4-9) suggest the duality of rural life in modern America—hardship and serenity—whereas contemporary photographer Robert Mapplethorpe (Fig. 4-4) drew the world's attention to what it was like to be gay and living in America at the turn of the millennium. The tumult of Germany in the years leading up to World War I can be felt in the dark palette, whirling brushstrokes, and **existentialist** expressions in Oskar

4-5 OSKAR KOKOSCHKA. *The Tempest* (1914). Oil on canvas. 71½″ × 86½″. Kunstmuseum Basel, Switzerland. Copyright Edimedia. Copyright 2003 Artists Rights Society (ARS), New York/ Pro Litteris, Zürich.

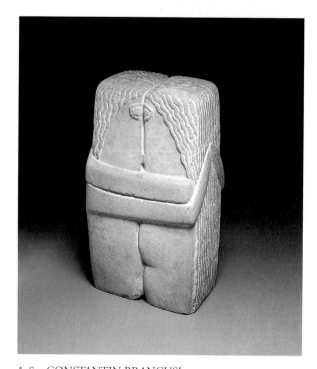

4-6 CONSTANTIN BRANCUSI. *The Kiss* (c. 1912). Limestone. H: 23″; W: 13″; D: 10″.

Philadelphia Museum of Art. Louise and Walter Arensberg Collection. Copyright 2003 Artists Rights Society (ARS), New York/ADAGP, Paris.

Kokoschka's *The Tempest* (Fig. 4-5). Donna Rosenthal's *He Said . . . She Said* (Fig. 4-10) seems to tap into some sort of collective unconscious ballroom in its unique yet universal ruminations. Constantin Brancusi's *The Kiss* (Fig. 4-6) could be said to transcend context in the simple accessibility or readability of its subject.

In their abstraction, Jackson Pollock's *Male and Female* (Fig. 4-7) and Barbara Hepworth's *Two Figures* (Fig. 4-8) are more difficult to decipher. Pollock's painting was created while he was undergoing psychoanalytic therapy and ought to be read in that context. It reveals a complex scheme of images that he believed were derived from his collective unconscious mind. Hepworth, by contrast, aims to disconnect her work from context by reducing her figures to their most common denominators—organic vertical shapes punctuated by softly modeled voids. Yet curiously, when we view *Two Figures* in the context of this grouping of "couples," it seems to belong, even if eyes may resist making a connection.

Context has a profound influence on style. We can see this in the similarities among artists of a specific era, regardless of their individual "signature." Claude Monet and Auguste Renoir, for example—both Impressionist artists working in nineteenth-century France—are recognized for their

*My aim in painting has always been the most exact transcription possible
of my most intimate impression of nature.*

—Edward Hopper

All the really good ideas I ever had came to me while I was milking a cow.

—Grant Wood

4-7 JACKSON POLLOCK.
Male and Female (1942).
Oil on canvas. $73\frac{1}{3}'' \times 49''$.

Philadelphia Museum of Art. Partial gift of Mrs. H. Gates Lloyd.
Copyright 2003 The Pollock-Krasner Foundation/
Artists Rights Society (ARS), New York.

4-8 BARBARA HEPWORTH (1903–1975).
Two Figures (Menhirs) (1954–1955).
Teak. H: 54″.

Art Institute of Chicago. Bridgeman Art Library. Copyright Bowness,
Hepworth Estate.

distinct styles, but they have more in common with each other than they do with, say, Rembrandt. And although you probably wouldn't mistake one for the other, the works of both artists are very much a product of their culture at a moment in time.

Styles in art are numerous, ever changing, and ever new. The vocabulary we use to discuss style, on the other hand, has been fairly standard for a long time.

I observe the effects of traditional and societal influences on the lives of women. . . .
I use text, repetition, and the cultural symbolism of clothing to expose the struggles between
the internal and external self. The manner in which I compose my work gives clues to age-old
personal and collective realities, the longings, presumptions, and predicaments of women.

—Donna Rosenthal

Realistic Art

Realism refers to the portrayal of people and things as they are seen by the eye or really thought to be, without idealization, without distortion. Wood's painting (Fig. 4-9) is described as realistic in terms of style. The term, with a capital *R*, also defines a specific school of art that flowered during the mid-nineteenth century in France. Realism featured subjects culled from daily life and experience and developed a new respect for the real substance of the artist's materials.

Grant Wood's renowned *American Gothic* is a painstakingly realistic portrait of the staid virtues of the rural life in America. It is also one of our more commercialized works of art; images derived from it have adorned boxes of breakfast cereal, greeting cards, and numerous other products. Note the repetition of the pitchfork pattern in the man's shirtfront, the upper-story window of the house, and in the plant on the porch. He is very much tied to his environment. Were it not for the incongruously spry curl falling from the mistress's otherwise tucked-tight hairdo, we might view this composition—as well as the sitters therein—as solid, stolid, and monotonous.

We think of most photographs as realistic. The very nature of the technique—shooting, capturing, documenting—suggests candid truth, unadulterated reality. Although photographers in the twentieth-century and beyond have pursued photography as an art form and strained against the bonds of representation, the impact of Mapplethorpe's photographs is largely due to his unflinching realism (Fig. 4-4).

Realistic versus Representational Art

The Lichtenstein couple (Fig. 4-2) is portrayed in a style that departs from strict Realism, yet the observer clearly identifies the caricature-like renderings of the figures as that of a man and woman. This is representational art. It presents natural objects in recognizable, though not realistic, form. *Forget it! Forget me!* is an example of Pop Art, which adopts the visual clichés of the comic strip. Donna Rosenthal's *He Said . . . She Said* (Fig. 4-10) also clearly depicts an interaction between a man and a woman, in this case capturing the verbal clichés of the human comedy. Both works can be described as representational.

The term **representational art,** often used synonymously with **figurative art,** is defined as art that portrays, however altered or distorted, things perceived in the visible world. The people in the Lichtenstein work may not be realistic, but they are clearly recognizable. The Mayan couple (Fig. 4-1) and Toulouse-Lautrec's *The Two Girlfriends* (Fig. 4-3) are similarly representational but not realistic.

Expressionistic Art

In expressionistic art, form and color are freely distorted by the artist in order to achieve a heightened emotional impact. **Expressionism** also refers to a modern art movement, but many earlier works are expressionistic in the broader sense of the term.

In *The Burial of Count Orgaz* (see Fig. 15-30), El Greco's expressionistic elongation of the heavenly figures seems to emphasize their ethereal spirituality. Postimpressionist Vincent van Gogh relied on both an expressionistic palette and brushwork to transfer emotion to his canvases.

Kokoschka's expressionistic painting *The Tempest* (Fig. 4-5) is marked by frenzied brushstrokes that mirror the torment of his inner life as well as the impending darkness of war in Germany. Reclining figures occupy the center of a dark, imaginary landscape. Images of earth, water, and flesh merge in a common palette and bevy of strokes; little distinguishes one from another. All seem caught up in a churning sky, very much in danger of being swept away.

Abstract Art

The term **abstract** applies to art that departs significantly from the actual appearance of things. Such art may be completely **nonobjective,** that is, it may make no reference whatsoever to nature or reality. On the other hand, abstract art may be rooted in nature, even though the finished product bears little resemblance to the source that inspired it. A number of aspects of the Brancusi sculpture (Fig. 4-6) are recognizable. One can discern an upper torso, arms, eyes, and hair. Yet the artist seems to have been more interested in the independent relationships of the shapes than in being true to the human form. For this reason we would more likely characterize *The Kiss* as abstract rather than representational.

Wood's *American Gothic* with Rosenthal's *He Said . . . She Said*

The style of a work of art refers to the characteristic ways in which artists express themselves and the times in which they live. In our consideration of the theme of couples, we were able to assess the way in which a full range of media, methods, and styles contributes to the uniqueness of each work. If we add to these the historical and cultural contexts of the works, we gain insight into the ways in which art reflects its place and time.

Consider Grant Wood's *American Gothic* and Donna Rosenthal's *He Said . . . She Said*. On a trip to Europe in the 1920s, Wood was influenced by the realistic works of fifteenth-century German and Flemish painters. His initial goal in *American Gothic* (Fig. 4-9) was to render realistically the rural Iowan house in the background of the painting. He enlisted a local dentist along with his own sister to pose as models for the farmer and his wife. The realism of their faces is so exacting and their expressions so intent that the viewer cannot but wonder what thoughts lie buried in their minds.

And then there is the expression "to wear one's heart on one's sleeve." In Rosenthal's *He Said . . . She Said* (Fig. 4-10), thoughts and feelings are broadcast plainly, as the (implied) individuals quite literally wear their thoughts on their clothes—a suit and party dress made from the pages of discarded books and newspapers. We know exactly what's on their minds, verbalized through cultural stereotypes of the conflicting wishes of males and females—his reluctance to make a commitment, her hope that he will still remember her in the morning. Other works by Rosenthal express man's desire for sex and woman's desire for security. Stereotypes are, of course, extreme; they represent conventional notions and not individual conceptions. Yet Rosenthal succeeds in her communication with the viewer in large part because we identify with these phrases.

As the physical couple is absent from the work, we are left with the notion that the clothes make the individual. This is conceptual art; that is, the ideas being expressed by the artist have greater meaning than their physical expression. ∎

4-9   GRANT WOOD.
American Gothic (1930).
Oil on beaverboard. 29⅞″ × 24⅞″.

Art Institute of Chicago. Friends of the American Art Collection. All rights reserved by the Art Institute of Chicago. Licensed by VAGA, New York.

4-10   DONNA ROSENTHAL.
He Said . . . She Said: "Let's get physical"–"Do you think I'm sexy" (1999).
Mixed media. Suit: 12″ × 12″ × 1½″; dress: 10″ × 8″ × 8″.
Courtesy, Bernice Steinbaum Gallery, Miami, FL.

Copy nature and you infringe on the work of our Lord. Interpret nature and you are an artist.

—Jacques Lipchitz

Abstract painting is abstract. It confronts you.

—Jackson Pollock

In *The Kiss,* the human torso is reduced to a simple block form. Twentieth-century proponents of **Cubism,** such as Pablo Picasso and Georges Braque (see Figs. 19-7 and 19-8) also transcribed natural forms into largely angular geometrical equivalents. To some degree, despite their reduction to essential geometrical components and line–shape relationships, the figures of Picasso and Braque remain somewhat decipherable. In any event, both artists—in spite of some brief dabbling in nonobjectivity—abstracted from reality.

Jackson Pollock's *Male and Female* (Fig. 4-7) "figures" are a great deal more difficult to discern than Brancusi's, but the totemic shapes bear some visual cues that suggest gender differences. At the time of the painting, Pollock was undergoing psychoanalysis, and he was quite convinced that the unconscious played a major role in his art. Using a method called **psychic automatism,** Pollock attempted to clear his mind of purpose and concerns so that inner conflicts and ideas could find expression through his work. The result in *Male and Female* is abstraction.

Although much of Barbara Hepworth's sculpture has been inspired by nature, it is not always derived from nature. That is why we characterize work such as *Two Figures* (Fig. 4-8) as nonobjective. That is, it is not intended to make any reference to reality. On the other hand, entitling the piece *Two Figures* places viewers in a quandary. It sends us searching for details that might represent the human form, even gender differences. Is the taller "figure" the male? Could the concave shapes in the shorter figure suggest femininity? Here the connection to reality may be fully in the eye of the beholder. The truth is that nonobjective artists do this type of thing quite a lot. Sometimes they label their paintings and sculptures *Untitled* partially as a way to discourage Rorschach-like readings of their work. At other times, they assign titles to their nonobjective works based on some association that is triggered by the work itself.

A case in point is Judy Pfaff's *Voodoo* (Fig. 4-11), a nonobjective painting in which highly saturated colors and jagged shapes comprise the content and spirit of the work. Though the elements and technique are the "subject" of the work, the title suggests the presence of mysterious figures undulating in a Caribbean jungle undergrowth. One of the issues that many viewers have with nonobjective art is that

4-11 JUDY PFAFF.
Voodoo (1981).
Contact paper collage on Mylar. 98″ × 60″ (framed).
Albright-Knox Art Gallery, Buffalo; Edmund Hayes Fund, 1983.

To give a body and a perfect form to your thought, this alone is what it is to be an artist.

—Jacques-Louis David

they want it to make sense. They want to connect it with something familiar—even if the "familiar" in this case is as abstruse as the title, *Voodoo.* But nonobjective art is just that—nonobjective—and viewers might come closer to the intention of the artist by allowing themselves to focus on what's there rather than to go on scavenger hunts for what probably isn't.

FORM

The form of a work refers to its totality as a work of art Form includes the elements, design principles, and composition of a work of art. A work's *form* might include, for example, the colors that are used, the textures and shapes, the illusion of three dimensions, the balance, rhythm, or unity of design. **Formalist criticism,** by extension, is an approach to art criticism that concentrates primarily on the elements and design of works of art rather than on historical factors or the biography of the artist.

CONTENT

The **content** of a work of art is everything that is contained in it. The content of a work refers not only to its lines or forms but also to its subject matter and its underlying meanings or themes.

The Levels of Content

We may think of works of art as containing three levels of content: (1) subject matter, (2) elements and composition, and (3) underlying or symbolic meanings or themes.

Consider a comparison between the subject matter of two visually similar paintings as a way of exploring these levels. In 1793, just a few years after the taking of the Bastille and the start of the French Revolution, Jacques-Louis David painted *Death of Marat* (Fig. 4-12), a memorial to a political martyr. Almost 200 years later, Sandow Birk appropriated David's image for *Death of Manuel* (Fig. 4-13), his graphic deposition on urban violence.

4-12   JACQUES-LOUIS DAVID.
Death of Marat (1793).
Oil on canvas. 63¾″ × 49⅛″.
Musées Royaux des Beaux-Arts de Belgique, Brussels/Erich Lessing/
Art Resource, New York.

4-13   SANDOW BIRK.
Death of Manuel (1992).
Oil on canvas. 33″ × 25″.
Koplin Gallery, Los Angeles.

David's *The Oath of the Horatii* with Kruger's *Untitled (We Don't Need Another Hero)*

The Oath of the Horatii (Fig. 4-14), by Jacques-Louis David, is one of the most readily recognizable works of the nineteenth century—indeed, the whole of the history of art. It is a landmark composition—symbolically and pictorially. David worked for the king of France in the days before the French Revolution. Ironically, although the *Oath* was painted for Louis XVI, who along with his wife, Marie Antoinette, would lose his head to the guillotine, the painting became an almost instant symbol of the Revolution. The loyalty, courage, and sacrifice it portrayed were an inspiration to the downtrodden masses in their uprising against the French

monarchy. David, because of his position, was imprisoned along with the members of the court and other French aristocracy, only to be—as it were—"bailed out" by another who could use his services as a painter. Thus David, court painter to the French king, would become painter to Napoleon Bonaparte, who would eventually crown himself emperor.

Pictorially, the work is also groundbreaking. It compresses space and forces us to concentrate on the meticulously rendered figures in the foreground. This treatment of space would open the door to the flattening of space in Modernist paintings. The tradition of treating the picture frame as a win-

4-14 JACQUES-LOUIS DAVID. *The Oath of the Horatii* (1784). Oil on canvas. 11' × 14'. Louvre Museum, Paris/RMN/Art Resource, New York

dow frame through which one peers into the infinite distance would be abandoned by many artists in favor of the two-dimensionality of the canvas.

Knowing something of the historical circumstances under which *The Oath of the Horatii* was created, and understanding what is new about it in terms of style and composition, helps us appreciate its significance. But our full comprehension and appreciation of the work can only occur with our consideration and interpretation of the subject matter. The subject of David's *The Oath of the Horatii* is, on the face of things, fairly easy to read. Three brothers—the Horatii—swear their allegiance to Rome on swords held high by their father. They pledge to come back victorious or not come back at all. Their forward thrusting and stable stance convey strength, commitment, bravery. And there is something else—something that has been referred to by feminist critics and scholars as a *subtext,* or additional level of content in the work. David's *Oath* is also a painting about the ideology of gender differences. The women in the painting collapse in the background, terrified at the prospect of the death of the brothers. To make matters worse, one of the Horatii sisters is engaged to be married to one of the enemy. She might lose her brother to the hands of her fiancé, or vice versa. The women's posture, in opposition to the men's, represents, according to historian Linda Nochlin, "the clear-cut opposition between masculine strength and feminine weakness offered by the ide-

ological discourse of the period." Whatever else the content of this painting is about, it is also about the relationship of the sexes and gender–role stereotypes.

A number of contemporary feminist artists have challenged the traditional discourse of gender ideology as damaging both to men and women. Barbara Kruger's *Untitled (We Don't Need Another Hero)* (Fig. 4-15) can be interpreted as an "answer" to David's *Oath.* In appropriating a Norman Rockwell illustration to depict the "innocence" of gender ideology—in this case, the requisite fawning of a little girl over the budding muscles of her male counterpart—Kruger violates the innocuous vignette with a cautionary band blazing the words *We don't need another hero.* The representation of the opposition between strength and weakness—male and female—is confronted and replaced with the gender discourse of a more socially aware era.

The subject matter of these works is strangely related, oddly linked. Visually, the works could not be more dissimilar. In David's composition, the subtext of gender ideology exits simultaneously with the main narrative—that of the soldiers preparing for battle. In Kruger's work, by contrast, the main narrative *is* gender ideology—and how to counteract it. In both, however, the essential nature of evaluating the content, or subject matter of the works we view, is underscored. They are, after all, really about the same thing, aren't they? ∎

4–15 BARBARA KRUGER. *Untitled (We Don't Need Another Hero)* (1987). Photographic silkscreen, vinyl lettering on Plexiglas. 109″ × 210″.

Collection of Emily Fisher Landau, New York. Courtesy of Mary Boone Gallery, New York.

The artist does not draw what he sees, but what he must make others see.
Only when he no longer knows what he is doing does the painter do good things.

—Edgar Degas

Visual formulation of our reaction to life.

—Josef Albers, on the content of art

There is a macabre similarity between the two paintings in their elements and composition. David's Marat is found dead in his bath—murdered by a counterrevolutionary fanatic named Charlotte Corday. The artist brings the viewer face-to-face with the slaughtered hero, whose arm drops lifeless and whose sympathetic facial expression leans toward us yearningly. Birk's *Manuel* is rendered in the same pose, although Marat's bath has been replaced with a Chevy Impala, riddled with bullets. Marat's left hand holds a false letter requesting a visit from the would-be murderer; Manuel's left hand grasps the steering wheel of his car. Marat's head is wrapped in a turban; Manuel's, in a brightly printed bandana. In both paintings, the figure is set in the extreme foreground and the backgrounds are monochromatic and nondescript. The spatial depth is severely limited. This dramatic silhouette effect, coupled with the strong linear style used to render the figure, creates the feeling of a sculptural frieze.

The underlying themes or symbolism in these works may not bear the same relationship as do the elements and composition. Yet the choice of the David prototype suggests ideas of revolution, heroism as it is defined within a group or culture, and the cold-blooded murder of the unsuspecting victim. The appropriation of the David image by Birk validates the historic significance of the eighteenth-century painting. Understanding the relationship between the two makes each more meaningful to the viewer.

Iconography

I prefer winter and fall, when you feel the bone structure in the landscape—the loneliness of it—the dread feeling of winter. Something waits beneath it—the whole story doesn't show.

—Andrew Wyeth

Winter is a perennial symbol of death and aloneness in the arts, and fall is a common symbol of either harvest or decline. Yet artists who paint the winter or the fall, or who write of them, may not directly speak of death or of the harvest. "The whole story" does not always show but rather may lie beneath a work of art.

Iconography is the study of the themes and symbols in the visual arts—the figures and images that lend works their underlying meanings. Bronzino's sixteenth-century masterpiece *Venus, Cupid, Folly, and Time (The Exposure of Luxury)* (Fig. 4-16) is a classic example of works in which there is much more than meets the eye. The painting weaves an intricate allegory, with many actors, many symbols. Venus, undraped by Time and spread in a languorous diagonal across the front plane, is fondled by her son Cupid. Folly prepares to cast roses on the couple, while Hatred and Inconstancy (with two left hands) lurk in the background. Masks, symbolizing falseness, and other objects, meanings known or unknown, complete the scene.

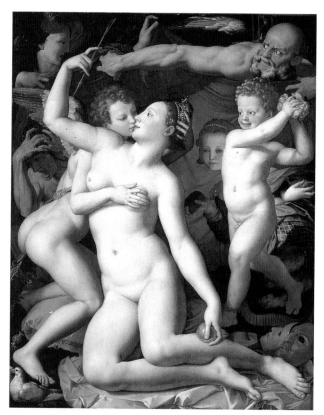

4-16 BRONZINO.
Venus, Cupid, Folly, and Time (The Exposure of Luxury)
(c. 1546).
Oil on wood. Approx. 61″ × 56¾″.
Courtesy of the Trustees of the National Gallery, London.

I would like to leave a will and testament to declare everything void at my death, and it's not unrealistic. I mean it, because only I know the work as it ought to be. All posthumous interpretations are less.

—Dan Flavin

Works such as these offer an intricate iconographic puzzle. Is Bronzino saying that love in an environment of hatred and that inconstancy is foolish or doomed? Is something being suggested about incest? self-love? Can one fully appreciate Bronzino's painting without being aware of its iconography? Is it sufficient to respond to the elements and composition, to the figure of a woman being openly fondled before an unlikely array of onlookers? No simple answer is possible, and a Mannerist artist such as Bronzino would have intended this ambiguity. Certainly one could appreciate the composition and the subject matter for their own sake, but awareness of the symbolism enriches the viewing experience.

Whereas Bronzino's painting illustrates a complex allegory, the symbolism of which would seem relevant only to the initiated, Willie Bester's *Semekazi (Migrant Miseries)* (Fig. 4-17) uses images and objects to communicate a tragic story to anyone who will listen. Bester is an artist who was classified as "colored" under South African apartheid rule and thus, as with most nonwhite artists, was deprived of opportunities for formal training in art. Collages such as *Semekazi* combine painting with found objects in a densely covered surface that seems, in its lack of space and air, to reflect the squalid living conditions among black Africans. The many images and objects serve as symbols of rampant oppression and deprivation affecting a whole people, while a single portrait of a worker in the center of the composition—peering from under bedsprings—serves as a single case study.

The paintings by Bronzino and Bester, as far apart in time, tenor, and experience as can be imagined, both supply the viewer with clear, familiar images intended to communicate certain underlying themes. But in some cases, the underlying themes may be at least in part the invention of the viewer. In Helen Frankenthaler's *Bay Side* (see Fig. 2-25), for example, we may interpret the juncture of the blue and tan fields as surf meeting sand. Did the artist intend this symbolism, however, or is it our own invention? Many of us love a puzzle and are willing to spend a great deal of time attempting to decipher the possible iconography of a work of art. In other cases, the subject matter of a work may be in the eye of the beholder.

Our exposition of the language of art is now complete. We have seen that artists use the visual elements of art in com-

4-17 WILLIE BESTER.
Semekazi (Migrant Miseries) (1993).
Oil, enamel paint, and mixed media on board.
49¼" × 49¼".
By courtesy of Sotheby's Picture Library. Copyright 2005 Willie Bester.

positions that employ various principles of design. Their compositions are usually created within certain traditional and contemporary styles. The totality of the form of their works—everything that we see in them—also has certain subject matter or content, which may exist on several levels. Our understanding of these various levels of content helps us appreciate the works.

Several chapters follow that show how artists apply the language of art to works in two dimensions and three dimensions. Then we survey the history of art, where we see how artists through the ages and around the globe have spoken a similar language. Although it may take us adults years to become fluent in the spoken languages of other peoples in other times and other places, we may find ourselves capable of more readily understanding the language in their visual works.

5

DRAWING

*Drawing . . . is the necessary beginning of everything in art,
and not having it, one has nothing.*

—Giorgio Vasari

The first sketch was probably an accident. Perhaps some Stone Age human idly ran a twig through soft clay and was astounded to find an impression of this gesture in the ground. Perhaps this individual then made such impressions as signs for family members (as in an arrow pointing "that way") and to record experiences, such as the hunt for a beast or a gathering around a fire. Similarly, a child may learn to trace a shell fragment through damp sand at the shore's edge. Soon the child is drawing sketches of geometric shapes, animals, toys, and people. Michelangelo was engaging in an essentially similar act when he sketched his models from life— albeit with a bit more skill and flair.

In this chapter we discuss drawing, the most basic of the two-dimensional art forms. In the next two chapters we will discuss two other forms of two-dimensional art—painting and printmaking. We shall see how people over the centuries have used a variety of materials, frequently from surprising sources, to express themselves through two-dimensional art forms.

I have always . . . wanted to copy and taken pleasure in copying, either from originals,

but above all from reproductions, every work of art that touched my feelings

or stirred my enthusiasm or just interested me particularly.

—Alberto Giacometti

In its broadest definition, **drawing** is the result of an implement running over a surface and leaving some trace of the gesture. But as we shall discover, the art of drawing goes far beyond this simple description.

The surface, or **support,** onto which an image is sketched is usually, although not always, two dimensional. Most often the support is **monochromatic** paper or parchment, although drawings can be found on a variety of surfaces. The implements can range from charcoal (which is burnt wood) to bristle brushes dipped in ink. Most drawings, by virtue of the implements, consist of black and tones of gray. But many full-color drawings have also been created with colored chalks, pastels, and wax crayons.

Some drawings are predominantly **linear;** others are constructed solely by tonal contrasts. The quality of line and the nature of shading are affected by the texture of the support. We shall see how the artist capitalizes on the idiosyncratic characteristics of the implements and support to capture a desired expression in the drawing.

CATEGORIES OF DRAWING

Drawing is basic to the visual arts. For centuries, painters and sculptors have made countless preparatory sketches for their major projects, working out difficulties on paper before approaching the more permanent medium of paint or bronze. Architects proceed in the same fashion, outlining buildings in detail before breaking ground. Drawing has also served artists as a kind of shorthand method for recording ideas.

Artists carry sketchbooks everywhere, and perhaps there is no one better known for his "little book of leaves" than Leonardo da Vinci, who advised artists to note everything and when the book was "full, [to] keep it to serve [their]

5-1 REMBRANDT VAN RIJN.
Copy of Leonardo da Vinci's
Last Supper.
Red chalk on paper.
14″ × 18¼″.

future plans, and take another and carry on with it." Leonardo's own work also served as inspiration for generations of artists who, like Rembrandt (Fig. 5-1), copied his masterpieces. Imitation has been said to be the sincerest form of flattery, and art-world luminaries and students alike have "gone to school on" the works of the masters. Copying permits the artist to, in a sense, retrace another artist's steps—from conception to completion. Far from being an exercise in mere duplication, the effort can lead to an understanding and feeling of form, of rhythm, of design. Sometimes such copies give us a bit of insight into how an artist might have changed a composition, in the artist's view, for the better. Although Leonardo's setting for the *Last Supper* is quite spare, with a simple rectangular window behind the figure of Jesus, Rembrandt has added an elaborate draped canopy and more architectural detail, no doubt more befitting of the event in his eyes. Rembrandt copied Leonardo's famed fresco from an engraving that another artist made after the original. Many artists in history have traveled well beyond their cities of origin, however, to meet the works of the masters and to unlock their secrets through the scrutiny of copying.

But drawing does not serve only a utilitarian purpose. In most cases, drawing is the most direct way of bringing what is in the artist's mind to the artist's surface. Many artists enjoy the sheer spontaneity of drawing, tracing a pencil or piece of chalk across a sheet of paper to capture directly their thoughts or to record the slightest movement of their hand.

Many drawings, by contrast, stand as complete works of art. Gary Kelley's sensual and rhythmic pastel drawing (Fig. 5-2) possesses all of the detail, all of the "finish" of a work of art in a medium that might be considered more "permanent." Its powerful zigzag composition contributes to the sense of life and movement, as do the contrasts between the harsh angularity of the male singer's zoot suit and the sinuous curves of the woman who writhes in response to his music. Kelley's drawing was commissioned as a promotional piece for the Mississippi Delta Blues Festival and was no doubt purposefully reminiscent of the Harlem jazz age as depicted by 1930s African American artists such as Archibald J. Motley Jr. (see Fig. 3-2).

Drawings may thus be said to fall into at least three categories:

1. Sketches that record an idea or provide information about something the artist has seen.

2. Plans or preparatory studies for other projects, such as buildings, sculptures, crafts, paintings, plays, and films.

3. Fully developed and autonomous works of art.

5-2 GARY KELLEY.
Promotion for the Mississippi Delta Blues Festival (c. 1989). Pastel. 24″ × 14″.
Courtesy of the artist and Richard Solomon.

DRAWING MATERIALS

Over the millennia, methods of drawing have become increasingly sophisticated and materials more varied and standardized. It would seem that we have come a long way from our prehistoric ancestors' use of twigs, hollow reeds, and lumps of clay. Drawing materials can be divided into two major groups: *dry media* and *fluid media*.

Dry Media

The **dry media** used in drawing include silverpoint, pencil, charcoal, chalk, pastel, and wax crayon.

Drawing is the honesty of the art. There is no possibility of cheating. It is either good or bad.

—Salvador Dalí

Silverpoint

Silverpoint is one of the oldest drawing media. It was used widely from the late Middle Ages to the early 1500s. Silverpoint drawings are created by dragging a silver-tipped implement over a surface that has been coated with a **ground** of bone dust or chalk mixed with **gum,** water, and **pigment.** This ground is sufficiently coarse to allow small flecks of silver from the instrument to adhere to the prepared surface as it is drawn across. These bits of metal form the lines of the drawing; they are barely visible at the start but eventually oxidize, becoming tarnished or darkened and making the image visible. Each silverpoint line, a soft gray to begin with, mellows and darkens to a grayish brown hue. If the artist desires to make one area of the drawing appear darker than others, it is necessary to build up a series of close, parallel, or cross-hatched, lines in that area to give the impression of deepened tone. Because they lack sharp tonal contrasts, the resultant drawings are often extremely delicate in appearance.

The technique of working in silverpoint is itself delicate. The medium allows for little or no correction. Thus, the artist is not in a position to experiment while working. There must be a fairly concrete notion of what the final product will look like, and the lines must be accurate and confidently drawn. The nineteenth-century *Head of a Man* (Fig. 5-3) by the French artist Alphonse Legros illustrates the way in which the artist must use techniques of cross-hatching and clusters of small lines to model form with the silverpoint medium. The portrait is a dramatic record of the topography of a man's face, rendered with the utmost clarity and control. Legros concentrates his efforts—and the viewer's attention—on the intent gaze of the face; the hair and collar are only faintly suggested. Working in silverpoint has its rewards. The drawings, painstakingly rendered, are flawless in execution, their finish exquisite and polished. But the technique is not for the fainthearted. Students interested in working in silverpoint are encouraged to create detailed preliminary sketches in hard pencil before launching into the other, more permanent and less forgiving medium.

Pencil

Silverpoint was largely replaced by the lead **pencil,** which came into use during the 1500s. Medieval monks, like the ancient Egyptians, ruled lines with metallic lead. Pencils as

5-3 ALPHONSE LEGROS.
Head of a Man (19th century).
Silverpoint on white ground.

we know them began to be mass-produced in the late eighteenth century.

A pencil is composed of a thin rod of **graphite** encased within wood or paper. The graphite is ground to dust and mixed with clay, and the mixture is baked to harden the clay. The relative hardness or softness of the implement depends on the quantity of clay in the mixture. The more clay, the harder the pencil.

Pencil is capable of producing a wide range of effects. Lines drawn with hard pencil can be thin and light in tone; those rendered in soft lead can be thick and dark. The sharp point of the pencil will create a firm, fine line suitable for meticulous detail. Softer areas of tone can be achieved through a buildup of parallel lines, smudging, or stroking the support with the side of the lead tip.

As seen in the contrasting works of Giorgio de Chirico and Albert Giacometti, pencil can be manipulated to achieve dramatically different effects that complement the subject. Chirico's mannequin (Fig. 5-4) is a controlled construction of wood pieces that have been fitted together to

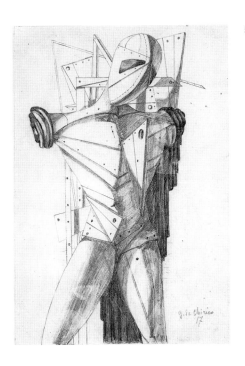

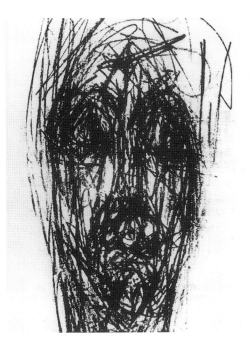

5-4 GIORGIO DE CHIRICO.
Condottiero (1917).
Pencil. 12⅜″ × 8½″.

Staatliche Graphische Sammlung,
Munich. Copyright Foundation
Giorgio de Chirico. Copyright 2003
Artists Rights Society (ARS),
New York/SIAE, Rome.

5-5 ALBERTO
GIACOMETTI.
Head (1946).
Pencil.
5⅞″ × 4¼″.

Copyright 2003
Artists Rights Society
(ARS), New York.

the likenesses of muscles, ligaments, and tendons. The precision of the construction is communicated through the fine lines of a hard pencil point.

Giacometti's drawing (Fig. 5-5), on the other hand, is a free expression of energy or, perhaps, anxiety. The highly abstracted head seems bound up in a frozen psychological state, one of inner turmoil created by the artist's agitated scribbling and reworking of bold pencil strokes. The contrast of thick black lines against the harsh white paper seems to echo the expressive nature of the drawing rather than convey the features of the subject. Giacometti was clearly not interested in creating a portrait likeness. Rather, he used his medium to render the distorted impression of an agitated figure, perhaps projecting his own inner conflict onto his subject. Chirico, by contrast, used pencil in a more static and controlled manner to present us with a factual duplication of his bizarre inanimate object.

Drawing is perhaps the most traditional of media. The exercise of drawing from life has been integral to the art academy experience for hundreds of years, a method by which the human form might be painstakingly analyzed and recorded. Perhaps this is why, in part, Adrian Piper chose the medium of drawing to render her dramatic *Self-Portrait Exaggerating My Negroid Features* (Fig. 5-6). With it, Piper invites the spectator to focus on those aspects of her physical genetic composition that reveal her mixed black and white parentage. The portrait gives us an unflinching record of Piper's countenance, but perhaps more important, the image

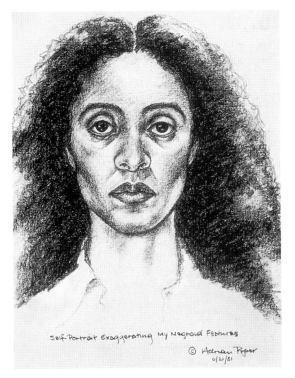

5-6 ADRIAN PIPER.
Self-Portrait Exaggerating My Negroid Features (1981).
Pencil on paper. 10″ × 8″.
Collection of the artist.

challenges us to confront our prejudices about the physical differences between the races.

Adrian Piper authored "calling cards" to hand out to people whom she overhears making racist remarks: "I regret any discomfort my presence is causing you, just as I am sure you regret the discomfort your racism is causing me."

Charcoal

Charcoal, like pencil, has a long history as a drawing implement. Used by our primitive ancestors to create images on cave walls, these initially crumbly pieces of burnt wood or bone now take the form of prepared sticks that are formed by the controlled charring of special hardwoods. Charcoal sticks are available in a number of textures that vary from hard to soft. The sticks may be sharpened with sandpaper to form fine and clear lines or may be dragged flat across the surface to form diffuse areas of varied tone. Like pencil, charcoal may also be smudged or rubbed to create a hazy effect.

When charcoal is dragged across a surface, bits of the material adhere to that surface, just as in the case of silverpoint and pencil. But charcoal particles rub off more easily, and thus the completed drawings must be sprayed with a solution of thinned varnish to keep them affixed. Also, because of the way in which the charcoal is dispersed over a surface, the nature of the support is evident in each stroke. Coarsely textured paper will yield a grainy image, whereas smooth paper will provide a clear, almost pencil-like line.

A self-portrait of the German Expressionist Käthe Kollwitz (Fig. 5-7) reveals one aspect of the character of the charcoal medium. Delicate lines of sharpened charcoal drawn over broader areas of subtle shading enunciate the

5-8   CLAUDIO BRAVO.
Package (1969).
Charcoal, pastel, and sanguine. $30\frac{7}{8}'' \times 22\frac{1}{2}''$.
Baltimore Museum of Art, Baltimore, MD.
Copyright Christies Images/Corbis.

two main points of interest: the artist's face and her hand. Between these two points—that of intellect and that of skill—runs a surge of energy described by aggressive, jagged strokes overlaying the lightly sketched contour of her forearm.

Values in the drawing range from hints of white at the artist's knuckles, cheekbone, and hair to the deepest blacks of the palm of her hand, eyes, and mouth. The finer lines override the texture of the paper, whereas the shaded areas, particularly around the neck and chest area, reveal the faint white lines and tiny flecks of pulp that are visual remnants of the papermaking process.

Charcoal can be expressive or descriptive, depending on its method of application. Claudio Bravo's *Package* (Fig. 5-8) is a finely rendered, trompe l'oeil drawing that bears almost no trace of the artist's gesture and almost no indication of the "dusty" quality of the media—primarily charcoal and pastel. The illusion of the smooth sheen and crinkled indentations of the wrapping paper, attributed to painstaking gradations in value, is so convincing that the implied texture of

5-7   KÄTHE KOLLWITZ.
Self-Portrait (1924).
Charcoal. $18\frac{3}{4}'' \times 25''$.
National Gallery of Art, Washington, DC. Rosenwald Collection.
Copyright 2003 Artists Rights Society (ARS), New York/VG Bild-Kunst, Bonn.

the package completely overrides the actual texture of the drawing materials. The viewer is enticed to touch the forbidden surfaces, just to test whether they are real.

Chalk and Pastel

The effects of charcoal, **chalk,** and **pastel** as they are drawn against the paper surface are very similar, though the compositions of the media differ. Chalk and pastel consist of pigment and a **binder,** such as **gum arabic,** shaped into workable sticks.

Chalks are available in a number of colors, some of which occur in nature. **Ocher,** for example, derives its dark yellow tint from iron oxide in some clays. **Umber** acquires its characteristic yellowish or reddish brown color from earth containing oxides of manganese and iron. Other popular "organic" or "earth" colors include white, black, and a red called **sanguine.**

Michelangelo used red chalk in a sketch for the Sistine Chapel (see Chapter 15), in which he attempted to work out certain aspects of the figure of the Libyan Sibyl (Fig. 5-9).

Quick, sketchy notations of the model's profile, feet, and toes lead to a detailed torso rendered with confident lines and precisely defined tonal areas built up from hatching. The exactness of muscular detail and emphasis on the edges of the body provide insight into the concerns of an artist whose forte was sculpture.

In contrast to Michelangelo's essentially linear approach to his medium, the *Portrait of a Woman* (Fig. 5-10) by the nineteenth-century French painter Jean-Baptiste Carpeaux appears to materialize from the background through subtle tonal contrasts. Whereas Michelangelo emphasized the edges of his model, Carpeaux was more interested in the subtle roundness of his model's form. Carpeaux capitalized on the effect of soft chalk drawn across a coarsely textured paper to create a hazy atmosphere that envelops the sitter.

Pastels consist of ground chalk mixed with powdered pigments and a binder. Whereas chalk drawings can be traced to prehistoric times, pastels did not come into wide use until the 1400s. They were introduced to France only in the 1700s, but within a century pastels captured the imagination of many important painters. Their wide range of brilliant colors offered a painter's palette for use in the more spontaneous medium of drawing.

One of the masters of pastel drawing was the nineteenth-century French painter and sculptor Edgar Degas. The directness and spontaneity of the medium was well

5-9 MICHELANGELO.
Studies for *The Libyan Sybil* (1510–1511).
Red chalk. 11⅜″ × 8⅜″.
The Metropolitan Museum of Art. Joseph Pulitzer Bequest, 1924 (24.197.2).
Copyright 1995 The Metropolitan Museum of Art, New York.

5-10 JEAN-BAPTISTE CARPEAUX.
Portrait of a Woman (1874).
Black chalk heightened with white, on buff paper.
7⅞″ × 5⅞″.
Sterling and Francine Clark Art Institute, Williamstown, MA.

If I could have had my own way, I would have confined myself entirely to black and white.

—Edgar Degas

5-11   EDGAR DEGAS.
Woman at Her Toilette (1903).
Pastel on paper. 30″ × 30½″.
Mr. and Mrs. Martin Ryerson Collection. Photograph courtesy of The Art Institute of Chicago.

5-12   JAUNE QUICK-TO-SEE SMITH.
The Environment: Be a Shepherd (1989).
Charcoal, colored chalk, and pastel. 47″ × 31¼″.
Collection of Lois Fichner-Rathus.

suited to some of his favorite subjects: ballet dancers in motion, horses racing toward a finish line, and women caught unaware in the midst of commonplace activities. Degas's *Woman at Her Toilette* (Fig. 5-11) is a veritable explosion of glowing color. The pastels are manipulated in countless ways to create a host of different effects. The contours of the figure are boldly sketched, whereas the flesh is composed of more erratic lines that create a sense of roundness through a spectrum of color. Degas scratched the pastels over the surface to form sharp lines or dragged them flatly to create more free-flowing strokes. At times the colors were left pure and intense, and at other times subtle harmonies were rendered through blending or smudging.

Jaune Quick-to-See Smith's *The Environment: Be a Shepherd* (Fig. 5-12) is an effective combination of drawing media: charcoal, colored chalk, and pastel. The earth tones of sepia, brown, greens, and grays evoke the desert Southwest and enhance the imagery of a Native American narrative. The upper right and lower left bear charcoal sketches of a horse and rural church; they are overworked, leaving ghostlike images of themselves reverberating in space. In the center, a shepherd's (priest's?) robe hovers with arms outstretched, like a spectre admonishing the abusers of the environment. Throughout the drawing, contrasting images that refer to intertwined cultural legacies are held together with tenuous, grasslike strokes. The media and the sketchy manner in which they are handled effectively creates the feeling of a "mental sketchbook"—fleeting memories sparked by incongruous objects.

Crayon

Strictly defined, the term **crayon** includes any drawing material in stick form. Thus, charcoal, chalk, and pastels are crayons, as are the wax implements you used on walls, floors, and occasionally coloring books when you were a child. One of the most popular commercially manufactured crayons for artists is the **conté crayon.** Its effects on paper are similar to those of chalk and pastel, although its harder texture makes possible a greater clarity.

A CLOSER LOOK

Life, Death, and Dwelling in the Deep South

Some years ago, African American sculptor Beverly Buchanan came to know Ms. Mary Lou Furcron. Both artists, one might say. Both the builders of structures. Both nurturing, creative, and colorful. Ever since this meeting, Buchanan's life and art have revolved around the art and life of the Southern shack dweller.

It's an existence unto itself, as the photographs indicate (Fig. 5-13). Ms. Furcron's shack reflects her life, and her life reflects the shack in which she lived. She devoted a part of each day to maintaining the structure, replacing rotted posts with new logs; using bark, lathing, and other odd materials to repair the siding. The shack stood as an organic and ever-evolving structure—an extension of Ms. Furcron herself. As the shack required her constant attention for its survival, her move to a nursing home brought its rapid disrepair. Just one month after Ms. Furcron's departure, the shack was unrecognizable as its former self.

Buchanan's art, in sculpture, and especially in drawing, reflects a structural approach to the creation of the shack image. As Ms. Furcron built with the recycled remnants of nature and human existence, so does Beverly Buchanan. Her mixed-media shacks are created from old pieces of wood, metal, and found objects, such as in *Hometown—Shotgun Shack* (Fig. 5-14). Her oil pastel drawing *Henriette's Yard* (Fig. 5-15) is vigorously and lovingly constructed of a myriad of vibrant strokes. These strokes at once serve as the building blocks of the shack image and the very stuff that reduces the structure to an almost indecipherable explosion of color. The precarious balance of the shacks in relation to one another and the uncertain ground in which they stand, further symbolize the precious and fragile nature of the shack dwelling, and human existence. ■

5-14 BEVERLY BUCHANAN.
Hometown—Shotgun Shack
(1992).
Wood, mixed media.
12″ × 9¼″ × 15″.
Courtesy of Bernice Steinbaum Gallery, Miami.

5-15 BEVERLY BUCHANAN.
Henriette's Yard (1995).
Oil pastel on paper. 60″ × 60″.
Collection of Lois Fichner-Rathus.
Courtesy of Bernice Steinbaum Gallery, Miami.

A

B

5-13 Photographs of Ms. Mary Lou Furcron's home.
Photo A shows the shack while Ms. Furcron was living in it and tending to it. Photo B shows the shack just one month after her placement in a nursing home.
Photographs courtesy of Bernice Steinbaum Gallery, Miami.

5-16 CHUCK CLOSE.
Self-Portrait / Conté Crayon (1979).
Conté crayon on paper. 29½″ × 22″.
Private collection. Courtesy of the Pace Gallery.

In his *Self-Portrait / Conté Crayon* (Fig. 5-16), Chuck Close seems less interested in clarity than in creating the illusion of a grainy and blurry photographic likeness. The artist superimposed a grid over his portrait and then transferred the "contents" of each of the squares of this grid to another, enlarged grid on a 29½″ × 22″ piece of drawing paper using conté crayon. By working square by square, Close could focus on the almost infinite tonal variations inherent in black-and-white photography and attempt to re-create them through scribbled, hatched, blurred, and smudged lines. The contrasts in value differentiate the details of the artist's portrait—from his bald head and eyeglasses to his mustache and beard. Many of the artist's unidealized portraits are based on this grid-transfer method, some featuring the vibrant colors of pastel and oil paint (see Fig. 3-21).

Wax crayons, like pastels, combine ground pigment with a binder—in this case, wax. Wax crayon moves easily over a support to form lines that have a characteristic sheen. These lines are less apt to smudge than charcoal, chalk, and pastels.

Fluid Media

The primary **fluid medium** used in drawing is ink, and the instruments used to carry the medium are pen and brush. Appearing in Egyptian **papyrus** drawings and ancient Chinese scrolls, ink has a history that stretches back thousands of years. Some ancient peoples made ink from the dyes of plants, squid, and octopus. By the second century CE, blue black inks were being derived from galls found on oak trees. The oldest-known type of ink is India or China ink, which is used in oriental **calligraphy** to this day. It is a solution of carbon black and water, and it is permanent and rich black in color.

As with the dry media, dramatically different effects can be achieved with fluid media through a variety of techniques. For example, the artist may alter the composition of the medium by diluting it with water to achieve lighter tones, or may vary the widths of brushes and pen points to achieve lines of different character.

Pen and Ink

Pens also have been used since ancient times. The earliest ones were hollow reeds that were slit at the ends to allow a controlled flow of ink. **Quills** plucked from live birds became popular writing instruments during the Middle Ages. These were replaced in the nineteenth century by the mass-produced metal **nib,** which is slipped into a wooden **stylus.** Many artists use these pens today.

Pen and ink are used to create drawings that are essentially linear, although the nature of the line can vary considerably according to the type of instrument employed. A fine, rigid nib will provide a clear, precise line that is uniform in thickness. Lines created by a more flexible quill tip, by contrast, will vary in width according to the amount of pressure the artist's hand exerts.

Jean Dubuffet all but fills his *Garden* (Fig. 5-17) with pen-and-ink scribbles of varying thicknesses outlining

5-17 JEAN DUBUFFET.
Garden (1952).
Pen and carbon ink on glazed white wove paper.
18¾″ × 23¾″.

The Art Institute of Chicago. Copyright 2003 Artists Rights Society (ARS), New York/ADAGP, Paris.

Paper Dolls for a Post-Columbian World

Mark Twain once wrote that the ink with which history has been written is fluid prejudice. Most of us are just beginning to understand that there are two sides to every historical event, and that any accurate examination of history must include the view of the vanquished, the story of the minority group, a look at the peripheral events that are part of the human story.

Native American artist Jaune Quick-to-See Smith has challenged our perception of Columbus's expedition to the New World by sardonically focusing on its destructive aftermath. She offers us her pen-and-pastel version of paper dolls, a familiar childhood pastime, which in her hands assumes all sorts of political connotations. Our Native American couple are called Barbie and Ken Plenty Horses (Fig. 5-18). Their clothing ensembles include some "ethnic wear" (politically correct) amidst a priest's robe, maid's uniform, saloon keeper's costume, and alternate sheaths of skin infested with smallpox. Is this what has become of the Native American population in the name of Western "civilization"? ■

5-18 JAUNE QUICK-TO-SEE SMITH.
Paper Dolls for a Post Columbian World with Ensembles Contributed by the U.S. Government (1991).
Pastel and pen on paper.
40″ × 29″.
Collection of Dr. and Mrs. Harold Steinbaum. Courtesy of Bernice Steinbaum Gallery, Miami.

Drawing is like making an expressive gesture with the advantage of permanence.

—Henri Matisse

mostly organic shapes. Just as a garden's plant life may give the eye a variegated experience of texture as well as color, Dubuffet's lines vary in length and thickness, sometimes culminating in little pools of ink. Here and there more angular, even craggy shapes suggest a path or an outcropping of rock, but the artist's aim is not to realistically depict any garden you might have visited. Rather, the high horizon line and the endless intertwining create an overall sense of being ensnared within a sea of shapes and textures.

Pen and Wash

Fine, clear lines of pure ink are often combined in drawings with **wash**—diluted ink that is applied with a brush. Wash provides a tonal emphasis absent in pen-and-ink drawings.

5-19   GIOVANNI BATTISTA TIEPOLO.
Hagar and Ishmael in the Wilderness (c. 1725–1735).
Pen, brush and brown ink, and wash, over sketch in black chalk. 16½″ × 11⅛″.
Sterling and Francine Clark Art Institute, Williamstown, MA.

In Giovanni Battista Tiepolo's eighteenth-century drawing (Fig. 5-19), the contours of the biblical figures are described in pen and ink, but their volume derives from a clever use of wash. An illusion of three-dimensionality is created by pulling the white of the untouched paper forward to function as form and enhancing it with contrasting areas of light and dark wash. The gestural vitality of the pen lines and the generous swaths of watery ink accentuate the composition's dynamic movement.

Brush and Ink

Brushes are extremely versatile drawing implements. They are available in a wide variety of materials, textures, and shapes that afford many different effects. The nature of a line in brush and ink will depend on whether the brush is bristle or nylon, thin or thick, pointed or flat tipped. Likewise, characteristics of the support—texture, absorbency, and the like—will influence the character of the completed drawing. Brush and ink touched to silk leaves an impression quite different from that produced by brush and ink touched to paper.

Japanese artists are masters of the brush-and-ink medium. They have used it for centuries for every type of

5-20   KATSUSHIKA HOKUSAI (1760–1849).
Boy Playing Flute.
Ink and brush on paper. 4½″ × 6¼″.
Courtesy of Freer Gallery of Art, Smithsonian Institution, Washington, DC.

It is only by much drawing, drawing everything, drawing unceasingly that one fine day
one is very surprised to find it possible to express something in its true spirit.

—Camille Pissarro

calligraphy, ranging from works of art to everyday writing. Their facility with the technique is most evident in seemingly casual sketches such as those done in the late eighteenth and early nineteenth centuries by Japanese artist Katsushika Hokusai (Fig. 5-20). Longer, flowing lines range from thick and dark to thin and faint, capturing, respectively, the heavy folds of the boy's clothing and the pale flesh of his youthful limbs. Short, brisk strokes humorously describe the similarity between the hemp of the woven basket and the youngster's disheveled hair. There is an extraordinary simplicity to the drawing attributable to the surety and ease with which Hokusai handles his medium.

Brush and Wash

The medium of brush and wash is even more versatile than that of brush and ink. Although it can duplicate the linearity of brush-and-ink drawings, it can also be used to create images solely through tonal contrasts. The ink can be diluted to varying degrees to provide a wide tonal range. Different effects can be achieved either by adding water directly to the ink or by moistening the support before drawing.

It is again surprising to note how adaptable the drawing media can be to different artistic styles or subjects. Consider the drawings by the Italian Renaissance master Leonardo da Vinci (Fig. 5-21) and the seventeenth-century French

5-21 LEONARDO DA VINCI.
Study of Drapery (c. 1473).
Brush, gray wash, heightened with white, on linen. 7⅜″ × 9¼″.
Louvre Museum, Paris. Copyright RMN/Art Resource, New York.

5-22　CLAUDE LORRAIN.
Tiber above Rome (c. 1640).
Brush and wash.
Courtesy of the trustees of the British
Museum/Edimedia/Corbis.

painter Claude Lorrain (Fig. 5-22). Even upon close inspection, one would not guess that both works were created in the same medium, despite their tonal emphasis. Leonardo captured the intricacies of drapery as it falls over the human form, dramatically lit to provide harsh contrasts between surfaces and crevices. The voluminous folds are realized through a meticulous study of tonal contrasts.

The shape of Lorrain's landscape also relies on tonal variations rather than line, but here the similarity ends. Leonardo's drawing is descriptive, and almost photographic in its realism. Lorrain's work is suggestive—a quick rendition of the artist's visual impression of the landscape. Whereas Leonardo worked his wash over linen, Lorrain worked on damp paper. By touching a brush dipped in ink to the wet surface, Lorrain made his forms dissolve into the surrounding field and lose their distinct contours. Broadly brushed liquid formations constructed of varying tones yield the impression of groves of trees on the bank of a body of water that leads to distant mountains. These nondescript areas of diffuse wash were here and there given more definition through bolder lines and brushstrokes applied after the

paper was dry. Leonardo used brush and wash to reveal form. Lorrain used it to define space.

CARTOONS

The word **cartoon** derives from the Italian *cartone,* meaning "paper." Originally, cartoons were full-scale preliminary drawings done on paper for projects such as fresco paintings, stained glass, or tapestries. The meaning of cartoon was expanded to include humorous and satirical drawings when a parody of fresco cartoons submitted for decoration of the Houses of Parliament appeared in an English magazine in 1843. Regardless of their targets, all modern cartoons rely on caricature, the gross exaggeration and distortion of natural features to ridicule a social or political target.

Honoré Daumier is perhaps the only famous painter to devote so great a part of his production—some 4,000 works—to cartoons. Known for his riveting images of social and moral injustices in nineteenth-century France, he also created caricatures in which he displayed a sharp, sardonic

Three Lawyers (c. 1855).
Pen and black ink, black chalk, brush and black and blue
black ink, gray and beige wash, and white gouache.
$12\frac{15}{16}'' \times 9\frac{3}{4}''$.
Copyright Edimedia.

wit. Daumier's *Three Lawyers* (Fig. 5-23) is a taunting illustration of what he perceived to be the grossly overstated importance of this professional group. Each lawyer strains to
raise his nose and eyebrows higher than those of his com-
rades, effectively communicating his self-adulation. The absurd superficiality of the trio's conversation is communicated
by their attempts to strike a meaningful pose in their clown-
like embodiments.

Cartoons have a long history of social commentary,
consciousness raising, and political activism. We are all
familiar with the children's books of Dr. Seuss, but few
of us are aware of Theodor Seuss Geisel's political cartoons
(Fig. 5-24). For two years during World War II, Dr. Seuss
was the chief editorial cartoonist for the New York tabloid
newspaper *PM*. During that time, he drew more than
400 cartoons, many of which pertained to the war effort.
It's fascinating to see Dr. Seuss's legendary, signature style
(and creatures) called into service for an altogether different
purpose.

5-24 DR. SEUSS.
Cages Cost Money!
Buy More U.S. Savings Bonds and Stamps!
From Dr. Seuss Collection, the Mandeville Special
Collections Library, University of California, San Diego.

Drawing is among the most personal things you can do. It doesn't have any rhetoric or anything to tell. It's a dialogue between the art and yourself.

—Santiago Calatrava, architect

NEWTON DISCOVERS SURREALISM

5-25 ROBERT JOLLEY.
New Yorker cartoon. *Newton Discovers Surrealism.*
Cartoon by Richard Jolley.
www.cartoonstock.com Used by permission.

Although cartoon drawing styles vary widely, what they often have in common is the visual pun, or play on words, images, or ideas—such as the *New Yorker* cartoon in Figure 5-25. A bit of a inside joke, so to speak, the artist combines the legend of Newton's apple—which fell out of a tree, popped him on the head, and initiated his reflections on the laws of gravity—with Dalí's infamous piano scene from his Surrealist film *Un Chien Andalou* (see Fig. 8-36). The cartoon artist has, through a play on visual images, managed to defang the more gruesome aspect of the Dalí film still and replace it with something that works as a humorous anachronism.

NEW APPROACHES TO DRAWING

Drawings display endless versatility in terms of their intended purposes, their media, and their techniques. It is not unusual to find drawings that are not "drawn" at all on materials that are far removed from traditional paper. You'd be right to ask, "What *is* a drawing after all?"

Jackson Pollock, an American artist working in the 1940s and 1950s, dripped and whipped enamel paint onto paper surfaces. His spontaneous gestures read like an almost-but-not-quite-recognizable calligraphy (Fig. 5-26). The expansive definition of drawing has led the medium from its traditional roots to one, like painting or printmaking, that is an end in itself. Galleries such as The Drawing Center in New York City feature exhibitions of drawings exclusively, concentrating on both historical and cutting-edge work (Fig. 5-27).

5-26 JACKSON POLLOCK.
Untitled (1950).
Pencil, duco on paper. 22″ × 59⅜″.

Graphische Sammlung, Staatsgalerie, Stuttgart.
Copyright 2005 Pollack-Krasner Foundation/Artists Rights Society (ARS),
New York

5-27 MARGARET HONDA
Exchange (2003–2004).
Vinyl on Mylar, 50 elements. Dimensions variable.

Photo Cathy Carver/The Drawing Center, New York.

6

PAINTING

Suddenly I realized that each brushstroke is a decision. . . . In the end I realize that whatever meaning that picture has is the accumulated meaning of ten thousand brushstrokes, each one being decided as it was painted.

—Robert Motherwell

The line between drawing and painting is sometimes blurred. The art historian will speak of linear aspects in painting or painterly qualities in drawing. At times the materials used in the two media will overlap. **Painting** is generally defined as the application of pigment to a surface. Yet we have already seen the use of pigment in pastel drawings.

Paint can be applied to a number of surfaces. It has been used throughout history to decorate pottery, enhance sculpture, and embellish architecture. In this section we shall explain the composition of paint and explore painting in works created on two-dimensional supports.

Just dash something down if you see a blank canvas staring at you. . . . You do not know how paralyzing it is, that blank staring of the canvas which says to the painter: You do not know anything.

—Vincent van Gogh

PAINT

To most of us, paint is synonymous with color. The color in a paint derives from its pigment. The pigment in powdered form is mixed with a binding agent, or **vehicle,** and a solvent, or **medium,** to form **paint**—the liquid material that imparts color to a surface.

Pigments are available in a wide chromatic range. Their color is derived from chemicals and minerals found in plant and animal life, clay, soil, and sand.

Different vehicles are employed in different painting media. The main criterion for a successful vehicle is that it hold the pigments together. Lime plaster, wax, egg, oil, acrylic plastic, water, and gum arabic are commonly used vehicles. Unfortunately, most vehicles are subject to long-term problems such as cracking, yellowing, or discoloration.

The task of a medium is to provide fluency to the paint so that the color may be readily dispersed over the surface.

Water or turpentine is frequently used as a thinning agent for this purpose.

TYPES OF PAINTING

A variety of supports and tools have been used throughout the history of art to create paintings. We shall discuss the characteristics of several types of painting.

Fresco

Fresco is the art of painting on plaster. **Buon fresco,** or true fresco, is executed on damp, lime plaster; **fresco secco** is painting on dry plaster. In buon fresco, the pigments are mixed only with water, and the lime of the plaster wall acts as a binder. As the wall dries, the painted image on it becomes permanent. In fresco secco—a less popular and less

6-1 GIOTTO.
Lamentation (c. 1305).
Fresco. 7'7" × 7'9".
Scrovegni Chapel, Padua, Italy/Alinair/
Art Resource, New York.

Remember that a picture—before being a horse, a nude, or some sort of anecdote— is essentially a flat surface covered with colors assembled in a certain order.

—Maurice Denis

permanent method—pigments are combined with a vehicle of glue that affixes the color to the dry wall.

Fresco painters encounter a number of problems. Because in true fresco the paint must be applied to fresh, damp plaster, the artist cannot bite off more than it is possible to chew—or paint—in one day. For this reason, large fresco paintings are composed of small sections, each of which has been painted in a day. The artist tries to arrange the sections so that the joints will not be obvious, but sometimes it is not possible to do so. In a fourteenth-century fresco painting by the Italian master Giotto (Fig. 6-1), these joints are clearly evident, particularly in the sky, where the artist was not able to complete the vast expanse of blue all at once. It is not surprising that sixteenth-century art historian Giorgio Vasari wrote that of all the methods painters employ, fresco painting "is the most masterly and beautiful, because it consists in doing in a single day that which, in other methods, may be retouched day after day, over the work already done."

Another problem: Although fresco paintings can be brilliant in color, some pigments will not form chemical bonds with lime. Thus, these pigments are not suitable for the medium. Artists in Giotto's era, for example, encountered a great deal of difficulty with the color blue. Such lime resistance limits the artist's palette and can make tonal transitions difficult.

Leonardo da Vinci, in his famous *The Last Supper* (Fig. 15-17), attempted to meet these nuisances head-on, only to suffer disastrous consequences. The experimental materials and methods he employed to achieve superior results were unsuccessful. He lived to see his masterpiece disintegrate beyond repair.

Despite these problems, fresco painting enjoyed immense popularity from prehistoric times until its full flowering in the Renaissance. Although it fell out of favor for several centuries thereafter, Mexican muralists revived the art of fresco after World War I.

Encaustic

One of the earliest methods of applying color to a surface was **encaustic.** It consists of pigment in a wax vehicle that has been heated to a liquid state. The ancient Egyptians and Greeks tinted their sculptures with encaustic to grant them

6-2 *Mummy Portrait of a Man* (Egypto-Roman, Faiyum, c. 160–179 CE).
Encaustic on wood. 14″ × 8″.
Albright-Knox Art Gallery, Buffalo, NY.
Charles Clifton Fund, 1938.

a lifelike appearance. The Romans applied encaustic to walls, using hot irons. Often, as in the Egyptian *Mummy Portrait of a Man* (Fig. 6-2) dating back to the second century CE, the medium was applied to small, portable wooden panels covered with cloth. As evidenced by the startling realism and freshness of the portrait, encaustic is an extremely durable medium whose colors remain vibrant and whose surface maintains a hard luster.

But encaustic is a difficult medium to manipulate: one must keep the molten wax at a constant temperature. For this reason, it has been used only by a handful of contemporary artists.

6-3 KAY WALKINGSTICK.
Solstice (1982).
Acrylic and wax on canvas. 48″ × 48″ × 3½″.
Collection of the artist.

Native American painter Kay Walkingstick derives a certain plasticity from her very different use of acrylic and wax on canvas (Fig. 6-3). In *Solstice,* two flattened arcs of sharply contrasting hues are about to merge in a viscous sea of mauve and purple. The canoelike image, although common to Native American symbolism, can also be viewed as an abstraction signifying the shifting of seasons from autumn to winter—a kind of quiet cosmological passage. Walkingstick builds her textural surface through successive layers of colored wax, gouging the field here and there with lines that reveal the palette of the lower layers. It is at once an image of power and of solitude.

Tempera

Tempera, like encaustic, was popular for centuries, but its traditional composition—ground pigments mixed with a vehicle of egg yolk or whole eggs thinned with water—is rarely used today. Tempera now describes a medium in which pigment can be mixed with an emulsion of milk, different types of glues or gums, and even the juices and saps of plants and trees. The use of tempera dates back to the Greeks and Romans. Tempera was the exclusive painting medium of artists during the Middle Ages. Not until the invention of oil paint in northern Europe in the 1300s did tempera fall out of favor.

Tempera offered many advantages. It was an extremely durable medium if applied to a properly prepared surface. Pure and brilliant colors were attainable. Colors did not become compromised by gradual oxidation. Also, the consistency and fluidity of the mixture allowed for a great deal of precision. Tempera, unlike oil paint, however, dries quickly and is difficult to rework. Also, unlike oils, it cannot provide subtle gradations of tone.

Tempera can be applied to wood or canvas panels, although the latter did not come into wide use until the 1500s. Both types of supports were prepared by covering the surface with a ground. The ground was generally a combination of powdered chalk or plaster and animal glue called **gesso.** The gesso ground provided a smooth, glistening white surface on which to apply color.

All that is desirable in the tempera medium can be found in Figure 6-4, the panel painting by the fifteenth-century Italian artist Gentile da Fabriano. Combined with the technique of **gilding**—the application of thinly hammered sheets of gold to the panel surface—the luminous reds and blues and pearly grays of the tempera paint provide a sumptuous display. The fine details of the ornate costumes testify to the precision made possible by **egg tempera.**

Several contemporary artists, such as the Swiss Photorealist painter Franz Gertsch, have also been enticed by the exactness and intricacies made possible by tempera. Suited to a methodical and painstaking approach to painting, this medium of the old masters yields unparalleled displays of contrasting textures and sharp-focused realism, as shown in Gertsch's large-scale portrait of *Silvia* (Fig. 6-5).

Oil

The transition from egg tempera to **oil paint** was gradual. For many years following the introduction of the oil medium, artists used it only to apply a finishing coat of glazes to an underpainting of tempera. **Glazing,** or the application of multiple layers of transparent films of paint to a surface, afforded subtle tonal variations and imparted a warm atmosphere not possible with tempera alone. Oil paints have been in wide use since the fifteenth century.

Oil paint consists of ground pigments combined with a linseed oil vehicle and turpentine medium or thinner. Oil paint is naturally slow in drying, but drying can be facilitated with various agents added to the basic mixture.

Oil painting's broad range of capabilities makes it a favorite among artists. It can be applied with any number of brushes or painting knives. Colors can be blended easily, offering a palette of almost limitless range. Slow drying facilitates the reworking of problem areas. When it is finely

6-4   GENTILE DA FABRIANO.
Adoration of the Magi (1423).
Tempera on wood panel. 9′10⅛″ × 9′3″.
Uffizi Gallery, Florence. Copyright Scala/Art Resource, New York.

6-5   FRANZ GERTSCH.
Silvia (1998).
Tempera on unprimed canvas. 9′6¼″ × 9′2¼″.
Copyright Museum Franzgertsch, Burgdorf, Switzerland.

A good painter is to paint two things, namely, man and the working of man's mind.

—Leonardo da Vinci

applied, oil paint can capture the most intricate detail. When it is broadly brushed, it can render diaphanous fields of pulsating color. Oil paint can be diluted to a barely tinted film to achieve subtle flesh tones, or it can be applied in thick impasto that physically constructs an image, as *Head of St. Matthew* (Fig. 6-6) by a follower of Rembrandt.

The first oil paintings were executed on wood panels, and then a gradual shift was made to canvas supports. Like wood panels, the canvas surface is covered with a gesso ground prior to painting. The pliability of fabric stretched over a wooden framework renders the working surface more receptive to the pressure of the artist's implement. The light

6-6 FOLLOWER OF
REMBRANDT VAN RIJN.
Head of St. Matthew (c. 1661).
Oil on wood. 9⅞″ × 7¾″.
National Gallery of Art, Washington, DC.
Widener Collection.

6-13 RALPH GOINGS.
Rock Ola (1992).
Watercolor on paper. 14″ × 20¾″.
Courtesy O. K. Harris Works of Art.

6-14 EMIL NOLDE.
Still Life, Tulips (c. 1930).
Watercolor on paper. 18½″ × 13½″.
Collection of the North Carolina Museum of Art, Raleigh.
Bequest of W. R. Valentiner.

to a minimum, as the painting emphasizes form over color, line over tonal patterns.

The broader appeal of watercolor, however, is not to be found in its capability of rendering meticulous detail. When the medium came into wide use during the sixteenth century, it was seen as having other, very different advantages. The fluidity of watercolor was conducive to rapid sketches and preparatory studies. Simple materials allowed for portability. Artists were able to cart their materials to any location, indoors or outdoors, and to register spontaneously their impressions of a host of subjects.

Of course, watercolor is also used for paintings that stand as completed statements. Artists such as the German Expressionist Emil Nolde (Fig. 6-14) were enticed by the transparency of tinted washes. Such washes permitted a delicate fusion of colors. As with the drawing medium of brush and wash, the effect is atmospheric. The edges of the forms are softened; they seem to diffuse into one another or the surrounding field. Unlike Dürer, who used watercolor in a descriptive, linear manner, Nolde creates his explosions of blossoms through delicately balanced patches of bold color and diaphanous washes. The composition is brightened by the white of the paper, which is brought forward to create forms as assertive as those in color.

Spray Paint

One can consider that spray painting has had a rather long history. The subtle coloration marking different species of animals on the walls of Paleolithic caves was probably achieved by blowing pigments onto a surface through hollowed-out reeds. Why are they there: decoration? ritual? history? Oddly enough, these questions can be asked of the contemporary graffiti artist and the thousands upon thousands of writings that range in definition from "tags" to "master" works. Why do they do it? Is it art? urban ritual? Will it speak in history to trials of inner-city living?

Everyone has seen graffiti, but the complexity of the work and the social atmosphere from which it is derived may not be common knowledge. Stylized signatures, or

Painting is self-discovery. Every good artist paints what he is.

—Jackson Pollock

6-15 CRASH (JOHN MATOS).
Arcadia Revisited (1988).
Spray paint on canvas. 96¼″ × 68″.
Courtesy of the artist.

walls. One such artist, Crash (or John Matos), created a parody of his own subway style in a complex canvas work called *Arcadia Revisited* (Fig. 6-15). All the tools and techniques of his trade—commercial cans of spray paint, the Benday dots of comic-strip fame, the sharp lines of the tag writer's logos, the diffuse spray technique that adds dimensionality to an array of otherwise flat objects—are used to describe a violent clash of cultural icons that are fragmented, superimposed, and barely contained within the confines of the canvas.

MIXED MEDIA

Contemporary painters have in many cases combined traditional painting techniques with other materials, or they have painted on nontraditional supports, stretching the definition of what has usually been considered painting. For example, in *The Bed* (Fig. 20-14), Pop artist Robert Rauschenberg splashed and brushed paint on a quilt and pillow, which he then hung on a wall like a canvas work and labeled a "combine painting." The Synthetic Cubists of the early twentieth century, Picasso and Braque, were the first to incorporate pieces of newsprint, wallpaper, labels from wine bottles, and oilcloth into their paintings. These works were called *papiers collés* and have come to be called **collages.**

The base media for Howardena Pindell's *Autobiography: Water / Ancestors, Middle Passage / Family Ghosts* (Fig. 6-16) are tempera and acrylic, but the work, on sewn canvas, also incorporates an array of techniques and substances—markers, oil stick, paper, photo-transfer, and vinyl tape. The detail achieved is quite remarkable. The artist seems to float in a shimmering pool of shallow water, while all around her images and objects of memory seem to enter and exit her consciousness. Included among them are the prominent white shape of an African slave ship, a reference to Pindell's African ancestry, and the whitened face of the artist's portrait that may have been influenced by Michael Jackson's "Thriller" makeup. The work resembles as much a weaving as a painting, further reflecting the tapestry-like nature of human recollection.

Miriam Schapiro is best known for her paint and fabric constructions, which she has labeled "femmage," to express what she sees as their unification of feminine imagery and materials with the medium of collage. In *Maid of Honour* (Fig. 6-17), Schapiro combines bits of intricately patterned fabric with acrylic pigments on a traditional canvas support

"tags," can be seen everywhere; it seems as though no urban surface—interior or exterior—is immune. Some are more likely to call this defacing public property than creating works of art, but how do we describe the elaborate urban "landscapes" that might cover the outside of an entire subway car, filling the space with a masterful composition of shapes, lines, textures, and colors? On the street, they are called masterworks, and their artists are indeed legendary.

Some graffiti writers have "ascended" to the art **gallery** scene, exchanging their steel "canvases" for some of fabric and their high-speed exhibition spaces for highbrow gallery to construct a highly decorative garment that is presented as a work of art. The painting is a celebration of women's experiences with sewing, quilting, needlework, and decoration.

The two-dimensional media we have discussed in Chapters 5 and 6, drawing and painting, create unique works whose availability to the general public is usually limited to photographic renditions in books such as this. Even the intrepid museum goer usually visits only a small number of collections. So let us now turn our attention to the two-dimensional medium that has allowed millions of people to own original works by masters—printmaking.

6-17 MIRIAM SCHAPIRO.
Maid of Honour (1984).
Acrylic and fabric on canvas. 60″ × 50″.
Collection of Lois Fichner-Rathus.

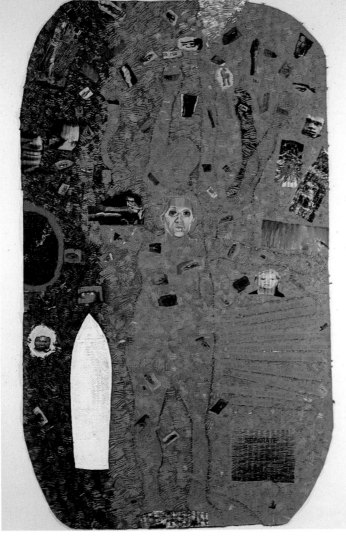

6-16 HOWARDENA PINDELL.
Autobiography: Water / Ancestors, Middle Passage / Family Ghosts (1988).
Acrylic, tempera, cattle markers, oil stick, paper, polymer photo-transfer, and vinyl tape on sewn canvas. 118″ × 71″.
Collection Wadsworth Atheneum, Hartford, CT. Ella Gallup Sumner and Mary Catlin Sumner Collection.

7

PRINTMAKING

*In comparison with painting and sculpture, engraving is a cosmopolitan art,
the immediate inter-relation of different countries being facilitated
by the portable nature of its creations.*

—Arthur M. Hind

The value of drawings and paintings lies, in part, in their uniqueness. Hours, weeks, sometimes years are expended in the creation of these one-of-a-kind works. Printmaking permits the reproduction of these coveted works as well as the production of multiple copies of original prints. Printmaking is an important artistic medium for at least two reasons. First, it allows people to study great works of art from a distance. Second, because prints are less expensive than unique works by the same artist, they make it possible for the general public, not just the wealthy few, to own original works. With prints, art has become accessible. Like some drawings, however, prints not only serve a functional purpose but may be considered works of art in themselves.

METHODS OF PRINTMAKING

The printmaking process begins with a design or image made in or on a surface by hitting or pressing with a tool. The image is then transferred to paper or a similar material. The transferred image is called the **print.** The working surface, or **matrix,** varies according to the printmaking technique. Matrices include wood blocks, metal plates, stone slabs, and silkscreens. There are special tools for working with each kind of matrix, but the images in printmaking are usually rendered in ink.

Printmaking processes are divided into four major categories: relief, intaglio, lithography, and serigraphy (Fig. 7-1). We shall examine a variety of techniques within each of them. Finally, we will consider the monotype and the combining of printmaking media with other media.

RELIEF

In **relief printing,** the matrix is carved with knives or gouges. Areas that are not meant to be printed are cut below the surface of the matrix (Fig. 7-1A), and areas that form the image and are meant to be printed are left raised. Ink is then applied to the raised surfaces, often from a roller. The matrix is pressed against a sheet of paper, and the image is transferred. The transferred image is the print. Relief printing includes woodcut and wood engraving.

Woodcut

Woodcut is the oldest form of printmaking. The ancient Chinese stamped patterns onto textiles and paper using carved wood blocks. The Romans used woodcuts to stamp symbols or letters on surfaces for purposes of identification. During the 1400s in Europe, woodcuts provided multiple copies of religious images for worshipers. After the invention of the printing press, woodcut assumed an important role in book illustration.

Woodcuts are made by cutting along the grain of the flat surface of a wooden board with a knife. Different types of wood and different gouging tools yield various effects.

Wood Engraving

The technique of **wood engraving** and its effects differ significantly from those of woodcuts. Whereas in woodcuts the flat surface of boards is used, in wood engraving many

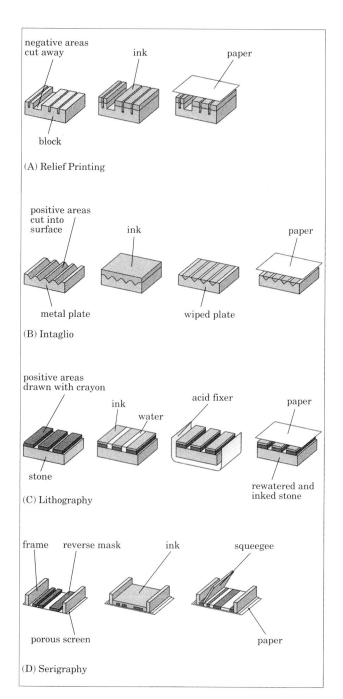

7-1   Printmaking technologies.

thin layers of wood are **laminated.** Then the ends of these sections are planed flat, yielding a hard, nondirectional surface. In contrast to the softer matrix used for the woodcut, the matrix for the wood engraving makes it relatively easy to work lines in varying directions. These lines are **incised** or

Hiroshige's *Rain Shower on Ohashi Bridge* with Xiaomo's *Family by the Lotus Pond*

7-2 ANDO HIROSHIGE.
Rain Shower on Ohashi Bridge (1857).
Color woodblock on paper. 13⅞″ × 9⅛″.
The Cleveland Museum of Art. Gift of J. J. Wade.

vide a delicate counterpoint to bold shapes and broad areas of color and create the illusion of a drawing.

The meticulous process by which Hiroshige achieved his sharply defined images is used to a very different effect in Zhao Xiaomo's *Family by the Lotus Pond* (Fig. 7-3). This contemporary Chinese printmaker uses a range of woodblock techniques to create complex, energetic compositions that often simulate oil paintings. Inspired by Chinese peasant paintings, as they are not bound by "academic rules," Xiaomo creates mosaic-like surfaces with bold, two-dimensional patterns.

How does the visual impact of these two works differ? Consider the use of line, shape, and color. ■

7-3 ZHAO XIAOMO.
Family by the Lotus Pond (1998).
Multiblock woodcut printed with water-soluble ink.
42.7 cm × 41.7 cm.
Art Institute of Chicago.

Ando Hiroshige, a nineteenth-century Japanese artist, achieved the finest detail in his works by choosing a close-grained wood and by tightly controlling the movement of his carving tools. Clean-cut, uniform lines define the steady rain and the individuals who tread huddled against the downpour across a wooden footbridge (Fig. 7-2). These fine lines pro-

7-4 Burin.

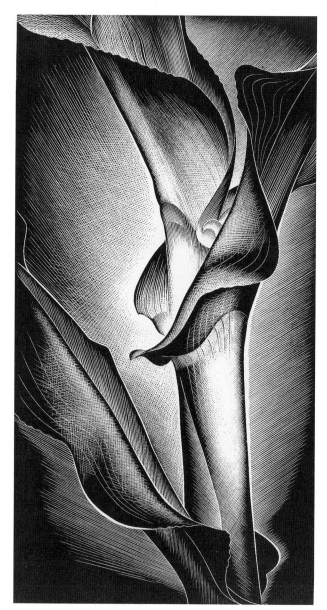

7-5 PAUL LANDACRE.
Growing Corn (1940).
Wood engraving. $8\frac{1}{2}" \times 4\frac{1}{4}"$.
Library of Congress, Washington, DC.

engraved with tools such as a **burin** or **graver** (Fig. 7-4) instead of being cut with knives and gouges. The lines can be extremely fine and are often used in close alignment to give the illusion of tonal gradations. This process was used to illustrate newspapers, such as *Harper's Weekly,* during the nineteenth century.

The razor-sharp tips of engraving implements and the hardness of the end-grain blocks make possible the exacting precision found in wood engravings such as that by Paul Landacre (Fig. 7-5), a well-known twentieth-century American printmaker. Tight, threadlike, parallel, and cross-hatched lines compose the tonal areas that define the form. The rhythmic, flowing lines of the seedling's unfurling leaves contrast dramatically with the fine, prickly lines that emanate like rays from the young corn plant. The print is a display of technical prowess in a most demanding and painstaking medium.

INTAGLIO

The popularity of relief printing declined with the introduction of the **intaglio** process. Intaglio prints are created by using metal plates into which lines have been incised. The plates are covered with ink, which is forced into the linear depressions, and then the surface is carefully wiped. The cut depressions retain the ink, whereas the flat surfaces are clean. Paper is laid atop the plate, and then paper and plate are passed through a printing press, forcing the paper into the incised lines to pick up the ink, thereby accepting the image. In a reversal of the relief process, then, intaglio prints are derived from designs or images that lie *below* the surface of the matrix (Fig. 7-1B).

Intaglio printing encompasses many different media, the most common of which are engraving, drypoint, etching, and mezzotint and aquatint. Some artists have used these techniques recently in interesting variations or combinations and have pioneered approaches using modern equipment such as the camera and computer.

Engraving

Although **engraving** has been used to decorate metal surfaces such as bronze mirrors or gold and silver drinking vessels since ancient times, the earliest engravings printed on paper did not appear until the fifteenth century. In engraving, the artist creates clean-cut lines on a plate of copper, zinc, or steel, forcing the sharpened point of a burin across the surface with the heel of the hand. Because the lines are transferred to paper under very high pressure, they not only reveal the ink from the grooves but have a ridgelike texture themselves that can be felt by running a finger across the print.

An early, famous engraving came from the hand of the fifteenth-century Italian painter Antonio Pollaiuolo (Fig. 7-6). Deep lines that hold a greater amount of ink define the contours of the ten fighting figures. As Landacre did, Pollaiuolo used parallel groupings of thinner and thus lighter lines to render the tonal gradations that define the exaggerated musculature. The detail of the print is described with the utmost precision, revealing the artist's painstaking mastery of the burin.

Drypoint

Drypoint is engraving with a simple twist. In drypoint, a needle is dragged across the surface, and a metal burr, or rough edge, is left in its wake to one side of the furrow. The burr retains particles of ink, creating a softened rather than crisp line when printed. The burr sits above the surface of the matrix and therefore is fragile. After many printings, it will break down, resulting in a line that simply looks engraved.

7-6   ANTONIO POLLAIUOLO.
Battle of Ten Naked Men (c. 1465–1470).
Engraving. 15½″ × 23³⁄₁₆″.
The Metropolitan Museum of Art, New York. Purchase, Joseph Pulitzer Bequest, 1917 (17.50.99). Photograph, all rights reserved, The Metropolitan Museum of Art.

7-7 REMBRANDT VAN RIJN.
Christ Crucified between the Two Thieves (1653).
Drypoint, 4th state. 15″ × 17½″.
Courtesy Museum of Fine Arts, Boston. Katherine E. Bullard Fund
in memory of Frances Bullard and bequest of Mrs. Russell W. Baker.

The characteristic velvety appearance of drypoint lines is seen in Rembrandt's *Christ Crucified between the Two Thieves* (Fig. 7-7). The more distinct lines were rendered with a burin, whereas the softer lines were created with a drypoint needle. Rembrandt used the blurriness of the drypoint line to enhance the sense of chaos attending the Crucifixion and the darkness of the encroaching storm. Lines fall like black curtains enshrouding the crowd, and rays of bright light illuminate the figure of Jesus and splash down onto the spectators.

Etching

Although they are both intaglio processes, **etching** differs from engraving in the way the lines are cut into the matrix. With engraving, the depth of the line corresponds to the amount of force used to push or draw an implement over the surface. With etching, minimal pressure is exerted to determine the depth of line. A chemical process does the work.

In etching, the metal plate is covered with a liquid, acid-resistant ground consisting of wax or resin. When the

What I am after, above all, is expression.

—Henri Matisse

ground has hardened, the image is drawn upon it with a fine needle. Little pressure is exerted to expose the ground; the plate itself is not scratched. When the drawing is completed, the matrix is slipped into an acid bath, which immediately begins to eat away, or etch, the exposed areas of the plate. This etching process yields the sunken line that holds the ink. The artist leaves the plate in the acid solution just long enough to achieve the desired depth of line. If a variety of tones is desired, the artist may pull the plate out of the acid solution after a while, cover lines of sufficient depth with the acid-resistant ground, and replace the plate in the bath for further etching of the remaining exposed lines. The longer

7-9 GIOVANNI DOMENICO TIEPOLO.
A Negro (1770).
Etching, 2nd state.
Courtesy Museum of Fine Arts, Boston. George R. Nutter Fund.

the plate remains in the acid solution, the deeper the etching. Deeper crevices hold more ink, and for this reason they print darker lines.

Etching is a versatile medium, capable of many types of lines and effects. The modern French painter Henri Matisse used but a few dozen uniformly etched lines to describe the essential features of a woman, *Loulou Distracted* (Fig. 7-8). The extraordinarily simple yet complete image attests to the delicacy that can be achieved with etching.

Whereas Matisse's figure takes shape through the careful placement of line, the subject of the etching by Giovanni Domenico Tiepolo (who was the son of Giovanni Battista Tiepolo) exists by virtue of textural and tonal contrasts (Fig. 7-9). This eighteenth-century Italian artist used a variety of wavy and curving lines to differentiate skin from cloth, fur from hair, figure from ground. Lines are spaced to provide a range of tones from the sharp white of the paper to the rich black of the man's clothing. The overall texture creates a hazy atmosphere that caresses the pensive figure.

7-8 HENRI MATISSE.
Loulou Distracted (1914).
Etching, printed in black. 7¹⁄₁₆″ × 5″.
The Museum of Modern Art, New York. Purchase. Copyright 2003 Succession H. Matisse, Paris/Artists Rights Society (ARS), New York/ Art Resource, New York.

Hung Liu: Chinese Traditions Unbound

In many ways, Hung Liu epitomizes the concerns and preoccupations of the Chinese artist whose life experiences during that country's Cultural Revolution have shaped their art, indeed their very existence. In 1984, Hung Liu arrived in the United States, in her words, with her "Five-thousand-year-old culture on my back. Late-twentieth-century world in my face. . . . My Alien number is 28333359." For four years in her home country, she was forced to work in the fields. In her chosen country, she is now a professor at Mills College and has had one-woman shows in New York, San Francisco, and Texas. Her art is one that focuses on what she has called "the peculiar ironies which result when ancient Chinese images are 'reprocessed' within contemporary Western materials, processes, and modes of display."

Figure 7-10 shows an untitled mixed-media print, whose main image consists of a photo-etching onto which are affixed small rectangular wooden blocks—mahjong pieces—bearing the "high-fashion" portraits of Chinese women. The inspiration for this print, and full oil paintings on the same theme, came from a series of photographs of Chinese prostitutes from the early 1900s that Hung Liu discovered on a recent return trip to China. When the Communist revolution took hold and all able-bodied individuals were forced into labor, these women were forced into prostitution because the traditions of oppression that led to the practice of binding their feet made them unfit for physical toil. They could barely walk.

Hung Liu feels the need to make known the pain, suffering, and degradation of generations of women before her:

Although I do not have bound feet, the invisible spiritual burdens fall heavy on me. . . . I communicate with the characters in my paintings, prostitutes—these completely subjugated people—with reverence, sympathy, and awe. They had no real names. Probably no children. I want to make up stories for them. Who were they? Did they leave any trace in history?

In Hung Liu's work we come to understand a piece of history. We are challenged to reflect, as she does, upon human rights and freedoms, spiritual and physical oppression, political expression, and silenced voices. ∎

7-10 HUNG LIU.
Untitled (1992).
Photo-etching, mixed media.
33″ × 22½″.

Collection of Lois Fichner-Rathus.
Photo courtesy of Bernice Steinbaum Gallery, Miami, FL.

The artist is a receptacle for the emotions that come from all over the place:
from the sky, from the earth, from a scrap of paper, from a passing shape, from a spider's web.

—Pablo Picasso

Mezzotint and Aquatint

Engraving, drypoint, and etching are essentially linear media. With these techniques, designs or images are created by cutting lines into a plate. The illusion of tonal gradations is achieved by altering the number and concentration of lines. Sometime in the mid-seventeenth century the Dutchman Ludwig von Siegen developed a technique whereby broad tonal areas could be achieved by nonlinear engraving, that is, engraving that does *not* depend on line. The medium was called **mezzotint,** from the Italian word meaning "half tint."

With mezzotint engraving, the entire metal plate is worked over with a curved, multitoothed implement called a **hatcher.** The hatcher is "rocked" back and forth over the surface, producing thousands of tiny pits that will hold ink. If printed at this point, the plate would yield an allover consistent, velvety black print. But the mezzotint engraver uses this evenly pitted surface as a point of departure. The artist creates an image by gradually scraping and burnishing the areas of the plate that are meant to be lighter. These areas will hold less ink and therefore will produce lighter tones.

The more persistent the scraping, the shallower the pits and the lighter the tone. A broad range of tones is achieved as the artist works from the rich black of the rocked surface to the highly polished pitless areas that will yield bright whites. Mezzotint is a rarely used, painstaking, and time-consuming procedure.

The subtle tonal gradations achieved by the mezzotint process can be duplicated with a much easier and quicker etching technique called **aquatint.** In aquatint a metal plate is evenly covered with a fine powder of acid-resistant resin. The plate is then heated, causing the resin to melt and adhere to the surface. As in line etching, the matrix is placed in an acid bath, where its uncovered surfaces are eaten away by the solution. The depth of tone is controlled by removing the plate from the acid and covering the pits that have been sufficiently etched.

Aquatint is often used in conjunction with line etching and is frequently manipulated to resemble tones produced by wash drawings. In *The Painter and His Model* (Fig. 7-11), Pablo Picasso brought the forms out of void space by defining their limits with dynamic patches of aquatint.

7-11 PABLO PICASSO.
The Painter and His Model
(1964).
Etching and aquatint.
12⅝" × 18½".

Courtesy Museum of Fine Arts, Boston. Lee M. Friedman Fund. Copyright 2003 Estate of Pablo Picasso/Artists Rights Society (ARS), New York.

These tonal areas resemble swaths of ink typical of wash drawings. Descriptive details of the figures are rendered in fine or ragged lines, etched to varying depths.

Other Etching Techniques

Different effects may also be achieved in etching by using grounds of different substances. **Soft-ground etching,** for example, employs a ground of softened wax and can be used to render the effects of crayon or pencil drawings. In a technique called **lift-ground,** the artist creates the illusion of a brush-and-ink drawing by actually brushing a solution of sugar and water onto a resin-coated plate. When the plate is slipped into the acid bath, the sugar dissolves, lifting the brushed image off the plate to expose the metal beneath. As in all etching media, these exposed areas accept the ink.

Given that the printing process implies the use of ink to produce an image, can we have prints without ink? The answer is yes—with the medium called **gauffrage,** or inkless intaglio. Joseph Albers, a twentieth-century American abstract artist, created *Solo V,* the geometric image shown in Figure 7-12, by etching the lines of his design to two different depths. Furrows in the plate appear as raised surfaces when printed. We seem to feel the image with our eyes, as light plays across the surface of the paper to enhance its legibility. Perceptual shifts occur as the viewer focuses now on

the thick, now on the thin lines. In trying to puzzle out the logic of the form, the viewer soon discovers that Albers has offered a frustrating illustration of "impossible perspective."

LITHOGRAPHY

Lithography was invented at the dawn of the nineteenth century by the German playwright Aloys Senefelder. Unlike relief and intaglio printing, which rely on cuts in a matrix surface to produce an image, the lithography matrix is flat. Lithography is a surface or **planographic printing** process (Fig. 7-1C).

7-13 HENRI DE TOULOUSE-LAUTREC.
The Seated Clowness (1896).
Lithograph printed in five colors. $20\frac{1}{2}'' \times 16''$.
The Metropolitan Museum of Art, New York. The Alfred Stieglitz Collection, 1949 (49.55.50). Photograph copyright 1984 The Metropolitan Museum of Art, New York.

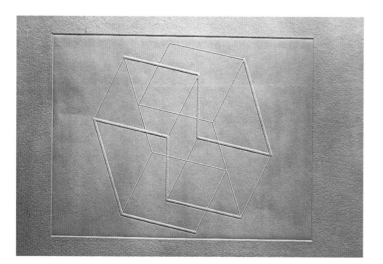

7-12 JOSEF ALBERS.
Solo V (1958).
Inkless intaglio. $6\frac{5}{8}'' \times 8\frac{5}{8}''$.
The Brooklyn Museum, Brooklyn, NY. Augustus A. Healy Fund. Copyright 2003 The Josef and Anni Albers Foundation/Artists Rights Society (ARS), New York.

7-14 KÄTHE KOLLWITZ.
The Mothers (1919).
Lithograph. 17¾″ × 23″.
Philadelphia Museum of Art. Given by Dr. and Mrs. William Wolgin. Copyright 2003 Artists Rights Society (ARS), New York/BG Bild-Kunst, Bonn.

In lithography, the artist draws an image with a greasy crayon directly on a flat stone slab. Bavarian limestone is considered the best material for the slab. Sometimes a specially sensitized metal plate is used, but a metal surface will not produce the often-desired grainy appearance in the print. Small particles of crayon adhere to the granular texture of the stone matrix. After the design is complete, a solution of nitric acid is applied as a fixative. The entire surface of the matrix is then dampened with water. The untouched areas of the surface accept the water, but the waxy crayon marks repel it.

A roller is then used to cover the stone with an oily ink. This ink adheres to the crayon drawing but repels the water. When paper is pressed to the stone surface, the ink on the crayon is transferred to the paper, revealing the image.

Different lithographic methods yield different results. Black crayon on grainy stone can look quite like the crayon drawing it is. Color lithographs employing brush techniques can be mistaken for paintings. Henri de Toulouse-Lautrec, a nineteenth-century French painter and lithographer, was well versed in the medium's flexibility, as is evident in his portrait of a woman clown (Fig. 7-13). The outlines of the figures were drawn with a crayon, and the broad areas of her tights and ruffled collar were brushed in with liquid crayon. The overall spray effect that dapples the surface of the print was probably achieved by his scraping a fingernail along a stiff brush loaded with the liquid substance.

The impact of Käthe Kollwitz's lithograph *The Mothers* (Fig. 7-14), which highlights the plight of lower-class German mothers left alone to fend for their children after World War I, could not be further removed from that of *The Seated Clowness.* The high contrast of the black and white and the coarse quality of the wax crayon yield a sense of desperation suggestive of a newspaper documentary photograph. All the imagery is thrust toward the picture plane, as in high relief. The harsh contours of protective shoulders, arms, and hands contrast with the more delicately rendered faces and heads of the children—all contributing to the poignancy of the work.

SERIGRAPHY

In **serigraphy**—also known as **silkscreen printing**—stencils are used to create the design or image. Unlike the case with other graphic processes, these images can be rendered in paint as well as ink.

One serigraphic process begins with a screen constructed of a piece of silk, nylon, or fine metal mesh stretched on a frame. A stencil with a cutout design is then affixed to the screen, and paper or canvas is placed beneath (Fig. 7-1D). The artist forces paint or ink through the open areas of the stencil with a flat, rubber-bladed implement called a **squeegee,** similar to those used in washing windows.

I think it was colors and weights and pushes and pulls and how to make a surface.

—Alex Katz, when asked what he learned from Matisse

7-15   ALEX KATZ.
Red Coat (1983).
Silkscreen, printed in color. 58″ × 29″.
The Museum of Modern Art, New York. John B. Turner Fund.
Copyright Alex Katz / Licensed by VAGA, New York.

The image on the support corresponds to the shape cut out of the stencil. Several stencils may be used to apply different colors to the same print.

Images can also be "painted" on a screen with use of a varnishlike substance that prevents paint or ink from passing through the mesh. This technique allows for more gestural images than cutout stencils would provide. Recently a serigraphic process called **photo silkscreen** has been developed; it allows the artist to create photographic images on a screen covered with a light-sensitive gel.

Serigraphy was first developed as a commercial medium and is still used as such to create anything from posters to labels on cans of food. The American Pop artist Andy Warhol raised the commercial aspects of serigraphy to the level of fine art in many of his silkscreen prints of the 1960s, such as *Four Marilyns* (see Fig. 1-9). These faithful renditions of celebrities and everyday items satirize the mass media's bombardment of the consumer with advertising. They also have their amusing side.

Alex Katz defines his forms with razor-sharp edges, fixing his subjects in an exact time and place by the details of their clothing and hairstyles. At the same time he transcends their temporal and spatial limits by simplifying and transforming their figures into something akin to icons. For example, the subject's intense red lips in his silkscreen *Red Coat* (Fig. 7-15) serve as a symbol of contemporary glamour. *Red Coat* looks something like a photograph transported into another medium. The individual shapes seem carved into a single plane like sawed jigsaw puzzle pieces. As in a photo, the edges of the silkscreen crop off parts of the image. The woman looks like a "supermodel," with her features exaggerated as they might be in a "cover girl" image.

MONOTYPE

Monotype is a printmaking process, but it overlaps the other two-dimensional media of drawing and painting. Like drawing and printmaking, monotype yields but a single image, and like them, therefore, it is a unique work of art.

In monotype, drawing or painting is created with oil paint or watercolor on a nonabsorbent surface of any material. Brushes are used, but sometimes fine detail is rendered by scratching paint off the plate with sharp implements. A

The Ballet Master (c. 1874).
Monotype in black ink. 22″ × 27½″.
Copyright 1994 National Gallery of Art. Washington, DC.
Rosenwald Collection.

piece of paper is then laid on the surface, and the image is transferred by hand rubbing the back of the paper or passing the matrix and paper through a press. The result, as can be seen in a monotype by Edgar Degas (Fig. 7-16), has all the spontaneity of a drawing and the lushness of a painting.

In Chapter 8 we conclude our discussion of two-dimensional media with an examination of imaging— photography, film, video, and digital arts. In Chapters 9 and 10 we turn our attention to sculpture and architecture. In drawing, painting, and printmaking, artists have frequently attempted to create the illusion of three-dimensionality. We shall see some of the opportunities and problems that attend actual artistic expression in three dimensions.

8

IMAGING: PHOTOGRAPHY, FILM, VIDEO, AND DIGITAL ARTS

—————————————

Look at the things around you, the immediate world around you. If you are alive,
it will mean something to you, and if you care enough about photography,
and if you know how to use it, you will want to photograph that meaning.

—Edward Weston

Technology has revolutionized the visual arts. For thousands of years one of the central goals of art was to imitate nature as exactly as possible. Today any one of us can point a camera at a person or an object and capture a realistic image. "Point-and-shoot" cameras no longer even require that we place the subject in proper focus or that we regulate the amount of light so as not to overexpose or underexpose the subject. Technology can do all these things for us.

Similarly, the art of the stage was once available only to those who lived in the great urban centers. Now and then a traveling troupe of actors might come by or local groups might put on a show of sorts, but most people had little or no idea of the ways in which drama, opera, dance, and other performing arts could affect their lives. The advent of motion pictures, or cinematography, suddenly brought a flood of new imagery into new local theaters, and a new form of communal activity was born. People from every station of life could flock to the movie theater on the week-end. Over time, cinematography evolved into an art form independent of its beginnings as a mirror of the stage.

More recently, television has brought this imagery into the home, where people can watch everything from the performing arts to sporting events in privacy and from the multiple vantage points that several cameras, rather than a single set of eyes, can provide. Fine artists have also appropriated television—or, more precisely, the technology that makes television possible—to produce **video art.** Technology has also given rise to the computer as a creative video-mediated tool. With the aid of artificial intelligence, we can instantly view models of objects from all sides. We can be led to feel as though we are sweeping in on our solar system from the black reaches of space, then flying down to the surface of our planet and landing where the programmer would set us down. Millions of children spend hours playing video games, such as *Tetris,* which challenges them to rotate plummeting polygons to construct a solid wall, or *Tomb Raider,* which requires them to evade or blast a host of enemies before their computer-drawn heroes and heroines plunge into an abyss. Computer technology and computer-generated

images have likewise been appropriated by fine artists in the creation of **digital art.** From illustrations of blue jeans that rocket through space, to snappy graphics that headline sporting events, to the web design that greets us every time we go online, computer-generated images punctuate our daily lives. DVDs, multimedia computers, and software that can blend or distort one shape or face into another are bringing a "virtual reality" into our lives that is in some ways more alluring than, well, "real reality."

In this chapter we discuss photography, film (cinematography), video, and digital arts. These media have given rise to unique possibilities for artistic expression.

PHOTOGRAPHY

Photography is a science and an art. The word *photography* is derived from Greek roots meaning "to write with light." The scientific aspects of photography concern the ways in which images of objects are made on a **photosensitive** surface, such as film, by light that passes through a **lens.** Chemical changes occur in the film so that the images are recorded. This much of the process—the creation of an objective image of the light that has passed through the lens—is mechanical.

8-1   ANSEL ADAMS.
Moon and Half Dome, Yosemite National Park, California (1960).

8-2   SHIRO SHIRAHATA.
Moon over Fuji (1972).
Universal Mountains Pictorial Museum, Echigo-Yuzawa, Japan

Photography records the gamut of feelings written on the human face, the beauty of the earth and skies that man has inherited and the wealth and confusion man has created.

—Edward Steichen

8-3 NASA.
Earthrise (1969).
Photo courtesy of NASA.

It would be grossly inaccurate, however, to think of the *art* of photography as mechanical. Photographers make artistic choices, from the most mundane to the most sophisticated. They decide which films and lenses to use, and which photographs they will retain or discard. They manipulate lighting conditions or printing processes to achieve dazzling or dreamy effects. Always, but always, they are in search of subjects—ordinary, extraordinary, universal, personal.

Photography is truly an art of the hand, head, and heart. The photographer must understand films and grasp skills related to using the camera and, in most cases, to developing **prints.** The photographer must also have the intellect and the passion to search for and to see what is important in things—what is beautiful, harmonious, universal, and worth recording.

Photography is a matter of selection and interpretation. Similar subjects seen through the eyes of different photographers will yield wildly different results. In Ansel Adams's *Moon and Half Dome, Yosemite National Park, California* (Fig. 8-1), majestic cliffs leap into a deep, cold sky. From our earthbound vantage point, the perfect order of the desolate, spherical moon contrasts with the coarseness of the living rock. Yet we know that its geometric polish is an illusion wrought by distance—the moon's surface is just as rough and chaotic. Adams's composition is as much about shape and texture as it is a photograph of a feature of the California landscape. Distance and scale come sharply into focus: This is a story of humans dwarfed by nature and nature dwarfed by the stars.

In *Moon over Fuji* (Fig. 8-2), photographer Shiro Shirahata renders Japan's extinct volcano with the etherealness and serenity of a Japanese scroll painting. The blackened peak recedes, deathlike, into the slate blue surroundings while the most piercing of moons hovers above, seemingly full of life. The vast space that separates the upper and lower portions of the narrow photograph is pregnant with suggestions of the relationships between the heavens and the earth.

In the early nineteenth century, when photography was invented, the stuff of which *Earthrise* (Fig. 8-3) is made would have been only fantasy. In this NASA photograph, taken during the first landing on the moon, the sharp lights and darks of the lunar landing module are silhouetted against the grays of the softly textured moon and balanced by the high-contrast values of black space and the arc of Earth above. The distance of the home planet lends it an abstract, geometric appearance. Out here, in space, the heavy landing module is very much closer and, despite its mechanical grotesqueness, it looks, frankly, much more like home.

Thus, the mood, stylistic inclinations, cultural biases, and technical preferences of the artist-photographer influence the nature of the creative product. As observers, we are as enriched by the diversity of this medium as by any other of the visual arts media.

Let us now consider two of the technical aspects of photography: cameras and films. Then we chronicle the history of photography.

Cameras

Cameras may look very different from one another and boast a variety of equipment, but they all possess certain basic features. As you can see in Figure 8-4, the camera is similar to the human eye. In both cases, light enters a narrow opening and is projected onto a photosensitive surface.

The amount of light that enters the eye is determined by the size of the *pupil,* which is an opening in the muscle called the *iris;* the size of the pupil responds automatically to the amount of light that strikes the eye. The amount of light that enters a camera is determined by the size of the open-

ing, or **aperture,** in the **shutter.** The aperture opening can be adjusted manually or, in advanced cameras, automatically. The size of the aperture, or opening, is the so-called **stop.** The smaller the f-stop, the larger the opening. The shutter can also be made to remain open to light for various amounts of time, ranging from a few thousandths of a second—in which case **candid** shots of fast action may be taken—to a second or more.

When the light enters the eye, the *lens* keeps it in focus by responding automatically to its distance from the object. The light is then projected onto the retina, which consists of cells that are sensitive to light and dark and to color. Nerves transmit visual sensations of objects from the retina to the brain.

In the same way, the camera lens focuses light onto a photosensitive surface such as **film.** A camera lens can be focused manually or automatically. Many photographers purposely take pictures that are out of focus, for their soft, blurred effects. **Telephoto lenses** magnify faraway objects and tend to collapse the spaces between distant objects that recede from us. **Wide-angle lenses** allow a broad view of objects within a confined area.

In their early days, cameras tended to be large and were placed on mounts. Today's cameras are usually small and held by hand. *The Steerage* (see Fig. 1-23) was shot with an early handheld camera. Many contemporary cameras contain angled mirrors that allow the photographer to see directly through the lens and thereby to be precisely aware of the image that is being projected onto the film.

Film

When an image is "shot," it is recorded on a device such as film or an electronic memory device such as a disk or "memory stick." Contemporary black-and-white films are very thin, yet they contain several layers, most of which form a protective coat and backing for the photosensitive layer. The "active" layer contains an **emulsion** of small particles of a photosensitive silver salt (usually silver halide) suspended in gelatin.

After the film is exposed to light and treated chemically, it becomes a **negative,** in which metallic silver is formed from the crystals of silver halide. In this negative, areas of dark and light are reversed. Because the negatives are transparent, light passes through them to a print surface, which becomes the final photograph, or print. Here the areas of light and dark are reversed again, now matching the shading of the original subject. Prints are also usually made significantly larger than the negative.

retina (photosensitive surface)

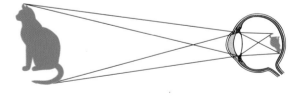

film (photosensitive surface)

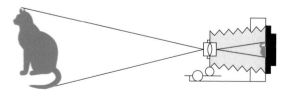

8-4   The camera and the human eye compared.

Black-and-white films differ in color sensitivity (the ability to show colors like red and green as different shades), in contrast (the tendency to show gradations of gray as well as black and white), in graininess (the textural quality, as reflective of the size of the silver halide crystals), and in speed (the amount of exposure time necessary to record an image). Photographers select films that will heighten the effects they seek to portray.

Color film is more complex than black-and-white film, but similar in principle. Color film also contains several layers, some of which are protective and provide backing. There are two basic kinds of color film: **color reversal film** and **color negative film.** Both types of color film contain three light-sensitive layers.

Prints are made directly from *color reversal film.* Therefore, each of the photosensitive layers corresponds to one of the primary colors in additive color mixtures: blue, green, or red. When color reversal film is exposed to light and treated chemically, mixtures of the primary colors emerge, yielding a full-color image of the photographic subject.

Negatives are made from *color negative film.* Therefore, each photosensitive layer corresponds to the complement of the primary color it represents. (Additive color mixtures and primary and complementary colors are explained in Chapter 2.)

Color films, like black-and-white films, differ in color sensitivity, contrast, graininess, and speed. But color films also differ in their appropriateness for natural (daylight) or artificial (indoor) lighting conditions.

Digital Photography

Today **digital photography** abounds. Digital cameras translate the visual images that pass through the lens into bits of digital information, which are recorded on an electronic storage device such as a disk, not on film. High-quality (translation: extremely expensive) digital cameras take photos whose **resolution**—that is, sharpness—rivals that of images recorded on film. The stored information can then be displayed on a computer monitor. Rather than have several prints made, the photographer can "back up" the information repeatedly. It can also be sent over the Internet in digital form. Printed images can also be scanned, of course, which coverts them into digital formats, and then stored on computer hard drives or sent over the Internet.

Digital photography has some advantages. One is that the photographer need not deal with film—loading and unloading it and having it developed. The images can be displayed immediately on a computer monitor or a screen built into the camera. Software then permits you to manipulate the images as desired. You can also print them out as you print out any other image or text.

The disadvantages are that (most) digital images do not have the sharpness of film images. They take a tremendous amount of storage space (several megabytes each!) on your hard drive. Also, your printer may not print images that approach the quality of film images, even if you have stored enough information to do so. To get "professional-quality" prints, you may have to invest in professional equipment or take your disk elsewhere, just as you have to take film to a lab or processor to be developed. But the price of this equipment is falling steadily, and it may soon be that nearly anyone will be able to afford digital equipment that rivals the resolution of more traditional photography.

History of Photography

The cameras and films described previously are rather recent inventions. Photography has a long and fascinating history. Although true photography does not appear much before the mid-nineteenth century, some of its principles can be traced back another 300 years, to the *camera obscura.*

The Camera Obscura

The **camera obscura**—literally, the covered-over or darkened room—was used by Renaissance artists to help them accurately portray depth, or perspective, on two-dimensional surfaces. The camera obscura could be a box, as shown in Figure 8-5, or an actual room with a small hole that admits light through one wall. The beam of light projects the outside scene upside down on a surface within the box. The

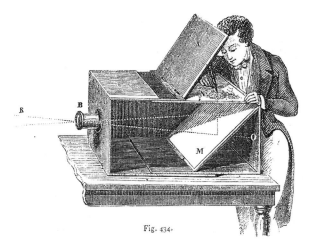

Fig. 434.

8-5   The camera obscura.
Illustration copyright Ann Ronan Picture Library, Oxfordshire, UK.

artist then simply traces the scene, as shown, to achieve a proper perspective—to truly imitate nature.

Development of Photosensitive Surfaces

The camera obscura could only temporarily focus an image on a surface while a person labored to copy it by tracing. The next developments in photography concerned the search for photosensitive surfaces that could permanently affix images. These developments came by bits and pieces.

In 1727 the German physicist Heinrich Schulze discovered that silver salts had light-sensitive qualities, but he never tried to record natural images. In 1802 Thomas Wedgwood, son of the well-known English potter, reported his discovery that paper soaked in silver nitrate did take on projected images as a chemical reaction to light. Unfortunately, the images were not permanent.

Heliography

In 1826 the Frenchman Joseph-Nicéphore Niepce invented **heliography. Bitumen,** or asphalt residue, was placed on a pewter plate to create a photosensitive surface. The bitumen was soluble in **lavender oil** if kept in the dark, but insoluble if struck by light. Niepce used a kind of camera obscura to expose the plate for several hours, and then he washed the plate in lavender oil. The pewter showed through where there had been little or no light, creating the image of the darker areas of the scene. The bitumen remained where the light had struck, however, leaving lighter values.

The Daguerreotype

The **daguerreotype** resulted from a partnership formed in 1829 between Niepce and another Frenchman, Louis-Jacques-Mandé Daguerre. The daguerreotype used a thin sheet of silver-plated copper. The plate was chemically treated, placed in a camera obscura, and exposed to a narrow beam of light. After exposure, the plate was treated chemically again.

Figure 8-6 shows the first successful daguerreotype, taken in 1837. Remarkably clear images could be recorded by this process. In this work, called *The Artist's Studio,* Daguerre, a landscape painter, sensitively assembled deeply textured objects and sculptures. The contrasting light and dark values help create an illusion of depth.

There were drawbacks to the daguerreotype. It had to be exposed from 5 to 40 minutes, requiring long sittings. The recorded image was reversed, left to right, and was so delicate that it had to be sealed behind glass to remain fixed. Also, the plate that was exposed to light became the actual

8-6 LOUIS-JACQUES-MANDÉ DAGUERRE.
The Artist's Studio (1837).
Société Française de Photographie, Paris.

daguerreotype. There was no negative, and consequently, copies could not be made. However, some refinements of the process did come rapidly. Within 10 years the exposure time had been reduced to about 30 to 60 seconds, and the process had become so inexpensive that families could purchase two portraits for a quarter. Daguerreotype studios opened all across Europe and the United States, and families began to collect the rigid, stylized pictures that now seem to reflect days gone by.

The Negative

The negative was invented in 1839 by British scientist William Henry Fox Talbot. Talbot found that sensitized paper, coated with emulsions, could be substituted for the copper plate of the daguerreotype. He would place an object, such as a sprig of a plant, on the paper and expose the arrangement to light. The paper was darkened by the exposure in all areas except those covered by the object. Translucent areas, allowing some passage of light, resulted in a range of grays. Talbot's first so-called photogenic drawings (Fig. 8-7), created by this process, seem eerie, though lyrically beautiful. The delicacy of the image underscores the impracticality of the process: How on earth would you "photograph" an elephant?

As with the daguerreotype, this process produced completed photographs in which the left and right of the image were reversed. In Talbot's photogenic drawings, the light and dark values of the image were also inverted. Talbot improved on his early experiments with his development of the **contact print**. He placed the negative in contact with a second sheet of sensitized paper and exposed them both to light. The resultant print was a "positive," with left and right, and light and dark, again as in the original subject. Many prints could be made from the negative. Unfortunately, the prints were not as sharp as daguerreotypes, because they incorporated the texture of the paper on which they were captured. Subsequent advances led to methods in which pictures with the clarity of daguerreotypes could be printed from black-and-white as well as color negatives.

Photography improved rapidly for the next 50 or 60 years—faster emulsions, glass-plate negatives, better camera lenses—and photographs became more and more available to the general public. The next major step in the history of photography came with the introduction by Louis Lumière of the "autochrome" color process in 1907. Autochromes were glass plates coated with three layers of dyed potato starch that served as color filters. A layer of silver bro-

8-8   LOUIS LUMIÈRE.
Young Lady with an Umbrella (1906–1910).
Autochrome.
Société Lumière, Paris.

8-7   WILLIAM HENRY FOX TALBOT.
Botanical Specimen (1839).
Photogenic drawing.
Royal Photographic Society, Bath, England. Heritage Image Partnership (HIP), heritage-images.com.

mide emulsion covered the starch. When the autochrome was developed, it yielded a positive color transparency. Lumière's autochrome photographs, such as *Young Lady with an Umbrella* (Fig. 8-8), are akin to paintings by Postimpressionist artist Georges Seurat (see Fig. 18-25), an avid student of color theory, as well as to works by other photographers in the pictorial style. Autochrome technology was not replaced until 1932, when Kodak began to produce color film that applied the same principles to more advanced materials.

Portraits

By the 1850s, photographic technology and the demands of a growing middle class in the wake of the American and French revolutions came together to create a burgeoning business in portrait photography. Having a likeness of oneself was formerly reserved for the wealthy, who could afford to commission painters. Photography became the democratic equalizer. The rich, the famous, and average bourgeois citizens could now become memorable, could now make their presence known long after their flesh had rejoined the elements from which it was composed.

Photographic studios spread like wildfire, and many photographers, such as Julia Margaret Cameron and Gaspard Felix Tournachon—called "Nadar"—vied for famous clientele. Cameron's impressive portfolio included portraits

8-9   NADAR.
Sarah Bernhardt (1859).
Bibliothèque Nationale, Paris. Copyright Photos 12, Paris.

of Charles Dickens; Alfred, Lord Tennyson; and Henry Wadsworth Longfellow. Figure 8-9 is Nadar's 1859 portrait of the actress Sarah Bernhardt. It was printed from a glass plate, which could be used several times to create sharp copies. Early portrait photographers such as Nadar imitated both nature and the arts, using costumes and props that recall Romantic paintings or sculpted busts caressed by flowing drapery. The photograph is soft and smoothly textured, with middle-range values predominating; Bernhardt is sensitively portrayed—pensive and brooding, but not downcast.

Photojournalism

Prior to the nineteenth century there were few illustrations in newspapers and magazines. Those that did appear were usually in the form of engravings or drawings. Photography revolutionized the capacity of the news media to bring realistic representations of important events before the eyes of the public. Pioneers such as Mathew Brady and Alexander Gardner first used the camera to record major historical events such as the U.S. Civil War. The photographers and their crews trudged down the roads alongside the soldiers, horses drawing their equipment behind them in wagons referred to by the soldiers as "Whatsits."

Equipment available to Brady and Gardner did not allow them to capture candid scenes, so there is no direct record of the bloody to and fro of the battle lines, no photographic record of each lunge and parry. Instead, they brought home photographs of officers and of life in the camps along the lines. Although battle scenes themselves would not hold still for Gardner's cameras, the litter of death and devastation caused by the war and pictured in Gardner's *Home of a Rebel Sharpshooter, Gettysburg* (Fig. 8-10) most certainly did. Despite their novelty and their accuracy, not many works of such graphic nature were sold. There are at least three reasons for this tempered success. First, the state of the art of photography made the photographs high priced. Second, methods for reproducing photographs on newsprint were not invented until about 1900; therefore, the works of the photojournalists were usually rendered as drawings, and the drawings translated into woodcuts before they appeared in the papers. Third, the American public might not have been ready to face the brutal realities they portrayed. In a similar vein, social commentators have suggested that the will of many Americans to persist in the Vietnam War was sapped by the incessant barrage of televised war imagery.

During the Great Depression of the 1930s, the conscience of the nation was stirred by the work of many photographers hired by the Farm Security Administration. Dorothea Lange and Walker Evans, among others, portrayed the lifestyles of migrant farmworkers and sharecroppers. Lange's *Migrant Mother* (Fig. 8-11) is a heartrending record of a 32-year-old woman who is out of work but cannot move on because the tires have been sold from the family car to purchase food for her seven children. The etching in the forehead is an eloquent expression of the mother's thoughts; the lines at the outer edges of her eyes tell the story of a woman who has aged beyond her years. Lange crops her photograph close to her subjects; they fill the print from edge to edge, forcing us to confront them rather than allowing us to seek comfort in a corner of the print not consigned to such an overt display of human misery. The migrant mother and her children, who turn away from the camera and heighten the futility of their plight, are as much constrained by the camera's viewfinder as they are by their circumstances.

Documentary photography records the social scene of our time. It mirrors the present and documents [it] for the future. Its focus is man in his relation to mankind. It records his customs at work, at war, at play. . . . It portrays his institutions. . . . It shows not merely their facades, but seeks to reveal the manner in which they function, absorb the life, hold the loyalty, and influence the behavior of human beings.

—Dorothea Lange

In the very year that Lange photographed the migrant mother, Robert Capa's fearless coverage of the Spanish Civil War resulted in such incredible photographs as *Death of a Loyalist Soldier* (see Fig. 3-18). During the early 1940s, photographers such as Margaret Bourke-White carried their handheld cameras into combat and captured tragic images of the butchery in Europe and in the Pacific. In 1929 Bourke-White became a staff photographer for *Fortune,* a new magazine published by Henry Luce. When Luce founded *Life* in 1936, Bourke-White became one of its original staff photographers. Like Dorothea Lange, she recorded the poverty of the Great Depression, but in the 1940s she traveled abroad to become one of the first female war photojournalists. As World War II was drawing to an end in Europe, Bourke-White arrived at the Nazi concentration camp

8-11 DOROTHEA LANGE.
Migrant Mother, Nipomo, California (1936).
Gelatin silver print. $12\frac{1}{2}" \times 9\frac{7}{8}"$.
Copyright The Dorothea Lange Collection. The Oakland Museum of Art. Gift of Paul S. Taylor.

8-10 ALEXANDER GARDNER.
Home of a Rebel Sharpshooter, Gettysburg (July 1863).
Wet-plate photograph.
Courtesy of the Chicago Historical Society.

8-12   MARGARET BOURKE-WHITE.
The Living Dead of Buchenwald, April 1945 (1945).
Time & Life Pictures/Getty Images.

of Buchenwald in time for its liberation by Gen. George S. Patton. Her photograph *The Living Dead of Buchenwald* (Fig. 8-12), published in *Life* in 1945, has become a classic image of the Holocaust, the Nazi effort to annihilate the Jewish people. The indifferent countenance of each survivor expresses, paradoxically, all that he has witnessed and endured. In her book *Dear Fatherland, Rest Quietly,* Bourke-White put into words her own reactions to Buchenwald. In doing so, she showed how artistic creation, an intensely emotional experience, can also have the effect of objectifying the subject of creation:

> I kept telling myself that I would believe the indescribably horrible sight in the courtyard before me only when I had a chance to look at my own photographs. Using the camera was almost a relief; it interposed a slight barrier between myself and the white horror in front of me . . . it made me ashamed to be a member of the human race.[1]

Dorothea Lange traveled rural America to photograph the effects of the Depression, and Margaret Bourke-White followed the U.S. troops abroad during World War II. As Bourke-White discovered, one of the keys to photojournalism is being in the right place at the right time—or in the wrong place at the wrong time. Photographer Ron Berard was also in the right—or wrong—place. He was living on an upper floor of an apartment building in Battery Park City, across a highway from the World Trade Center, on September 11, 2001, when Arab terrorists hijacked commercial aircraft and flew them into the twin towers, causing

---

[1] Margaret Bourke-White, *Dear Fatherland, Rest Quietly* (New York: Simon and Schuster, 1946), 73.

8-13   RON BERARD.
Untitled (2001).
Copyright Ron J. Berard.

their collapse and the loss of nearly 3,000 lives. His photograph (Fig. 8-13) captures the hellish quality of the destruction—the shard of the curtain wall that remained, the pile of rubble, the charred facade of a still-standing neighbor. The eerie smoke that rose from the pit would continue to rise for two months.

Another of Berard's photographs—an American flag flying, flapping, snapping against the grim background of the devastation of the World Trade Center site—was picked up by *Time* magazine. Yet perhaps the best-known photo from the tragedy of September 11 is the one taken a day later by Thomas E. Franklin, a staff photographer for *The Record,* a local New Jersey newspaper. That image (Fig. 8-15) of firefighters raising the flag amidst the rubble—a symbol of survival, heroism, and pride—was made into a U.S. postage stamp. Its content, design, and

The Raising of the Flag at Iwo Jima with the Raising of the Flag at the World Trade Center

They were both photographs taken by people who just happened to be there. They were both photographs that captured heroes of the moment, ordinary fighters from ordinary ranks giving loft to hope amidst death and destruction. And they were both photographs destined to become American icons—symbols of strength and liberty woven of the threads of their time into the fabric of history.

Joe Rosenthal's photograph (Fig. 8-14) of marines raising an American flag on the Japanese island of Iwo Jima gained such celebrity that it was used as the basis for a memorial in Washington, D.C. Thomas E. Franklin's record of firefighters raising the American flag (Fig. 8-15) up a felled pole became such a visual symbol for Ground Zero that the scene is commemorated on a U.S. postage stamp. The relationship between the two images was coincidental but immediately recognized by news commentators along with the rest of us who were familiar with the indelible images of World War II. Beyond the visual similarities, which were clear enough, lay the desire to mark the war against terror as equivalent to the war against Fascism and Nazism. The connection between the two photographs also enabled Americans to assign victory—the circumstances of the Iwo Jima image—to what appeared to be the depths of defeat—the utter destruction of the World Trade Center towers and the loss of thousands of innocent lives. ■

8-15 THOMAS E. FRANKLIN.
The Flag Raising at Ground Zero (2001).
Copyright 2001 The Record (Bergen County, NJ),
Thomas E. Franklin/Corbis SABA.

8-14 JOE ROSENTHAL.
Old Glory Goes Up on Mt. Suribachi, Iwo Jima (1945).
Gelatin silver print. 34.5 cm × 26.7 cm.
Joe Rosenthal/AP Photo.

It gradually began to dawn on me that something must be wrong with the art of painting as practiced at that time. With my camera I could procure the same results as those attained by painters. . . . I could express the same moods. Artists who saw my earlier photographs began to tell me that they envied me; that they felt my photographs were superior to their paintings, but that, unfortunately, photography was not an art. . . . There and then I started my fight— or rather my conscious struggle for the recognition of photography as a new medium of expression, to be respected in its own right, on the same basis as any other art form.

—Alfred Stieglitz

emotional impact have been compared with the equally famous photograph of U.S. Marines raising the flag on the Pacific island of Iwo Jima during World War II.

Photography as an Art Form

Photographers became aware of the potential of their medium as an art form more than 100 years ago. Edward Weston, Paul Strand, Edward Steichen, and others argued that photographers must not attempt to imitate painting but must find modes of expression that are truer to their medium. Synergistically, painters were free to move toward abstraction because the "obligation" to faithfully record nature was now assumed by the photographer. Why, after all, do what a camera can do better? In 1902 Alfred Stieglitz founded the Photo-Secession, a group dedicated to advancing photography as a separate art form. Stieglitz himself enjoyed taking pictures under adverse weather conditions and at odd times of day to show the versatility of his medium and the diversity of his expression.

Edward Steichen's *The Flatiron Building—Evening* (Fig. 8-16), photographed a century ago, is among the foremost early examples of the photograph as a work of art. It is an exquisitely sensitive nocturne of haunting shapes looming in a rain-soaked atmosphere. The branch in the foreground provides the viewer with a psychological vantage point as it cuts across the composition like a bolt of lightning or an artery pulsing with life. The values are predominantly middle grays, although here and there, beaconlike, street lamps sparkle in the distance. The infinite gradations of gray in the cast-iron skyscraper after which the picture is named, and in the surrounding structures, yield an immeasurable softness. Although much is present that we cannot readily see, there is nothing gloomy or frightening about the scene. Rather, it

seems pregnant with wonderful things that will happen as the rain stops and the twentieth century progresses.

It was not long before artists began to manipulate their medium so that they, too, could venture beyond mere imitation. The first steps were tentative, building on the familiar and the readily acceptable. Photographer James VanDerZee, known for his visual narrative of life in New York's Harlem, experimented with painted backgrounds and double-exposed images in otherwise traditional portraits. *Future Expectations* (Fig. 8-17) is both a visual record of a young

8-16 EDWARD STEICHEN.
The Flatiron Building—Evening (1906).
Courtesy of the Library of Congress.

couple on their wedding day and a symbol of their hopes and anticipations—a comfortable home with a blazing hearth, and beautiful children, secure in their love.

In the realm of photography and fantasy, we may take a quantum leap to the present day, when technology is such that the only impediment to the most innovative results is the artist's ability to fathom the unfathomable. In what sharp contrast to VanDerZee's interior stands Sandy Skoglund's *Radioactive Cats* (Fig. 8-18)! Hopes and expectations for the "good life" fade into the dullness of gray, as a phlegmatic elderly couple live out their colorless lives. Yet sparks of life and humor permeate the deadly pallor of their environment—in the form of neon green cats. Skoglund sculpted the plaster cats herself and painted the room gray, controlling every aspect of the set before she shot the scene. Yet it is the photograph itself that stands as the completed work of art.

From cats to dogs . . . artist-photographer William Wegman happened upon his most famous subject when his Weimeraner puppy virtually insisted on performing before his lights. Man Ray, named by Wegman after the Surrealist photographer, posed willingly in hundreds of staged sets that range from the credible to the farcical. *Blue Period*

8-17 JAMES VANDERZEE.
Future Expectations (c. 1915).
Gelatin silver print.

8-18 SANDY SKOGLUND.
Radioactive Cats (1980).
Cibachrome. 30″ × 40″.
Collection of the artist.

8-19 WILLIAM WEGMAN.
Blue Period (1981).
Color Polaroid photograph. 24″ × 20″.
Copyright William Wegman. Courtesy PaceWildenstein MacGill.

8-20 CINDY SHERMAN.
Untitled (1984).
Color photograph. 71″ × 48½″.
Metro Pictures, New York.

(Fig. 8-19) is a spoof on Pablo Picasso's painting *The Old Guitarist* (see Fig. 19-6), enframed in a souvenir version in the left lower foreground. In both works a guitar cuts diagonally across the composition, adding the only contrasting color to the otherwise monochromatic blue background. The heads of the old man and of Man Ray hang, melancholy, over the soulful instrument. As Picasso gave the old man's flesh a bluish cast, so did Wegman tint the Weimaraner's muzzle. In Wegman's photograph, however, we find the pièce de résistance—an object laden with profound meaning for the guitarist's stand-in: a blue rubber bone.

In contemporary photography, artists often use themselves as subjects. Cindy Sherman adopts diverse personae for her photographs. She recalls a mundane, early inspiration for her approach:

> I had all this makeup. I just wanted to see how transformed I could look. It was like painting in a way.[2]

[2] Cindy Sherman, in Gerald Marzorati, "Imitation of Life," *Artnews 82* (September 1983): 84–85.

Soon she set herself before elaborate backdrops, costumed in a limitless wardrobe. Dress designers began to ask her to use their haute couture in her photographs, and works such as *Untitled* (Fig. 8-20) were actually shot as part of an advertising assignment for French *Vogue.* The result is less a sales device than a harsh view of the fashion industry. Sherman appears as a disheveled model with a troubling expression. Something here is very wrong. Regimented stripes go awry as the fabric of her dress is stretched taut across her thighs and knees. Her hands rest oddly in her lap, fingertips red with what seems to be blood. And then there is the smile— an unsettling leer implying madness.

Skoglund, Wegman, and Sherman are photographers who work, by their own admission, as painters. Painter David Hockney has used photography to construct unified compositions whose sum total of parts has a far greater impact than the whole. In the process of photographing a subject like *Pearblossom Highway 11–18th April 1986 #2* (Fig. 8-21), Hockney fragments the panorama, only to rebuild it in his studio. It is almost as if he were reconstruct-

I see my work as a pictorial excursus on the topic of feminism and contemporary Islam—
a discussion that puts certain myths and realities under the microscope and comes to the conclusion
that these are much more complex than many of us had thought.

—Shirin Neshat

8-21 DAVID HOCKNEY.
Pearblossom Highway
11—18th April 1986 #2 (1986).
Photographic collage.
78″ × 111″.
Copyright 1986 David Hockney.

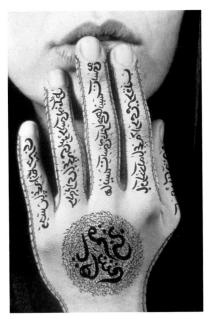

8-22 SHIRIN NESHAT.
Untitled (Women
of Allah) (1994).
Gelatin silver print,
ink. 36 cm × 28 cm.
Courtesy of Thomas
Rehbein Gallery, Köln,
Germany.

ing the scene as most of us do from fragmented memories. The result is a shimmering mosaic that elevates the commonplace to the level of fine art.

Iranian-American photographer and video artist Shirin Neshat came to the United States as a teenager, before the shah was removed from power, and returned in 1990 to witness a nation transformed by the rule of Islamic clergy. She was particularly concerned about how life had changed for Iranian women, who now had limited opportunities outside the home and were veiled behind black chadors. Figure 8-22 is one of a series called *Women of Allah,* in which guns or flowers are frequently juxtaposed with vulnerable though rebellious faces and hands that emerge from beneath the veil. The exposed flesh is overwritten with sensual or political texts by Iranian women in the native tongue of Farsi. To a non-Arabic-speaking Westerner, the calligraphic writing may first appear to be little more than a mélange of elegant and mysterious patterns and designs. Yet there is no mistaking its purpose as one of resistance. The photos are unlikely to be seen and "decoded" by the eyes of Iranians living in Iran, but the message of the artist to the world outside is clear.

Evolving technology has made it possible for photographers to achieve dazzling images such as the one in Harold Edgerton's *Fan and Flame Vortices* (Fig. 8-23). Edgerton is an electrical engineer who invented the strobe light, a device that emits brief and brilliant flashes of light that seem to slow or stop the action of people or objects in motion. *Fan and Flame Vortices* is a high-speed photograph of a metal fan blade rotating at 3,600 revolutions per minute through the flame emitted by an alcohol burner. Changes in the density of the air and other gases are responsible for the fluctuating colors. Edgerton, like many other contemporary photographers, has used technological innovations to transform some of the mundane objects of the real world into vibrant abstract images.

8-23   HAROLD EDGERTON.
Fan and Flame Vortices (1973).
Dye transfer print. 13″ × 20″.
Copyright Kim Vandiver & Harold Edgerton. Courtesy of Palm Press, Inc.

Photographs have the capacity to stir us; because of their size, our relationship to them is intimate. At times they speak frankly to us; sometimes they leave much to the imagination. Because they are frozen moments in time, we can only wonder about what had gone before and what came after. This capacity to stir us is intensified, expanded, and altered in the art of cinematography. A large screen, movement, and—since the 1930s—sound capture the visual and auditory senses of the audience like no other medium.

CINEMATOGRAPHY

The magic of **cinematography**—the art of making motion pictures—envelops our senses. Some members of the audience demand to be so encompassed that they sit in the front row, with the screen looming above them like a tidal wave. What associations does cinematography evoke for you? The big screen? The silver screen? The drive-in, with long lines for hot dogs and french fries? Speakers blasting from the walls? Popcorn? Ushers complaining about bringing drinks to the seats? Gum sticking to your shoe? Teenagers laughing, shouting, and necking? All these are part of Americana. Couples not only have their "song"; they often have their "movie"—what they saw on one of their first dates, what spoke to them deeply in their emotional vulnerability.

Varieties of Cinematographic Techniques

Despite their power to move us, motion pictures, or "movies," do not really move themselves. The illusion of movement is created by stroboscopic motion, which is the presentation of a rapid progression of images of stationary objects. The audience is shown 16 to 24 pictures or frames per second, like those shown in the series of Muybridge photographs (Fig. 8-24). Each picture or frame differs slightly from that preceding it. Showing them in rapid succession creates the illusion of movement. (Children similarly draw series of shapes or figures along the outer margins of books, then flip the pages to create the illusion of movement.)

At a rate of 22 or 24 frames per second, the "motion" in a film seems smooth and natural. At fewer than 16 or so frames per second, it is choppy. For that reason, **slow motion** is achieved by filming 100 or more frames per second. When they are played back at 22 or 24 frames per second, movement appears to be very slow yet smooth and natural.

A film is—or should be—more like music than like fiction. It should be a progression of moods and feelings. The theme, what's behind the emotion, the meaning, all that comes later.

—Stanley Kubrick

8-24   EADWEARD MUYBRIDGE.
Galloping Horse (1878).
International Museum of Photography at George Eastman House, Rochester, NY.

Eadweard Muybridge's *Galloping Horse* sequence was shot in 1878 by 24 cameras placed along a racetrack and was made possible by new fast-acting photosensitive plates. (If these plates had been developed 15 years earlier, Brady could have bequeathed us a photographic record of Civil War battle scenes.) Muybridge had been commissioned to settle a bet as to whether racehorses ever had all hooves off the ground at once. He found that they did, but also that they never assumed the "rocking-horse" position in which the front and back legs are simultaneously extended.

Muybridge is generally credited with performing the first successful experiments in cinematography. He fashioned a device that could photograph a rapid sequence of images, and he invented the **zoogyroscope,** which projected these images onto a screen.

The motion-picture camera and projector were perfected by the inventor of the light bulb, Thomas Edison, toward the end of the nineteenth century. In 1893 the photographer Alexander Black made a motion picture of the president of the United States. In 1894 Thomas Edison's assistant Fred Ott was immortalized on film in the act of sneezing. Out of these inauspicious beginnings, a new medium for the visual arts was suddenly born.

Within a few short years, commercial movie houses sprang up across the nation and motion-picture productions were distributed for public consumption. Sound was added to visual sensations by means of a **sound track,** and a number of silent film stars with noncompelling voices fell by the wayside.

Additional innovations have had a checkered history. There have been expansions to wider and wider screens, including Cinemascope, Cinerama, Panavision, and films that are projected completely around the audience on a 360-degree strip wall or on the inner surface of a hemispherical dome. Stereophonic sound has been introduced. Three-dimensional (3-D) movies requiring special eyeglasses

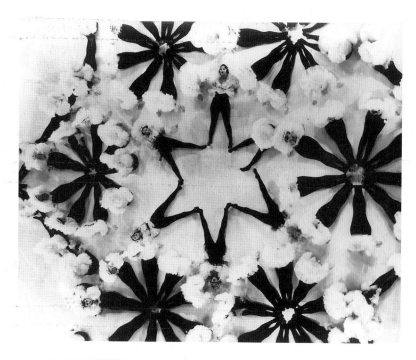

have been made. Today stereophonic sound, color, and reasonably wide screens remain in common use. But what photographers have noted about the role of photographic equipment seems also to apply to cinematography: the vision or creativity of the cinematographer is more important than technical advances.

Let us now consider a number of cinematographic techniques more closely: use of the fixed camera, the moving camera, editing, color, animation, and special effects.

Fixed Cameras and Staged Productions

With a stage play, the audience is fixed and must observe from a single vantage point. Similarly, many early motion pictures used a single camera that was more or less fixed in place. Actors came onstage and exited before them.

For the most part, the Busby Berkeley musicals of the 1930s (Fig. 8-25) were shot on indoor stages that pretended to be nothing but stages. The motion picture had not yet broken free from the stage that had preceded it. Many directors used cinematography to bring the stages of the great urban centers to small cities and rural towns. We can note that the musicals of the 1930s were everything that the photographs of Dorothea Lange and the other Depression photographers were not: they were bubbly, frivolous, light, even saucy. Perhaps they helped Americans make it through. Some musicals of the 1930s showed apple-cheeked "kids" getting their break on the Great White Way. Others portrayed the imaginary shenanigans of the wealthy few in an innocent era when Hollywood believed that they would offer amusement and inspiration to destitute audiences rather than stir feelings of social conflict through depiction of conspicuous consumption and frivolity.

8-26 D. W. GRIFFITH.
Scene from *Birth of a Nation* (1915).
Copyright Ann Ronan Picture Library, Oxfordshire, UK.

The Mobile Camera

Film critics usually argue that motion pictures should tell their stories in ways that are inimitable through any other medium. One way is through the mobile camera. Film pioneer D. W. Griffith is credited with making the camera mobile. He attached motion-picture cameras to rapidly moving vehicles and used them to **pan** across expanses of scenery and action, as in the battle scenes in his *Birth of a Nation* (Fig. 8-26). Today it is not unusual for cameras to be placed aboard rapidly moving vehicles and also to **zoom** in on and away from their targets.

Editing

Griffith is also credited with making many advances in film editing. **Editing** is the separating and assembling, sometimes called "patching and pasting," of sequences of film. Editing helps make stories coherent and heightens dramatic impact.

In **narrative editing,** multiple cameras are used during the progress of the same scene or story location. Then shots are selected from various vantage points and projected in sequence. Close-ups may be interspersed with **longshots,** providing the audience with abundant perspectives on the action while advancing the story. Close-ups usually better communicate the emotional responses of the actors, whereas longshots describe the setting, as in Alfred Hitchcock's thriller, *North by Northwest* (Fig. 8-27).

In **parallel editing,** the story shifts back and forth from one event or scene to another. Scenes of one segment of a battlefield may be interspersed with events taking place on another or back home, collapsing space. Time may also be collapsed through parallel editing, with the cinematographer shifting back and forth between past, present, and future.

In the **flashback,** one form of parallel editing, the story line is interrupted by the portrayal or narration of an earlier episode, often through the implied fantasies of a principal character. Orson Welles's *Citizen Kane* (Fig. 8-28) innovated the use of the flashback. The flashback usually gives current action more meaning. In the **flash-forward,** editing permits the audience glimpses of the future. The flash-forward is frequently used at the beginning of dramatic television shows to capture the interest of the viewer who may be switching channels.

Motion pictures may proceed from one scene to another by means of **fading.** The current scene becomes gradually dimmer, or *fades out.* The subsequent scene then grows progressively brighter, or *fades in.* In the more rapid, current technique of the **dissolve,** the subsequent scene becomes brighter and the current scene fades out so that the first scene seems to dissolve into the second.

8-27 ALFRED HITCHCOCK.
Film still from *North by Northwest.*
Copyright 1959 Metro-Goldwyn-Mayer. Copyright Ann Ronan Picture Library, Oxfordshire, UK.

8-28 ORSON WELLES.
Film still from *Citizen Kane.*
Copyright 1941 RKO Radio Pictures. Copyright Ann Ronan Picture Library, Oxfordshire, UK.

I love Mickey Mouse more than any woman I have ever known.

—Walt Disney

In **montage,** a sequence of abruptly alternating images or scenes conveys associated ideas or the passage of time. Images can suddenly flash into focus or whirl about for impact, as in a series of newspaper headlines meant to show the progress of the actors over time.

Color

Color came into use in the 1930s. One early color film, *The Wizard of Oz,* depicted the farm world of Kansas in black and white and the imaginary Oz in glorious, often expressionistic color. Madonna sort of reverses the pattern in *Truth or Dare,* where her stage performances (fantasy?) are in color and her (real?) backstage life is in black and white. Yet interestingly, this pattern is now frequently reversed in music videos, where fantasy is often portrayed in black and white and reality in (everyday, natural?) color.

The screen version of Margaret Mitchell's *Gone with the Wind* (Fig. 8-29) was one of the first color epics, or "spectaculars." It remains one of the highest-grossing works of all film eras. In addition to the sweeping **panoramas** of the Civil War battlefield wounded and the burning of Atlanta, *Gone with the Wind* included close-ups of the passion and fire communicated by Clark Gable as Rhett Butler and Vivien Leigh as Scarlett O'Hara.

8-29   VICTOR FLEMING.
"The Burning of Atlanta," a film still from
Gone with the Wind.
Selznick/MGM/The Kobal Collection.

8-30   BRAD BIRD.
Film still from *The Incredibles* (2004),
a Walt Disney Production.
Topfoto/The Image Works.

Animation

Animation is the creation of a motion picture by photographing a series of drawings, each of which shows a stage of movement that differs slightly from the one preceding it. As a result, projecting the frames in rapid sequence creates the illusion of movement. The first cartoons were in black and white and employed a great deal of repetition.

During the 1930s, Walt Disney's studios began to produce full-color stories and images that have become part of our collective unconscious mind. Disney characters such as Mickey Mouse, Donald Duck, Bambi, Snow White, and Pinocchio are national treasures. In recent years, Disney has collaborated with Pixar Animation Studios to create a new generation of animated films, including *Toy Story; Finding Nemo; Monsters, Inc.;* and *The Incredibles* (Fig. 8-30).

Special Effects

Over the years, filmmakers have raised the technical bar for special effects in their action movies. The industry has come a long way from tiny exploding capsules planted in the ground to simulate gunfire to the extravaganzas of effects in films such as *The Lord of the Rings, Star Wars,* or *Batman Begins* (Fig. 8-31). Complex motorized, remote-controlled models (the great white shark in *Jaws,* dinosaurs in *Jurassic*

Christian Bale as Batman in *Batman Begins* (2005), a Warner Brothers film.
The Everett Collection.

Park, starships and out-of-this-world inhabitants in *Star Wars,* prototype vehicles like the batmobile in *Batman Begins*) and extensive computer graphics combine to create an extreme illusion of the director's reality.

Varieties of Cinematographic Experience

No discussion of cinematography can hope to recount adequately the richness of the motion-picture experience. Broadly speaking, motion pictures are visual experiences that entertain or move us. For example, as in novels, we identify with characters and become wrapped up in plots.

Like other artists, cinematographers make us laugh (consider the great films of the Marx Brothers and Laurel and Hardy); create propaganda, satire, social commentary, fantasy, and symbolism; express artistic theories; and reflect artistic styles. Let us consider some of these more closely.

Propaganda

Although there are some early (and choppy) film records of World War I, cinematography was ready for World War II. In fact, while many American actors were embattled in Europe and the Pacific, former president Ronald Reagan was making films for the United States that depicted the valor of the Allied soldiers and the malevolence of the enemy.

Our adversaries were active as well. Prior to the war, in fact, German director Leni Riefenstahl made what is considered one of the greatest (though also most pernicious) propaganda films of all time, *Triumph of the Will* (Fig. 8-32). Riefenstahl transformed the people and events of a historic event, the 1935 Nürnberg Congress, into abstract, symbolic patterns through the juxtaposition of longshots and close-

ups, and aerial and ground-level views. Her montage of people, monuments, and flag-bedecked buildings unified flesh and stone into a hymn to Nazism. The United States, England, Canada, and some other nations paid a backhanded compliment to the power of *Triumph of the Will* by banning it.

Satire

Satire is the flip side of propaganda. Although Riefenstahl glorified national socialism in Germany, American filmmakers derided it. In one cartoon, for example, Daffy Duck clubs a realistic-looking, speechifying Adolf Hitler over the head with a mallet. Hitler dissolves into tears and calls for his mommy. British-American filmmaker Charlie Chaplin added to the derision of the führer in *The Great Dictator* (Fig. 8-33). The film and television series *M*A*S*H* was set during the Korean War, but it satirized authoritarianism through the ages.

Social Commentary

Filmmakers, like documentary photographers, have made their social comments. *The Grapes of Wrath* (Fig. 8-34), based on the John Steinbeck novel, depicts one family's struggle for survival during the Great Depression, when the banks failed and the Midwest farm basket of the United States turned into the Dust Bowl. Like a Dorothea Lange photograph, the camera comes in to record hopelessness and despair. Cinematographers have commented on everything from *Divorce, American Style* to *The Killing Fields* of Southeast Asia to the excesses of *Wall Street*.

I can make an audience laugh, scream with terror, smile, believe in legends, become indignant, take offense, become enthusiastic, lower itself or yawn with boredom. I am, then, either a deceiver or—when the audience is aware of the fraud—an illusionist. I am able to mystify, and I have at my disposal the most precious and the most astounding device [the motion-picture camera] that has ever, since history began, been put into the hands of the juggler.

—Ingmar Bergman

8-35   ROBERT WIENE.
Film still from *The Cabinet of Dr. Caligari* (1919).
Copyright Ann Ronan Picture Library, Oxfordshire, UK.

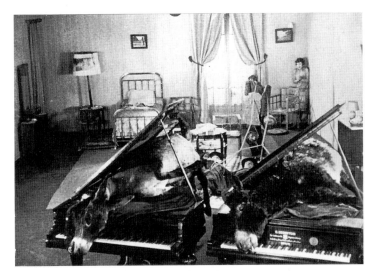

8-36   SALVADOR DALÍ AND LUIS BUÑUEL.
Film still from *Un Chien Andalou* (1928).
Copyright 2003 Artists Rights Society (ARS)/New York.

Fantasy

Fantasy and flights of fancy are not limited to paintings, drawings, and the written word. In the experimental films of Robert Wiene and Salvador Dalí and Luis Buñuel, events are not confined to the material world as it is; they occupy and express the inmost images of the cinematographer. The sets for Wiene's *The Cabinet of Doctor Caligari* (Fig. 8-35) were created by three painters who employed Expressionist devices such as angular, distorted planes and sheer perspectives. The hallucinatory backdrop removes the protagonist, a carnival hypnotist who causes a sleepwalker to murder people who displease him, from the realm of reality. The muddy line between the authentic and the fantastic is further obscured by the film's ending, in which the hypnotist becomes a mental patient telling an imaginary tale. (It is akin to the ravings of the mad Salieri, who, through flashbacks, recounts his actual and fantasized interactions with Mozart in the film *Amadeus*.)

Caligari has a story, albeit an unusual one, but Dalí and Buñuel's surrealistic *Un Chien Andalou* (Fig. 8-36)

has a script (if you can call it a script) without order or meaning in the traditional sense. In the shocking opening scene, normal vision is annulled by the slicing of an eyeball. The audience is then propelled through a series of disconnected, dreamlike scenes.

Symbolism

In writing about *Un Chien Andalou,* Buñuel claimed that his aims were to evoke instinctive reactions of attraction and repulsion in the audience, but that nothing in the film *symbolized* anything.[3] Fantastic cinematographers often portray their depths of mind literally. They create on the screen the images that dwell deep within. Other cinematographers, such as Ingmar Bergman, do frequently express aspects of the inner world through symbols.

---

[3] Luis Buñuel, "Notes on the Making of *Un Chien Andalou*," in *Art in Cinema,* a symposium held at the San Francisco Museum of Art (repr., New York: Arno Press, 1968).

8-37 INGMAR BERGMAN. Film still from *The Seventh Seal* (1956).

Copyright Ann Ronan Picture Library, Oxfordshire, UK.

Since the 1950s, filmgoers have been struck by Bergman's mostly black-and-white films (Fig. 8-37). As in so much other art, nature serves as counterpoint to the vicissitudes of the human spirit in Bergman's films. The Swedish summers are short and precious. The bleak winters seem, to Bergman, to be the enduring fact of life. Against their backdrop, he portrays modern alienation from comforting religion and tradition. Bergman's films have ranged from jocular comedies to unrelieved dark dramas, and his bewitching screen images have brought together Nordic mythology and themes of love, death, and ultimate aloneness.

VIDEO

Video is used in television and in experimental video and mixed-media works that incorporate video monitors. The techniques of cinematography—methods of editing and so on—also apply to video.

Over a period of about 60 years, television has radically altered American life and placed the American lifestyle before the world. Commercial television broadcasts many of the images that reflect and create our common contemporary culture—from the pop world of Britney to the underworld of *The Sopranos.* Children spend as many hours in front of a TV set as they do in school. Congressional committees debate the impact of televised violence. For many people, television is an indispensable companion.

"Live" coverage enabled hundreds of millions of TV viewers to witness Neil Armstrong's first steps on the Moon. Many millions watched in horror the "live" assassination of John F. Kennedy and the explosion of the *Challenger* space shuttle. Viewers who came to be called "gulf potatoes" seemed to be addicted to the televising of the Gulf War, the nation's first real video war—which began with CNN's "live" description of fighter-bombers over Baghdad in 1991. In 2001 viewers watched the destruction of the World Trade Center "live"—whether from the suburbs of New York or from Chicago or Los Angeles. We were a single community connected by wireless broadcasting and by cable.

The sights and sounds that are recorded by the television camera are transformed into electronic messages in the form of lengthy digital codes (a pattern of ones and zeroes). The digital information is transmitted wirelessly or by cable.

8-38 NAM JUNE PAIK.
Global Groove (1973).
Videotape still.
Courtesy Electronic Arts Intermix (EAI), New York.

The television set then reconstructs the digital information into visual images and sounds.

Commercial television is most often used to transmit news, sporting events, staged events, and films to viewers. Korean-born Nam June Paik and other fine artists, however, have appropriated video as their medium in the creation of works of art—video art. Video art is to be distinguished from the commercial efforts of the television establishment.

Paik's *Global Groove* (Fig. 8-38) flashes fragmented segments of Japanese Pepsi commercials, Korean drummers, a videotaped theater group, poet Allen Ginsberg reading from his work, women tap dancers, and a musical piece in which a cellist draws her bow across a man's back. The stream of consciousness is somewhat surrealistic, but the imagery provides a reasonably recognizable pastiche of television worldwide.

In *Three Mountains* (Fig. 8-39), Japanese artist Shigeko Kubota incorporates video into a pyramidal sculptural piece, a combination intended to re-create the experience of the open western landscape. Video monitors are installed in a plywood base—the cutouts lined with mirrors. The mixed-media work confronts the viewer with multiple images of

the Grand Canyon, as seen from a helicopter; a drive along Echo Cliff, Arizona; a Taos, New Mexico, sunset; and a Teton sunset. Kubota commented:

> My mountains exist in fractured and extended time and space. My vanishing point is reversed, located behind your brain. Then, distorted by mirrors and angles, it vanishes in many points at once. Lines of perspective stretch on and on, crossing at steep angles, sharp, like cold thin mountain air.[4]

---

[4] Shigeko Kubota, *Video Sculptures* (Berlin: Daadgalerie; Essen: Museum Folkwang; Zurich: Kunsthaus, 1982), 37.

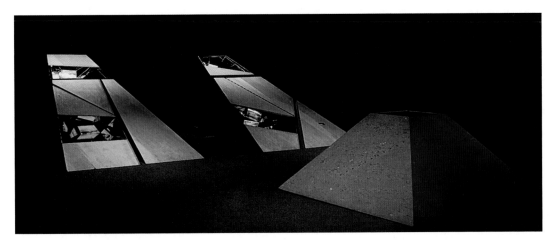

8-39 SHIGEKO KUBOTA.
Three Mountains (1976–1979).
Four-channel video installation with 3 mountains, constructed of plywood and plastic mirrors, containing 7 monitors; Mountain I: 38″ × 17″ at top and 59″ × 59″ at base;
Mountains II and III: 67″ × 21″ at top and 100″ × 60″ at base; 4 color videotapes, each 30 minutes.
Collection of the artist. Courtesy Electronic Arts Intermix, New York.

8-40   DARA BIRNBAUM.
PM Magazine (1982).
Installation at San Francisco Museum of Modern Art,
May 9–September 16, 1997; five-channel color video
and sound installation. Installation panel 6′ × 8′.

San Francisco Museum of Modern Art. Purchased through a gift of Rena
Bransten and the Accessions Committee Fund. Gift of Collectors Forum,
Doris and Donald G. Fisher, Evelyn and Walter Haas Jr., Byron R. Meyer,
and Norah and Norman Stone.

8-41   BILL VIOLA.
The Crossing (1996).
Two-channel color video and stereo-sound installation,
continuous loop. 192″ × 330″ × 684″ (487.7 cm ×
838.2 cm × 1,737.4 cm).

Solomon R. Guggenheim Museum, New York. Gift, The Bohen Foundation (2000.2000.61). Photograph by Sally Ritts. © The Solomon R.
Guggenheim Foundation, New York.

Dara Birnbaum's provocative videotapes and multimedia installations contribute to the contemporary discourse on art, television, and feminism. Her works appropriate and subvert the power of mass-media images to
comment on the myths and stereotypes of our culture. Her
installation *PM Magazine* (Fig. 8-40) appropriated and
modified footage from the former network magazine–
format show to reveal how news and entertainment formats
can exploit women. (How many older, unglamorous female
TV news anchors and reporters do we see? How many "important" stories involve bizarre incidents of sex and violence?)

Bill Viola's *The Crossing* (Fig. 8-41) is a video/sound
installation that engulfs the senses and attempts to transport
the viewer into a spiritual realm. In this piece the artist
simultaneously projects two video channels on separate
16-foot-high screens or on the back and front of the same

screen. In each video a man enveloped in darkness appears
and approaches until he fills the screen. On one channel, a
fire breaks out at his feet and grows until the man is apparently consumed in flames (the content is not what we would
call graphic or disturbing, however). On the other channel,
the one shown here, drops of water fall onto the man's head,
develop into rivulets, and then inundate him. The sound
tracks accompany the screenings with audio images of tor-
rential rain and of a raging inferno. The dual videos wash
over the viewer with their contrasts of cool and hot colors
and their encompassing sound. Critics speak about the
spiritual nature of Viola's work, but it is also about the here-
and-now reality of the sensory experiences created by his
art form.

In *Getaway #2* (Fig. 8-42), Tony Oursler projects a
videotape with a sound track onto the cloth face of a life-
size doll "hiding" adolescent-like beneath a mattress. A
critic described his experiences as he and a companion observed another couple viewing the work in Williamstown,
Massachusetts:

Tony Oursler is super-clever. He knows that we unreflectively absorb television images and voices, making their public content part of our private lives, so he literally makes television part of us— our heads—and uses it to project our inner lives back into the outer world.

—Donald Kuspit

8-42   TONY OURSLER.
Getaway #2 (1994).
Mattress, cloth, LCD projector, VCR, videotape.
16″ × 117½″ × 86″ overall.
Whitney Museum of American Art, New York.
Purchased with funds from the Contemporary Painting
and Sculpture Committee.

We followed a couple into the gallery, and I saw one of them later taking great pains to get down on the ground to better see a piece consisting of a life-size doll whose head is underneath a mattress. The doll's projected face is yelling, "Hey, you! Get outta here!," plus various obscenities and epithets; and the aforementioned viewer, upon a heroic struggle to get up again after that better look, exclaimed, "Whew! I almost became part of that piece!"[5]

I can empathize. I usually have to drag my youngest child through exhibitions, but when *Getaway #2* was "doing its thing" (that is, arguing with her and insulting her) at the Whitney a couple of years back, she was spellbound and would not leave the gallery in which the piece was installed and uttering its R-rated phrases. It took weeks before we stopped hearing her parrotlike renditions of the doll's naughty verbal bits. The message of many of Oursler's video works seems to be that people are unusually receptive to video images. They absorb them and then spout them. Television creates some of the most salient of the images we share in our culture—both video and audio—and as with

[5] Devon Damonte, "Vital Video in Williamstown: Personal Reflections on Some New Museum Exhibits in Western Mass," September 1999. http:// www.newenglandfilm.com/news/archives/99september/museum.htm.

The role of the artist has to be different from what it was fifty or even twenty years ago. I am continually amazed at the number of artists who continue to work as if the camera were never invented, as if Andy Warhol never existed, as if airplanes, and computers, and videotape were never heard of.

—Keith Haring

any effort to define or describe the individual, we must wonder where the person's "individuality" leaves off and cultural influences begin. Perhaps they become so enmeshed that it is impossible to define the borders. Oursler seems to be saying that the border is porous.

DIGITAL ART

As we enter the new millennium in the arts, most readers undoubtedly have toyed with computer programs like Microsoft's *Paint* or *Paintbrush*. Software such as this, typically part of the computer manufacturer's standard package, enables the user—artistic or otherwise—to create illustrations by manipulating stock shapes, drawing "freehand," "spray painting" color fields, or enhancing the images with a variety of textural patterns—all of which are selected by directing the mouse to a menu of techniques and design elements. The resultant shapes or drawings can be flipped and rotated or stretched in any direction. Even word-processing programs such as Word and WordPerfect can be used to distort and otherwise play with images. The user-artist needn't have the talent to draw a straight line, simply the ability to point and click. For most of us, the results are literally "child's play," but career artists who have sealed their reputations in other media have also been tempted by the computer as an artistic tool. Keith Haring, the infamous subway graffittist-turned-mainstream-artist, created *Untitled* (Fig. 8-43) on the Images paint system of the New York Institute of Technology. Haring's paintings are characterized by animated, mostly featureless figures bounded by thick, signature outlines, and his computer-generated image bears a close resemblance to his other work. Drawing on a computer screen must have seemed a natural segue for Haring. Haring is an experimenter by nature, an artist who challenged and pushed the limits, so his exploration of the possibilities of the computer as tool is not surprising. Yet when Haring created *Untitled* in 1983, he probably could only have imagined the directions that computer art would take in the coming decades.

Only within the last century have the horizons of artists been expanded by technological advances encompassing anything and everything from the development of quick-drying acrylic paints to the advent of film and video. The computer has greatly expanded what can be achieved in these media and others. Today computer graphics software programs offer palettes of more than 16 million colors, which can be selected and produced on the monitor almost instantaneously. Compositions can be recolored in seconds. Effects of light and shade and simulated textured surfaces

8-43   KEITH HARING.
Untitled (1983).
35 mm slide of work created on the New York Institute of Technology's Images paint system.
Courtesy of the New York Institute of Technology.

8-44   ROBERT LAZZARINI.
Study for *Payphone* (2001).
Mixed media. 108″ × 84″ × 48″.
Collection of the artist. Courtesy Pierogi, Brooklyn, NY.

8-45   YAEL KARANEK.
Digital landscape in the sunset/sunrise desert terrain of
World of Awe (2000).
Courtesy of the artist.

can be produced with the point and click of a mouse. Software programs enable artists to create three-dimensional representations with such astounding realism that they cannot be distinguished from photos or films of real objects in space. They can be viewed from any vantage point and in any perspective. Images can be saved or stored in any stage of their development, be brought back into the computer's memory at will, and modified as desired, without touching the original image. It is difficult to believe that these images are stored in computers as series of zeroes and ones, and not as pictures, but they are.

The herd of galloping dinosaurs in *Jurassic Park* was made possible by computer animation. Computer graphics is used to create environments as in video games (for example, the "tombs" raided by Lara Croft) or the virtual-reality world of the 1999 film *Matrix*.

Figure 8-43 is an example of *digital art*. Broadly speaking, digital art is the production of images by artists with the assistance of the computer. Just as artists have adapted the technical possibilities of photography, film, and video, so too have they appropriated the computer.

Digital artists can distort the commonplace according to meticulous mathematical formulas. Robert Lazzarini uses the computer to alter everyday objects, like the pay phones we find along the streets of cities (Fig. 8-44), and then he builds sculptures based on the modified images. The sculptures are fabricated from the materials used in the actual objects. The viewer might try to get a visual handle on such works by viewing them from the "proper" angle, but no vantage point will "straighten out" these objects. The viewer is compelled to take a new look at the familiar, a goal of art for millennia.

Yael Karanek's digital landscape in *World of Awe* (Fig. 8-45) is a screenshot of an interactive digital "journal" that was purportedly found on a laptop computer in Silicon Canyon. The "traveler" who enters this virtual world will find love letters, travel logs, and a variety of navigation tools that can be used to find a "treasure." The work builds on the notion of "interfaces" (to use a nice digital term) between travel, storytelling, creation, and technology.

Visual artists as well as commercial filmmakers use digital techniques to modify and embellish ordinary imagery. In

Video and interactive systems became a means of following the trail of personal history. That gave me the clue to my real place in the cultural context.

—Lynn Hershman

the storyboard from *Winchester* (Fig. 8-46), Jeremy Blake combines film, drawings, and computer-generated imagery to narrate what he imagines to be the psychological state of Sarah Winchester, the widow of the founder of the Winchester rifle company, who believed that she was being pursued by the ghosts of people who had been killed with her husband's rifles. Over a span of 38 years, she added numerous rooms to her San Jose home, shown here in a spongy space–time continuum, to house friendly apparitions and ward off hostile spirits with noisy construction. The unreality of the resultant DVD reflects the unreality of this peculiar home environment.

Artists not only appropriate the technology of the day but they also appropriate images that have special meaning within a culture. Lynn Hershman's *Digital Venus* (Fig. 8-47) starts with Titian's well-known Renaissance painting *Venus of Urbino* (see Fig. 15-28) and substitutes digital imagery for the sumptuous glazes that defined the body. Many of Hershman's works comment on the voyeurism we find in the video medium, and *Digital Venus* is a way of showing how frequently the images that affect us are composed of pixels—microscopically small bits of digital information that fool our senses into believing we are somehow connecting with a corporeal reality. And like the work of Dara Birnbaum, it addresses feminist issues pertaining to the male gaze and the exploitation of women.

Artists are now only scratching the surface of digital art as a medium. Art courses in digital arts and interactive multimedia have never been more in demand. Just as photography was once termed a "democratizer" in the visual arts—enabling anyone with a camera to capture anything—so has the ubiquitousness of the digital camera and computer opened the door to limitless experimentation among artists and "outsiders" alike (Fig. 8-48).

8-46   JEREMY BLAKE.
Winchester (2002).
Sequence from DVD with sound for plasma or projection, 18-minute continuous loop.
Courtesy Feigen Contemporary, New York.

8-47 LYNN HERSHMAN.
Digital Venus (1996).
Iris print. 102 cm × 152 cm.
Courtesy of the artist. Hotwire Productions.

8-48 LOIS FICHNER-RATHUS.
Hudson River Landscape (2004).
Digital print.
Courtesy of the author.

9

SCULPTURE

A sculptor is a person obsessed with the form and shape of things, and it's not just the shape of one thing, but the shape of anything and everything: the hard, tense strength, although delicate form of a bone; the strong, solid fleshiness of a beech tree trunk.

—Henry Moore

What is a stone? To a farmer it is an obstacle to be dug and carted from the field. To a Roman warrior it was a powerful missile. To an architect it is a block, among many, to be assembled into a home or a bridge. But to a sculptor it is the repository of inner forms yearning for release. What is a steel girder? To an architect it is part of the skeleton of a skyscraper. To a sculptor it is the backbone of a fantastic animal or machine that never was, except in the imagination.

Stone, metal, wood, clay, plastics, light, and earth—these are some of the materials and elements that we have carved, modeled, assembled, and toyed with to create images of ourselves and to express our inmost fears and fantasies. Each of them affords the artist certain opportunities and limitations for self-expression. In this chapter we will see how they have been used in sculpture to grant three-dimensional reality to ideas. In the next chapter we will see how architects have used them to create aesthetic structures that protect us from the elements and provide settings for communal and intimate activities.

According to Greek myth, Pygmalion, the king of Cyprus, fell in love with the idealized statue of a woman. Aphrodite, goddess of love, heard his prayers and brought the statue to life. In one version of the myth, the statue becomes the goddess herself. In still another, Pygmalion was the sculptor who created the statue. In this myth we find the elements of the human longing for perfection. We glimpse the emotionality that sculptors can pour into their works.

SCULPTURE

Sculpture is the art of carving, casting, modeling, or assembling materials into three-dimensional figures or forms. Within this broad definition, architecture could be seen as a type of sculpture. But architecture serves the utilitarian purpose of providing housing and other structures for work and play, whereas sculptures need serve no practical purpose at all.

It could be argued that sculpture is more capable of grasping the senses than are the two-dimensional art forms of drawing, painting, and printmaking. We view two-dimensional works from vantage points to the front of the support. We might move closer or farther away, or squat or stand on tiptoe to gain new perspective, but the work itself, even if thickly laden with impasto, is essentially flat. **Relief sculptures** are similar to two-dimensional works in that their three-dimensional forms are raised from a flat background. In low relief, or **bas-relief,** especially, the forms project only slightly from the background; in **high relief,** figures project by at least half their natural depth.

But **freestanding sculptures** have fronts, sides, backs, and tops. They invite the viewer to walk around them. Sometimes viewers may climb on them, walk through them, or, as in the case of a Calder mobile, look up at them from beneath. As we move about a sculpture, we are impressed by new revelations. The spaces or voids in and around the work may take on as much meaning as the sculpted forms themselves.

Two-dimensional art forms are not meant to be touched, but much of the pleasure of appreciating a sculpture derives from imagining what it would be like to run one's hands over sensuous curving surfaces of cool marble or hand-rubbed walnut. In many cases we may be prevented by ropes and guards—or by self-control—from touching sculptures, but many are made purposefully to be caressed. Some fool the eye, such as the "leather" jacket modeled from clay (see Fig. 11-2).

Recently developed forms of sculpture may interact with the viewer in other ways. The viewer may become involved in watching a kinetic sculpture run full cycle, or in trying to decipher just what the cycle is. Some kinetic sculptures and light sculptures may also literally be turned on and off, sometimes by the viewer.

Sculpture is a highly familiar medium. For thousands of years we have used sculpture to portray our visions of the gods, saints, and devils. Religious people in earlier times and some even now believe that their gods actually dwell within the stone they chisel or the wood they carve. We have carved and modeled the animals and plants of field and forest. We have exalted our heroes and leaders and commemorated our achievements and catastrophes in stone and other materials. The size of a sculpture has often been commensurate with the power ascribed to the hero or with the magnitude of the event. In addition to serving community and religious functions, sculptures are decorative. They adorn public buildings and parks. They sit on pedestals in walkways and stand in fountains, impervious to the spray, or perhaps contributing to the pool from the mouth or nether parts. Sculptures, of course, also serve as vehicles to express an artist's ideas and feelings.

In our discussion of sculpture, we will first distinguish between subtractive and additive sculpture and describe the techniques of each. Then we will examine the characteristics of a number of works that have been rendered in the traditional materials such as stone, wood, clay, and metal. Finally, we will explore several modern materials and methods, ranging from new metals and found objects to kinetic sculpture, light sculpture, and earthworks.

SUBTRACTIVE AND ADDITIVE TYPES OF SCULPTURE

Sculptural processes are either subtractive or additive. In a **subtractive process,** such as carving, unwanted material is removed. In the **additive processes** of modeling, casting, and constructing, material is added, assembled, or built up to reach its final form.

Carving

In **carving,** the sculptor begins with a block of material and cuts portions of it away until the desired form is created. Carving could be considered the most demanding type of sculpture because the sculptor, like the fresco painter, must have a clear conception of the final product at the outset. The material chosen—stone, wood, ivory—strongly influences the mechanics of the carving process and determines the type of creation that will emerge.

*No painter ought to think less of sculpture than of painting
and no sculptor less of painting than of sculpture.*

—Michelangelo

9-1   MICHELANGELO.
*The Cross-Legged
Captive*
(c. 1530–1534).
Marble. H: 7'6½".
Galleria dell'Accademia,
Florence. Copyright
Scala/Art Resource,
New York.

Modeling

In **modeling,** a pliable material such as clay or wax is shaped
into a three-dimensional form. The artist may manipulate
the material by hand and use a variety of tools. Unlike carving, in which the artist must begin with a clear concept of
the result, in modeling the artist may work and rework the
material until pleasing forms begin to emerge.

Casting

The transition from modeling to casting can be easily seen
in Louise Bourgeois's *Portrait of Robert* (Fig. 9-2). Here the
artist has expressionistically modeled a pliable material and

9-2   LOUISE BOURGEOIS.
Portrait of Robert (1969).
Cast bronze with white patina. 13" × 12½" × 10".
Courtesy Cheim & Read, New York. Copyright Louise Bourgeois. Licensed
by VAGA, New York.

Michelangelo believed that the sculptor liberated forms
that already existed within blocks of stone. *The Cross-Legged
Captive* (Fig. 9-1) is one of a series of unfinished Michelangelo statues in which the figures remain partly embedded in
marble. In its unfinished state, the tension and twisting in
the torso almost cause us to experience the struggle of the
slave to free himself fully from the marble and, symbolically,
from his masters. Despite the massiveness of the musculature, the roughness of the finish imparts a curious softness
and humanity to the figure, which further increase our empathy. When we view this sculpture, it's as if we await the
emergence of perfection from the imperfect—from the
coarse and irregular block of stone. It is Michelangelo's genius that allows the figure to transcend its humble origins.

converted the work to the more permanent bronze medium through a casting process. The white patina she has applied to finish the sculpture curiously subverts the material's typical sheen and grants the work a claylike appearance—the very material with which the artist started.

In the **casting** process, a liquid material is poured into a **mold.** The liquid hardens into the shape of the mold and is then removed. In casting, an original model, made of a material such as wax, clay, or even Styrofoam, can be translated into a more durable material such as bronze. The mold is like a photographic negative, but one of form and not of color; the interior surfaces of the mold carry the reversed impressions of the model's exterior.

Any material that hardens can be used for casting. Bronze has been used most frequently because of its appealing surface and color characteristics, but concrete, plaster, liquid plastics, clay diluted with water, and other materials are also appropriate. Once the mold has been made, the casting may be duplicated a number of times.

The Lost-Wax Technique

Bronze casting is usually accomplished by means of the **lost-wax technique** (Fig. 9-3), which has changed little over the centuries. In this technique, an original model is usually sculpted from clay, and a mold of it is made, usually from sectioned plaster or flexible gelatin. Molten wax is then brushed or poured into the mold to make a hollow wax model. If the wax has been brushed onto the inner surface of the mold, it will form a hollow shell. If the wax is to be poured, a solid core can first be placed into the mold and the liquid wax poured around the core. After the wax hardens, the mold is removed, and the wax model stands as a

hollow replica of the clay. The hollow wax model is placed upside down in a container, and wax rods called **gates** are connected to it. Then a sandy mixture of silica, clay, and plaster is poured into and around the wax model, filling the shell and the container. The mixture hardens into a fire-resistant mold, or **investiture.** Thus, the process uses two models and two molds: models of clay and wax, and molds of plaster or gelatin and of the silica mixture.

The silica mold, or investiture, is turned over and placed in a **kiln.** As the investiture becomes heated, the wax turns molten once more and runs out. Hence the term *lost-wax technique.* The investiture is turned over again while it is still hot, and molten bronze is poured in. As the metal flows into the mold, air escapes through the gates so that no air pockets are left within. The bronze is given time to harden. Then the investiture and core are removed, leaving the bronze sculpture with strange projections where the molten metal had flowed up through the gates as it filled the mold. The projections are removed, and the surface of the bronze is **burnished** or treated chemically to take on the texture and color desired by the sculptor, as we shall see in the following bronze sculptures.

A statue by the French Impressionist Edgar Degas has an interesting history and metamorphosis from wax to bronze. As Degas grew blind, he turned to sculpture so that he could work out anatomical problems through the sense of touch. With one exception, his wax or clay experiments were left crumbling in his studio or discarded, although the intact figures were cast as a limited edition of bronze sculptures after his death. The exception was *The Little Dancer* (Fig. 9-4), which he showed as a wax model at the 1881 Impressionist exhibition and later cast in bronze. This diminutive painted wax figure startled the public and critics alike with its innovative sculptural realism: It sported real hair,

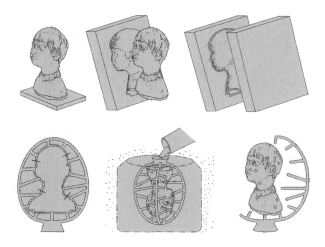

9-3 The lost-wax technique.

9-4 EDGAR DEGAS.
The Little Dancer, 14 Years Old
(1880–1881).
Bronze. H: 39″.
Copyright Sterling and Francine Clark Art Institute, Williamstown, MA.

Plaster is an incredible recorder of what is there, more effective to me than the movie camera.

—George Segal

9-5 SHERRIE LEVINE.
Fountains after Duchamp (1991).
Bronze. Installation view at Sherrie Levine Exhibition
in the Zürich Kunsthalle (2.11.1991–3.1.1992),
Zürich, Switzerland.
Courtesy of the Jablonka Gallery, Köln, Germany.

a satin hair ribbon, a canvas bodice, and a tulle skirt. The
styles of hair and clothing make the 14-year-old ballerina
very much a product of her time and place.

Sherrie Levine's *Fountains after Duchamp* (Fig. 9-5)
consists of a series of bronze urinals, turned on their backs
and displayed on pedestals as if to invite serious study
and contemplation. The urinals pay homage to Marcel

Duchamp's Dada masterpiece, *Fountain* (see Fig. 1-32), and
in so doing, they represent what lies at the heart of Levine's
artistic concept and strategy: the critical appropriation of
objects and images that already exist in the visual lexicon of
high art and mass culture. If Duchamp invested his readymades with a new *idea*—the reconsideration of ordinary objects in the artist's self-defined and self-imposed context of
fine art—Levine's objects and reproductions are invested
with a reconsideration of issues such as authorship and originality in relation to art making. Many contemporary artists
come upon the art scene at a time when it seems that perhaps everything that can be done has been done. Some push
to develop new styles, new subjects, new ways of conceptual-
izing and defining art. Sherrie Levine, the foremost representative of "appropriation art," embraces what she believes
to be the reality of working during a time when the major
accomplishments in modernism have already been recorded
as history. Her point of departure seems to be "There is
nothing new under the sun. Now where does that take me?"

Casting of Human Models

Three Figures and Four Benches (Fig. 9-6) by George Segal
features intriguing variation on the casting process. Segal
produced ghostlike replicas of human beings by means of

9-6 GEORGE SEGAL.
Three Figures and Four Benches (1979).
Painted bronze. 52″ × 144″ × 58″.
Theo Anderson, Allentown, PA.

plaster casts. Live models were covered in plaster-soaked cloth, which was molded and kneaded by the artist's hands. When the plaster was dry, the cast was removed in sections and then reassembled into whole figures. *Three Figures and Four Benches* was then cast in bronze, but the white surface of the original plaster cast was retained. Segal's figures are literally and figuratively shells. In unimaginable aloneness, his apparitions occupy an urban landscape of buses, gas stations, diners, and other settings. The amorphousness of the surface textures is not unlike that of the Nakian sculpture, placing the figures further into what seems a kind of limbo of contemporary life. Although the figures are connected by virtue of their common medium, they do not seem to speak to one another or interact in any way. They are at once connected and disconnected, sharing a place and time and yet lost in their inner worlds.

Construction

In construction, or **constructed sculpture,** forms are built from materials such as wood, paper and string, sheet metal, and wire. As we shall see in works by Picasso, Louise Nevelson, and other artists, traditional carving, modeling, and casting are abandoned in favor of techniques such as pasting and welding.

TYPES OF MATERIALS

Sculptors have probably employed every known material in their works. Different materials tend to be worked in different ways, and they can also create very different effects. In this section we will explore the varieties of ways in which sculptors have worked with the traditional materials of stone, wood, clay, and metal. In the section on modern and contemporary materials and methods, we shall see how sculptors have worked with nontraditional materials, such as plastic and light.

Stone

Stone is an extremely hard, durable material that may be carved, scraped, drilled, and polished. The durability that makes stone so appropriate for monuments and statues that are meant to communicate with future generations also makes working with stone a tedious process. The granite

used by ancient Egyptians was extremely resistant to detailed carving, which is one reason that Egyptian stone figures were simplified and resemble the shape of the quarried blocks. The Greeks used their abundant white marble to embody the idealized human form in action and in repose. However, they painted their marble statues, suggesting that they valued the material more for its durability than for its color or texture.

The hand tools used with stone—such as the chisel, mallet, and **rasp**—have not changed much over the centuries. But contemporary sculptors do not find working with stone to be quite so laborious because they can use power tools for chipping away large areas of unwanted material and for polishing the finished piece.

The Stone Age *Venus of Willendorf* (see Fig. 12-2) has endured for perhaps 25,000 years. The same stone that lent such durability to this rotund fertility figure apparently pressed the technological limits of the sculptor. There are clues that the artist found the stone medium arduous. As with ancient Egyptian sculpture, the shape of the figurine probably adheres closely to that of the block or large pebble from which it was carved. The rough finish further suggests the primitive nature of the artist's flint tools.

It is a leap from the stone art of the Stone Age to the sculpture of, say, Michelangelo in *The Cross-Legged Captive* (Fig. 9-1) or the *David* (see Fig. 15-26). The *Captive,* like the *Venus,* does not stray far from the shape of the block or precariously extend its limbs. But except for the eternal nature of the *David,* the statue belies the nature of the material. The furrowed brow, the taut muscles, the veins in the hand all breathe life into the work.

The *Apollo and Daphne* (see Fig. 2-69) of the Italian Baroque sculptor and architect Gianlorenzo Bernini shows us yet more of the potential of marble. Marble can also capture the softness and sensuousness of flesh and the textures of hair, leaves, and bark. Observe the hundreds of slender projections, and imagine the intricacy of cutting away the obstinate stone to reveal them. In his *David* (see Fig. 15-27), Bernini portrays the moment in which the youth is twisting in preparation to fire the sling. David bites his marble lips; the muscles and veins of the left arm reflect the tightening of the hand; even his marble toes grip the rock beneath. When we view this sculpture, perhaps our own muscles tighten in empathy.

In *Eyes* (Fig. 9-7), by Louise Bourgeois, two precisely tooled spheres are perched atop a marble cube, some of which has been chiseled to create hollows and other irregularities. The carved circular openings in the spheres suggest the penetrating pupils of eyes, a commonly used symbol among Surrealist artists (see Chapter 19). For Bourgeois, who often incorporated gender allusions in her work, the eyes may represent the female anatomy and the marble block, a house. The two strong shapes in contrast to each other may suggest a woman's relationship to her domestic role, a theme that Bourgeois revisited numerous times in her long career. Although Bourgeois's technique results in a finished work that remains close to the quarried marble block, the perfectly round "eyes," the polish of the surfaces, and the carved "interruptions" create a striking contrast between a deliberate absence and an assertive presence of the artist's hand.

Wood

Wood, like stone, may be carved, scraped, drilled, and polished. But unlike stone, wood may also be permanently molded and bent. Under heat, in fact, plywood can be bent to take on any shape. Wood, like stone, varies in hardness and grain, but it is more readily carved than stone.

Although wooden objects may last for many hundreds of years, wood does not possess the durability of stone and tends to warp and crack. But wood appeals to sculptors because of its grain, color, and workability. Wood is warm to the touch, whereas stone is cold. When polished, wood is sensuous. Wood's **tensile strength** exceeds that of stone, so

9–7 LOUISE BOURGEOIS.
Eyes (1982).
Marble. $74\frac{3}{4}'' \times 54'' \times 45\frac{3}{4}''$.
The Metropolitan Museum of Art, New York. Anonymous gift (1986.397). Licensed by VAGA, New York. Photograph copyright 1987 The Metropolitan Museum of Art. Copyright Louise Bourgeois.

The Vietnam Veterans Memorial—
A Woman's Perspective

It terrified me to have an idea that was solely mine to be no longer a part of my mind, but totally public.

—Maya Ying Lin, on her design for the Vietnam Veterans Memorial in Washington, D.C.

When we view the expanses of the Washington Mall, we are awed by the grand obelisk that is the Washington Monument. We are comforted by the stately columns and familiar shapes of the Lincoln and Jefferson memorials. But many of us do not know how to respond to the two 200-foot-long black granite walls that form a V as they recede into the ground. There is no label—only the names of 58,000 victims chiseled into the silent walls:

As we descend along the path that hugs the harsh black granite, we enter the very earth that, in another place, has accepted the bodies of our sons and daughters. Each name is carved not only in the stone, but by virtue of its highly polished surface, in our own reflection, in our physical substance. We are not observers, we are participants. We touch, we write [letters to our loved ones], we leave parts of ourselves behind. This is a woman's vision—to commune, to interact, to collaborate with the piece to fulfill its expressive potential. . . .

Maya Ying Lin has foregone the [format of the triumphal monument]. She has given us [the earth mother] Gaea, who, pierced by the ebony scar of suffering death, takes back her children, as she has done since the dawn of humanity.*

This is Maya Ying Lin's Vietnam Veterans Memorial (Fig. 9-8), completed in 1982 on a two-acre site on the Mall. In order to read the names, we must descend gradually into the earth, and then just as gradually work our way back up. This progress is perhaps symbolic of the nation's involvement in Vietnam. As did the war it commemorates, the eloquently simple design of the memorial also stirs controversy.

This dignified understatement in stone has offended many who would have preferred a more traditional memorial. One conservative magazine branded the design a conspiracy to dishonor the dead. Architecture critic Paul Gapp of *The Chicago Tribune* argued, "The so-called memorial is bizarre . . . neither a building nor sculpture." One Vietnam veteran had called for a statue of an officer offering a fallen soldier to heaven. The public expects a certain heroic quality in its monuments to commemorate those fallen in battle. Lin's work is antiheroic and antitriumphal. Whereas most war monuments speak of giving up our loved ones to a cause, her monument speaks only of giving up our loved ones.

How did the Vietnam Memorial come to be so uniquely designed? It was chosen from 1,421 entries in a national competition. The designer, Maya Ying Lin, is a Chinese American woman who was all of 22 years old at the time she submitted her entry. A native of Ohio, Lin had just graduated from Yale University, where she majored in architecture. Lin recognized that a monumental sculpture or another grand building would have been intrusive in the heart of Washington. Her design meets the competition criteria of being "neither too commanding nor too deferential" and is yet another expression of the versatility of stone. ∎

9-8 MAYA YING LIN.
Vietnam Veterans Memorial, Washington, DC (1982).
Polished black granite.
L: 492′.
Copyright Maya Ying Lin and Bluffton Educational College.

*Lois Fichner-Rathus, "A Woman's Vision of the War," *The New York Times,* August 18, 1991, H6.

projecting wooden parts are less likely than their stone counterparts to break off. In recent years, wood has also become commonly used in assemblages.

The capacity of wood to yield beautiful, rough-hewn beauty is shown in the mask called *Kagle* (Fig. 9-9), by a sculptor of the African Dan people. The Dan of Sierra Leone, the Ivory Coast, and Liberia have carved masks for use in rituals and celebrations. Some Dan masks are polished and refined; others are intentionally crude. *Kagle* is a powerful work of thrusting and receding planes. The abstracted, geometric voids are as commanding as the wooden form itself. Such a mask is believed to endow its wearer with the powers of the bush spirits and is an essential element in the garb of tribal law-enforcement officers.

British sculptor Barbara Hepworth's abstraction *Two Figures* (see Fig. 4-8) is carved from elm wood. Hepworth pierces solid masses to give contour to negative shapes. The concavities, which are painted white, and the voids in her carved figures have as much "shape-meaning"—to use Henry Moore's term—as the solids. The viewer feels the urge to identify each form as male or female, but the sculp-

9-9   Poro Secret Society mask (*Kagle*). Liberian, Dan people. Wood. H: 9″.

Yale University Art Gallery. Gift of Mr. and Mrs. James Osborn.

9-10   PO SHUN LEONG.
Figure (1993).
Mahogany with hidden drawers.
H: 50″.
Courtesy of the artist.

tural "evidence" is too scant to allow such classification. At first glance it might seem that a similar artistic effect could have been achieved by carving these figures from marble, but the wood grain imparts a warmth to the surface that would not have been attained in marble. Also, the painting of the concavities lends them a "durability" and hardness not found in the outer surface. Ironically, the voids attain more visual solidity than the outer surfaces.

There is an implied massiveness to both the *Kagle* mask and Hepworth's *Two Figures.* But wood can also be used to create figures and forms of great complexity, delicacy, and intricacy. The rich mahogany surfaces of Po Shun Leong's *Figure* (Fig. 9-10) have been polished, carved, striated, and gouged. There is a restlessness to the patterns, which, coupled with a host of hidden drawers punctuating the form—some open, some closed—creates a sense of constant motion.

One starts to get young at the age of sixty and then it is too late.

—Pablo Picasso

Clay

Clay is more pliable than stone or wood. The modeling of clay is personal and direct; the fingerprints of the sculptor may be found in the material. Children, like sculptors, enjoy the feel and smell of clay.

Unfortunately, clay has little strength, and it is not usually considered a permanent material, even though an **armature** may be used to prevent clay figures from sagging. Because of its weakness, clay is frequently used to make three-dimensional sketches, or models, for sculptures that are to be executed in more durable materials. As was noted earlier, clay models may be translated into bronze figures. In ceramics, clay is fired in a kiln at high temperatures so that it becomes hardened and nonporous. Before firing, clay can also be coated, or glazed, with substances that provide the ceramic object with a glassy monochromatic or polychromatic surface.

Metal

Metal has been used by sculptors for thousands of years. Metals have been cast, **extruded, forged, stamped,** drilled, filed, and burnished. The process of producing cast bronze sculptures has changed little over the centuries. But in recent years artists have also assembled **direct-metal sculptures** by welding, riveting, and soldering. Modern adhesives have also made it possible to glue sections of metal together into three-dimensional constructions.

Different metals have different properties. Bronze has been the most popular casting material because of its pleasing surface and color characteristics. Bronze surfaces can be made dull or glossy. Chemical treatments can produce colors ranging from greenish blacks to golden or deep browns. Because of oxidation, bronze and copper surfaces age to form rich green or greenish blue **patinas.**

The French artist Auguste Rodin is considered by many to be the greatest sculptor of the nineteenth century. Nevertheless, Rodin's *The Walking Man* and similar sculptural fragments were not well received in his day because they have an unfinished look. They were not incomplete, of course. Instead, they reflected Rodin's obsession with the correct rendition of anatomical parts.

MODERN AND CONTEMPORARY MATERIALS AND METHODS

Throughout history sculptors have searched for new forms of expression. They have been quick to experiment with the new materials and approaches that have been made possible by advancing technology. During the past century, technological changes have overleaped themselves, giving rise to new materials, such as plastics and fluorescent lights, and to new ways of working traditional materials.

In this section we will explore a number of new materials and approaches, including constructed sculpture, assemblage, readymades, mixed media, light sculpture, kinetic sculpture, and earthworks. Although the search for novelty has been exhausting, this list is by no means exhaustive.

Constructed Sculpture

In constructed sculpture the artist builds or constructs the sculpture from materials such as cardboard, celluloid, translucent plastic, sheet metal, or wire, frequently creating forms that are lighter than those made from carving stone, modeling clay, or casting metal. Picasso inspired a movement in this direction with works such as *Mandolin and Clarinet* (Fig. 9-11). As critic Robert Hughes remarked, such works were "everything that statues had not been: not monolithic, but open, not cast or carved, but assembled from flat planes."[1] In spirit and style, reliefs from this era were very close to Picasso's paintings. But the unorthodox materials—wood, sheet metal, wire, found objects—challenged all traditions in art making. Sculpture would never be the same.

A Russian visitor to Picasso's Paris studio, Vladimir Tatlin, is credited with having realized the three-dimensional potential of constructed sculpture, which was then further developed in Russia by the brothers Antoine Pevsner and

[1] Robert Hughes, "The Liberty of Thought Itself," *Time,* September 1, 1986, 87.

*I began using found objects. I had all this wood lying around
and I began to move it around, I began to compose.*

—Louise Nevelson

Naum Gabo. Naum Gabo's *Column* (see Fig. 19-17) epitomizes the ascendance of form and space over mass that is
characteristic of many constructed sculptures. Gabo's
translucent elements transform masses into planes that
frame geometric voids. "Mass" is created in the mind of the
viewer by the empty volumes.

Pop artist Claes Oldenburg's *Soft Toilet* (Fig. 9-12) is
constructed of vinyl, kapok, cloth, and Plexiglas. Our sensibilities are challenged in a lighthearted work: A familiar object that we know to be hard, cold, and unmovable is rendered soft, supple, and pliable—and certainly unusable.

Assemblage

Assemblage is a form of constructed sculpture in which preexisting, or found, objects, recognizable in form, are integrated by the sculptor into novel combinations that take on

9-11   PABLO PICASSO.
Mandolin and Clarinet (1913).
Wood construction and paint.

Musée Picasso, Paris. Copyright Giraudon/Art Resource, New York.
Copyright 2003 Estate of Pablo Picasso/Artists Rights Society (ARS),
New York.

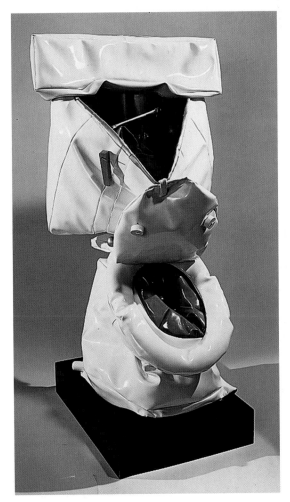

9-12   CLAES OLDENBURG.
Soft Toilet (1966).
Vinyl filled with kapok painted with Liquitex, and wood.
$57^{1}/_{16}'' \times 27^{5}/_{8}'' \times 28^{1}/_{16}''$.

Collection Whitney Museum of American Art, New York. 50th anniversary
gift of Mr. and Mrs. Victor W. Ganz.

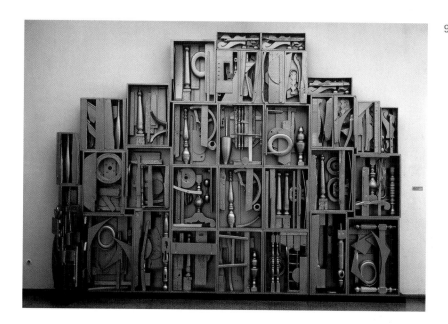

9-13 LOUISE NEVELSON.
Red Tide IV (1960).
Wood, with gold-spray technique.
323 cm × 446 cm × 55 cm.
Rheinisches Bildarchiv, Köln, Germany.
Copyright 2003 Estate of Louise Nevelson/
Artists Rights Society (ARS), New York.

a life and meaning of their own. American artist Louise Nevelson's *Red Tide IV* (Fig. 9-13), like many of her wooden sculptures, is a compartmentalized assemblage of rough-cut geometric shapes and lathed wooden objects with previous lives, such as finials. Similar assemblages include banal objects such as bowling pins, chair slats, and barrel staves and may be painted white or black, as well as gold.

Why walls? Nevelson explains:

> I attribute the walls to this: I had loads . . . and loads of creative energy. . . . So I began to stack my sculptures into an environment. . . . I think there is something in the consciousness of the creative person that adds up, and the multiple image that I give, say, in an enormous wall gives me so much satisfaction.[2]

The overall effect of Nevelson's collections is one of nostalgia and mystery. They suggest the pieces of the personal and collective past, of lonely introspective journeys among the cobwebs of Victorian attics—of childhoods that never were. Perhaps they are the very symbol of consciousness, for what is the function of intellect if not to impose order on the bits and pieces of experience?

Nature is the point of departure for Betye Saar's *Ancestral Spirit Chair* (Fig. 9-14). In a work that was influenced by Saar's African ancestry and tribal beliefs concerning ancestor worship, the artist combines remnants of nature and common objects of human existence. The chair is constructed of tree branches that have been sawed, shaped, or left in their natural state, reaching skyward like fingers on a hand. These "fingertips" are capped by a collection of glass saltshakers, and other found objects make their appearance here and there. The chair's surface is adorned with rhythmic white markings suggesting the body painting common to some African peoples. It is a curious piece, inviting, yet seeming to welcome only those who belong.

Perhaps the best-known assemblage is Picasso's *Bull's Head* (Fig. 9-15). Consisting of the seat and handlebars of an old bicycle, the work possesses a rakish vitality. It is immediately and whimsically recognizable as animal—so much so that on first impression, its mundane origins are obscured.

Readymades

The assemblages of Nevelson and Picasso are constructed from found objects. Early in the twentieth century Marcel Duchamp declared that found objects, or readymades, such as bottle racks and urinals, could be literally elevated as works of art by being placed on pedestals—literally or figuratively. No assembly required. The urinal in Figure 1-32—appropriated some 80-plus years later by Sherrie Levine for

---

[2] Louise Nevelson, *Louise Nevelson: Atmospheres and Environments* (New York: C. N. Potter in association with the Whitney Museum of American Art, 1980), 77.

9-14　BETYE SAAR.
Ancestral Spirit Chair (1992).
Painted wood, bone, glass, plastic, metal, and vine.
60″ × 46″ × 32″.
Smith College Museum of Art, Northampton, MA. Purchased 1992.

Mixed Media

In **mixed-media** constructions and assemblages, sculptors use materials and ready-made or found objects that are not normally the elements of a work of art. Contemporary painters also sometimes "mix" their media by attaching objects to their canvases. Robert Rauschenberg, discussed in Chapter 19, has attached ladders, chairs, and electric fans to his paintings and run paint over them as if they were continuations of the canvas. What do we call the result—painting or sculpture?

her *Fountains after Duchamp* (Fig. 9-5)—was turned on its back, put into a new context, and given the title *Fountain*. These adjustments were said by the artist to invest the object with a new *idea*. Duchamp argued that the dimension of taste, good or bad, was irrelevant. The function of the readymade—not that it needed one—was to prompt the spectator to think, and to think again.

Duchamp recognized that artists could take advantage of the concept of the ready-made object and substitute cleverness for solid work should the "making" of readymades become a habit. For this reason Duchamp advised that artists elevate common objects to the realm of art only a few times each year.

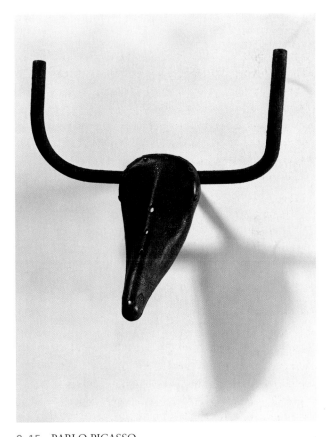

9-15　PABLO PICASSO.
Bull's Head (1943).
Bronze cast of parts of a bicycle. H: 16⅛″.
Réunion des Musées Nationaux, France. Copyright Réunion des Musées Nationaux/Art Resource, New York. Copyright 2003 Estate of Pablo Picasso/Artists Rights Society (ARS), New York.

9-16 SIMON RODIA.
Simon Rodia Towers in Watts (1921–1954).
Cement with various objects. H: 98′.

Cultural Affairs Department, Los Angeles.
Copyright Nik Wheeler/CORBIS/RM.

9-17 GEORGE RICKEY.
Cluster of Four Cubes (1992).
Stainless steel.

National Gallery of Art Sculpture Garden, Washington, DC. Gift of George Rickey and Patrons' Permanent Fund 1992. Copyright Estate of George Rickey. Licensed by VAGA, New York.

patterns of contrasting and harmonious colors. The towers took 33 years to erect and were built by Rodia's own hands. Rodia, by the way, knew nearly nothing of the world of art.

Kinetic Sculpture

Sculptors have always been concerned with the portrayal of movement, but **kinetic sculptures** actually do move. Movement may be caused by the wind, magnetic fields, jets of water, electric motors, variations in the intensity of light, or the active manipulation of the observer. During the 1930s, the American sculptor Alexander Calder was one of the early pioneers of the first form of art that made motion as basic an element as shape or color—the mobile. As in his monumental mobile in the East Wing of the National Gallery of

The sculptural environment known as the *Simon Rodia Towers in Watts* (Fig. 9-16) was constructed by an Italian-born tile setter who immigrated to Watts, a poor neighborhood in Los Angeles. Rodia's whimsical towers are built sturdily enough—of cement on steel frames, the tallest one rising nearly 100 feet. As a mixed-media assemblage, the towers are coated with debris, such as mirror fragments, broken dishes, shards of glass and ceramic tile, and shells. The result is a lacy forest of spires that glisten with magical

I just enjoy making people have to rethink what painting and sculpture are.

—Michael Hayden

We all have a need to decorate Mother Nature because it all belongs to us.

—Marco Evaristti

Art (see Fig. 2-67), carefully balanced weights are suspended on wires such that the gentlest current of air sets them moving in prescribed orbits.

George Rickey's welded, stainless steel cubes bear the mark of Calder's mobile constructions. Much of the work of both artists responds to the flow of currents of air. In

Rickey's *Cluster of Four Cubes* (Fig. 9-17), burnished steel "boxes" are attached by ball bearings to arms that branch from a trunklike post. The cubes are weighted and balanced to turn effortlessly in light breezes.

Light Sculpture

Natural light has always been an important element in defining sculpture, but only in the past century did sculptors begin to experiment with the use of artificial light in their compositions. Their concern has been with the physical and psychological effects of color and, at times, with the creation of visual illusions.

For more than three decades Michael Hayden has used light in his "Lumetric" sculptures, some of which have been hundreds of feet long and weighed many tons. *Arpeggio* (Fig. 9-18) was commissioned by the Nashville Airport Authority to illuminate the pathway that leads to the terminal. The work consists of two pairs of tapered helixes (spirals) that are illuminated with LED (light-emitting diode) sections of blue, red, green, and amber. The artist has written about his fascination with iridescence in nature—from the skin of the mahi-mahi to butterfly wings and the fine-feathered throats of hummingbirds—and his attempt to emulate or at least suggest this phenomenon in his works.

9-18 MICHAEL HAYDEN.
Arpeggio (2000).
Work (light sculpture) installed at the Metro Nashville Airport.
Copyright Michael Hayden. New York.

Land Art

Land art is site-specific work that is created or marked by an artist within natural surroundings. Sometimes large amounts of earth or land are shaped into sculptural forms, as in the **earthworks** of the 1960s and 1970s. These works could be temporary or permanent and included great trenches and drawings in the desert, collections of rocks, shoveled rings in ice and snow, and even installations of mounds of dirt on floors of the urban galleries. Robert

9-19 ROBERT SMITHSON.
Spiral Jetty, Great Salt
Lake, Utah (1970).
Black rocks, salt, earth,
water, and algae.
L: 1500′; W: 15′.

Copyright Estate of Robert
Smithson. Licensed by VAGA,
New York.

9-20 MARCO EVARISTTI.
The Ice Cube Project (2004).
Red dye and seawater,
Greenland coast.

EPA/HO/Landov.

The body is our common denominator for our pleasures and our sorrows.
I want to express through it who we are, how we live and die.

—Kiki Smith

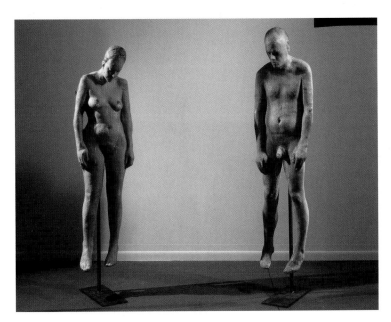

9-21 KIKI SMITH.
Untitled (1990).
Beeswax and microcrystalline wax figures on
metal stands; female figure installed height
6′1½″; male figure installed height 6′4¹⁵⁄₁₆″.
Collection Whitney Museum of American Art, New York.
Purchased with funds from the Painting and Sculpture
Committee. Photograph by Jerry L. Thompson.

A Portfolio of More Recent Sculpture

Sculpture today is where it has always been and where it has never been before. It has always been traditional and innovative; it has always been enduring and transient. It has always represented the artist's perception of what art is, or conception of what it could be, at any given time in history.

Figurative sculpture, for example, is alive and well as we cross into the third millennium. The figures in Kiki Smith's *Untitled* (Fig. 9-21) are hung up, hanging down, hanging around—perhaps being hung out to dry. There is something about them—the hang-dog faces, even the body shapes that makes them sort of "now," but they are not all there, or anywhere.

The artist's realism is, in a sense, more realistic than realism has ever been—even when compared to the "Photorealism" of artists such as Duane Hanson (see Fig. 20-29). The realism in Kiki Smith's couple is almost too painful to observe, too close to the realities of our own physical selves. Smith notes, "Most of the functions of the body are hidden . . . from society," and she thus has aimed to bring them out into the open. Smith has focused her artistic eye on body parts and body by-products; one of her installations consisted of jars filled with bodily fluids from saliva to blood, reflecting her experience as an emergency medical service technician in New York City. In their superrealistic state of age and deterioration, the individuals in Smith's untitled work have lost control over emission of bodily fluids. The woman's figure is stained with, or drained of, milk that drips from her nipples. Semen drips down the man's leg. They are suspended in space, isolated in their loss of control, sharing the frailties of the human condition.

Smithson's *Spiral Jetty* (Fig. 9-19) is composed of rocks and earth bulldozed into a spiral formation in Utah's Great Salt Lake. Over time, salt deposits and algae have accumulated on the jetty, which lay underwater for many years. With a prolonged drought, the jetty began to reemerge in 1999.

Art that "makes marks" in nature is often temporary, however. In March 2004, Danish artist Marco Evaristti set sail in two icebreakers to find the perfect "frozen canvas" among the icebergs off the coast of Greenland. For two hours, a crew of 20 sprayed 780 gallons of red dye onto an almost 10,000-square-foot iceberg (Fig. 9-20). The dye, diluted with seawater, was the same that is used for tinting meat. Evaristti's work can be found—for the time being, at least—near Ilullissat (which means "icebergs" in the Greenlandic language), a town of 4,000 that is popular among tourists for its spectacular and *artistic* scenery.

Christo and Jeanne-Claude: *The Gates, Central Park, New York City, 1979–2005*

As if intentionally timed to shake New York City out of its winter doldrums, 7,503 sensuous saffron panels were gradually released from the tops of 16-foot-tall gates along 23 miles of footpaths throughout Central Park. It was the morning of February 12, 2005—a date that marked the end of artists Christo and Jeanne-Claude's 26-year-long odyssey to bring a major project to their adopted city. For a brief 16 days, the billowy nylon fabric fluttered and snapped and obscured and enframed our favorite park perspectives (Fig. 9-22). Olmsted's and Vaux's majestic plan of ups and downs, of lazy loops and serpentine curves, was being seen or reseen for the first time as we—the participants—wove our walks according to the patterns of the gates. The artists have said that "the temporary quality of their projects is an aesthetic decision," that it "endows the works of art with a feeling of urgency to be seen." For a brief 16 days, it was clear from the crowds in a winter park, from the constant cluster of buses at the 72nd Street entrance, and from the rubbernecking traffic on the streets and avenues bordering the park that the urgency of which Christo and Jeanne-Claude speak was very real.

As with all of artists Christo and Jeanne-Claude's works of environmental art, every aspect of *The Gates* project was financed and fought for by the artists themselves. They developed the concept for *The Gates* back in 1979, but their first proposal to the city in 1981 was rejected. Mayor Michael R. Bloomberg granted permission for the 2005 version of the project on January 22, 2003. The "vital statistics" of *The Gates, Central Park, New York City, 1979–2005,* are staggering. Placed at 12- to 15-foot intervals, 7,503 vinyl gates, 16 feet high, varying in width from 5 feet 6 inches to 18 feet, covered 23 miles of footpaths (Fig. 9-23). The free-hanging, saffron-colored fabric panels dropped from the top of each rectangular vinyl gate to 7 feet

9-22   CHRISTO AND JEANNE-CLAUDE.
The Gates, Central Park, New York City (1979–2005).
Andrew Gombert/EPA/Landov.

9-23　Aerial view of *The Gates* in Central Park with Manhattan skyline.
Photograph by Andrea Mohin / The New York Times.

above the ground—just low enough for small children on their father's shoulders to sneak a touch. The project required more than 1 million square feet of vinyl and 5,300 tons of steel. Hundreds of paid volunteers assembled, installed, maintained, and removed the work, and most of the materials were to be recycled. The estimated cost of the project—borne by the artists alone—was $20 million.

The artists finance their environmental sculptures, which have included *Wrapped Reichstag, Berlin, 1971–95; Surrounded Islands, Biscayne Bay, Greater Miami, Florida, 1980–83; Running Fence, Sonoma and Marin Counties, California, 1972–76;* and others, by selling preparatory drawings and early works by Christo. Much of the funds thus accumulated have been used to cover the cost of the materials used in the project, to pay workers, and, when necessary, for legal fees to combat suits brought by concerned environmentalists (as was the case with the *Running Fence* project).

The environmental art projects of artists Christo and Jeanne-Claude have been seen by millions, who have been enticed to experience their familiar surroundings with a heightened sensibility. Like the artists, I, too, live in New York City. I walked *The Gates* many times over 16 days, with each group of family members and friends who made the pilgrimage. As I read the artists' response to the question, Why was it so important to realize this work in Central Park? ("When our son was a little boy, we used to take him to Central Park every day—he loved to climb the beautiful rocks. Central Park was a part of our life."), I thought of my own daughter, whose school holds gym class on the park's Great Lawn. The Central Park that she will remember as a part of her life growing up in New York will forever include the 16 days when, in clear and in cold and a glorious snowfall, a "golden river" snaked through a barren winter scene, lighting the landscape with flashes of color. ∎

I decided to open up the continuum of space. I wanted to remove the work from the limitations of the object, or the definition of the specific object.

—Richard Serra

9-24 JANINE ANTONI.
Chocolate Gnaw (1992).
Chocolate (600 lb before biting), gnawed by the artist.
24″ × 24″ × 24″ (61 cm × 61 cm × 61 cm).
Collection of the Museum of Modern Art, New York. Photo by Brian Forest. Courtesy of the artist and Luhring Augustine, New York.

9-25 SYLVIE FLEURY.
Dog Toy 3 (Crazy Bird) (2000).
Styrofoam, paint. 260 cm × 210 cm × 180 cm.
Courtesy of Mehdi Chouaki.

Janine Antoni's *Chocolate Gnaw* (Fig. 9-24) may be overall reminiscent of a minimalist cube by an artist such as Donald Judd or Tony Smith, but it holds some sensory surprises: Antoni's medium is chocolate, and her sculptural tools consist of what nature has endowed her with—a good set of teeth. The artist's gesture, signature, the art-making process itself, even the "gnawing" question "Is it art?"—so long a part of the critical evaluation of works of art—take on new meaning. Add to that the issue of whether the work is in good taste.

Sylvie Fleury's *Dog Toy 3 (Crazy Bird)* (Fig. 9-25), like Antoni's *Chocolate Gnaw,* seems part and parcel of the "why not" school of contemporary art media. Permanence is clearly not a goal. Chocolate will melt in your mouth or, with a bit of heat, into a nondescript and gooey pool. Neither does Styrofoam endure like the marble of "eternal" works; it can be dented with the point of a pencil, violated with the pressure of a thumb, bitten into to form a perfect impression. Fleury takes a familiar, nonthreatening, squeaky toy animal and raises it to the same nightmarish proportions that turned the smiling marshmallow man in the film *Ghostbusters* into a menacing monster crushing everything in his wake. Fleury invaded the art world in the 1990s with her series of *Shopping Bags*—installations of designer-labeled bags that appeared to have been left by visitors on the floors of galleries after a day of binge buying in upscale clothing stores. In the tradition of the "bad boy–bad girl" artist, Fleury elevated consumer readymades to art objects as Andy Warhol had done some 30 years earlier.

Nothing could be further removed from Sylvie Fleury's whimsical but clearly identifiable *Dog Toy 3 (Crazy Bird)* than Richard Serra's extraordinary permanent installation of eight bent-steel sculptures (Fig. 9-26) at the Guggenheim Museum in Bilbao, Spain (see Fig. 2-21). Like Christo and Jeanne-Claude's environmental art, Serra's work is intended to be walked into, around, and through—intended to be experienced rather than viewed. The sheets of steel might enclose the visitor in a protected, almost private space or lead that same visitor, by way of an undulating path, to a more public, socially interactive space. Serra seems to have met his professed goal of "opening up the continuum of space." The mass is solid and the texture is tough, but the concept seems to reflect a nonmaterial realm—a gateway to something other within the real worlds we traverse every day. Unlike the transient "stuff" of Styrofoam—good for packing objects in cartons, useful for holding a cup of coffee—Serra's massive steel pieces convey an instant sense of eternity.

For decades, Richard Serra has been listening to the nature of one of his favorite materials—steel—and using it to create minimalist (in form, certainly not in scale) sculptural objects that express its powerful physical qualities. Like most of the Bilbao installation, many of his works have been monumental in size and site specific. But unlike infamous early pieces such as his *Tilted Art,* which was designed specifically for Foley Square in New York City and was removed shortly after installation because it hampered the progress of pedestrians, the Bilbao works represent an aesthetic whose time has come. Serra's steel surfaces grow more richly textured as time and oxidation work their effects upon them, serving as an apt metaphor for the effect on the visitor's memory that the experience of the installation might have.

In the next chapter we will turn our attention to the shaping of materials into structures that house our work, our play, our family life, our worship, and our sleep—architecture.

9-26 RICHARD SERRA.
Installation view, Guggenheim Museum, Bilbao, Spain.
Photograph by Vincent West/Reuters/Landov.

ART TOUR

New York

W hen we look at New York and the arts, the Big Apple is the big show. For the performing arts—theater and music and dance—there's nothing like Broadway and Lincoln Center.

In terms of the visual arts, New York is renowned, and rightly so, for its museums and architecture, and for its public art, including Central Park and statues popping up everywhere. The Metropolitan Museum of Art houses one of the greatest and broadest collections in the world, including Egyptian, Greek and Roman, Asian, Islamic, Pacific Island, European, American, and contemporary art (which, of course, comes from anywhere and everywhere).

Even the most reluctant museumgoer will be charmed by the nineteenth-century European collection, which includes great paintings by the likes of Cézanne, Monet, Manet, Renoir, Degas, and van Gogh, and sculpture by Rodin. In the contemporary wing, you'll find paintings by Jackson Pollock, Georgia O'Keeffe, and Andy Warhol, for example. During the summer months, the roof of the Met is an outdoor sculpture garden. Take the elevator up for the art and for grand views of Central Park and the city. The main museum sits on Fifth Avenue, within Central Park, in the lower 80s. The Cloisters, which is part of the Met, is devoted to European medieval art and architecture and is located in northern Manhattan's Fort Tryon Park, which seems like a Manhattan island untouched by civilization.

Frank Lloyd Wright's Solomon R. Guggenheim Museum sits across Fifth Avenue from Central Park, about 10 blocks up from the Met, in New York's "Museum Mile." The main exhibition hall houses transient exhibitions. Marcel Breuer's Whitney Museum of American Art is found on Madison Avenue, which parallels Fifth Avenue, one block east, at 75th Street. The Whitney is devoted to American art, and its exhibitions include some of the edgiest and most controversial art in New York. My youngest daughter was captivated by Tony Oursler's *Getaway #2*, which was lying on the floor, repeatedly asking "Are you lookin' at me?" and cursing museumgoers. You can catch lunch in any of these museums.

The Museum of Modern Art (MOMA) has recently undergone a major renovation. The collection of the MOMA contains many familiar and beloved works, works not to be missed: van Gogh's *Starry Night* (Fig. 18-27), Rousseau's *The Sleeping Gypsy* (Fig. 2-33), Picasso's *Les Demoiselles d'Avignon* (Fig. 2-22), Chagall's *I and the Village* (Fig. 1-14), Boccioni's *Dynamism of a Soccer Player* (Fig. 2-73), Dalí's *The Persistence of Memory* (Fig. 19-28), Pollocks, Monets, and . . . the list is, for all practical purposes, endless.

There are almost too many other museums and art galleries to mention. The Morgan Library on Madison Avenue in midtown contains one of the few remaining copies of the Gutenberg Bible (dated 1455). When visiting Harlem, check out the exhibitions at the Studio Museum on 125th Street. The Museo del Barrio is on Fifth Avenue in the 100s (don't forget the charming garden within Central Park across from the Museo). As you're heading back down Fifth Avenue toward the 90s and the Museum Mile, you will find it worthwhile to visit the Jewish Museum and the Cooper-Hewitt National Design Museum. Down in the 70s, past the Met, you'll find the Frick Collection.

New York is also an architecture buff's dream. The Guggenheim and Whitney Museums are to be appreciated as works of art themselves, not just as houses for art. Some of the churches of the city are, well, divine, including the Cathedral of St. John the Divine, on Amsterdam Avenue and

FRANK LLOYD WRIGHT, Guggenheim Museum.
Rafael Macia/PR.

SOL LEWITT, *Splotch #15,* on the roof at the Met.
© 2005 Sol LeWitt/Artists Rights Society (ARS), New York.

THE WHITNEY MUSEUM OF AMERICAN ART.
Jeff Goldbert/Esto.

112th Street. This is the largest cathedral in the world (really), and St. Patrick's Cathedral, on Fifth Avenue at 50th Street, is the largest Catholic cathedral in the United States. The Cathedral of St. John the Divine was begun in 1892 and is about two-thirds finished.

When (and if) sufficient funds are raised, completion will require only about another half century. It is a very people- and environment-oriented cathedral, with chapels containing children's art and fish tanks that illustrate the ecology of the Hudson River.

New York is looking up. That is, visitors to New York are always looking up. Look for the Art Deco stainless steel spire of the Chrysler Building (Lexington Avenue at 42nd Street), which resembles the grille of a car of the 1920s (its gargoyles resemble hood ornaments). It's worth a visit to check out the Art Deco doors of the elevators. The Empire State Building, at Fifth Avenue and 34th Street, provides wonderful views of the city. (King Kong enjoyed a visit to the top in 1933.) If you walk up Park Avenue from midtown, you'll come across the famed Waldorf Astoria Hotel; the Byzantine St. Bartholomew's Church (St. Bart's), with its wonderful ornate detail and gold dome; and prime examples of the steel-cage architecture of the 1950s, Lever House (Fig. 10-15) and the Seagram Building.

Do not forget to spend time in Central Park, one of the city's greatest works of art, regardless of the time of year. It's never too hot to sunbathe or too cold to enjoy the Wolman Skating Rink or a horse-drawn carriage ride (there are blankets in the carriages). Designed by Frederick Law Olmsted, the park is a rectangular strip of grass, trees, hills, and lakes some 21.2 miles long (running from 59th Street to 110th Street) and almost a mile wide (running from Fifth Avenue to Central Park West, which is the equivalent of Eighth Avenue). It forms the geographical and spiritual heart of Manhattan. Museums and other landmarks line its edges. Joggers circle the reservoir, young (and old) children guide miniature yachts in the sailboat pond, animals stretch and growl in the zoo, and lovers meander along its paths. New Yorkers pay a premium for apartments with a view of the park. Multiple roadways pass above and below one another so that through traffic, pedestrian walkways, and bridle paths all function simultaneously. Forty-six bridges and arches—all different—contribute to the harmonious functioning of the transportation system or simply provide decoration. Next to the lake (many blocks below the reservoir), you'll find Bethesda Fountain, where dozens of movies have been shot. A path around the lake will take you into wooded areas that might be 100 miles upstate.

It's worth the extra dollars to eat at the Boathouse (on the lake near Bethesda Fountain) or at Tavern on the Green ("the Green" is Central Park). In the summer, enjoy the amateur acrobats and break-dancers at the fountain, the beat of African drums, and the Rollerblade dancers nearby.

Then there is the unexpected. One summer, for example, New York was invaded by cows. We know that Rockefeller Center has a grand Christmas tree during the holiday season, but unusual pieces of art also show up, like big yellow elephants.

CHINATSU BAN, *VWX Yellow Elephant / HIJ Kiddy Elephant.*
Chiantsu Ban, VWX Yellow Elephant Underwear/HIJ Kiddy Elephant Underwear, 2005. Sculpture at Doris C. Freedman Plaza, 60th Street and Fifth Avenue. A Project of Public Art Fund and the Japan Society. Courtesy Marianne Boesky Gallery, New York. Photo by Tom Powel Imaging. © 2005 Chinatsu Ban/Kaikai Kiki Co., Ltd. All rights reserved.

 To continue your tour and learn more about New York City, go to our website.

10

ARCHITECTURE

The mother art is architecture. Without an architecture of our own
we have no soul of our own civilization.

—Frank Lloyd Wright

Early humans found their shelters—the mouth of a yawning cave, the underside of a ledge, the boughs of an overspreading tree. But for thousands of years we having been building shelters and fashioning them to our needs. Before we became capable of transporting bulky materials over vast distances, we had to rely on local possibilities. Native Americans constructed huts from sticks and bark and conical teepees from animal skins and wooden poles. They carved their way into the sides of cliffs. African villagers wove sticks and grass into walls and plastered them with mud; their geometrically pure cone roofs sit atop cylindrical bases. Desert peoples learned to dry clay in the sun in the form of bricks. From ice, the Inuit fashioned the dome-shaped igloo.

Architecture is the art and science of designing buildings, bridges, and other structures to help us meet our personal and communal needs. Of all the arts, architecture probably has the greatest impact on our daily lives. For most of us, architecture determines the quality of the environments in which we work, play, meditate, and rest.

Architecture is also a vehicle for artistic expression in three dimensions. More than any other art form, architecture is experienced from within as well as without, and at great length. If sculptures have fronts, backs, sides, tops, and bottoms, buildings have **facades,** foundations, roofs, and a variety of interior spaces that must be planned. If some sculptures are kinetic and some are composed of light sources, buildings may contain complex systems for heating, cooling, lighting, and inner transportation.

Architects, like sculptors, must work within the limits of their materials and the technology of the day. In addition to understanding enough of engineering to determine how materials may be used efficiently to span and enclose sometimes vast spaces, architects must work with other professionals and with contractors who design and install elements of the **service systems** of their buildings.

In a sense the architect is not only an artist but a mediator—a compromiser. The architect mediates between the needs of the client and the properties and aesthetic possibilities of the site. (Today's technology permits the erection of 20-story-high, 20-foot-wide "sliver skyscrapers" on expensive, narrow urban sites, but at what aesthetic cost to a neighborhood of row houses?) The architect balances aesthetics and the building codes of the community. (Since the 1930s, architects in New York City have had to comply with the so-called setback law and step back or contour their high-rises from the street in order to let the sun shine in on an environment that seemed in danger of devolving into a maze of blackened canyons.) Climate, site, materials, building codes, clients, contractors, service systems, and the amount of money available—these are just some of the variables that the architect must employ or contend with to create an aesthetically pleasing, functional structure.

In this section we will explore traditional and modern ways in which architects have come to terms with these variables. We will survey the traditional materials and methods associated with building in stone and wood. Then we will examine a number of modern and contemporary architectural materials and methods, including those associated with cast-iron and steel-cage construction, use of reinforced concrete, and steel cable.

STONE ARCHITECTURE

As a building material, stone is massive and virtually indestructible. Contemporary wood-frame homes frequently sport stone fireplaces, perhaps as a symbol of permanence

10-1 Cliff Dwellings, Mesa Verde, Colorado (Native American, Pre-Columbian).
Topfoto/The Image Works.

Architecture completes nature.

—Giorgio De Chirico

and strength as well as of warmth. The Native American cliff dwellings at Mesa Verde, Colorado (Fig. 10-1), could be considered something of an "earthwork high relief." The cliff itself becomes the back wall or "support" of more than 100 rectangular apartments. Circular, underground **kivas** served as community centers. Construction with stone, **adobe,** and timber creates a mixed-media functional fantasy. Early humans also assembled stone temples and memorials.

Post-and-Lintel Construction

The prehistoric Stonehenge (see Fig. 12-5) probably served religious or astronomical purposes. Its orientation toward the sun and its layout in concentric circles are suggestive of the amphitheaters and temples to follow. Stonehenge is an early example of **post-and-lintel** construction (Fig. 10-2A). Two stones were set upright as supports, and a third was

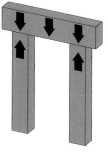

10-2A   Post-and-lintel construction.

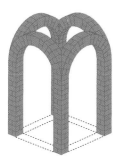

10-2B   Rounded arches enclosing square bay.

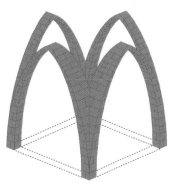

10-2C   Pointed arches enclosing rectangular bay.

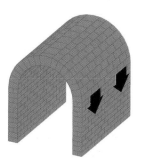

10-2D   Tunnel or barrel vault.

10-2E   Groin vault.

10-2F   Groin vault showing ribs that carry greatest loads.

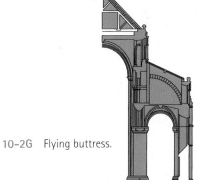

10-2G   Flying buttress.

10-2H   Dome.

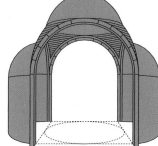

10-2I   Pendentives.

10-2J   Geodesic dome.

10-3 Walls of Fortress
of Machu Picchu,
Urubamba Valley,
Peru (Incan,
1490–1530).
Topfoto/The Image
Works.

placed across them, creating an opening beneath. How the massive blocks of Stonehenge were transported and erected remains a mystery.

Early stone structures were erected without benefit of mortar. Their **dry masonry** relied on masterly carving of blocks, strategic placement, and sheer weight for durability. Consider the imposing ruin of the fortress of Machu Picchu, perched high above the Urubamba River in the Peruvian Andes. Its beautiful granite walls (Fig. 10-3), constructed by the Incas, are pieced together so perfectly that not even a knife blade can pass between the blocks. The faces of the Great Pyramids of Egypt (see Fig. 12-14) are assembled as miraculously, perhaps even more so considering the greater mass of the blocks.

10-4 Temple of Amen-Re, Karnak (Egyptian, XVIII dynasty, 1570–1342 BCE).
Copyright George Holton/Photo Researchers, Inc., New York.

An arch is two curves trying to fall.

—Andy Rooney

Stone became the favored material for the public buildings of the Egyptians and the Greeks. The Egyptian Temple of Amen-Re at Karnak (Fig. 10-4) and the Parthenon (see Fig. 13-9) of the Classical period of Greece begin to speak of the elegance as well as the massiveness that can be fashioned from stone. The Temple of Amen-Re is of post-and-lintel construction, but the paintings, relief sculptures, and overall smoothness of the columns belie their function as bearers of stress (see Fig. 12-17). The virtual forest of columns was a structural necessity because of the weight of the massive stone lintels. The Parthenon is also of post-and-lintel construction. Consistent with the Greeks' emphasis on the functional purpose of columns, the surfaces of the marble shafts are free from ornamentation. The Parthenon, which may be the most studied and surveyed building in the world, is discussed at length in Chapter 13.

Arches

Architects of stone also use **arches** to span distances (Figs. 10-2B and 10-2C). Arches have many functions, including supporting other structures, such as roofs, and serving as ac-

tual and symbolic gateways. An Arch of Triumph, as in the city of Paris, provides a visual focus for the return of the conquering hero. Eero Saarinen's Gateway Arch (Fig. 10-5), completed in St. Louis in 1965, stands 630 feet tall at the center and commemorates the westward push of the United States after the Louisiana Purchase of 1803. The Pont du Gard (see Fig. 13-21) near Nîmes, France, employs the arch in a bridge that is part of an aqueduct system. It is a marvel of Roman engineering. Early masonry arches were fashioned from **bricks;** each limestone block of the Pont du Gard weighs up to two tons, and they were assembled without benefit of mortar. The bridge stands and functions today, two millennia after its creation.

In most arches, wedge-shaped blocks of stone, called **voussoirs,** are gradually placed in position ascending a wooden scaffold called a **centering.** When the center, or **keystone,** is set in place, the weight of the blocks is all at once transmitted in an arc laterally and downward, and the centering can be removed. The pull of gravity on each block serves as "cement"; that is, the blocks fall into one another so that the very weight that had made their erection a marvel now prevents them from budging. The **compressive**

10-5 EERO SAARINEN. Jefferson National Expansion Memorial, Gateway Arch, St. Louis, MO (1966).
Topfoto/The Image Works.

strength of stone allows the builder to place additional weight above the arch. The Pont du Gard consists of three **tiers** of arches, 161 feet high.

Vaults

An extended arch is called a **vault.** A tunnel or **barrel vault** (Fig. 10-2D) simply places arches behind one another until a desired depth is reached. In this way impressive spaces may be roofed and tunnels may be constructed. Unfortunately, the spaces enclosed by barrel vaults are dark, because piercing them to let in natural light would compromise their strength. The communication of stresses from one arch to another also requires that the centering for each arch be kept in place until the entire vault is completed.

Roman engineers are credited with the creation of the **groin vault,** which overcame limitations of the barrel vault, as early as the third century CE. Groin vaults are constructed by placing barrel vaults at right angles to cover a square space (Fig. 10-2E). In this way the load of the intersecting vaults is transmitted to the corners, necessitating **buttressing** at these points but allowing the sides of the square to be open. The square space enclosed by the groin vault is called a **bay.** Architects could now construct huge buildings by assembling any number of bays. Because the stresses from one groin vault are not transmitted to a large degree to its neighbors, the centering used for one vault can be removed and reused while the building is under construction.

The greatest loads in the groin vault are thrust onto the four arches that compose the sides and the two arches that run diagonally across them. If the capacity of these diagonals is increased to carry a load, by means of **ribs** added to the vault (Fig. 10-2F), the remainder of the roof can be fashioned from stone **webbing** or other materials much lighter in weight. A true stone skeleton is created.

Note in Figure 10-2B that rounded arches can enclose only square bays. One could not use rounded arches in rectangular bays because the longer walls would have higher arches. Architects over the centuries solved the rectangular bay problem in a number of ingenious ways. The most important of these is found in **Gothic** architecture, discussed in Chapter 14, which uses ribbed vaults and **pointed arches.** Pointed arches can be constructed to uniform heights even when the sides of the enclosed space are unequal (Fig. 10-2C). Gothic architecture also employed the so-called **flying buttress** (Fig. 10-2G), a masonry strut that transmits part of the load of a vault to a buttress positioned outside a building.

Most of the great cathedrals of Europe achieve their vast, open interiors through the use of vaults. Massive stone rests benignly above the heads of worshipers and tourists alike, transmitting its brute load laterally and downward. The **Ottonian** St. Michael's (see Fig. 14-11), built in Germany between 1001 and 1031 CE, uses barrel vaulting. Its bays are square, and its walls are blank and massive. The **Romanesque** St. Sernin (see Fig. 14-13), built in France between about 1080 and 1120, uses round arches and square bays. The walls are heavy and blunt, with the main masses subdivided by buttresses. St. Étienne (see Fig. 14-15), completed between 1115 and 1120, has high, rising vaults—some of the earliest to show true ribs—that permit light to enter through a **clerestory.** Stone became a fully elegant structural skeleton in the great Gothic cathedrals such as those at Laon (see Figs. 14-20 and 14-21) and Chartres (see Fig. 14-23) and in the Notre-Dame of Paris (see Fig. 14-22). Lacy buttressing and ample **fenestration** lend these massive buildings an airy lightness that seems consonant with their mission of directing upward the focus of human awareness.

Domes

Domes are hemispherical forms that are rounded when viewed from beneath (see Figs. 10-2H and 10-2J). Like vaults, domes are extensions of the principle of the arch and are capable of enclosing vast reaches of space. (Buckminster Fuller, who designed the American Pavilion [Fig. 10-25] for the 1967 World's Fair in Montreal, proposed that the center of Manhattan should be enclosed in a weather-controlled transparent dome two miles in diameter.) Stresses from the top of the dome are transmitted in all directions to the points at which the circular base meets the foundation, walls, or other structures beneath.

The dome of the Buddhist temple or Stupa of Sanchi, India, completed in the first century CE, rises 50 feet above the ground and causes the worshiper to contemplate the dwelling place of the gods (see Fig. 17-28). It was constructed from stones placed in gradually diminishing concentric circles. Visitors find the domed interior of the Pantheon of Rome (see Fig. 13-28), completed during the second century CE, breathtaking. Like the dome of the Stupa, the rounded inner surface of the Pantheon, 144 feet in diameter, symbolizes the heavens.

The dome of the vast Hagia Sophia (see Fig. 1-13) in Constantinople is 108 feet in diameter. Its architects, building during the sixth century CE, used four triangular surfaces called **pendentives** (Fig. 10-2I) to support the dome on a square base. Pendentives transfer the load from the base of the dome to the **piers** at the corners of the square beneath.

Stone today is rarely used as a structural material. It is expensive to quarry and transport, and it is too massive to handle readily at the site. Metals are lighter and have greater tensile strength, so they are suitable as the skeletons or reinforcers for most of today's larger structures. Still, buildings with steel skeletons are frequently dressed with thin facades, or **veneers,** of costly marble, limestone, and other types of stone. Many tract homes are granted decorative patches of stone across the front facade, and slabs of slate are frequently used to provide minimum-care surfaces for entry halls or patios in private homes.

WOOD ARCHITECTURE

Wood is as beautiful and versatile a material for building as it is for sculpture. It is an abundant and, as many advertisements have proclaimed, renewable resource. It is relatively light in weight and is capable of being worked on the site with readily portable hand tools. Its variety of colors and grains as well as its capacity to accept paint or to weather charmingly when left in its natural state make wood a ubiquitous material. Wood, like stone, can be used as a structural element or as a facade. In many structures it is used as both.

Wood also has its drawbacks. It warps and cracks. It rots. It is also highly flammable and stirs the appetite of termites and other devouring insects. However, modern technology has enhanced the stability and strength of wood as a building material. Chemical treatments decrease wood's vulnerability to rotting from moisture. **Plywood,** which is built up from sheets of wood glued together, is unlikely to warp and is frequently used as an under layer in the exterior walls of small buildings and homes. Laminated wood beams possess great strength and are also unlikely to become distorted in shape from exposure to changing temperatures and levels of humidity.

Architect Paul Schweikher's contemporary northern Arizona home (Fig. 10-6) is a Japanese-inspired clean design of glass and wood in which sturdy but graceful fir timbers provide both a structural system and a primary source of decoration. The cedar **siding** exudes both warmth and crisp elegance. Timbers and siding are integrated into the surrounding red rock country by means of a crushed red sandstone driveway, a rock path bordered in red gravel, and a floor throughout of 4-inch by 8-inch **quarry tile.** There are times during the day when the light is such that the huge panels of glass seem to melt away, and the house is very much one with the Sedona butte on which it sits.

10-6 PAUL SCHWEIKHER.
Schweikher House, Sedona, AZ
(1972).
Courtesy of Fine Home Building Magazine,
Taunton Press.

Post-and-Beam Construction

Schweikher's house is of **post-and-beam** construction (Fig. 10-7A), which is similar to post-and-lintel construction; vertical and horizontal timbers are cut and pieced together with wooden pegs. The beams span openings for windows, doors, and interior spaces, and they can also support posts for another story or roof trusses.

Trusses

Trusses are lengths of wood, iron, or steel pieced together in triangular shapes of the sort shown in Figure 10-7B in order to expand the abilities of these materials to span distances. Trusses acquire their strength from the fact that the sides of a triangle, once joined, cannot be forced out of shape. In many buildings, roof trusses are exposed and become elements of the design.

Balloon Framing

Balloon framing (Fig. 10-7C), a product of the industrial revolution, dates back to the beginning of the twentieth century. In balloon framing, factory-cut studs, including the fa-

miliar two-by-four, are mass-produced and assembled at the site using thousands of factory-produced metal nails. Several light, easily handled pieces of wood replace the heavy timber of post-and-beam construction. Entire walls are framed in place or on their sides and then raised into place by a crew of carpenters. The multiple pieces and geometric patterns of balloon framing give it a sturdiness that rivals that of the post and beam, permitting the support of slate or tile roofs. However, the term *balloon* was originally a derisive term: inveterate users of post and beam were skeptical that the frail-looking wooden pieces could provide a rugged building.

Balloon framing, of course, has now been used on millions of smaller buildings, not only homes. Sidings for balloon-framed homes have ranged from **clapboard** to asbestos shingle, brick and stone veneer, and aluminum. Roofs have ranged from asphalt or cedar shingle to tile and slate. These materials vary in cost, and each has certain aesthetic possibilities and practical advantages. Aluminum, for example, is lightweight, durable, and maintenance-free. However, when aluminum siding is shaped like clapboard and given a bogus grain, the intended trompe l'oeil effect usually fails and can create something of an aesthetic embarrassment.

Two other faces of wood are observable in American architect Richard Morris Hunt's Griswold House (Fig. 10-8),

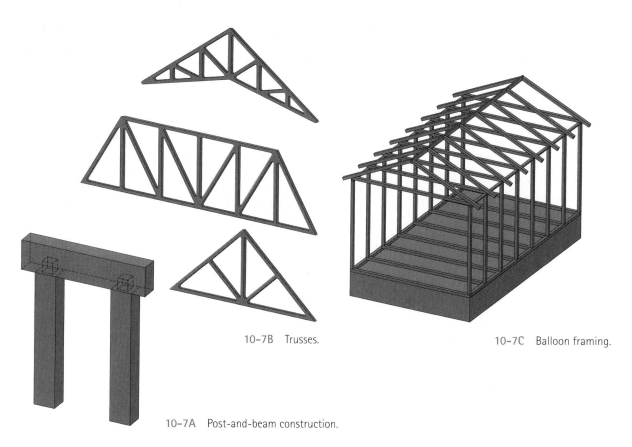

10-7B   Trusses.

10-7C   Balloon framing.

10-7A   Post-and-beam construction.

10-8 RICHARD M. HUNT.
J. N. A. Griswold House, Newport, RI
(1862–1863).
Courtesy of the Newport Art Museum.

built at Newport, Rhode Island, in 1862–1863 in the *Stick style,* and in the Cape Cod–style home in Levittown, Long Island, a suburb of New York City (Fig. 10-9). The Griswold House shows the fanciful possibilities in wood. The Stick style sported a skeletal treatment of exteriors that remind one of an assemblage of matchsticks, open interiors, and a curious interplay of voids and solids and horizontal and vertical lines. Shapes proliferate in this short-lived movement. Turrets and gables and dormers poke the roof in every direction. Trellised porches reinforce a certain wooden laciness. One cannot imagine the Griswold House constructed in any material but wood.

The house at Levittown is more than a home; it is a socio-aesthetic comment on the need for mass suburban housing that impacted so many metropolitan regions during the marriage and baby boom that followed World War II. This house and 17,000 others almost exactly like it were built, with few exceptions, on 60-foot by 100-foot lots that had been carved out from potato fields. In what was to become neighborhood after neighborhood, bulldozers smoothed already flat terrain and concrete slabs were poured. Balloon frames were erected, sided, and roofed. Trees were planted; grass was sown. The houses had an eat-in kitchen, living room, two tiny bedrooms, one bath on the first floor, and an expansion attic. Despite the tedium of the repetition, the original Levittown house achieved a sort of architectural integrity, providing

10-9 Cape Cod–style houses built by Levitt & Sons, Levittown, NY (c. 1947–1951).
Hulton Archive/Getty Images.

living space, the pride of ownership, and an inoffensive facade for a modest price. Driving through Levittown today, it seems that every occupant thrust random additions in random directions as the family grew, despite the limitations of the lots. The trees only partly obscure the results.

No person who is not a great sculptor or painter can be an architect. . . . He can only be a builder.

—John Ruskin

CAST-IRON ARCHITECTURE

Nineteenth-century industrialization also introduced **cast iron** as a building material. It was one of a number of structural materials that would change the face of architecture. Cast iron was a welcome alternative to stone and wood. Like stone, iron has great strength, is heavy, and has a certain brittleness, yet it was the first material to allow the erection of tall buildings with relatively slender walls. Slender iron beams and bolted trusses are also capable of spanning vast interior spaces, freeing them from the forests of columns that are required in stone.

At the mid-nineteenth-century Great Exhibition held in Hyde Park, London, Sir Joseph Paxton's Crystal Palace (Fig. 10-10) covered 17 acres. Like subsequent iron buildings, the Crystal Palace was **prefabricated.** Iron parts were cast at the factory, not the site. The new railroads facilitated their transportation, and it was a simple matter to bolt them together at the exhibition. It was also a relatively simple matter to dismantle the structure and reconstruct it at another site. The iron skeleton, with its myriad arches and trusses, was an integral part of the design. The huge plate-glass paneled walls bore no weight. Paxton asserted that "nature" had been his "engineer," explaining that he merely copied the system of longitudinal and transverse supports that one finds in a leaf. Earlier architects were also familiar with the structure of the leaf, but they did not have the structural materials at hand that would permit them to build, much less conceptualize, such an expression of natural design.

The Crystal Palace was moved after the exhibition, and until heavily damaged by fire, it served as a museum and concert hall. It was demolished in 1941 during World War II, after it was discovered that it was being used as a landmark by German pilots on bombing runs.

The Eiffel Tower (Fig. 10-11) was built in Paris in 1889 for another industrial exhibition. At the time, Gustave Eiffel was castigated by critics for building an open structure lacking the standard masonry facade. Today the Parisian symbol is so familiar that one cannot visualize Paris without the tower's magnificent exposed iron trusses. The pieces of the 1,000-foot-tall tower were prefabricated, and the tower was assembled at the site in 17 months by only 150 workers.

Structures such as these encouraged **steel-cage construction** and the development of the skyscraper.

10–11   GUSTAVE EIFFEL.
Eiffel Tower, Paris (1889).
Topfoto/The Image Works.

10–10   Engraving of Sir Joseph Paxton's Crystal Palace, London (1851).
Copyright Ann Ronan Picture Library, Oxfordshire, UK.

STEEL-CAGE ARCHITECTURE

Steel is a strong metal of iron alloyed with small amounts of carbon and a variety of other metals. Steel is harder than iron, and more rust and fire resistant. It is more expensive than other structural materials, but its great strength permits it to be used in relatively small quantities. Light, narrow, prefabricated I-beams have great tensile strength. They resist bending in any direction and are riveted or welded together into skeletal forms called **steel cages** at the site (Fig. 10-12). Facades and inner walls are hung from the skeleton and frequently contribute more mass to the building than does the skeleton itself.

The Wainwright Building (Fig. 10-13), erected in 1890, is an early example of steel-cage construction. Architect Louis Sullivan, one of the fathers of modern American

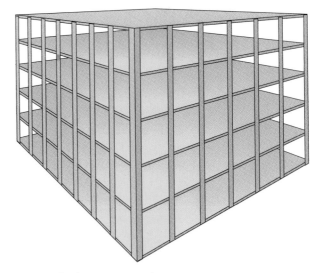

10-12   Steel-cage construction.

10-13   Louis Sullivan.
Wainwright Building, St. Louis, MO
(1890).
Courtesy Bill Hedrich, Hedrich-Blessing/
Chicago Historical Society.

Less is more.

—Miës van der Rohe

architecture, emphasized the verticality of the structure by running **pilasters** between the windows through the upper stories. Many skyscrapers run pilasters up their entire facades. Sullivan also emphasized the horizontal features of the Wainwright Building. Ornamented horizontal bands separate most of the windows, and a severe decorated **cor-** **nice** crowns the structure. Sullivan's motto was "form follows function," and the rigid horizontal and vertical processions of the elements of the facade suggest the regularity of the rectangular spaces within. Sullivan's early "skyscraper"— in function, in structure, and in simplified form—was a precursor of the twentieth-century behemoths to follow.

10-14   GORDON BUNSHAFT. Lever House, New York (1951–1952).
Copyright Angelo Homak/CORBIS.

Architecture is the first manifestation of man creating his own universe.

—Le Corbusier

Well, now that he's finished one building, he'll go write four books about it.

—Frank Lloyd Wright on Le Corbusier

10-15   BURGEE ARCHITECTS WITH
PHILIP JOHNSON.
Sony Plaza (formerly AT&T Building),
New York (1984).
Photo courtesy of Norman McGrath.

One of these behemoths is New York City's Modernist Lever House (Fig. 10-14). Lever House was designed by Gordon Bunshaft of Skidmore, Owings, and Merrill, a firm that quickly became known for its "minimalist" rectangular solids with their "curtain walls" of glass. The nation was excited about the clean, austere look of Lever House and about its donation of open plaza space to the city. The plaza prevents the shaft from overwhelming its site. The evening light angles down across the plaza and illuminates the avenue beneath.

By the mid-1970s, the clean Modernist look of buildings such as Lever House was overwhelming the urban cityscape. A few buildings of the kind—even a few dozen buildings of the kind—would have been most welcome, but now architectural critics were arguing that a national proliferation of steel-cage rectangular solids was threatening to bury the nation's cities in boredom. Said John Perrault in 1979, "We are sick to death of cold plazas and 'curtain wall' skyscrapers."

By the end of the 1970s, a new steel-cage monster was being bred throughout the land—one that utilized contemporary technology but drew freely from past styles of ornamentation. These **Postmodernist** structures reject the formal simplicity and immaculate finish of **Modernist** architecture in favor of whimsical shapes, colors, and patterns. Postmodern architects revived the concept of the decorative in architecture, an absolute "no-no" for decades in the twentieth century.

One of most interesting aspects of Postmodern architecture is its appropriation of historical motifs; Philip Johnson and John Burgee's AT&T Building in New York City (subsequently sold to Sony) (Fig. 10-15) is one of the earliest examples. The massive tower sits on a forest of columns, reminiscent—to Johnson—of an Egyptian hypostyle hall (Figure 10-4). Its pale pink facade is punctuated with fenestration, although the prominent stone grid lines regulate the pace of the upward sweep. The building is crowned with a broken roof pediment referencing the Chippendale style, which originated with the eighteenth-century

10-16 LUDWIG MIËS VAN DER ROHE.
Farnsworth House, Fox River, Plano, IL (1950).
Courtesy Hedrich-Blessing. Copyright 2000 Artists Rights Society (ARS),
New York / VG Bild-Kunst, Bonn.

British cabinetmaker Thomas Chippendale. Beneath the ornamentation lies a steel-cage structure, now visually all but disguised.

A more surprising, and unusual, example of steel-cage architecture is found in Miës van der Rohe's Farnsworth House (Fig. 10-16). The rhythmic procession of white steel columns suspends it above the Illinois countryside. In its perfect technological elegance, it is in many ways visually remote from its site. Why steel? Less expensive wood could have supported this house of one story and short spans, and wood might have appeared more natural on this sylvan site. The architect's choices, of course, may be read as a symbol of our contemporary remoteness from our feral past. If so, the architect seems to believe that the powerful technology that has freed us is to the good, for the house is as beautiful as it is austere in ornamentation. The Farnsworth House has platforms, steps, and a glass curtain wall that allows the environment to flow through. The steps and platforms provide access to a less well-ordered world below.

REINFORCED CONCRETE ARCHITECTURE

Although cement was first produced in the early 1800s, the use of **reinforced concrete** is said to have begun with a French gardener, Jacques Monier, who proposed strengthening concrete flower pots with a wire mesh in the 1860s. In reinforced concrete, or **ferroconcrete,** steel rods and/or steel mesh are inserted at the points of greatest stress into concrete slabs before they harden. In the resultant slab, stresses are shared by the materials.

Ferroconcrete has many of the advantages of stone and steel, without some of the disadvantages. The steel rods increase the tensile strength of concrete, making it less susceptible to tearing or pulling apart at stress points. The concrete, in turn, prevents the steel from rusting. Reinforced concrete can span greater distances than stone, and it supports more weight than steel. Perhaps the most dramatic ad-

10-17 LE CORBUSIER.
Chapel of Notre-Dame-du-Haut,
Ronchamp, France (1950–1954).
Copyright 2003 Artists Rights Society (ARS), New York/ADAGP, Paris/FLC.

10-18 LE CORBUSIER.
Interior, south wall, Chapel of Notre-Dame-du-Haut.
Copyright 2003 Artists Rights Society (ARS), New York/ADAGP, Paris/FLC.

vantage of reinforced concrete is its capacity to take on natural curved shapes that would be unthinkable in steel or concrete alone. Curved slabs take on the forms of eggshells, bubbles, seashells, and other organic shapes that are naturally engineered for the even spreading of stress throughout their surfaces and are, hence, enduring.

Reinforced concrete, more than other materials, has freed the architect to think freely and sculpturally. There are limits to what ferroconcrete can do, however; initial spatial concepts are frequently somewhat refined by computer-aided calculations of marginally more efficient shapes for distributing stress. Still, it would not be far from the mark to say that buildings of almost any shape and reasonable size are possible today, if one is willing to pay for them. The architects of ferroconcrete have achieved a number of buildings that would have astounded the ancient stone builders—and perhaps Joseph Paxton.

Le Corbusier's chapel of Notre-Dame-du-Haut (Figs. 10-17 and 10-18) is an example of what has been referred to as the "new brutalism," deriving from the French *brut,* meaning "rough, uncut, or raw." The steel web is spun, and the concrete is cast in place, leaving the marks of the wooden forms on its surface. The white walls, dark roof, and white towers are "decorated" only by the texture of the curving reinforced concrete slabs. In places the walls are incredibly thick. Windows of various shapes and sizes expand from small slits and rectangles to form mysterious light tunnels; they not so much light the interior as draw the observer outward. The massive voids of the window apertures recall the huge stone blocks of prehistoric religious structures.

Frank Lloyd Wright's Kaufmann House (Fig. 10-19), which has also become known as "Fallingwater," shows a

10-19 FRANK LLOYD WRIGHT.
Kaufmann House ("Fallingwater"), Bear Run, PA (1936).
Scott Frances/ESTO.

very different application of reinforced concrete. Here cantilevered decks of reinforced concrete rush outward into the surrounding landscape from the building's central core, intersecting in strata that lie parallel to the natural rock formations. Wright's **naturalistic style** integrates his building with its site. In the Kaufmann House, reinforced concrete and stone walls complement the sturdy rock of the Pennsylvania countryside.

For Wright, modern materials did not warrant austerity; geometry did not preclude organic integration with the site. A small waterfall seems mysteriously to originate beneath the broad white planes of a deck. The irregularity of the structural components—concrete, cut stone, natural stone, and machine-planed surfaces—complements the irregularity of the wooded site. The Kaufmann House, naturalistic, might have always been there. It is right. The Farnsworth House, although not "wrong," is a technological surprise on its landscape.

Israeli architect Moshe Safdie's Habitat (Fig. 10-20) is another expression of the versatility of concrete. Habitat was erected for Expo 67 in Montreal as one solution to the housing problems of the future. Rugged, prefabricated units were stacked like blocks about a common utility core at the site, so that the roof of one unit would provide a private deck for another. Only a couple of Safdie-style "apartment houses" have been erected since, one in Israel and one in Puerto Rico, so today Safdie's beautiful sculptural assemblage evokes more nostalgia than hope for the future. Its unique brand of rugged, blocky excitement is rarely found in mass housing, and this is our loss.

10-20   MOSHE SAFDIE.
Habitat, Expo 67, Montreal (1967).
Copyright Magma Photo, Quebec.

STEEL-CABLE ARCHITECTURE

The notion of suspending bridges from cables is not new. Wood-and-rope suspension bridges have been built in Asia for thousands of years. Iron suspension bridges, such as the Menai Strait Bridge in Wales and the Clifton Bridge near Bristol, England, were erected during the early part of the nineteenth century. But in the Brooklyn Bridge (Fig. 10-21), completed in 1883, John Roebling exploited

10-21   JOHN A. ROEBLING.
Brooklyn Bridge, New York
(1869–1883).
Copyright Superstock
Photography, Jacksonville, FL.

A doctor can bury his mistakes, but an architect can only advise his clients to plant vines.

—Frank Lloyd Wright

*We may live without architecture, and worship without her,
but we cannot remember without her.*

—John Ruskin

the great tensile strength of steel to span New York's East River with **steel cable.** In such a cable, many parallel wires share the stress. Steel cable is also flexible, allowing the roadway beneath to sway, within limits, in response to changing weather and traffic conditions.

Roebling used massive vaulted piers of stone masonry to support parabolic webs of steel, which are rendered lacy by the juxtaposition. In many more recent suspension bridges, steel cable spans more than a mile, and in bridges such as the Golden Gate, the George Washington, and the Verrazzano Narrows, the effect is aesthetically stirring.

There is another stirring aspect to the photograph of the Brooklyn Bridge. In the background you see the twin towers of the World Trade Center, which collapsed in the terrorist attack of September 11, 2001. Within months following September 11, dozens of architects and planners were submitting concepts to New York City for "Ground Zero," which included a memorial to those who had been killed in the attack and new buildings that might recapture the upward spirit of the city. At one point in the decision-making process, the commission was awarded to Studio Daniel Libeskind, whose original design for the World Trade Center site appears in Figure 10-22. The twisting structures, about the same height of the original towers, were designed to reduce the dynamic effects of wind, much as the aerodynamic contours of an automobile do. They were to be significantly stronger; a combination of steel on the outside and concrete within would better resist the natural forces of wind and gravity, and the unnatural forces of a terrorist assault. Accompanying the lower buildings was a broadcast tower that would have been the tallest structure in the world. The elements of the plan would have seemed a perfect compromise, taking into account the sobering realities of doing business in a super high-rise skyscraper in a post-9/11 world and the desire of most Americans to build high and build proud. And although these tall structures would reassert the lower Manhattan skyline, which now dips mournfully into the harbor, the twisted planes of the building facades seem to bear some acknowledgment of vulnerability in the wake of the attack by foreign enemies on U.S. soil.

10-22   STUDIO DANIEL LIBESKIND.
Computer-generated drawings of the design selected to rebuild the World Trade Center site, New York City.
Copyright archimation. Courtesy, Studio Daniel Libeskind.

In Lights at Ground Zero, Steps toward Illumination*

For a month in the spring of 2002, twin towers of light at "Ground Zero" served as an architectural memorial to the twin towers of glass and steel that had been felled by terrorists, even if the medium could not be clutched by the hands. It was called *Tribute in Light* (Fig. 10-23), and architectural critic Herbert Muschamp wrote about it in *The New York Times:*

> *"Tribute in Light" was a moving piece of urban spectacle. The project's impact surpassed even the dramatic digital renderings. In the renderings, the twin light towers appeared to be saying something. As realized, they seemed to be looking for something. More a question than a statement, the project set a rhetorical tone worthy of emulation by those who will be shaping the future of Lower Manhattan in days to come.*
>
> *The project was conceived independently by two architects, John Bennett and Gustavo Bonevardi, and two artists, Paul Myoda and Julian LaVerdiere. On learning of each other's work, the two teams joined. Another architect, Richard Nash Gould, was later added. The lighting genius Paul Marantz executed the concept.*
>
> *As realized, the concept gave the impression of an image revealed, rather than designed, as if two lustrous columns have been excavated by an archaeological team from the darkness of time. Like classical columns, the towers were fluted, an effect of the 44 individual high-power lamps used to create each one. Extra lamps at the corners reinforced the architectonic illusion.*
>
> *The effect was similar to that made by missiles thrusting off into space. Though stationary, the light towers appeared aimed for the arrival of signs from above. The eye wanted to follow, not just behold them.*
>
> *Light, Marshall McLuhan reminded us, is a medium. Indeed, in his influential book* Understanding Media, *the Canadian thinker devoted his chapter on architecture to developing that idea. Light is a "pure" communication medium whose power to shape environments is independent of content. In artificial form, light reshaped the boundaries of buildings and entire cities. We encounter that form in its purest state at night, when gazing up at a skyline, or gazing down from an airplane window at suburban sprawl.*
>
> *Ancient builders designed monuments to align sacred sites with the positions of sun and moon. The lightness of Gothic construction was inseparable from the biblical narratives inscribed in stained glass for the benefit of those who couldn't read.*
>
> *But where have our two towers gone? "For the moment I can only cry out that I have lost my splendid mirage," F. Scott Fitzgerald wrote in 1945. "Come back, come back, O glittering and white!"* ∎

10–23 *Tribute in Light*
(March–April, 2002).
Topfoto/The Image Works.

structure filled with windmills at the top of the building will generate 20 percent of the building's energy. This part of the building is designed as cable-suspension structure.

Daniel Libeskind's design was originally chosen from a distinguished group of finalists, including the firm of David Childs. It was the individual who owns the lease on the ill-fated twin towers who appointed Childs the lead architect, putting Childs and Libeskind into what the latter has called "a forced marriage." One critic described the result of the compromise a "Freedom Bunker" in place of Freedom Tower. As this book goes to press, city planners, businesspeople, politicians, architects, families of the victims, and other citizens continue to debate the proper uses of lower Manhattan—of Ground Zero and its adjoining areas and neighborhoods. Even though Child's design appears to be the final vision for the moment, some believe that the process is not yet over. One can only hope for a solution that fits the spirit of the nation and also remains sensitive to the needs of the families of those who lost their lives.

SHELL ARCHITECTURE

Modern materials and methods of engineering have made it possible to enclose spaces with relatively inexpensive shell structures. Masonry domes have been replaced by lightweight shells, which are frequently flatter and certainly capable of spanning greater spaces. Shells have been constructed from reinforced concrete, wood, steel, aluminum, and even plastics and paper. The concept of shell architecture is as old as the canvas tent and as new as the geodesic dome (Fig. 10-25) designed by Buckminster Fuller for the

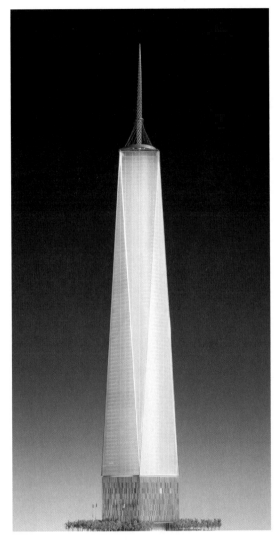

10-24   DAVID CHILDS IN COLLABORATION WITH DANIEL LIBESKIND.
Freedom Tower.
Skidmore, Owings and Merrill / Landov.

But Libeskind's integrated design would not survive the tangle of bureaucratic red tape that gripped (some say crippled) the process. What emerged was a compromise solution between two main architects—Libeskind and David Childs. The so-called Freedom Tower, which Libeskind designed to rise 1,776 feet, was an important symbolic aspect of the plan. According to the architect, that number reflects "a date [America's year of independence from Britain] that speaks to the whole world." Although the tower will still top out at 1,776 feet, its original slender and graceful lines have been replaced by Childs with a much more obviously fortified design (Fig. 10-24) that speaks "safety first." Only the first 70 floors will be occupied by office space, and these sit on a base of concrete and steel about 200 feet high. A lattice

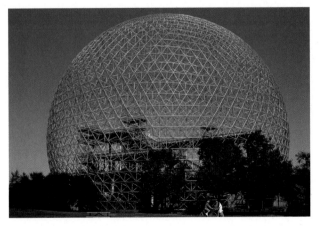

10-25   BUCKMINSTER FULLER.
United States Pavilion, Expo 67, Montreal (1967).
Topfoto / The Image Works.

American Pavilion at Expo 67 in Montreal. In a number of sports arenas, fabric roofs are held up by keeping the air pressure inside the building slightly greater than that outside. Like balloons, these roof structures are literally inflated.

Fuller's shell is an assemblage of lightweight metal trusses into a three-quarter sphere that is 250 feet in diameter. Looking more closely, one sees that the trusses compose six-sided units that give the organic impression of a honeycomb. Light floods the climate-controlled enclosure, creating an environment for any variety of human activity—and any form of additional construction—within. Such domes can be covered with many sorts of weatherproofing, from lightweight metals and fabric to translucent and transparent plastics and glass. Here the engineering requirements clearly create the architectural design.

NEW MATERIALS, NEW VISIONS

In architecture studios and schools, the saying goes, "Convention gets built; innovation gets published." But this adage is systematically being proven wrong as scientists and engineers have combined forces to turn architects' dreams into reality: "If you can think it, we can build it."

In 1997 Frank Gehry transformed architectural design with the use of titanium in the same way that reinforced concrete altered the look of the exterior "skin" of buildings in the 1950s and 1960s. His Guggenheim Museum in Bilbao, Spain (see Fig. 2-21), set a new artistic course for Gehry in terms of his own style and nurtured the adaptation of high-tech metals by architects worldwide. Gehry's Ray and Maria Stata Center (Fig. 10-26), which opened in 2005 on the MIT campus, stands as a visual summation of his most recent designs, materials, and theories of spatial relationships. The 730,000-square-foot complex will be a hub for research in the fields of computer science, linguistics, and philosophy. The assertive clashing of shapes signifies the disparate disciplines that will be housed in the structure, while communal lounges and shared interior spaces encourage interaction, collaboration, and the cross-fertilization of ideas. Gehry said of the Stata center, "It reflects the different groups, the collision of ideas, the energy of people and ideas. . . . That's what will lead to the breakthroughs and the positive results."

Architect Peter Testa's view is that there is a "need to rethink how we assemble buildings" and that it is time to design in collaboration with materials manufacturers and to explore the potential of nascent technologies. Testa and his partner, Devyn Weiser, have designed a high-rise tower out of composite materials (Fig. 10-27). Their skyscraper would be held erect by a cross-hatched lattice made of carbon fiber—a material several times stronger than the traditional steel. The "woven building" would have an interior that is completely open (except for elevator shafts) and void of structural support.

The use and reuse of unorthodox materials by some contemporary architects is also worth noting. Shigeru Ban, a Tokyo architect who has designed public buildings on the principle that art should not be only for the privileged, uses paper tubes and plastic sheets among other materials typically associated with other circumstances. Some of his works include the Paper Refugee Shelter for the United Nations, the Paper Museum and Paper Church in Japan, and a paper-tube arch in the Museum of Modern Art, New York, sculpture garden. He also designed the 45,000-square-foot No-

10-26 FRANK GEHRY.
Ray and Maria Stata Center for Computer, Information, and Intelligence Sciences at MIT, Cambridge, MA (2005).
Gehry Partners, LLC.

10-27 PETER TESTA AND DEVYN WEISNER, TESTA ARCHITECTURE AND DESIGN.
Carbon Tower.
© 2005 Testa Architecture/Design, Los Angeles.

10-28 SHIGERU BAN.
Nomadic Museum (2005).
Tyler Hicks, *The New York Times.*

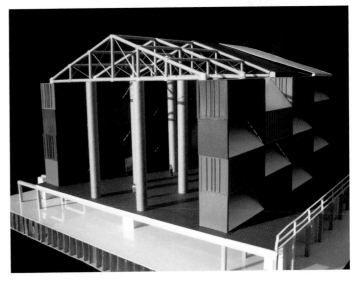

10-29 SHIGERU BAN.
Model of Nomadic Museum showing shipping containers, paper-tube columns, and roof trusses.
Shigeru Ban Architects.

madic Museum (Figs. 10-28 and 10-29)—a mobile structure whose walls are composed of 148 steel cargo containers; a roof and columns made of paper tubes; and a ceiling made of 1 million used, pressed, paper teabags (tea leaves removed). The museum was constructed to display the work of Gregory Colbert, a Canadian-born artist whose photographs of elephants, whales, and human–animal relationships seem to have a visual and environmental affinity with the structure surrounding them. Sited at one point on Manhattan's historic Pier 54, the Nomadic Museum has an itinerary that includes Santa Monica Pier in California, as well as the Vatican in Rome. According to architect Ban, "It can be seen by more people all over the world if it moves. Maybe it remains in your memory if it's gone."

ART TOUR

Chicago

Go for the lake and the miles of beaches. Go for the deep-pan pizza and hotdogs with the works. Go to cheer for the Chicago Cubs or the Bulls. Go to see Oprah! But while you're in Chicago—for goodness' sake—make time in your day for the most magnificent art and architecture you can imagine.

Situated at the literal crossroads between the East and Midwest, Chicago grew rich on trade opportunities and began to take shape as a major commercial and cultural center in the nineteenth century. The Great Chicago Fire of 1871, however, destroyed most of the downtown buildings in a conflagration that lasted 36 hours. Out of this devastation, after which one-third of the city population was homeless, came one of the greatest building campaigns in U.S. history.

Experiencing Chicago starts with getting to know its neighborhoods—77 in all—and its unique topographic features—such as the Chicago River, which wends its way amidst skyscrapers, or Lake Michigan, which provides 15 miles of recreational beaches. At its heart is the Loop, but the long list contains neighborhoods such as the Magnificent Mile, River North, River West, the Gold Coast, Old Town, Lincoln Park, Wrigleyville, Lakeview, South Loop, and Chinatown.

We all know how good it feels to "be in the loop." But that expression couldn't more meaning than when it's used to describe the city of Chicago. The Loop in this town refers to the very center of the downtown core and takes its name from the elevated train tracks that encircle the area.

The city of Chicago has always been synonymous with architectural innovation and world-class buildings. Balloon-frame construction (still one of the most common residential building types in the United States today, and so called because it was said to be as simple and easy as blowing up a balloon) originated in 1833 with a Chicago developer. Although most structures of this kind went up in flames in the 1871 fire, you can still see a few of them in the North Side area of the city. After the fire, wood was banned as a building material and cast iron and terra-cotta took its place. Those materials—along with steel—made their most significant impact on the city's commercial architecture. It was here that the first skyscraper was built and the Chicago School of architecture—an internationally celebrated style—was born.

One of the weirder structures in the downtown core is the Monadnock Building, the two halves of which represent old-style and new-style architectural design and materials. One half—the northern half—was designed in 1891 by the firm of Burnham and Root. At 16 stories, it was the tallest masonry building ever to have been constructed. Two years later, the other, southern half was constructed, this time of a steel skeleton covered with a sheath of terra-cotta. This design, by the firm of Holabird and Roche, was pivotal for the future of the skyscraper. Many followed—the Rookery, the Reliance Building, the Marquette Building, to name a few. All of these can be seen within

THE MONADNOCK BUILDING.
Robert Frerck/Odyssey.

the downtown core. Keep your eye out for the signature "Chicago windows" on some of these buildings. They were a stylistic by-product of the Chicago School's structural innovations and consist of a wide central glass pane that doesn't open flanked by two thinner windows that do.

Among the sentimental favorites of Chicago architecture are the Marshall Field and Company and the Carson Pirie Scott department stores. Marshall Field's began as a Renaissance-revival building that ultimately grew to accommodate 124,400 square miles of retail space; its southern atrium features a spectacular glass mosaic dome whose installation was supervised by Louis Comfort Tiffany himself. Louis Sullivan, one of the city's most prolific and beloved architects of the Chicago School, finished the exterior of his steel-frame Carson Pirie Scott building with white terracotta and graced the first two stories of the entrance with ornamental cast-iron motifs consisting of organic and geometric forms. You can still pick out the initials *L.H.S.* above the entrance.

Surveying the architectural wonders of Chicago can keep a tourist busy. These historic examples are but the tip of the iceberg. Within the downtown core you'll find Beaux Arts—style gems such as the Chicago Theatre, Neoclassical monuments such as the Chicago Cultural Center and the Art Institute of Chicago (more later on this phenomenal collection), and on the opposite end of the style spectrum, the Sears Tower. Opened in 1974 after three years under construction, the building had, then lost, and then regained the title as the world's tallest building (thanks to the addition of one very tall antenna). Not surprisingly, its sky deck offers unparalleled views of the city, Lake Michigan, and beyond.

THE TRIBUNE TOWER.
Copyright John Zich/zrImages/Corbis.

Extending your tour a bit north, you'll come to the Miracle Mile. There you'll get a glimpse of the Wrigley Building (seat of the chewing gum empire), Marina City's corncob towers, Miës van der Rohe's exposed steel-frame IBM Building, and the Tribune Tower (home to one of the country's most influential newspapers). The Tribune Tower that you see was the winning design in a 1922 international competition calling upon architects to design the most beautiful office building in the world. The entrance features sculptures of figures from Aesop's fables, and gargoyles abound in the upper reaches of the facade. Most peculiar, perhaps, is the collection of stone fragments from the world's great architectural sites embedded in the outer walls of the building. You'll find pieces from London's Westminster Abbey, the Colosseum in Rome, and the Great Wall of China; a rock from Antarctica and one from the moon. Believe it or not, most of these stones were pilfered by *Tribune* foreign correspondents at the behest (command?) of one of the paper's early publishers.

Among Chicago's newest additions to its architecture hall of fame is Frank Gehry's music pavilion for Millennium Park, an extension of Grant Park. Gehry's band shell, home to the Grant Park Symphony, is renowned for a sound system that reaches all of its 14,000 audience members.

Although architecture in Chicago has a way of monopolizing the spotlight, its art collections merit a significant piece of the action. For one thing, the Art Institute of Chicago, a venerable museum of art that was founded in 1879, has what some of us like to call "The Room." This term of endearment refers to a cluster of spaces featuring some of the best-known examples of Impressionist, Post-impressionist, and early twentieth-century art—Monet haystacks, Degas dancers, a van Gogh self-portrait; Cezanne's *Still Life with Basket of Apples* (Fig. 18-26), Picasso's *Old Guitarist* (Fig. 19-6), Hopper's

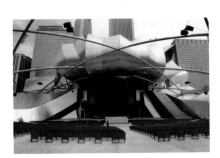

FRANK GEHRY, Pritzker Pavilion for Millennium Park.
Copyright John Zich/Corbis.

Nighthawks (Fig. 1-25), Wood's *American Gothic* (Fig. 4-9), Toulouse-Lautrec's *At the Moulin Rouge* (Fig. 18-30), and one of Chicago's most prized possessions, Seurat's *A Sunday Afternoon on the Island of La Grand Jatte* (Fig. 18-25)—and more. Students remark that their textbooks unfold before their eyes as they wander these galleries.

Chicago's museums go far beyond the Institute. The Museum of Contemporary Art has an impressive permanent collection (Alexander Calder, Andy Warhol, Cindy Sherman—to mention but a few artists featured in your textbook) mixed with cutting-edge rotating exhibitions by new and established contemporary artists. The Terra Museum of American Art, founded and funded by a man who invented fast-drying ink, is one of the only U.S. collections designed to feature exclusively works by American artists. It includes paintings of the Hudson River School, George Caleb Bingham, and Edward Hopper. The University of Chicago is also the site of both the Oriental Institute (specializing in Middle Eastern antiquities) and the Smart Museum (known for its old master prints, Asian paintings, and postwar Chicago artwork and craft). These museums, and the university, are in Chicago's South Side area, the location also of the famed Frank Lloyd Wright Robie

FRANK LLOYD WRIGHT, Robie House.
Art Resource, NY.

House, designed for the bicycle manufacturer-magnate Frederick Robie. Wright's signature unity among all of the parts—exterior design, interior function, interior decoration—makes this one of the quintessential examples of Wright's Prairie style of architecture.

So grab a hotdog (which, in Chicago, has its own sort of architecture) with ketchup, mustard, relish, onions, and hot peppers and get yourself moving. You still have to meet Sue (the most complete *Tyrannosaurus rex* anywhere, on display at the Field Museum) before you catch the best jazz and blues in the world.

 To continue your tour and learn more about Chicago, go to our website.

11

CRAFT AND DESIGN

I think art can exist within any craft tradition. Craft is just another way of saying means. I think it's a question of conscious intention, finally, and personal gifts, or giftedness. It seems that in art there is a primacy of idea over both means or craft, and function. Idea has to transcend both. I think this is probably why it's so difficult to make art out of something functional, or in a realm where craft has been nurtured for its own sake.

—Martin Puryear

An Attic vase, a Navajo rug, Tiffany glass, a Chippendale desk—which is art? Which is craft? Art critics and historians once had certain answers to these questions. Now, however, the perception of the relationship among functional objects, craft materials and techniques, and works of fine art has changed. Consider this story concerning one of the Metropolitan Museum of Art's most precious acquisitions, as retold by art critic Arthur C. Danto.[1] According to Thomas Hoving, the director of the museum at the time of the purchase, the vase in Figure 11-1 is "the single most perfect work of art I ever encountered . . . an object of total adoration." In his memoirs, Hoving further described his feelings upon his first encounter with the piece: "The first thought that came to mind was that I was gazing not at a vase, but at a painting." The director was obviously swept off his feet by

[1] Arthur C. Danto, "Fine Art and the Functional Object," *Glass,* no. 51 (Spring 1993): 24–29.

Musée Toulouse-Lautrec, Albi, France/Erich Lessing/Art Resource, New York.

11-1 EUPHRONIOS AND EUXITHEOS.
Calyx Krater (1st quarter of 5th century BCE).
Ceramic. H: 18″; D: 21 11/16″.
The Metropolitan Museum of Art. Bequest of Joseph H. Durkee.
Gift of Darious Ogden Mills, and gift of C. Buxton Love. By exchange
(1972.11.10). Copyright 1999 The Metropolitan Museum of Art,
New York.

this masterpiece of Greek art—a terra-cotta vessel painted with the scene of the *Dead Sarpedon Carried by Thanatos and Hypnos* and signed by both the potter and the painter. But why did Hoving diminish the significance of the potter's craft by essentially dismissing the pot as a mere support for an extraordinary painting? Danto suggests that Hoving's reaction is indicative of an art-world prejudice of sorts—one that attaches less importance to functional objects and decoration of any kind. He warns that "the painting [on the vase] is there to decorate an object of conspicuous utility" and cannot be considered without reference to the vase itself. In fact, doing so precludes any real understanding of the work in the historical and artistic context in which it was created.

What purpose does this esoteric argument have for us who, as students, are trying to understand art? Simply this: The distinction between fine art and functional object is linked to the historical and cultural context in which a work was created. As Danto pointed out, the Greek philosophers praised craftspeople as somewhere between artists and philosophers, but held the view that no one was lower than the artist. Danto paraphrases Plato in *The Republic:* "The carpenter knows how to fashion in real life what the painter can merely imitate; therefore . . . artists have no real knowledge at all, trafficking only in the outward appearance of

things."[2] More than 2,000 years later, a French philosopher would declare, "Only what serves no purpose is truly beautiful."[3] Today, many painters are turning their talent to utilitarian objects or creating paintings with techniques traditional to craft. Ceramic artists are creating works of sculpture, and sculptors are finding innovative ways to manipulate clay, wood, and metal. The glassmaker's art has reached new heights of experimentation while employing centuries-old techniques. For many artists, the distinction between art and craft is an artificial and limiting one. Any and all options should be exercised in pursuit of artistic expression. And the aesthetic and artistic merit of any creative work ought to be recognized.

In this chapter we discuss a variety of media and categories of artistic expression. We consider the materials traditional to craft—clay, glass, fiber, metal, and wood—using historical and contemporary works as evidence of the broad technical and stylistic ranges of the media. We also examine graphic design, industrial design, web design, and urban design. In the realm of design, as with crafts, the distinction between art for art's sake and art for utility's sake is also sometimes blurred.

CERAMICS

Ceramics refers to the art or process of making objects of baked clay. Ceramics includes many objects that range from the familiar pots and bowls of **pottery,** to clay sculptures, to building bricks and the extremely hard tiles that protect the surface of the space shuttles from the intense heat of atmospheric reentry.

Methods of Working with Clay

Ceramics is a venerable craft that was highly refined in the ancient lands of the Middle East and in China. For thousands of years people have modeled, pinched, and patted various types of wet clay into useful vessels and allowed them to dry or bake in the sun, creating hard, durable containers. They have rolled clay into rope shapes, which they coiled around an open space. They have rolled out slabs of clay like dough, cut them into pieces, fastened them together, and smoothed them with simple tools, as Native Americans still do today.

---

[2] Ibid.
[3] Théophile Gautier, Preface to his novel *Mademoiselle de Maupin*, 1835.

11-2   MARILYN LEVINE.
        John's Jacket (1981).
        Ceramic, zipper, and metal fasteners. 36″ × 23½″ × 7″.
        Courtesy of the artist.

They discovered that if they allowed clay vessels to dry, then fired them in a type of oven called a kiln, or over coals, they became waterproof and more durable.

Marilyn Levine's mostly clay *John's Jacket* (Fig. 11-2) shows the whimsical use of materials that sometimes defines the aesthetic of the craftsperson. In galleries we circle suspiciously around works such as these. We are drawn to test out our visual sensations by touching them, and perhaps we are simultaneously amused by and annoyed at the craftsperson who would push our senses to the limit. Perhaps we are also on the lookout for gallery employees who might frown on our using our hands to test what we sense with our eyes, and for fellow patrons who might doubt our intelligence or criticize our quest for tactile sensation. Ultimately, the combination of the phony and the real shock the sense of touch.

Levine's jacket is, in reality, composed of rolled-out slabs of clay that have the look of leather, and the work also contains stitching and real metal snaps and a zipper. The shifting back and forth between illusion and reality functions as a metaphor for what arts and crafts are all about: in so many instances they transform the world that they represent.

The Potter's Wheel

The potter's wheel (Fig. 11-3) was first used in the Middle East in about 4000 BCE and seems to have come into common use a thousand years later. A pot can be **thrown** quite rapidly and effortlessly on a wheel once the techniques have been mastered, in contrast to the more laborious and time-consuming process of building a pot by coiling. In **coiling,** ropes of clay are fashioned, then stacked upon one another. The walls of the pot are then scraped to a smooth finish and molded to the desired vessel shape. The walls of a wheel-thrown pot tend to be thinner and more uniform in thickness than coiled pots, and the outer and inner surfaces are smoother. This does not suggest, however, that coiled pots in the hands of some craftspeople do not approach wheel-thrown pots in their accomplishment. For example, Native Americans of the southwestern United States have never

11-3   *The Hands of the Potter.*
        Conrad Knowles forming a tray and a bowl
        for his collection of artful pottery.
        Copyright 2005 Fritz Henle Estate.

11-4 MARIA MARTINEZ.
Long-neck Avanyu Vase, black on black (c. 1925–1930).
H: 13″; D: 8½″.
Courtesy Adobe Gallery, Albuquerque.

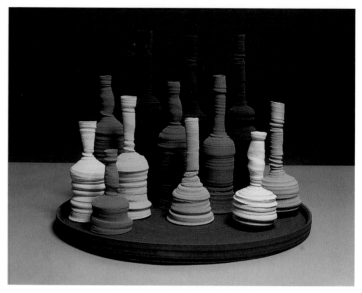

11-5 JAMES MAKINS.
Junihitoe (1992).
Porcelain. 14½″ × 20″ × 20″.
Courtesy of Barry Rosen & Jaap van Liere Modern and Contemporary Art, collection of the Everson Museum, Syracuse, NY.

used the potter's wheel, yet their hand-built pots can be as thin walled and symmetrical as their wheel-thrown counterparts. A wonderful example of coiling can be found in works by the famous Native American potter Maria Martinez. Her black-on-black vessels (Fig. 11-4), adorned with stylized natural forms, flowers, and animals, are among the finest works of the Pueblo people.

Anyone who has been a student in a ceramics class appreciates the difficulty experienced in mastering the potter's wheel. The body movement, rhythm of the wheel, placement, and force of the fingers must come together like a smoothly choreographed dance. The goal, generally, is to achieve perfect symmetry and a smooth contour. How ironic, then, are the works of James Makins (Fig. 11-5), which, when seen alone, may look like the failed efforts of "frustrated student, Ceramics 101." These objects—vases? vessels? bottles?—are, in effect, records of variations in men-

tal concentration, hand pressure, wheel speed, and glaze experimentation. Set on trays as they are, they suggest ritual or domestic objects or, to some, figures on a stage. The entire composition—incidentally an exceptional example of variety within unity—appears foremost as a sculpture, probably because these bottles seem far from utilitarian.

Glazing

Variation in color and texture is secured by the choice of clay and by glazing. The earliest-known glaze dates from about 3000 BCE and is found on tile from the tomb of the Egyptian king Menes.

Glazes, which contain finely ground minerals, are used in liquid form. They are brushed, sprayed, or poured on ceramics after a preliminary **bisque firing** removes all water. During the second firing, the glaze becomes glasslike, or **vitrifies,** fusing with the clay. It gives the clay a glassy, **nonporous** surface coating that can be shiny or dull, depending on its composition. Glazing can create intricate, glossy patterns across otherwise uniform and dull surfaces.

Contrast the simple, pure form of the vase by Chester Nealie (Fig. 11-6) with the unrefined forms of James Makins. The deep but mellow glaze of the Nealie "bottle" is modulated by light to impart a glowing intensity, in contrast to the opaque and uniform glazes of Makins. In both groups, the glazes complement the potters' techniques. The graceful contours of the Nealie vase would lose their sensuality and delicacy with the bold colors and matte finish of the Makins piece. Similarly, the spontaneity, brusqueness, and uniqueness of those lilting bottles would be lost if they were to be enshrouded in a uniform, pearlescent glaze.

Robert Arneson's *Jackson Pollock* (Fig. 11-7) provides a very different example of a glazed ceramic work and illustrates how blurred the line between craft and fine art can be.

11-7 ROBERT ARNESON.
Jackson Pollock (1983).
Glazed ceramic. 23″ × 13″ × 7″.
Collection of Dr. Paul and Stacy Polydoran. Courtesy of George Adams Gallery, New York. Copyright Estate of Robert Arneson. Licensed by VAGA, New York.

11-6 CHESTER NEALIE.
Bottle (2000).
Celadon glaze. H: 30 cm.
Courtesy of the artist, Chester Nealie, woodfire potter.

Arneson's figures are purposefully unrefined, intentionally flawed, mirroring the ceramic artist's view of human nature as imperfect. The subject of the work, Jackson Pollock, was an Abstract Expressionist who became renowned for his drip paintings (see Chapter 19). Arneson's clay portrait unifies the artist and his works by providing the illusion of overall dripping and splattering on the bust.

Types of Ceramics

Ceramic objects and **wares** are classified according to the type of clay and the temperature at which they are fired.

11-8 Mangbetu Portrait Bottle, Zaire
(19th–20th centuries).
Terra-cotta. H: 11⅜″.

The Metropolitan Museum of Art, New York.
The Michael C. Rockefeller Collection.
Bequest of Nelson Rockefeller, 1979. (1979. 206. 246).
Photograph © 1991 The Metropolitan Museum of Art.

Earthenware derives its name from the fact that it is usually red or tan in color. It is made from coarse clay or shale clay and is usually fired at 1,000 to 2,000 degrees Fahrenheit. It is somewhat porous and is used for common bricks and coarse pottery. The Mangbetu bottle from Zaire (Fig. 11-8) is made from **terra-cotta,** a heavy clay earthenware product fired at a higher temperature of about 2,070 to 2,320 degrees Fahrenheit. The head is an effigy or portrait of a Mangbetu citizen. Note that the textural decoration is reminiscent of a basket weave. It was probably fired in the open, on a bed of straw and twigs.

Stoneware is usually gray but may be tan or reddish. It is fired at about 2,300 to 2,700 degrees Fahrenheit. It is slightly porous or fully nonporous and is used for most dinnerware and much ceramic sculpture.

Claudi Casanovas's *Block #43* (Fig. 11-9) is a cubic form ceramic sculpture built around a hollow inner space. The work emphasizes the massive, angular forms inherent in hardened clay; the colors complement the natural earthen materials of the sculpture—black, brown, and beige, even a hint of gold—that we might find in the strata of the planet. The texture and fissures would have it seem that the work has been exposed to harsh elements from without and within. Yet it will endure. Casanovas, a visual artist and poet, wrote about his "blocks":

> *Each piece is a silence*
> *If I were a poet, I would inscribe words there*
> *To bring us closer to the truth*
> *Which urges us on from within*
> *If I were a philosopher, or writer, I would*
>   *inscribe words so*
> *That the heart would overflow with knowledge*
> *And the meaning of clarity*
> *If I were a monk I would inscribe prayers in which*
>   *all spirit might find repose*
> *And glory in the same Being*
> *Only I am a simple mortal*
> *Surrounded by simple obscurity*
> *And unfailing silences*
> *Each piece is a silence*
> *That is filled with the sounds of your gaze.*[4]

[4] Translated from the Catalan by Marilyn McCull, in Miguel Jimenez, "Claudi Casanovas' Blocks," *Ceramics: Art and Perception,* no. 49 (2002): 45. Reprinted with permission.

*Ceramic sculptural works are more specific than traditional sculpture
with its expressive force coming from the surface of the body. The surface
of the sculpture can be bare clay or clay with oxides and glazes;
however, this surface tells us as much about the purpose
of the sculpture as does the form itself.*

—Tania De Brukyner

11-9   CLAUDI CASANOVAS.
Block #43 (2001).
30 cm × 30 cm × 26 cm.
Copyright Claudi Casanovas.
Photo courtesy of Lois Fichner-Rathus.
Photo reproduced by kind permission of Galerie Besson.

Porcelain is hard, nonporous, and usually white or gray in color. It is made from fine, white kaolin clay and contains other minerals such as feldspar, quartz, and flint in various proportions. It is usually fired at 2,400 to 2,500 degrees Fahrenheit, and it is used for fine dinnerware. Chinese porcelain, or **china,** is white and fired at low temperatures. It is glasslike or vitreous and nonporous, and it may be translucent. It makes a characteristic ringing sound when struck with a fingernail. Porcelain has been used by various cultures for vases and dinnerware for thousands of years. Like other kinds of wares, it has also provided a vehicle for artistic expression.

Harumi Nakashima's *Porcelain Form* (Fig. 11-10) illustrates how the smooth, sophisticated surfaces of fine porcelain stand in contrast

11-10   HARUMI NAKASHIMA.
Porcelain Form (2001).
Porcelain. Inlaid decoration.
50 cm × 45 cm × 40 cm.
European Ceramic Work Centre, The Netherlands.
Photograph by Corné Bastiaansen.

to the rough-hewn, rocklike textures often given center stage in earthenware. Here, the rounded surfaces have a biomorphic or organic quality. The repetition in the polka-dotted glaze complements the rhythms found in the budding protuberances. Whereas the colors of the Casanovas piece connect it with earth and reality, the unnatural blue of Nakashima's dots against the purity of the white surfaces disconnect the work from anything in our tangible experience.

One of the fascinating features of clay is its versatility. Clay can be used to form the refined vessels of Chester Nealie and the crude, slablike structures of both primitive and contemporary workers. It is said that one test of the integrity of a work is its trueness to its material. In the case of ceramics, however, one would be hard pressed to point to any one of the products of clay as representative of its "true" face.

GLASS

Glass, like ceramics, has had a long history and has been used to create fine art and functional objects. The Roman historian Pliny the Elder traced the beginnings of glassmaking (albeit accidental) to an account of Phoenician sailors preparing a meal on a beach. They set their pots on lumps of *natron*—an alkali they had on deck to embalm the dead—lit a fire, and when the hot natron mixed with the sand of the beach, molten glass flowed. In fact, glass predates the Phoenicians and the Romans, and the tale as recounted by Pliny probably has some gaps. But the truth is that the recipe for glass is quite simple; as researchers have found in trying to replay the sailor's experience, it could happen![5] The result may not have been that wondrous substance—transparent or translucent—that has the power to transform light into an ephemeral, jewel-like palette. But it was surely glass.

Techniques of Working Glass

Glass is generally made from molten sand, or **silica,** mixed with minerals such as lead, copper, cobalt, cadmium, lime, soda, or potash. Certain combinations of minerals afford the glass a rich quality as found in the stained-glass windows of the great cathedrals and in the more recent stained-glass works of Henri Matisse and Marc Chagall.

As Beethoven created his magnificent final symphony after he became deaf, Henri Matisse achieved something similar in scope in the visual works he created once he became bedridden with a serious illness. Rather than surrender to despair, Matisse found opportunity in disability and experimented with media that permitted him to express himself despite his physical limitations. Whereas he had been primarily known as a painter and sculptor, he turned to pasted paper cutouts, which he had previously used to plan large decorative compositions. Perhaps the incentive for these new works was found after Matisse moved to the Riviera town of Vence, where he was cared for by Dominican nuns while he was ill. To show his appreciation, Matisse designed for them a chapel complete with stained-glass windows, murals, and all the liturgical accoutrements—priests' vestments, an altar, candlesticks, and a crucifix. His stained-glass window, *The Tree of Life* (Fig. 11-11), consists of twin elongated arches—shapes that are familiar in the tradition of stained glass in religious architecture—alive with what appear to be overlays of falling leaves. The luminosity of the color is such that the viewer is dazzled by the sense of growth and movement. Blues and greens "cool down" the light streaming through the window, whereas the brilliant yellow of the shapely oak leaves reinforces the feeling of warmth, of life.

Like ceramics, glass is versatile. Molten glass can be modeled, pressed, rolled, blown, and even spun into threads. **Fiberglass** is glass that has been spun into fine filaments. It can be woven into yarn for textiles, used in woolly masses for insulation, and pressed and molded into a plastic material that is tough enough to be used for the body of an automobile. About 4,000 years ago the Egyptians modeled small bottles and jars from molten glass. Contemporary machine-made glassware is usually pressed. Molten glass is poured into molds and then forced into shape by a plunger. The plate glass used for windows and mirrors is made by passing rollers over molten glass as it cools.

Just as the potter's wheel transformed the making of clay vessels both in terms of quality and quantity, so did the technique of **glassblowing** change the nature of glass production. This technique was developed by the Romans, who created pieces of all shapes, sizes, colors, and functions, making glass containers commonplace. In this method, a hollow tube or blowpipe is dipped into molten glass and then removed. Air is blown through the tube,

[5] William S. Ellis, "Glass: Capturing the Dance of Light," *National Geographic* 184, no. 6 (December 1993): 37–69.

11-11 HENRI MATISSE.
Interior of the Chapel of the Rosary, Vence.
At left: *The Tree of Life*, stained glass.

causing the hot glass to form a spherical bubble whose contours are shaped through rolling and pulling with various tools. The process is usually quite rapid, but the glass can be reheated if it must be worked extensively.

Once the desired shape has been achieved, the surface of the glass can be decorated by cutting or **engraving** planes that reflect light in certain patterns, by etching, or by printing.

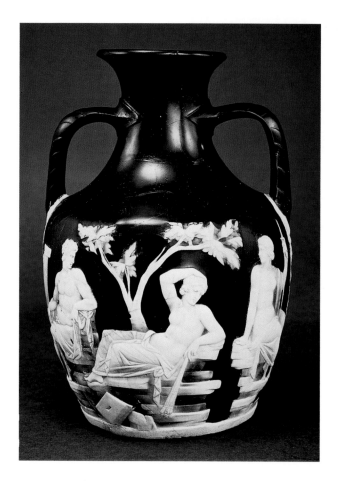

11–12　Portland Vase (Roman, 3rd century).
Cameo-cut glass.

British Museum, London. Heritage Image Partnership (HIP),
heritage-images.com.

One of the earliest and best-known pieces of glass-ware is the Roman Portland Vase (Fig. 11-12), which survives from the third century CE. The refinement of the piece testifies to the long tradition of glassmaking in Rome even before that time. The Portland Vase was created in three steps. The underlying form was blown from dark blue glass. Next, a coating of semi-opaque white glass was added to the surface of the basic blue form. Finally, the white glass was carved away to provide the bas-relief of figures and vegetation that circumscribe the vase. The relief consists of many subtle gradations. Where it is thinnest, the blue from beneath shows through to provide a shaded quality. Imagine the patience of the cameo cutter who meticulously chipped glass away from glass, leaving unscratched the brittle blue surface that serves as background for the figures.

In various eras, different world centers became renowned for glassmaking. For example, during the Middle Ages, Venetian glass became known for its lightness and delicacy.

Eighteenth-century Stiegel glass, made in Pennsylvania, became known for its use of flint (lead oxide) to achieve hardness and brightness. So-called **flint glass** is used for lenses of optical instruments and for crystal. Nineteenth-century Sandwich glass—from the town of Sandwich, Massachusetts—was pressed into molds to take on the appearance of a cut pattern. Ornamental Sandwich glass pieces in the shapes of cats, dogs, hens, and ducks became common home decorations.

During the second half of the nineteenth century, Louis Comfort Tiffany designed some of the most handsome **Art Nouveau** interiors. His glassware (Fig. 11-13) attains a similar marriage of simplicity and exotic refinement. Graceful botanical forms swell and become attenuated. The translucent or iridescent glass is decorated by spiral shapes,

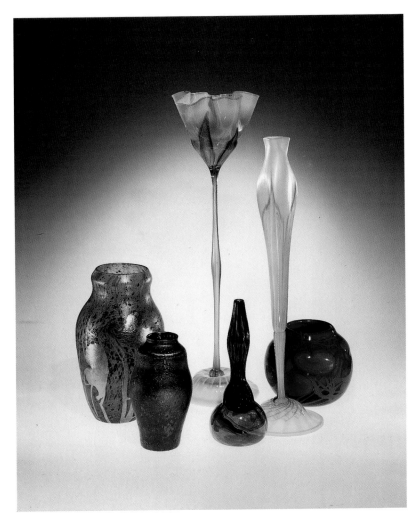

11-13 LOUIS COMFORT TIFFANY.
Six pieces of glassware in Art Nouveau
style made by the Tiffany Studio.
Glass, favrile. Height, left to right:
$8^9/_{16}''$; $5^7/_8''$; $18^{11}/_{16}''$; $7^5/_8''$; $16^1/_4''$; $4^1/_2''$.
The Metropolitan Museum of Art, New York
(96.17.42; 41.121.9; 51.121.17–.18; 55.213.22;
55.213.28). Photograph copyright 1987
The Metropolitan Museum of Art, New York.

swirling lines, and floating forms that seem to grow naturally out of the glassblowing process. They keep faith with the Art Nouveau creed that decoration should be a natural expression of the manufacturing process. Tiffany also fashioned many fine candlesticks, lamps, and lighting fixtures from bronze that show the same botanical whimsy he expressed in his glassware.

FIBER ARTS

Fibers are slender, threadlike structures that are derived from animals (for example, wool or silk), vegetable (cotton or linen), or synthetic (rayon, nylon, or fiberglass) sources.

The fiber arts refer to a number of disciplines in which fibers are combined to make functional or decorative objects or works of art. They include, but are not limited to, weaving, embroidery, crochet, and macramé.

Weaving

Weaving was known to the Egyptians, who placed patterned fabrics before the thrones of the pharaohs 5,000 years ago. Only royalty could tread on certain fabrics. According to ancient Greek legend, King Agamemnon showed excessive pride by walking upon purple fabrics that were intended for the gods.

The Chandeliers of Dale Chihuly

They're going to think we're nuts over there, and of course
we are a little nuts, but we'll get this thing built.

—Dale Chihuly (about the Icicle Creek chandelier)

11-14 DALE CHIHULY.
Rio delle Torreselle Chandelier (1996), Venice, Italy.
A chandelier installation in the Rio Delle Torre Stelle,
part of the Chihuly over Venice project, Venezia Aperto Vetro.
Photo: Russell Johnson, courtesy Chihuly Studio.

"A little bit nuts." Artists, and even the rest of us, may have felt this way or been characterized this way at some point or another—especially when we were seeing things in an unconventional way. Glass artist Dale Chihuly has redefined the conventional definition and function of "chandelier" by designing works he describes by this name for public spaces from Venice to Jerusalem, from the world's great museums to the wilderness of the great outdoors. Although many chandeliers, in the traditional sense, are ornamental, they are also functional objects used, with candles or electricity, to illuminate an environment. But Chihuly's chandeliers are a different species. They do not emit light of their own. Rather, they reflect and transform ambient light—batteries not included.

Chihuly's extraordinary glassworks capture, amplify, and channel light. In their unusual stylistic juxtaposition with their surroundings, his chandeliers compel passersby to take another look at the context in which they are set—whether the Byzantine architecture and canals we find in Venice (Fig. 11-14), the ancient ruins in Jerusalem, or in the wilderness, the literal natural state of affairs.

Chihuly designed the chandelier shown in Figure 11-15 for the Sleeping Lady mountain retreat at Icicle Creek in the state of Washington. He erected it on an ancient granite boulder among the grand pines of a primeval setting, surrounded by a river and a profusion of wildlife. The chandelier reflects and amplifies the frosted serenity of the site in winter. It enriches visitors' relationship with the area surrounding the retreat and with nature as a whole. The chandelier also adds Chihuly's—and humankind's—personal stamp to a pristine wooded site. It also says something about the vision and the passion of the artist—unique in this case to Dale Chihuly, though made visual by a team of glassblowers and technicians. Does the work have deeper symbolic meanings, meanings that connect it with the history of

Chihuly is a luminist. He uses glass as a literal and metaphorical prism through which he projects both ambient and intense theatrical light to produce sublime, luminous effects. This connects him to the long history of art in which light is cherished, "otherworldly," and implies divine presence.

—Jack Cowart

art and civilization, meanings that connect it with contemporary technology and modes of expression? Much of the answer to that question lies in you. Perhaps you would like to consider these lines from Wallace Stevens's poem "Anecdote of the Jar":

> *I placed a jar in Tennessee,*
> *And round it was, upon a hill.*
> *It made the slovenly wilderness*
> *Surround that hill.*
> *The wilderness rose up to it,*
> *And sprawled around, no longer wild.** ∎

---

*From *The Collected Poems of Wallace Stevens* by Wallace Stevens, © 1945 by Wallace Stevens and renewed 1982 by Holly Stevens. Used by permission of Alfred A. Knopf, a division of Random House, Inc.

11–15   DALE CHIHULY.
Icicle Creek Chandelier (1996).
Photo courtesy of the artist.

11-16 Arbadil carpet, probably Tabriz (1539–1540). Woolen pile. 34″ × 17½″.

Victoria and Albert Museum, London/Art Resource, New York.

The **weaving** of fabric or cloth is accomplished by interfacing horizontal and vertical threads. The length-wise fibers are called the **warp,** and the crosswise threads are called the **weft** or **woof.** The material and type of weave determine the weight and quality of the cloth. Wool, for example, makes soft, resilient cloth that is easy to dye. Nylon is strong, more durable than wool, mothproof, resistant to mildew and mold, nonallergenic, and easy to dye.

There are a number of types of weaves. The **plain weave** found in burlap, muslin, and cotton broadcloth is the strongest and simplest: the woof thread passes above one warp fiber and beneath the next. In the **satin weave,** woof threads pass above and beneath several warp threads. Warp and woof form broken diagonal patterns in the **twill weave.** In **pile weaving,** which is found in carpeting and in velvet, loops or knots are tied; when the knotting is done, the ends are cut or sheared to create an even surface. In sixteenth-century Persia, where carpet weaving reached an artistic peak, pile patterns often had as many as 1,000 knots to the square inch.

The Persian rug shown in Figure 11-16 was woven in the seventeenth century. Like others of its kind, it portrays the old Islamic concept of Paradise as a garden. Here, a light-colored tree and an assortment of other plants grow on a claret red background. The date palm, the iris, a symbolic tree of life, hyacinths, and tulips were frequently depicted on such rugs.

Weaving is typically carried out by the hand **loom** or a power loom. The Alaskan Chilkat robe (Fig. 11-17), however, was woven by Native American women without benefit of a loom. Chilkat women achieved a very fine texture with a thread made from a core of a strand of cedar bark covered with the wool from a mountain goat. Clan members used robes such as these on important occasions to show off the family crest. Here a strikingly stylized, winged animal occupies the center of a field of eyes, heads, and mysterious symbols.

Traditional weaving techniques may surface in innovative ways in the hands of contemporary artists. Ed Rossbach's wall hanging (Fig. 11-18), which, in overall shape, is not unlike the Chilkat robe, is worlds apart in its choice of materials and strong political message. Rossbach plaits construction paper in such a manner that his image emerges subtly from an overall mottled background.

The surfaces of fabrics can be enhanced by printing, embroidery, tie-dyeing, or batik. Hand printing has been known since ancient times, and Oriental traders brought the practice to Europe. A design was stamped on a fabric with a carved wooden block that had been inked. Contemporary

11-17 DORICA JACKSON.
Chilkat robe (1976).
Cedar bark warp; sheep's wool wefts. W: 60″.
The Courtesy of the U.S. Department of the Interior. National Park Service.
Sitka National Historical Park, Sitka, AK.

11-19 Ceremonial feathered basket with bead and shell
pendants. Pomo, CA (American Indian, Pomo, 1900).
H: 3½″.
Phoebe A. Hearst Museum of Anthropology, University of California,
Berkeley.

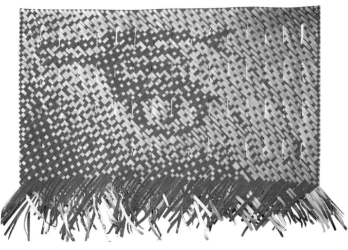

11-18 ED ROSSBACH.
Handgun (1975).
Plaited construction paper. 40″ × 54″.
The Collection of Craft Alliance. Courtesy of the artist.

machine printing uses inked rollers in the place of blocks, and fabrics can be printed at astonishingly rapid rates. In **embroidery,** the design is made by needlework.

Tie-dyeing and batik both involve dyeing fabrics. In **tie-dyeing,** designs are created by sewing or tying folds in the cloth to prevent the dye from coloring certain sections of fabric (Figs. 11-21 and 11-22). In **batik,** applications of wax prevent the dye from coloring sections of fabric that are to be kept light or white. A series of dye baths and waxings can be used to create subtly deeper colors.

Basketry

In **basketry,** or basket weaving, fibers are also woven together in various patterns. The delightful Pomo gift basket (Fig. 11-19) was woven from grass and glass beads. Triangles of warm primary red leap out from a backdrop of cool primary blue and pale straw. Native Americans from California made extremely fine basketry, with as many as 60 stitches to the inch. Barks, roots, and other fibers supplemented grass, and precious feathers and shells were sometimes used.

METALWORK AND JEWELRY

The refining and working of metals has been known for thousands of years. Iron and its alloys have been used to fashion horseshoes and arrowheads and, more recently, the skeletons of skyscrapers. **Stainless steel** is used in kitchen utensils and furniture. Lightweight aluminum is used in cookware and in aircraft. Bronze is the favorite metal of sculptors. **Brass** is seen everywhere from andirons to candlesticks to beds.

Silver and gold have been prized for millennia for their rarity and their appealing colors and textures. They are used in jewelry, fine tableware, ritual vessels, and sacred objects. In jewelry these precious metals often serve as settings for equally precious gems or polished stones, or their surfaces can be **enameled** by melting powdered glass on them. These metals even find use as currency; in times of political chaos,

The Fiber Arts of Faith Ringgold

Faith Ringgold was born in Harlem in 1930 and educated in the public schools of New York City. Raised with a social conscience, she painted murals and other works inspired by the civil rights movement in the 1960s and, a decade later, took to feminist themes after her exclusion from an all-male exhibition at New York's School of Visual Arts. Ringgold's mother, a fashion designer, was always sewing, the artist recalls, and at this time the artist herself turned to sewing and related techniques—needlepoint, beading, braided ribbon, and sewn fabric—to produce soft sculptures such as those in *Mama Jones, Andrew, Barbara, and Faith* (Fig. 11-20), from her series *The Family of Women*. African garments inspired the clothing of these family members, and the faces are reminiscent of African masks.

More recently, Ringgold is most well known for her narrative quilts, such as the highly acclaimed *Tar Beach* (see Fig. 1-24), which combine traditions common to African Americans and women—storytelling and quilting. *Matisse's Chapel* (Fig. 11-21) is from Ringgold's *French Collection,* which inserts contemporary American artists, other colleagues, and family members into French settings. In one quilt, *Dancing at the Louvre,* friends, including the children of one, are shown in high spirits before the Mona Lisa. In *Picasso's Studio,* the famed Spanish artist (literally) draws inspiration for *Les Demoiselles d'Avignon* from a black model. In an ironic twist on Manet's *Luncheon on the Grass* (see Figure 18-12), a nude Picasso sits on the grass in the company of clothed women. *Matisse's Chapel* places a wedding party composed of the artist's family in the chapel made famous by dint of Matisse's contributions, including *The Tree of Life* (Fig. 11-11).

Crown Heights Children's Story Quilt (Fig. 11-22) is on permanent display at a Brooklyn public school. The quilt pictures 12 folktales of peoples who have contributed to the life of New York, including Jamaicans and West Africans (the top three on the left), the Dutch (upper right), two Native American peoples, Asians, Puerto Ricans, Italian Americans, and Jewish Americans. True to the genre of quilting, the artist uses her skills to patch together the myths and stories of different peoples in a nation composed of diverse ethnic groups. ■

11-20   FAITH RINGGOLD.
Mama Jones, Andrew, Barbara, and Faith (1973).
Embroidery and sewn fabric. 74″ × 69″.
From *The Family of Women* series. Copyright Faith Ringgold.
Artist's collection.

11-21 FAITH RINGGOLD.
Matisse's Chapel (1991).
Acrylic on canvas; tie-dyed,
pieced fabric border.
74″ × 79½″.

From *The French Collection* series,
Part I, #6. Private collection.
Copyright 1994 Faith Ringgold.
Photo courtesy of the New Museum
of Contemporary Art.

11-22 FAITH RINGGOLD.
*Crown Heights Children's Story
Quilt* (1994).
Painted and pieced fabric.
108″ × 144″.

Collection of NYC Board of Education,
New York. Copyright 1994 Faith
Ringgold / The New York City Board
of Education.

11-23 Pectoral piece from Ordzhonikidze, Russia (4th century BCE). Gold. D: 12″.
Historical Museum, Kiev.

gold and silver are sought even as the value of paper money drops off to nothing. Threads of gold and silver find their way onto precious china and into the garments and vestments of clergy and kings. Gold leaf adorns books, paintings, and picture frames.

Metals can be hammered into shape, **embossed** with raised designs, and cast according to procedures described for bronze in Chapter 9. Each form of working metal has its own tradition and its advantages and disadvantages.

Ancient Greek goldsmiths wrought some of the finest gold jewelry. The pectoral piece shown in Figure 11-23 was meant to be worn across the breast of some nomadic chieftain from southern Russia and probably buried with him. Fortunately, it was not. People and animals are depicted

with a realism that renders the fanciful **griffins** in the lower register as believable as the horses, dogs, and grasshoppers found elsewhere in the piece. The figures are balanced by the refined scrollwork in the central register, and all are contained by the magnificent coils.

The Renaissance sculptor and goldsmith Benvenuto Cellini created a gold and enamel saltcellar (Fig. 11-24) for the French king Francis I that shows the refinement of his art. Its allegorical significance is merely an excuse for displaying the skill of Cellini's craft. Salt, drawn from the sea, is housed in a boat-shaped salt container and watched over by a figure of Neptune. The pepper, drawn from the earth, is contained in a miniature triumphal arch and guarded by a female personification of Earth. Figures on the base repre-

11-24 BENVENUTO CELLINI.
Saltcellar of Francis I (1539–1543).
Gold and enamel. H: 10⅛″; L: 13¹/₁₆″.
Kunsthistorisches Museum, Vienna. Copyright Art Resource, New York.

11-25 Nose ornament, crayfish, Peru (Loma Negra, 3rd century CE).
Gold, silver, turquoise inlay. H: 4¾″.

The Metropolitan Museum of Art, New York. The Michael C. Rockefeller Memorial Collection. Bequest of Nelson A. Rockefeller, 1979 (1979.206.1236) Photograph copyright 1998 The Metropolitan Museum of Art, New York.

11-26 KIFF SLEMMONS.
Transport (1990).
Sterling silver, aluminum, gauze, mesh, tape, tubing, pearls. 5″ × 14″ × 4½″.

Courtesy of the artist. Photo by Rod Slemmons.

sent the seasons and the segments of the day—all on a piece 13 inches long. Unfortunately, the saltcellar is Cellini's sole major work in gold that survives.

Body ornament, ever growing in popularity to this day, spans history and geography. Consider the nose ornament from Peru in Figure 11-25. The piece is fashioned of gold, silver, and turquoise inlay and is a characteristic example of the ancient Peruvian facility in handling complex metal techniques. Much of the jewelry available for us to see today has been unearthed from tombs of the very wealthy among

Peruvian society. The images and their symbolism remain mostly undeciphered, but archeologists have nonetheless constructed a view of these people from such artifacts.

Kiff Slemmons's *Transport* (Fig. 11-26) is a miniature sculpture that again bridges the supposed gulf between fine art and the functional object. It was constructed for the *Artworks for AIDS* exhibition that was held in Seattle in 1990. It is a miniature two-wheeled cart that refers to the history of mass deaths. Throughout the ages, such carts have been used in cities to truck away the victims of epidemics. The wheels of the cart are clocks with human hands, seeming to tick away as the number of deaths due to AIDS mounts. Hospital waste and a stylized "progress" chart with an alarming indicator of the rising toll of the epidemic complete the political message.

WOOD

Some relatively sophisticated technology is require to convert glass, metal, and clay into something of use. Wood, however, has only to be cut and carved to form a functional object.

Three wood vases hint at the versatility of the medium. The soft, flowing contours of Melvyn Firmager's vase (Fig. 11-27) highlight the swirling grain patterns of the wood, which almost take on the character of glazing on a

11-27 MELVYN FIRMAGER.
Untitled (1993).
Destroyed in 1994 Los Angeles earthquake. Eucalyptus gunnii.
H: 13½″; D: 8″.

Photo courtesy of Del Mano Gallery, Los Angeles.

Successful designs . . . stand out because . . . they raise the human spirit and make life a little easier.

—Wolf Von Eckardt

*An artist is someone who produces things that people don't need to have but that he—
for some reason—thinks it would be a good idea to give them.*

—Andy Warhol

11–28 DAVID ELLSWORTH.
Vessel (1992).
Norway maple burl. H: 4″; D: 7″.
Courtesy of the artist.

ceramic vase. The simple roundness, highly polished surface, and inherent grain patterns in David Ellsworth's vase (Fig. 11-28) create the illusion of stone.

DESIGN

An array of design disciplines touches us in our daily lives—from every advertisement we see to every product we use. Good design raises our quality of life, even if we are not consciously aware of it. Let us consider the disciplines of graphic design, industrial design, web design, and urban design.

Graphic Design

Graphic design refers to visual arts in which designs or patterns are made for commercial purposes. Examples of graphic design include the postage stamp, greeting cards, book design, advertising brochures, newspaper and maga-

zine ads, billboards, product packages, posters, signs, trademarks, and logos. Frequently, graphic design includes written copy that is set in type. **Typography** refers to the related art or process of setting and arranging type for printing. Once projects, including type, have been designed, they are usually mass-produced by one of the types of printing discussed in Chapter 7, through use of blocks, plates, or screens.

Package Design

The packaging of products is a complicated process. Packaging must catch the eye as a consumer wanders down the aisles of a supermarket or surfs the Internet. It must quickly and effectively communicate something about the nature and quality of the product and, at the same time, reflect the aesthetic preferences of the targeted group of consumers.

The familiarity of many product packages provided fertile inspiration for Pop Art. Andy Warhol was perhaps best known for his series of silkscreens of Campbell's soup cans, but he also produced multiple images of Coca-Cola bottles and oversized assemblages of Brillo boxes made from acrylic silkscreen on wood (Fig. 11-29). Manufacturers use the same silkscreen process for printing many of their packages.

Posters

Posters are mass-produced, often illustrated paperworks that are designed to widely publicize or advertise products or events. Posters are affordable choices for wall art, to which students in residence halls attest, yet vintage signed posters in limited editions can fetch thousands of dollars.

Henri de Toulouse-Lautrec, a late nineteenth-century French artist, is seen by some as the father of the color lithograph poster. Toulouse-Lautrec dwelled in nighttime Paris—its cafés, music halls, nightclubs, and brothels. The posters that he designed for concerts and other performances are among the most well known in the history of art. His designs (Fig. 11-30) are successful because they capture, in a single image, the spirit and personality of the establishment and the performer. Areas of unmodulated color and high-contrast values in the poster design evoke theater lighting

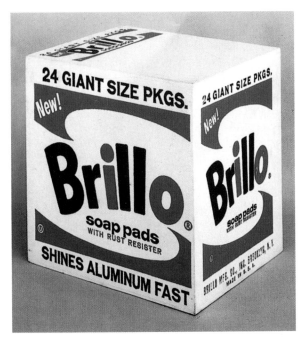

11-29 ANDY WARHOL.
Brillo (1964).
Acrylic silkscreen on wood. 17″ × 17″ × 13″.
Leo Castelli Gallery, New York. Copyright 2003 Andy Warhol
Foundation for the Visual Arts/Artists Rights Society (ARS), New York.

11-30 HENRI DE TOULOUSE-LAUTREC. (1864–1901).
Le Divan Japonais (1892).
Color lithograph. 31⅝″ × 23⅞″.
Musée Toulouse-Lautrec, Albi, France/Erich Lessing/Art Resource, New York.

11-31 MTV logo.
© Jane Butchofsky-Houser/Corbis.

and costuming. The lyrical shapes and undulating lines, coupled with an oblique perspective and bold patterns influenced by Japanese prints, combine to catch the eye and draw the patron to the party. Can you think of some of your favorite posters for rock concerts? Why were the images memorable?

Logos

A **logo** is an emblematic design used to identify and advertise a company or an organization. The most successful corporate identity designs are ones that will spring to mind immediately when you think of the entities that they represent. The next time you are watching MTV (Fig. 11-31), note the persistent

11-32 Cingular Wireless logo.
Courtesy Cingular Wireless.

logo in the corner of your screen. It is instantly recognizable. Whether or not your wireless service is provided by Cingular (Fig. 11-32), you are no doubt familiar with the androgynous orange character that represents the company. Both of these logos appear in print ads but also have their animated counterparts in video versions you see on TV. MTV's "M" pulsates and changes contours and colors; the Cingular "man" leaps and hops and somersaults.

One of today's most visually exciting and successful design campaigns—from product to marketing—is the one for the Apple iPod (Fig. 11-33). From packaging and posters, to its distinctive logo and industrial design, all of the elements interface with and enhance one another. In choosing an iPod MP3 player, the consumer is not only buying a product but buying into a lifestyle.

Industrial Design

Industrial design refers to the planning and artistic enhancement of industrial products ranging from space shuttles and automobiles to microcomputers and MP3 players. To a large degree, the functional and mechanical aspects of these products are the work of engineers. Designers wrap the inner workings in attractive skins or housings.

Form and Function

Consider the forms of the lunar landing module shown in the photograph *Earthrise* (see Fig. 8-3) and of the space shuttle. The forms of each were determined largely by their functions. The lunar landing module needed only to travel from outer space down to the lunar surface and then back from the Moon to an orbiting spacecraft. It never navigated through an atmosphere, so it did not need to be aerodynamic; it could afford its odd shape and many protrusions. The space shuttle, on the other hand, must glide from outer space down to the surface of Earth. To a large degree, its shape is designed mathematically so that the atmosphere will provide a maximum of lift to the underside of its bulky body. The instrument panels in both spacecraft were designed by experts in human psychology and engineering. They had to be placed in strategic locations and differenti-

11-33 Apple iPod logo.
Jackson Tack/Alamy.

11-34 NATHAN GEORGE HORWITT.
Watch Face (1947).
D: 1³⁄₈″.
Specially designed face without numerals; with
silver hands and simple silver dot indicating position
of number 12.
Collection of the Museum of Modern Art, New York.
Gift of the designer. Copyright Art Resource, New York.

ated from one another. In order not to hamper the work
of pilots and navigators, their forms had to suggest their
functions.

In most cases, designers have a larger influence on the
final appearance of a product than they did with the lunar
landing module and the space shuttle. The factors that usually enter into an industrial design include utility (that is, in
what form is the equipment easiest to use?), cost, and aesthetic considerations. The aesthetic appeal of an industrial
product not only provides a sense of satisfaction for the designer and the manufacturer but also affects sales.

New York's Museum of Modern Art has an extensive
collection of superior industrial designs. It includes an end-
lessly broad range of products—chairs, teapots, wrist-
watches, lighting fixtures—assembled with one criterion in
mind: excellence in design. The minimalist appearance of
the Movado watch (Fig. 11-34) is pure and elegant and
signifies efficiency. Rody Graumans's *85 Lamps Lighting Fixture* (Fig. 11-35) brings out the whimsical in the industrial in
its unadulterated clustering of naked light bulbs and wiring.

Web Design

Websites are an inextricable part of the information superhighway. Any of us cyberspace surfers can go online, access
the website of a popular consumer magazine, and get the lat-

11-35 RODY GRAUMANS.
85 Lamps Lighting Fixture (1992).
Light bulbs, cords, and sockets. H: 39³⁄₈″ (100 cm);
D: 39³⁄₈″ (100 cm).
Droog Design, The Netherlands, MOMA/Art Resource, New York.

est reviews on the new car we're drooling over. We can research without books, order books, book reservations, bid
on a special reserve wine. And a big part of what keeps us attached to our PC's mouse at the end of an electronic umbili-
cal cord is the visual feedback we get when we click. The
better the design of the website, the more tantalizing the
product or service—a clear fact not lost on the thousands
upon thousands of businesses, organizations, agencies, and
individuals for whom the website is the new face and first
face to the consumer in the age of electronics.

11-36 Website: Home page
of the Louvre.

Copyright Louvre Museum, Paris.

We can think of web design as having two key tasks. One is technical and involves programming—how users click their way around a web page, how hot links to other pages and sites are established, and how to insert still images or animated clips and sound. The other task is an aesthetic one, encompassing art and design.

Art museums are among the untold numbers of organizations that can be accessed through websites. The home page of the website of the Louvre (Fig. 11-36) (http://www.louvre.fr) includes a photograph of the exterior of the building, featuring its now famous glass pyramid entrance. Once "inside," users can click their way to some of the more popular works of art in the collection. The Louvre invites you to take a *visite virtuelle en ligne* (a virtual visit online), with text in a number of languages, including English, Spanish, and Japanese. The more mundane but essential information about museum hours and current exhibits is reliably posted, but the functionality of the web design almost pales in comparison to its ability to transport virtual visitors to one of the world's great cultural centers from the comfort of their ergonomically designed computer chairs.

You can visit ArtMuseum.net (http://www.artmuseum.net) to view art "exhibitions" from various participating museums online. When you take your virtual tour of one of these sites, clicking on a "thumbnail" illustration of a work in the collection might enlarge it or display descriptive text. Some websites let you walk through a building or another environment and look in various directions as you do—something like "Super Mario Brothers Visit the Art Institute of Chicago," without the punching, flying, or shooting.

As you surf the web, you have no doubt been struck by the endless variety, quality, and quantity of web design—from sophisticated to tacky, from "high art" to "low art." I, like you, come across interesting websites almost every day, so it was hard to settle for just one or two to highlight in this chapter among the wealth of riches and rags. Some current "faves": websites for the Alvin Ailey American Dance Theater in New York City (known for its brilliant, mind- and body-stretching choreography) (Fig. 11-37) and BBDO (one of the world's premier advertising agencies) (Fig. 11-38). These and other websites feature hot spots that the user can click on to navigate the site for related web pages and information.

Web design is a big business, and many graphic designers set up shop in this realm. Students can now take web design in their college courses, whereas the rest of us can learn

11-37 Website: Alvin Ailey
American Dance Theater.

Photo copyright Andrew Eccles.
Courtesy of Alvin Ailey
American Dance Theater.

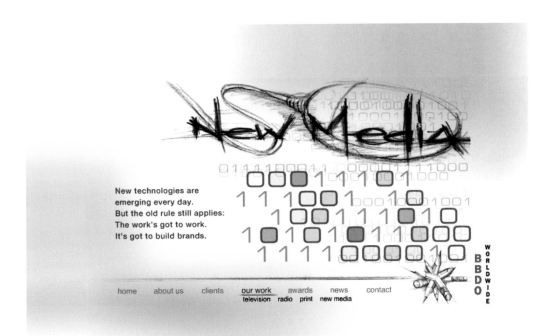

11-38 A web page within
the website of the
advertising agency
BBDO Worldwide.

Courtesy BBDO
Worldwide.

about it in how-to books such as *Web Design for Dummies*. Many individuals, like organizations, have websites on which they include text and uploaded photos and video clips. They serve as anything from electronic business cards to ways for families to keep in touch. Cyberspace collapses the distance that separates us from the important people in our lives.

Urban Design

Perhaps it is in urban design that our desire for order and harmony achieves its most majestic expression. Throughout history most towns and cities have more or less sprung up. They have pushed back the countryside in all directions, as necessary, with little evidence of an overall guiding concept. As a result, the masses of great buildings sometimes press against other masses of great buildings, and transportation becomes a worrisome afterthought. The Rome of the early Republic, for example, was an impoverished seat of empire, little more than a disordered assemblage of seven villages on seven hills. Later, the downtown area was a jumble of narrow streets winding through mud–brick buildings. Not un-

til the first century BCE were the major building programs undertaken by Sulla and then the Caesars.

The new towns of the Roman Empire were laid out largely on a rectangular grid. This pattern was common among centrist states, where bits of land were parceled out to the subjects of mighty rulers. The gridiron was also found to be a useful basis for design throughout history—from the ancient Greeks to the colonial Americans. Many cities of the Near and Middle East, such as Baghdad, have a circular tradition in urban design, which may reflect the belief that they were the hubs of the universe. The throne room of the palace in eighth-century Baghdad was at the center of the circle. The palace—including attendant buildings, a game preserve, and pavilions set in perfumed gardens—was more than a mile in diameter, and the remainder of the population occupied a relatively narrow ring around the palace.

Washington, D.C.

Few urban designs are as simple and rich as Pierre-Charles L'Enfant's plan for Washington, D.C. (Fig. 11-39). The city is cradled between two branches of the Potomac River, yielding an uneven, overall diamond shape. Within the dia-

11–39 PIERRE-CHARLES L'ENFANT.
Plan for Washington, D.C. (1792).
Courtesy of the National Archives.

11-40 REM KOOLHAAS.
Design for Les Halles, Paris.
Rem Koolhaas/OMA/photograph by Hans Werlemann.

mond, a rectangular grid of streets that run east-west and north-south was laid down. Near the center of the diamond, with its west edge at the river, an enormous Mall or green space was set aside. At the east end of the Mall is the Capitol Building. To the north, at its west end, is the president's house (which is now the White House). Broad boulevards radiate from the Capitol and from the White House, cutting across the gridiron. One radiating boulevard runs directly between the Capitol and the White House, and other boulevards parallel it.

The design is a composition in which the masses of the Capitol Building and White House balance one another, and the rhythms of the gridiron pattern and intersecting diagonal boulevards create contrast and unity. The Mall provides an open central gathering place that is as much a part of American culture as it is respite from the congestion of the city.

L'Enfant's plan for Washington, D.C., was inspired by the art and architecture of Neoclassical France. Today, a visitor to both cities will note that avenues and grand boulevards culminate in monuments that punctuate the end of a long vista. Paris is often called the most beautiful city in the world, a title achieved after massive renovations to the city plan by Raoul Haussmann in the nineteenth century. Then, as now, Paris was not without its pockets of urban problems requiring creative and politically sensitive solutions. The Parisian area of Les Halles has long been home to park and commercial spaces as well as a major transit hub. Architect Rem Koolhaas and his firm, OMA, bring together the disparate parts in a transparent design that makes all of the amenities visible to the surrounding neighborhood (Fig. 11-40). Shape and color dominate the plan, with circular gardens and luminous towers rising above the city's infrastructure. The dark, discontinuous, and chaotic environs of the old Les Halles will be transformed, through an innovative and practical urban design, into a signature city monument.

ART TOUR
Washington, D.C.

On July 14, 1789, in what became the defining symbolic moment of the French Revolution, the Bastille prison was stormed by revolutionaries who freed a grand total of seven prisoners. Four years later, with the founding of a new Republic, the doors of the Louvre Museum (containing about 200 works that had belonged to the king) opened to the public.

The point to this story lies in its contrast with the next: In 1936, Andrew Mellon (an American statesman and financier) gave his art collection to the United States of America and built the National Gallery of Art in Washington, D.C., to house it. In subsequent years, other collectors followed suit until the "nation's collection" outgrew its space. Unlike many of the world's great art museums, such as the Louvre, the museums you will see in Washington, D.C., did not begin as private royal collections made accessible to the public only after revolution and democratization. The core of Washington's holdings came from entrepreneurs who willingly, even affectionately, gave their art to their fellow citizens. Much of what you will see in Washington, D.C., is yours by virtue of your citizenship in the United States of America. And seeing just about all of it costs you nothing.

If you're coming to Washington by train, come hungry. You will arrive, most likely, at Union Station—itself a fine example of the Beaux Arts architectural style. From the three main archways that define the entry (based on the Arch of Constantine in Rome!) to the magnificent gilded barrel-vaulted ceiling, Union Station is not simply a transit center to move through—linger and look. It opened in 1907, and for more than 50 years this station was the largest in the world. After careful and costly restoration in 1988, this is now the second most visited site in Washington, D.C. Union Station is home to one of the most fantastic food courts you will ever come upon, with selections to entice every palate. Take a spin around the stalls before you commit to that Maryland crab-cake sandwich.

Union Station is a well-situated starting point for your art tour of the capital. From there, a short stroll along Delaware or Louisiana Avenue will bring you to the U.S. Capitol and the Mall, the site of many museums and memorials. It is here that you will experience the *feeling* of the nation's capital—its Classical architecture (inspired, as was the new democratic government, by Greek and Roman ideals), expanses of tree-lined grassy lawn, reflecting pools, marble and granite monuments. The Capitol Building (Fig. 3-10) is at the "top"—or eastern end—of the Mall and has much to offer to the art seeker. The dome, designed by Thomas U. Walter, is one of the largest in the world. The rotunda (the large, circular space in the interior beneath the dome) contains many paintings and sculptures and is capped by Constantino Brumidi's mural depicting the *Apotheosis of Washington* (bring your binoculars and your sense of humor).

Outside the Capitol, the Mall is arrayed before the visitor, offering a perspective toward the Washington Monument on the west end and all that lies between. The Mall was designed by the French architect Pierre L'Enfant, who imported many of his elements of city planning (grand boulevards, elegant residences, well-situated monuments) from Paris. The first museum on your tour is the National Gallery of Art. The collection is divided between two buildings—East and West. The West (Neoclassical) Building is the earlier museum—the one financed by Andrew Mellon and designed by John Russell Pope. Here the visitor will find Western art spanning the thirteenth through the nineteenth centuries, featuring stellar examples of works by such artists as Giotto, Botticelli, Leonardo da Vinci, Raphael (*The Alba Madonna*), Rembrandt, Rubens (*Daniel in the Lion's Den*), El Greco, Monet (*Woman with a Parasol—Mme Monet and Her Son*), Cassatt, Cézanne, Toulouse-Lautrec (*Quadrille at the Moulin Rouge*), Homer (*Breezing Up*), and Whistler (*Symphony in White, No. 1: The White Girl*), among many, many others of fame and note. And that's just the west wing. The entire East Building, designed by I. M. Pei and one of the few Modernist works of architecture in the city, houses the country's collection of twentieth-century art. A dramatic, soaring

UNION STATION.
Corbis.

Entrance lobby of the National Gallery of Art, Washington, D.C., with sculpture of children holding hands.

SMITHSONIAN CASTLE.

atrium, featuring an enormous mobile by Alexander Calder (Fig. 2-67) and works by Henry Moore, Joan Miró, and Andrew Goldsworthy, is flanked by balconies and galleries in which one will find works from the permanent collection as well as traveling exhibitions. Both museums (connected underground) have wonderful restaurants and bookshops.

One of the highlights of the Mall is the Sculpture Garden of the National Gallery of Art, poised between the West Building and the National Museum of Natural History. Works of modern sculpture pepper the sections of lawn surrounding a refreshing fountain in summer and delightful skating rink in winter. Viewers can walk among and around pieces by Claes Oldenberg, Roy Lichtenstein, Louise Bourgeois, Joan Miró, and others. And from these fun-filled, art-filled surroundings, one can cross over a broad expanse of lawn to another collection of outdoor sculpture belonging to the Hirshhorn Museum, a private-turned-public collection displayed in a cylindrical building affectionately referred to as "the doughnut." Rodin's *The Burghers of Calais* (Fig. 18-40) finds itself in equally prestigious company in this collection.

The Mall contains a staggering number of museums, galleries, and monuments. The old Smithsonian Castle, the building that once housed works that are now found in other sites along the Mall (don't miss wandering through its splendid gardens); the spectacular National Air and Space Museum; such small jewels as the Arthur M. Sackler Gallery of Asian Art, the National Museum of African Art, and the United States Holocaust Memorial Museum just beyond the Washington Monument merely scratch the surface of what one might discover on an art tour of the capital. And to these we must add artistic memorials such as the Vietnam Veterans Memorial, the Korean War Veterans Memorial, and the Franklin D. Roosevelt Memorial, all of which have altered the very concept of meaningful memorials for Washington, D.C., and the country.

For many students in the United States, "the family trip to Washington" was viewed as essential to child rearing. For others, "the school trip to Washington" was the first "independent" trip away from home—traveling on a rowdy bus with one's peers to take in the sights and watch history come alive. Memories of these experiences traverse generations.

MAYA YING LIN, Vietnam Veterans Memorial. Names and Reflections on the Wall.

We have always understood the importance of symbols to American history. Our own art tours of the nation's capital enable us to understand the importance of art to American people.

 To continue your tour and learn more about Washington, D.C., go to our website.

GLOSSARY

Abstract art A form of art characterized by simplified (abstracted) or distorted rendering of an object that has the essential form or nature of that object; a form of *nonobjective art* in which the forms make no reference to visible reality.

Abstract Expressionism A style of painting and sculpture of the 1950s and 1960s in which artists expressionistically distorted abstract images with loose, gestural brushwork. Also see *expressionistic*.

Academic art A neoclassical, nonexperimental style promoted by the Royal French Academy during the eighteenth and nineteenth centuries.

Achromatic Without color.

Acquisition Purchase (of a work of art) for a museum or a formal collection.

Acropolis The fortified upper part of a Greek city; literally, "city on a hill."

Acrylic paint A paint in which pigments are combined with a synthetic plastic medium that is durable, water soluble, and quick drying.

Action painting A contemporary method of painting characterized by *implied motion* in the brushstroke and splattered and dripped paint on the canvas.

Actual balance Equal distribution of weight. Contrast with *pictorial balance*.

Actual line The path made by a moving point; a connected and continuous series of points. Contrast with *implied line*.

Actual mass The physical mass of an object as determined by its weight. Contrast with *implied mass*.

Actual motion The passage of a body or an object from one place to another. Contrast with *implied motion*.

Actual texture The texture of an object or picture, as determined by the sense of touch. Contrast with *visual texture*.

Additive process In sculpture, adding or assembling materials, as in modeling and constructing. Contrast with *subtractive process*.

Adobe Brick that has been dried in the sun rather than fired in a kiln.

Afterimage The lingering impression from a stimulus that has been removed. The afterimage of a color is its complement. Also see *complementary color*.

Allegory A narrative in which people and events have been given consistent symbolic meanings; extended metaphor.

Altar A raised platform or stand used for sacred ceremonial or ritual purposes.

Alternate a-b-a-b support system An architectural support system in which every other nave wall support sends up a supporting rib that crosses the vault as a transverse arch.

Alternate support system An architectural support system in which alternating structural elements bear the weight of the walls and the load of the ceiling.

Ambulatory In a church, a continuation of the side aisles of a *Latin cross plan* into a passageway that extends behind the choir and apse and allows traffic to flow to the chapels, which are often placed in this area (from *ambulare,* Latin for "to walk").

Amorphous Without clear shape or form.

Amphitheater A round or oval open-air theater with an arena surrounded by rising tiers of seats.

Analogous colors Colors that lie next to one another on the color wheel and share qualities of hue as a result of the mixture of adjacent hues; harmonious hues.

Analytic Cubism The early phase of Cubism (1909–1912) during which objects were dissected or analyzed in a visual information-gathering process and then reconstructed on the canvas.

Animation Creation of an animated cartoon; the photographing of a series of drawings, each of which shows a stage of movement that differs slightly from the previous one, so that figures appear to move when projected in rapid succession.

Annunciation The angel Gabriel's announcement to Mary that she would give birth to Jesus.

Aperture Opening.

Apocalypse The ultimate triumph of good over evil foretold in Judeo-Christian writings.

Apse A semicircular or polygonal projection of a building with a semicircular dome, especially on the east end of a church.

Aquarelle A watercolor technique in which a transparent film of paint is applied to a white, absorbent surface.

Aquatint An etching technique in which a metal plate is colored with acid-resistant resin and heated, causing the resin to melt. Before printing, areas of the plate are exposed by a needle, and the plate receives an acid bath. Aquatinting can be manipulated to resemble washes.

Aqueduct A bridgelike structure that carries a canal or pipe of water across a river or valley (from Latin roots meaning "to carry water").

Arch A curved or pointed structure consisting of wedge-shaped blocks that span an open space and support the weight of material above by transferring the load outward and downward over two vertical supports, or piers.

Archaic period A period of Greek art dating roughly 660–480 BCE. The term *archaic* means "old" and refers to the art created before the Classical period.

Architectural style A style of Roman painting in which walls were given the illusion of opening onto a scene.

Architecture The art and science of designing aesthetic buildings, bridges, and other structures to help people meet their personal and communal needs.

Architrave In architecture, the lower part of an *entablature,* which may consist of one or more horizontal bands.

Archivolts In architecture, concentric moldings that repeat the shape of an arch.

Armature In sculpture, a framework for supporting plastic material.

Art Nouveau A highly ornamental style of the 1890s characterized by floral patterns, rich colors, whiplash curves, and vertical attenuation (French for "new art").

Assemblage A work of art that consists of three-dimensional objects assembled to create an image. Artists often manipulate preexisting objects in various ways and incorporate them with other media, such as painting or printmaking.

Asymmetrical balance Balance in which the right and left sides of a composition contain different shapes, colors, textures, or other elements and yet are arranged or "weighted" so that the overall impression is one of balance. Contrast with *symmetrical balance*.

Athena The Greek goddess of wisdom, skills, and war.

Atmospheric perspective An illusion of depth created through grades of texture and brightness, color saturation, and warm and cool colors. An indistinct or hazy effect produced by distance and the illusion of distance in visual art (the term derives from recognition that the atmosphere between the viewer and the distant objects would cause the effect).

Atrium A hall or entrance court.

Automatic writing Writing based on free association, practiced by Dadaists and Surrealists.

Automatist surrealism An outgrowth of automatic writing in which the artist attempts to derive the outlines of images from the unconscious through free association.

Avant-garde The leaders in new, unconventional movements; the vanguard (from French, "advance guard").

Balance The distribution of the weight, mass, or other elements of a work of art so as to achieve harmony.

Balloon framing In architecture, a wooden skeleton of a building constructed from prefabricated studs and nails.

Balustrade A railing held up by small posts, or balusters, as on a staircase.

Baroque A seventeenth-century European style characterized by ornamentation, curved lines, irregularity of form, dramatic lighting and color, and exaggerated gestures.

Barrel vault A roofed-over space or tunnel constructed as an elongated arch.

Basalt A dark, tough volcanic rock.

Basketry The craft of making baskets.

Bas-relief Sculpture that projects only slightly from its background (from *bas,* French for "low"). Contrast with *high relief.*

Batik The process of making designs in cloth by waxing fabric to prevent dye from coloring certain areas; a cloth or design made in this way.

Bay In architecture, the area or space spanned by a single unit of vaulting that may be marked off by piers or columns.

Bevel To cut at an angle.

Bilateral symmetry Mirror-type similarity between the sides of a composition. Also termed "pure" or "formal" symmetry.

Binder A material that binds substances together.

Biomorphic Having the form of a living organism.

Bisque firing In ceramics, a preliminary firing that hardens the body of a ware.

Bitumen Asphalt.

Black-figure painting A three-stage firing process that gives vases black figures on a reddish ground. In the first, oxidizing phase of firing, oxygen in the kiln turns the vase and slip red. In the second, reducing phase, oxygen is eliminated from the kiln and the vase and slip turn black. In the third, reoxidizing phase, oxygen is reintroduced into the kiln, turning the vase red once more.

Bohemian Literally, of Bohemia, a section of the Czech Republic. Because Gypsies, or

Roma, in transit to Western Europe passed through Bohemia, the term has come to signify a nonconformist, unconventional style of life.

Brass A yellowish alloy of copper and zinc.

Brick A hard substance made from clay, fired in a kiln or baked in the sun, and used in construction.

Brightness gradient The relative degree of intensity in the rendering of nearby and distant objects, used to create an illusion of depth in a two-dimensional work.

Buddha An enlightened man.

Buon fresco True fresco, executed on damp lime plaster. Contrast with *fresco secco.*

Burin A pointed cutting tool used by engravers.

Burnish To make shiny by rubbing or polishing.

Buttress To support or prop up construction with a projecting structure, usually built of brick or stone; a massive masonry structure on the exterior wall of a building that presses inward and upward to hold the stone blocks of arches in place. Also see *flying buttress.*

Byzantine A style associated with Eastern Europe that arose after 300 CE, the year that Emperor Constantine moved the capital of his empire from Rome to Byzantium and renamed the city Constantinople (present-day Istanbul). The style was concurrent with the Early Christian style in Western Europe.

Calligraphy Beautiful handwriting; penmanship; ornamental writing with a pen or brush.

Camera obscura An early camera consisting of a large dark chamber with a lens opening through which an image is projected onto the opposite surface in its natural colors.

Candid In photography, unposed, informal.

Canon of proportions A set of rules governing the proportions of the human body as they are to be rendered by artists.

Capital In architecture, the area at the top of the shaft of a column that provides a solid base for the horizontal elements above. Capitals provide decorative transitions between the cylinder of the column and the rectilinear *architrave* above.

Caricature The gross exaggeration or distortion of natural features for the purpose of benign or malevolent satire.

Carolingian Referring to Charlemagne or his period. Charlemagne was emperor of the Holy Roman Empire from 800 to 814 CE.

Cartoon Originally, a preparatory drawing made for a fresco, usually on paper and drawn to scale; a drawing that caricatures or satirizes an event or person of topical interest. Also see *animation.*

Carving In sculpture, the process of cutting away material, such as wood.

Cast iron A hard alloy of iron containing silicon and carbon that is made by casting.

Casting The process of creating a form by pour-

ing a liquid material into a mold, allowing it to harden, and then removing the mold.

Catacomb A vault or gallery in an underground burial place.

Cella The small inner room of a Greek temple, used to house the statue of the god or goddess to whom the temple is dedicated. Located behind solid masonry walls, the cella was accessible only to the temple priests.

Centering In architecture, a wooden scaffold used in the construction of an arch.

Central plan A design for a church or a chapel with a primary central space surrounded by symmetrical areas around each side. Contrast with *longitudinal plan.*

Ceramics The art of creating baked clay objects, such as pottery and earthenware.

Chalk A form of soft limestone that is easily pulverized and can be used as a drawing implement.

Charcoal A form of carbon produced by partially burning wood or other organic matter; it can be used as a drawing implement.

Chiaroscuro An artistic technique in which subtle gradations of value create the illusion of rounded three-dimensional forms in space; also termed *modeling* (from Italian for "light-dark").

China Whitish or grayish porcelain that rings when struck.

Cinematography The photographic art of creating motion pictures.

Cinerary urn A vessel used for keeping the ashes of the cremated dead.

Clapboard In architecture, siding composed of thin, narrow boards placed in horizontal, overlapping layers.

Classical Art Art of the Greek Classical period, spanning roughly 480–400 BCE; also known as Hellenic Art (from "Hellas," the Greek name for Greece).

Clerestory In a *Latin cross plan,* the area above the *triforium* in the elevation of the nave, which contains windows to provide direct lighting for the nave.

Close-up In cinematography or video, a "shot" made from very close range, providing intimate detail.

Coffer A decorative sunken panel.

Coiling A pottery technique in which lengths of clay are wound in a spiral fashion.

Collage An assemblage of two-dimensional objects to create an image; works of art in which materials such as paper, cloth, and wood are pasted to a two-dimensional surface, such as a wooden panel or canvas (from *coller,* French for "to paste").

Colonnade A series of columns placed side by side to support a roof or a series of arches.

Color negative film Film from which color negatives are made.

Color reversal film Film from which color prints ("positives") are made directly, without the intervening step of creating negatives.

Color-field painting Painting that uses visual

elements and principles of design to suggest that areas of color stretch beyond the canvas to infinity; figure and ground are given equal emphasis.

Combine painting A contemporary style of painting that attaches other media, such as found objects, to the canvas.

Complementary color One of a specific pair of colors (e.g., red and green) that most enhance, or exaggerate, one another by virtue of their simultaneous contrast. Each pair of complementary colors contains one primary color plus the secondary color made by mixing the other two primaries. Because the complements do not share characteristics of hue and are as unlike as possible, the eye readily tells them apart. When complementary colors are placed next to one another, the effects are often jarring.

Composition The organization of the visual elements in a work of art.

Compound pier In Gothic style, a complexly shaped vertical support to which a number of colonnettes (thin half columns) are often attached.

Compressive strength The degree to which a material can withstand the pressure of being squeezed.

Computer art The production of images with the assistance of the computer. Artists can use the computer to create art for its own sake or as a design tool, as in architecture and graphic design.

Computer-assisted design (CAD) The use of the computer to assist artists and designers working in other media, such as architecture. CAD permits interior designers and architects to view their designs from various vantage points and to see how the modification of one element affects the entire design.

Conceptual Portrayed as a person or object is known or thought (conceptualized) to be; not copied from nature at any given moment. Conceptual figures tend to be stylized rather than realistic.

Conceptual art An anticommercial movement begun in the 1960s in which works of art are conceived and executed in the mind of the artist. The commercial or communal aspect of the "work" is often a set of instructions for what exists in the artist's mind.

Conceptual space Space that is depicted as conceptualized by the artist rather than in realistic perspective.

Conceptual unity Unity in a work that is achieved through the relationship between the meaning and function of the images.

Constructed sculpture Sculpture in which forms are built up from such materials as wood, paper, string, sheet metal, and wire.

Constructivism A sculptural outgrowth of Cubist collage in which artists attempt to use a minimum of mass to create volumes in space.

Contact print A photographic print that is made by placing a negative in contact with a sheet of photosensitive paper and exposing both to light so that the second sheet of paper acquires the image.

Conté crayon A wax crayon with a hard texture.

Content All that is contained in a work of art: the visual elements, subject matter, and underlying meaning or themes.

Contour line A perceived line that marks the edge of a figure as it curves back into space.

Contrapposto A position in which a figure is obliquely balanced around a central vertical axis. Also see *weight-shift principle.*

Cool color A color such as a blue, green, or violet that appears to be cool in temperature and tends to recede spatially behind warm colors.

Corbel A supportive, bracket-shaped piece of metal, stone, or wood.

Corinthian order The most ornate of the Greek architectural styles, characterized by slender, fluted columns and capitals with an acanthus leaf design.

Cornice In architecture, a horizontal molding that projects along the top of a wall or a building; the uppermost part of an *entablature.*

Cosmetic palette A palette for mixing cosmetics, such as eye makeup, with water.

Crayon A small stick of colored wax, chalk, or charcoal.

Cross-hatching Intersecting sets of parallel lines used to shade a drawing.

Crossing square In architecture, the area that defines the right-angle intersection of the vaults of the nave and the transept of a church.

Cubism A twentieth-century style developed by Picasso and Braque that emphasizes the two-dimensionality of the canvas, characterized by multiple views of an object and the reduction of form to cubelike essentials.

Cuneiform Wedge-shaped; descriptive of the characters used in ancient Akkadian, Assyrian, Babylonian, and Persian alphabets.

Curvilinear Consisting of a curved line or lines.

Dada A post–World War I movement that sought to use art to destroy art, thereby underscoring the paradoxes and absurdities of modern life.

Daguerreotype A photograph made from a silver-coated copper plate; named after Louis Daguerre, the innovator of the method.

Deconstructivist architecture A Postmodern approach to the design of buildings that disassembles and reassembles the basic elements of architecture. The focus is on the creation of forms that may appear abstract, disharmonious, and disconnected from the functions of the building. Deconstructivism challenges the view that there is one correct way to approach architecture.

Der Blaue Reiter (The Blue Rider) A twentieth-century German Expressionist movement that focused on the contrasts between, and combinations of, abstract form and pure color.

Design The combination of the visual elements of art according to such principles as balance and unity.

De Stijl An early twentieth-century movement that emphasized the use of basic forms, particularly cubes, horizontals, and verticals.

Diagonal rib In architecture, a *rib* that connects the opposite corners of a groin vault.

Die Brücke (The Bridge) A short-lived German Expressionist movement characterized by boldly colored landscapes and cityscapes and by violent portraits.

Digital art Art that makes use of—or is developed with the assistance of—electronic instruments, such as computers, that store and manipulate information through the use of series of zeros and ones (digits); including but not limited to web design, *graphic design,* and *digital photography.*

Digital photography Photography that stores visual information electronically rather than on film.

Direct-metal sculpture Metal sculpture that is assembled by such techniques as welding and riveting rather than *casting.*

Dissolve In cinematography and video, a fading technique in which the current scene grows dimmer as the subsequent scene grows brighter.

Dome In architecture, a hemispherical structure that is round when viewed from beneath.

Doric order The earliest and simplest of the Greek architectural styles, consisting of relatively short, squat columns, sometimes unfluted, and a simple, square-shaped capital. The Doric *frieze* is usually divided into *triglyphs* and *metopes.*

Drawing The art of running an implement that leaves a mark over a surface; a work of art created in this manner.

Dry masonry Brick or stone construction without use of mortar.

Dry media Drawing materials that do not involve the application of water or other liquids. Contrast with *fluid media.*

Drypoint A variation of engraving in which the surface of the matrix is cut with a needle to make rough edges. In printmaking, rough edges make soft rather than crisp lines.

Dynamism The Futurist view that force or energy is the basic principle that underlies all events, including everything we see. Objects are depicted as if in constant motion, appearing and disappearing before our eyes.

Earthenware Reddish tan, porous pottery fired at a relatively low temperature (below 2,000°F).

Earthwork A work of art in which large amounts of earth or land are shaped into a sculpture.

Eastern Orthodox A form of Christianity dominant in Eastern Europe, western Asia, and North Africa.

Editing In cinematography and video, rearranging a film or video record to provide a more coherent or interesting narrative or presentation of the images.

Egg tempera A painting medium in which ground pigments are bound with egg yolk.

Emboss To decorate with designs that are raised above a surface.

Embroidery The art of ornamenting fabric with needlework.

Emphasis A design principle that focuses the viewer's attention on one or more parts of a composition by accentuating certain shapes, intensifying value or color, featuring directional lines, or strategically placing the objects and images.

Empire period The Roman period from about 27 BCE to 395 CE, when the empire was divided.

Emulsion A suspension of a salt of silver in gelatin or collodion used to coat film and photographic plates.

Enamel To apply a hard, glossy coating to a surface; a coating of this type.

Encaustic A method of painting in which the colors in a wax medium are burned into a surface with hot irons.

Engraving Cutting; in printmaking, an *intaglio* process in which plates of copper, zinc, or steel are cut with a burin and the ink image is pressed onto paper.

Entablature In architecture, a horizontal structure supported by columns, which, in turn, supports any other element, such as a pediment, that is placed above; from top to bottom, the entablature consists of a *cornice,* a *frieze,* and an *architrave.*

Entasis In architecture, a slight convex curvature of a column used to provide the illusion of continuity of thickness as the column rises.

Equestrian portrait A depiction of a figure on horseback.

Etching In printmaking, an *intaglio* process in which the matrix is first covered with an acid-resistant ground. The ground is removed from certain areas with a needle, and the matrix is dipped in acid, which eats away at the areas exposed by the needle. These areas become grooves that are inked and printed.

Etruscan From ancient Etruria, located along the northwestern shores of present-day Italy.

Existentialism A literary and philosophical movement of the early twentieth century characterized by the belief that human beings are free and responsible for their behavior and actions. This freedom, according to proponents Søren Kierkegaard, Jean-Paul Sartre, and Margin Heidegger, leads to humanity's pain and anguish.

Expressionism A modern school of art in which an emotional impact is achieved through agitated brushwork, intense coloration, and violent, hallucinatory imagery.

Expressionistic Emphasizing the distortion of color and form to achieve an emotional impact.

Extreme unity Unification of all elements in a composition.

Extrude To force metal through a die or small holes to give it shape.

Facade A French term for the face or front of a building.

Fading In cinematography and video, the gradual dimming or brightening of a scene, used as a transition between scenes.

Fantastic art The representation of fanciful images, sometimes joyful and whimsical, sometimes horrific and grotesque.

Fauvism An early twentieth-century style of art characterized by the juxtaposition of areas of bright colors that are often unrelated to the objects they represent, and by distorted linear perspective (from French for "wild beast").

Fenestration The arrangement of windows and doors in a structure, often used to create balance and rhythm as well as light, air, and access.

Ferroconcrete Same as *reinforced concrete.*

Fertile Crescent The arable land lying between the Tigris and Euphrates rivers in ancient Mesopotamia.

Fertile Ribbon The arable land lying along the Nile River in Egypt.

Fetish figure An object believed to have magical powers.

Fiber A slender, threadlike structure or material that can be woven.

Fiberglass Fine spun-glass filaments that can be woven into textiles.

Figurative art Art that represents the likeness of human and other figures.

Figure–ground relationship The relationship between the primary subject (figure) and other parts of the composition (ground or background).

Figure–ground reversal A shift in a viewer's perception of a composition in which what at one moment appears to be the figure becomes the ground (or background), and vice versa.

Film A thin sheet of cellulose material coated with a photosensitive substance.

Flashback In cinematography and video, an interruption of the story line with the portrayal of an earlier event.

Flash-forward In cinematography and video, an interruption of the story line with the portrayal of a future event.

Flint glass A hard, bright glass containing lead oxide.

Fluid media Liquid-based drawing materials. Contrast with *dry media.*

Flying buttress A buttress that is exterior to a building but connected in a location that permits the buttress to support an interior vault.

Focal point A specific part of a work of art that seizes and holds the viewer's interest.

Foreshortening Diminishing the size of the parts of an object that are represented as farthest from the viewer. Specifically, rendering parts of an object as receding from the viewer at angles oblique to the picture plane so that they appear proportionately shorter than parts of the object that are parallel to the picture plane.

Forge To form or shape metal (usually heated) with blows from a hammer, press, or other implement or machine.

Form The totality of what the viewer sees in a work of art; a product of the composition of visual elements.

Formalist criticism An approach to art criticism that concentrates on the elements and design of works of art rather than on historical factors or the biography of the artist.

Forum An open public space, particularly in ancient Rome, used as a market and a gathering place.

Freestanding sculpture Sculpture that is carved or cast in the round, unconnected to a wall, and thereby capable of being viewed in its entirety by walking around it. Freestanding sculpture can also be designed for a niche, which limits the visible portion of the sculpture.

Fresco A type of painting in which pigments are applied to a fresh, wet plaster surface or wall and thereby become part of the surface or wall (from Italian for "fresh").

Fresco secco Dry fresco; painting executed on dry plaster. Contrast with *buon fresco.*

Frieze In architecture, a horizontal band between the *architrave* and the *cornice* that is often decorated with sculpture.

Futurism An early twentieth-century style that portrayed modern machines and the dynamic character of modern life and science.

Gate In the lost-wax technique of casting, one of a number of wax rods connected to the mold; as molten bronze flows into the mold, gates allow air to escape.

Gauffrage An inkless *intaglio* process.

Genre painting Simple human representations; realistic figure painting that focuses on themes taken from everyday life.

Geometric period A period of Greek art from about 900 to 700 BCE during which works of art emphasized geometric patterns.

Geometric shape A shape that is regular, easy to measure, and easy to describe, as distinguished from *organic* or *biomorphic shape,* which is irregular, difficult to measure, and difficult to describe.

Gesso Plaster of Paris that is applied to a wooden or canvas support and used as a surface for painting or as the material for sculpture (from Italian for "gypsum").

Gild To apply thin sheets of gold leaf or gold-like substance to a surface.

Glassblowing The art of shaping molten glass

into glass objects by blowing air through a tube.

Glaze In painting, a semitransparent coating on a painted surface that provides a glassy or glossy finish. In ceramics, a hard, glossy coating formed by applying a liquid suspension of powdered material to the surface of a ware, which is then dried and fired at a temperature that causes the ingredients to melt together.

Golden mean The principle that a small part of a work should relate to a larger part of the work in proportion to the manner in which the larger part relates to the whole.

Golden rectangle A rectangle based on the *golden mean* and constructed so that its width is 1.618 times its height.

Golden section Developed in ancient Greece, a mathematical formula for determining the proportional relationship of the parts of a work to the whole.

Gothic A Western European style developed between the twelfth and sixteenth centuries CE, characterized in architecture by ribbed vaults, pointed arches, flying buttresses, and steep roofs.

Gouache Watercolor paint that is made opaque by mixing pigments with a particular gum binder.

Graphic design Design for advertising and industry that includes design elements such as typography and images for communication purposes.

Graphite A soft black form of carbon used as a drawing implement (from *graphein,* Greek for "to write").

Graver A cutting tool used by engravers and sculptors.

Greek cross plan A cross-shaped design, particularly of a church, in which the arms (nave and transept) are equal in length.

Griffin A mythical creature with the body and back legs of a lion, and the head, talons, and wings of an eagle.

Groin vault In architecture, a vault that is constructed by placing *barrel vaults* at right angles so that a square is covered.

Ground The surface on which a two-dimensional work of art is created; a coat of liquid material applied to a surface that serves as a base for drawing or painting. Also, the background in a composition. Also see *figure–ground relationship.*

Gum A sticky substance found in many plants, used to bind pigments as found, for example, in silverpoint, chalk, and pastel drawings.

Gum arabic A gum obtained from the African acacia plant.

Haniwa A hollow ceramic figure placed at ancient Japanese burial plots.

Hard-edge painting A contemporary style in which geometric forms are rendered with precision but with no distinction between foreground and background.

Hatcher An engraving instrument that produces thousands of tiny pits that will hold ink.

Hatching Fine parallel lines drawn or engraved to represent shading.

Heliography A photographic process in which bitumen is placed on a pewter plate to create a photosensitive surface that is exposed to the sun (from *helios,* Greek for "sun").

Hellenism The culture, thought, and ethical system of ancient Greece.

Herringbone perspective A portrayal of space in which *orthogonals* vanish to a specific point along a vertical line that divides a canvas.

Hierarchical scaling The use of relative size to indicate the comparative importance of the depicted objects or people.

High relief Sculpture that projects from its background by at least half its natural depth. Contrast with *bas relief.*

Horizon In linear perspective, the imaginary line (frequently, where the earth seems to meet the sky) along which converging lines meet. Also see *vanishing point.*

Horizontal balance Balance in which the elements on the left and right sides of the composition seem to be about equal in number or visual emphasis.

Horus The ancient Egyptian sun god.

Hudson River School A group of nineteenth-century American artists whose favorite subjects included the scenery of the Hudson River Valley and the Catskill Mountains of New York State.

Hue Color; the distinctive characteristics of a color that enable us to label it (as blue or green, for example) and to assign it a place in the visible spectrum.

Humanism A system of belief in which humankind is viewed as the standard by which all things are measured.

Hypostyle In architecture, a structure with a roof supported by rows of piers or columns.

Ibex A wild goat.

Iconography A set of conventional meanings attached to images; as an artistic approach, representation or illustration that uses the visual conventions and symbols of a culture.

Iconology The study of visual symbols, which frequently have literary or religious origins.

Idealism The representation of forms according to a concept of perfection.

Illumination Illustration and decoration of a manuscript with pictures or designs.

Illusionistic surrealism A form of *surrealism* that renders the irrational content, absurd juxtapositions, and changing forms of dreams in a highly illusionistic manner that blurs the distinctions between the real and the imaginary.

Imam A prayer leader in a mosque; a religious and temporal ruler of a Muslim community or state.

Imbalance A characteristic of works of art in which the areas of the composition are unequal in *actual weight* or *pictorial weight.*

Impasto Application of a medium such as oil or acrylic paint so that an actual texture is built up on a surface.

Implied line A line that is completed by the viewer; a discontinuous line that the viewer perceives as being continuous; a line suggested by series of points or dots or by the nearby end-points of series of lines; or a line evoked by the movements and glances of the figures in a composition. Contrast with *actual line.*

Implied mass The apparent mass of a depicted object as determined, for example, by the use of forms or fields of color. Contrast with *actual mass.*

Implied motion An impression of movement created by the use of visual elements, composition, or content. Contrast with *actual motion.*

Implied time An impression of time's passage through the depiction of events that occur over a period of time.

Impressionism A late nineteenth-century style characterized by the attempt to capture the fleeting effects of light by painting in short strokes of pure color.

Incise To cut into with a sharp tool.

Industrial design The planning and artistic enhancement of industrial products.

Installation A work of art created for a specific gallery space or outdoor site.

Intaglio A printing process in which metal plates are incised, covered with ink, wiped, and pressed against paper. The print receives the image of the areas that are below the surface of the matrix.

Intarsia A style of decorative mosaic inlay.

International Gothic style A refined style of painting in late fourteenth-century and early fifteenth-century Europe characterized by splendid processions and courtly scenes, ornate embellishment, and attention to detail.

International style A post–World War I school of art and architecture that used modern materials and methods and expressed the view that form must follow function.

Investiture The fire-resistant mold used in metal casting.

Ionic order A moderately ornate Greek architectural style introduced from Asia Minor and characterized by spiral scrolls (*volutes*) on capitals and a continuous *frieze.*

Jamb In architecture, the side post of a doorway, window frame, fireplace, etc.

Jasper A kind of porcelain (also called jasperware) developed by Josiah Wedgwood that is characterized by a dull green or blue surface and raised white designs.

Ka figure According to ancient Egyptian belief, an image of a body in which the soul would dwell after death.

Keystone In architecture, the wedge-shaped stone placed in the top center of an arch to prevent the arch from falling inward.

Kiln An oven used for drying and firing ceramics.

Kinetic art Art that moves, such as the mobile.

Kinetic sculpture Sculpture that actually moves (as opposed to providing the illusion of movement).

Kiva A circular, subterranean structure built by Native Americans of the Southwest for community and ceremonial functions.

Kore figure A clothed female figure of the Greek Archaic style, often adorned with intricate carved detail. A counterpart to the male kouros figure.

Kouros figure The male figure as represented in the sculpture of the geometric and Archaic styles (from Greek for "boy").

Labyrinth Maze.

Lamination The process of building up by layers.

Lapis lazuli An opaque blue, semiprecious stone.

Latin cross plan A cross-shaped church design in which the nave is longer than the transept.

Lavender oil An aromatic oil derived from plants of the mint family.

Lens A transparent substance with at least one curved surface that causes the convergence or divergence of light rays passing through it. In the eye and the camera, lenses are used to focus images onto photosensitive surfaces.

Lift-ground etching A technique in which a sugar solution is brushed onto a resin-coated plate, creating the illusion of a brush-and-ink drawing.

Light The segment of the spectrum of electromagnetic energy that stimulates the eyes and produces visual sensations.

Linear Determined or characterized by the use of line.

Linear perspective A system of organizing space in two-dimensional media in which lines that are in reality parallel and horizontal are represented as converging diagonals. The method is based on foreshortening, in which the space between the lines grows smaller until it disappears, just as objects appear to grow smaller as they become more distant.

Linear recession Depth as perceived through the convergence of lines at specific points in the composition, such as the horizon line.

Lintel In architecture, a horizontal member supported by posts.

Lithography A surface printing process in which an image is drawn onto a matrix with a greasy wax crayon. When dampened, the waxed areas repel water while the material of the matrix absorbs it. An oily ink is then applied, which adheres only to the waxed areas. When the matrix is pressed against

paper, the paper receives the image of the crayon.

Living rock Natural rock formations, as on a mountainside.

Local color The hue of an object created by the colors its surface reflects under normal lighting conditions (contrast with *optical color*). Color that is natural rather than symbolic for the depicted objects.

Logo A distinctive company trademark or signature (short for "logogram" or "logotype").

Longitudinal plan A church design in which the nave is longer than the transept and in which parts are symmetrical against an axis. Contrast with *central plan.*

Longshot In cinematography and video, an image or sequence made from a great distance, providing an overview of a scene.

Loom A machine that weaves thread into yarn or cloth.

Lost-wax technique A bronze-casting process in which an initial mold is made from a model (usually clay) and filled with molten wax. A second, fire-resistant mold is made from the wax, and molten bronze is cast in it.

Lunette A crescent-shaped space or opening (French for "little moon").

Magazine In architecture, a large supply chamber.

Mandala In Hindu and Buddhist traditions, a circular design symbolizing wholeness or unity.

Mannerist art A sixteenth-century, post-Renaissance style characterized by artificial poses and gestures, vivid—sometimes harsh—color, and distorted, elongated figures.

Manuscript illumination Illustration or decoration of books and letters with pictures or designs.

Mass In painting, a large area of one form or color; in three-dimensional art, the bulk of an object. Also see *implied mass* and *actual mass.*

Matrix In printmaking, the working surface of the block, slab, or screen. In sculpture, a mold or hollow shape used to give form to a material that is inserted in a plastic or molten state.

Measure Extent, dimensions, or capacity as determined by a standard.

Medium The materials and methods used to create an image or object in drawing, painting, sculpture, and other arts (from Latin for "means").

Megalith A huge stone, especially as used in prehistoric construction.

Megaron A rectangular room with a two-columned porch.

Mesolithic Of the Middle Stone Age.

Metope In architecture, the panels containing *relief sculpture* that appear between the *triglyphs* of the *Doric frieze.*

Mezzotint A nonlinear engraving process in which the *matrix* is pitted with a *hatcher.*

Middle Ages The thousand-year span (400–1400 CE) from the end of Roman Classical Art to the rebirth of Classical traditions in the Renaissance. Although this period is sometimes referred to as the Dark Ages, it was actually a time of important contributions to economics, science, and the arts.

Mihrab A niche in the wall of a mosque that faces Mecca and thus provides a focus of worship.

Mimesis The practice of exact imitation in artistic representation.

Minaret A tall, slender tower of a mosque from which Muslims are called to prayer.

Minimal art Contemporary art that adheres to the Minimalist philosophy.

Minimalism A twentieth-century style of *non-objective art* in which a minimal number of visual elements are arranged in a simple fashion.

Mixed media The use of two or more media to create a single image.

Mobile A type of *kinetic* sculpture that moves in response to air currents.

Modeling In two-dimensional works of art, the creation of the illusion of depth through the use of light and shade (*chiaroscuro*). In sculpture, the process of shaping a pliable material, such as clay or wax, into a three-dimensional form.

Modernism A contemporary style of architecture that deemphasizes ornamentation and uses recently developed materials of high strength.

Mold A pattern or matrix for giving form to molten or plastic material; a frame on which something is modeled.

Monochromatic Literally, "one-colored"; descriptive of images that are executed in a single color or with so little color contrast as to appear uniform in hue.

Monolith A single, large block of stone; in sculpture, monolithic refers to a work that retains much of the shape of the original block of stone.

Monotype In printmaking, a technique in which paint is brushed onto a matrix that is pressed against a sheet of paper, yielding a single print.

Montage In cinematography or video, the use of flashing, whirling, or abruptly alternating images to convey connected ideas, suggest the passage of time, or provide an emotional effect.

Mortuary temple An Egyptian temple of the New Kingdom in which the pharaoh worshiped and was worshiped after death.

Mosaic A medium in which the ground is wet plaster on an architectural element, such as a wall, into which small pieces (tesserae) of colored tile, stone, or glass are assembled to create an image.

Muezzin Crier who calls Muslims to prayer five times a day from a *minaret.*

Mummification A process by which a body is preserved, often by removing all moisture.

Mural Image(s) painted directly on a wall or intended to cover a wall completely (from *muralis,* Latin for "of a wall").

Mural quality A surface suitable for mural painting.

Narrative editing In cinematography or video, selecting from multiple images of the same subject to advance a story.

Narthex A church vestibule that leads to the nave, constructed for use by the catechumens (individuals preparing to be baptized).

Naturalism Representation that strives to imitate nature rather than to express intellectual theory.

Naturalistic style A style prevalent in Europe during the second half of the nineteenth century that depicted the details of ordinary life.

Nave The central aisle of a church, constructed for use by the congregation at large.

Negative In photography, an exposed and developed film or plate on which values—that is, light and dark—are the reverse of what they are in the actual scene and in the print, or *positive.*

Negative shape Space that is empty or filled with imagery that is secondary to the main objects or figures depicted in the composition. Contrast with *positive shape.*

Neoclassical style An eighteenth-century revival of Classical Greek and Roman art, characterized by simplicity and straight lines.

Neo-Expressionism A violent, figurative style of the second half of the twentieth century that largely revived the German Expressionism of the early twentieth century.

Neolithic Of the New Stone Age.

Neutrals "Colors" (black, white, and gray) that do not contribute to the hue of other colors with which they are mixed.

New image painting An art style of the second half of the twentieth century that sought to reconcile abstraction and representation through the use of simplified images to convey the grandeur of abstract shapes without dominating visual elements such as color and texture.

New Objectivity (Neue Sachlichkeit) A post–World War I German art movement that rebelled against German Expressionism and focused on the detailed representation of objects and figures.

Nib The point of a pen; the split and sharpened end of a quill pen.

Nirvana In Buddhist belief, a state of perfect blessedness in which the individual soul is absorbed into the supreme spirit.

Nonobjective art Art that does not portray figures or objects; art without real models or subject matter.

Nonporous Not containing pores and thus not permitting the passage of fluids.

Nonrepresentational art Art that does not represent figures or objects.

Ocher A dark yellow color derived from an earthy clay.

Oculus In architecture, a round window, particularly one placed at the apex of a dome (from Latin for "eye").

Offset lithography A variation of *lithography* in which the image is hand drawn by the artist on Mylar.

Oil paint Paint in which pigments are combined with an oil medium.

One-point perspective Linear perspective in which a single vanishing point is placed on the horizon.

Op Art A style of art dating from the 1960s that creates the illusion of vibrations through afterimages, disorienting perspective, and the juxtaposition of contrasting colors. Also called "optical art" or "optical painting."

Optical Portrayal of objects as they are seen at the moment, especially depicting the play of light on surfaces. The painting of optical impressions is a hallmark of *Impressionism.*

Optical art See *Op Art.*

Optical color The perception of the color of an object, which may vary markedly according to atmospheric conditions. Contrast with *local color.*

Oran A praying figure.

Organic shape A shape characteristic of living things and thus appearing soft, curvilinear, and irregular. Contrast with *geometric shape.*

Orthogonal Composed of right angles.

Ottonian Of the period characterized by the consecutive reigns of German kings named Otto, beginning in 936 CE.

Oxidizing phase See *black-figure painting.*

Paint A mixture of a pigment with a vehicle or medium.

Painting The application of a pigment to a surface; a work of art created in this manner.

Palatine chapel A chapel that is part of a palace.

Palette A surface on which pigments are placed and prepared and from which the artist works; the artist's choice of colors as seen in a work of art.

Pan To move a motion picture or video camera from side to aide to capture a comprehensive or continuous view of a subject.

Panel painting A painting, usually in tempera but sometimes in oil, whose ground is a wooden panel.

Panorama An unlimited view in all directions.

Papyrus A writing surface made from the papyrus plant.

Parallel editing In cinematography or video, shifting back and forth from one event or story line to another.

Pastel A drawing implement made by grinding coloring matter, mixing it with gum, and forming it into a crayon.

Pastoral Relating to idyllic rural life, especially of shepherds and dairymaids.

Patina A fine crust or film that forms on bronze or copper because of oxidation. It usually provides a desirable greenish or greenish blue tint to the metal.

Patrician A member of the noble class in ancient Rome.

Pattern painting A decorative contemporary style that uses evocative signs, symbols, and patterns.

Pediment In architecture, any triangular shape surrounded by *cornices,* especially one that surmounts the *entablature* of the *portico facade* of Greek temple. The Romans frequently placed pediments without support over windows and doorways.

Pencil A rod-shaped drawing instrument with an inner shaft that is usually made of *graphite.*

Pendentive In architecture, a spherical triangle that fills the wall space between the four arches of a *groin vault* in order to provide a circular base on which a dome may rest.

Peplos In Greek Classical Art, a heavy woolen wrap.

Photography The creation of images by exposure of a photosensitive surface to light.

Photorealism A movement dating from the 1960s in which subjects are rendered with hard, photographic precision.

Photosensitive Descriptive of a surface that is sensitive to light and therefore capable of recording images.

Photo silkscreen A variation of *serigraphy,* or *silkscreen printing,* that allows the artist to create photographic images on a screen covered with a light-sensitive gel.

Piazza An open public square or plaza.

Pictograph A simplified symbol of an object or action; for example, a schematized or abstract form of an ancestral image, animal, geometric form, anatomic part, or shape suggestive of a cosmic symbol or microscopic life.

Pictorial balance The distribution of the apparent or *visual weight* of elements in two-dimensional works of art. Contrast with *actual balance.*

Picture plane The flat, two-dimensional surface on which a picture is created. In much Western art, the picture plane is viewed as a window opening onto deep space.

Pier In architecture, a columnlike support with a rectilinear rather than cylindrical profile. Piers generally support arches.

Pigment Coloring matter that is usually mixed with water, oil, or other substances to make paint.

Pilaster In architecture, a decorative element that recalls the shape of a structural *pier.* Pilasters are attached to the wall plane and project very little. They may have all the visual elements of piers, including base, shaft, *capital,* and *entablature* above.

Pile weave A weave in which knots are tied, then cut, forming an even surface.

Plain weave A weave in which the woof thread passes above one warp fiber and below the next.

Planar recession Perspective in which the illusion of depth is created through parallel planes that appear to recede from the picture plane.

Planographic printing Any method of printing from a flat surface, such as *lithography.*

Plastic elements Those elements of a work of art, such as line, shape, color, and texture, that artists manipulate to achieve desired effects.

Plasticity Capacity of a material to be molded or shaped.

Plebeian class In ancient Rome, the common people.

Plywood Sheets of wood that resist warping because they are constructed of layers glued together with the grain oriented in different directions.

Pointed arch An arch that comes to a point rather than curves at the top.

Pointillism A systematic method of applying minute dots of unmixed pigment to the canvas; the dots are intended to be "mixed" by the eye when viewed. Also called "divisionism."

Pop Art An art style originating in the 1960s that uses commercial and popular images and themes as its subject matter.

Porcelain A hard, white, translucent, nonporous clay body. The *bisque* is fired at a relatively low temperature and the *glaze* at a high temperature.

Portico The entrance facade of a Greek temple, adapted for use with other buildings and consisting of a *colonnade, entablature,* and *pediment* (from Greek for "porch").

Positive shape The spatial form defined by the objects or figures represented in works of art. Contrast with *negative shape.*

Post-and-beam construction Construction in which vertical elements (posts) and horizontal timbers (beams) are pieced together with wooden pegs.

Post-and-lintel construction Construction in which vertical elements (posts) are used to support horizontal crosspieces (lintels). Also termed "trabeated structure."

Postimpressionism A late nineteenth-century style that relies on the gains made by Impressionists in terms of the use of color and spontaneous brushwork but that employs these elements as expressive devices. The Postimpressionists, however, rejected the essentially decorative aspects of Impressionist subject matter.

Postmodernism A contemporary style that arose as a reaction to Modernism and that returns to ornamentation drawn from Classical and historical sources.

Pottery Pots, bowls, dishes, and similar wares made of clay and hardened by heat; a shop at which such objects are made.

Poussiniste Those Neoclassical artists who took Nicolas Poussin as their model. Contrast with *Rubeniste.*

Prefabricate In architecture, to build beforehand at a factory rather than at the building site.

Pre-Hellenic Of ancient Greece before the eighth century BCE.

Primary color A hue—red, blue, or yellow—that is not obtained by mixing other hues; all other colors are derived from primary colors.

Print In printmaking, a picture or design made by pressing or hitting a surface with a plate or block; in photography, a photograph, especially one made from a negative.

Prism A transparent, polygonal body that breaks down white light into the colors of the visible spectrum.

Proportion The relationship of the size of the parts to the whole.

Propylaeum In architecture, a gateway building leading to an open court in front of a Greek or Roman temple; specifically, such a building on the Acropolis.

Psychic automatism A process of generating imagery through ideas received from the unconscious mind and expressed in an unrestrained manner.

Quarry tile Reddish brown tile, similar to terracotta.

Quatrefoil In architecture, a design made up of four converging arcs that are similar in appearance to a flower with four petals.

Quill A pen made from a large, stiff feather.

Radial balance Balance in which the design elements radiate from a center point.

Radiating chapel An apse-shaped chapel, several of which generally radiate from the *ambulatory* in a *Latin cross plan.*

Rasp A rough file that has raised points instead of ridges.

Rationalism The belief that ethical conduct is determined by reason; in philosophy, the theory that knowledge is derived from the intellect, without the aid of the senses.

Readymade Found objects that are exhibited as works of art, frequently after being placed in a new context with a new title.

Realism A style characterized by accurate and truthful portrayal of subject matter; a nineteenth-century style that portrayed subject matter in this manner.

Rectangular bay system A church plan in which rectangular *bays* serve as the basis for the overall design. Contrast with *square schematism.*

Rectilinear Characterized by straight lines.

Reducing phase See *black-figure painting.*

Reformation A social and religious movement of sixteenth-century Europe in which various groups attempted to reform the Roman Catholic Church by establishing rival religions (Protestant sects).

Register A horizontal segment of a structure or work of art.

Regular repetition The systematic repetition of the visual elements in a work to create *rhythm.*

Reinforced concrete Concrete that is strengthened by steel rods or mesh. Same as *ferroconcrete.*

Relative size The size of an object or figure in relation to other objects or figures or the setting. See *scale.*

Relief printing Any printmaking technique in which the matrix is carved with knives so that the areas not meant to be printed (that is, not meant to leave an image) are below the surface of the matrix.

Relief sculpture Sculpture that is carved to ornament architecture or furniture, as opposed to *freestanding sculpture.* Also see *bas-relief* and *high relief.*

Renaissance A period spanning the fourteenth and fifteenth centuries CE in Europe. The Renaissance (French for "rebirth") rejected medieval art and philosophy; it first turned to Classical antiquity for inspiration and then developed patterns of art and philosophy that paved the way toward the modern world.

Reoxidizing phase See *black-figure painting.*

Representational art Art that presents natural objects in recognizable form.

Republican period The Roman period lasting from the victories over the Etruscans to the death of Julius Caesar (527–509 BCE).

Resolution In video and digital photography, the sharpness of a picture as determined by the number of lines or pixels composing the picture.

Rhythm The orderly repetition or progression of the visual elements in a work of art.

Rib In Gothic architecture, a structural member that reinforces the stress points of *groin vaults.*

Rococo An eighteenth-century style during the Baroque era that is characterized by lighter colors, greater wit, playfulness, occasional eroticism, and yet more ornate decoration.

Romanesque style A style of European architecture of the eleventh and twelfth centuries that is characterized by thick, massive walls, the *Latin cross plan,* the use of a *barrel vault* in the *nave,* round arches, and a twin-towered facade.

Romanticism A nineteenth-century movement that rebelled against academic Neoclassicism by seeking extremes of emotion as enhanced by virtuoso brushwork and a brilliant palette.

Root five rectangle A rectangle whose length is 2.236 (the square root of 5) times its width that can be constructed by rotating the diagonal of a half square left and right.

Rosette A painted or sculpted circular ornament with petals and leaves radiating from the center.

Rose window A large circular window in a Gothic church, assembled in segments that resemble the petals of a flower, usually adorned with stained glass and plantlike ornamental work.

Rubeniste Those Romantic artists who took Peter Paul Rubens as their model. Contrast with *Poussiniste.*

Salon An annual exhibition of the French Academy held in the spring during the eighteenth and nineteenth centuries.

Salon d'Automne An independent exhibition of experimental art held in the autumn of 1905; named the "Salon of Autumn" to distinguish it from the Academic salons that were usually held in the spring.

Sanguine Blood colored, ruddy; cheerful and confident (from Latin for "blood").

Sarcophagus A coffin or tomb, especially one made of limestone.

Satin weave A weave in which the woof passes above and below several warp threads at a time.

Saturation The degree of purity of hue measured by its intensity or brightness.

Scale The relative size of an object compared to other objects, the setting, or people.

Sculpture The art of carving, casting, modeling, or assembling materials into three-dimensional figures or forms; a work of art made in such a manner.

S curve Developed in the Classical style as a means of balancing the human form, consisting of the distribution of tensions so that tension and repose are passed back and forth from one side of the figure to the other, resulting in an S shape; *contrapposto.*

Seal A design or stamp placed on a document as a sign of authenticity.

Secondary color A color that is derived from mixing pigments of primary colors in equal amounts. The secondary colors are orange (obtained by mixing red and yellow), violet (red and blue), and green (blue and yellow).

Serigraphy A printmaking process in which stencils are applied to a screen of silk or similar material stretched on a frame. Paint or ink is forced through the open areas of the stencil onto paper beneath. Also termed *silkscreen printing.*

Service systems In architecture, mechanical systems that provide structures with transportation, heat, electricity, waste removal, and other services.

Shade The degree of darkness of a color determined by the extent of its mixture with black.

Shaft grave A vertical hole in the ground in which one or more bodies are buried.

Shape An area within a composition that has boundaries that separate it from its surroundings.

Shaped canvas A canvas that departs from the traditional rectangle and often extends the work into three-dimensional space, thus challenging the traditional orientation of a painting.

Shinto A major religion of Japan that emphasizes nature and ancestor worship.

Shiva The Hindu god of destruction and regeneration.

Shrine A repository for sacred relics and art objects intended to arouse feelings of religious devotion. A small structure or area intended for private religious devotion; a site or structure used in religious devotion.

Shutter In photography, a device for opening and closing the aperture of a lens so that the film is exposed to light.

Siding In architecture, a covering for an exterior wall.

Silica A hard, glossy mineral compound of silicon and oxygen.

Silkscreen printing A printmaking process in which stencils are applied to a screen of silk or similar material stretched on a frame. Paint or ink is forced through the open areas of the stencil onto paper beneath. Also termed *serigraphy.*

Silverpoint A drawing medium in which a silver-tipped instrument inscribes lines on a surface that has been coated with a *ground* or pigment.

Slip In ceramics, clay that is thinned to the consistency of cream for use in casting, decorating, or cementing.

Slow motion A cinematographic process in which action is made to appear fluid but slower than actual motion by shooting a greater than usual number of frames per second and then projecting the film at the usual number of frames per second.

Soft-ground etching An etching technique in which a ground of softened wax yields effects similar to those of pencil or crayon drawings.

Sound track An area on the side of a strip of motion picture film that carries a record of the sound accompanying the visual information.

Square schematism A church plan in which the crossing square serves as the basis for determining the overall dimensions of the building. Contrast with *rectangular bay system.*

Squeegee A T-shaped tool with a rubber blade used to remove liquid from a surface.

Stainless steel Steel that has been alloyed with chromium or other metals to make it virtually immune to corrosion.

Stamp To impress or imprint with a mark or design.

Steel A hard, tough metal composed of iron, carbon, and other metals, such as nickel or chromium.

Steel cable A strong cable composed of multiple intertwined steel wires.

Steel-cage construction A method of building that capitalizes on the strength of steel by piecing together slender steel beams to form the skeleton of a structure.

Stele (or **stela**) An engraved stone slab or pillar that serves as a grave marker.

Stereoscopy An illusion of three-dimensionality created by simultaneously viewing two photographs of a scene taken from slightly different angles (as the scene would be seen by a pair of eyes).

Stippling Drawing or painting small dots or dabs to create shading or a dappled effect.

Stoicism The philosophy that the universe is governed by natural laws and that people should follow virtue, as determined by reason, and remain indifferent to passion or emotion.

Stoneware A ceramic that is fired at 2,300°F–2,700°F. The resulting object is usually gray but can be tan or reddish. Stoneware is nonporous or slightly porous and is used in dinnerware and ceramic sculpture.

Stop In photography, the aperture of a lens, which is typically adjustable; the "f-number."

Stopped time In photography, an image that captures action in midmovement by exposing the film very briefly.

Stroboscopic motion The creation of the illusion of movement by the presentation of a rapid progression of stationary images, such as the frames of a motion picture.

Stupa A dome-shaped Buddhist shrine.

Style A characteristic manner or mode of artistic expression or design.

Stylobate A continuous base or platform that supports a row of columns.

Stylus A pointed, needlelike tool used in drawing, printmaking, making impressions on electronic media, and so on.

Subtractive process In sculpture, the removal of material, as in carving. Contrast with *additive process.*

Subversive texture Texture that is chosen or created by artists to foil or undermine our ideas about the objects that they depict.

Support A surface on which a two-dimensional work of art is made.

Surrealism A twentieth-century art style whose imagery is believed to stem from unconscious, irrational sources and that therefore takes on *fantastic* forms. Although the imagery is fantastic, it is often rendered with extraordinary realism.

Symmetrical balance Balance in which imagery on one side of a composition is mirrored on the other side. Symmetrical balance can be pure, or it can be *approximate,* in which case the whole of the work has a symmetrical feeling but with slight variations that provide more visual interest than would a mirror image. Contrast with *asymmetrical balance.*

Symmetry Similarity of form or arrangement on both sides of a dividing line.

Synthetic Cubism The second phase of Cubism, which emphasized the form of the object and constructing rather than disintegrating that form.

Synthetism Gauguin's theory of art, which advocated the use of broad areas of unnatural color and primitive or symbolic subject matter.

Telephoto lens A lens that is shaped and distanced from the photosensitive surface so that it produces large images of distant objects.

Tempera A kind of painting in which pigments are mixed with casein, size, or egg—particularly egg yolk—to create a dull finish.

Tenebrism A style of painting in which the artist goes rapidly from highlighting to deep shadow, using very little modeling.

Tensile strength The degree to which a material can withstand being stretched.

Terra-cotta A hard, reddish brown earthenware used in sculpture and pottery; usually left unglazed.

Tertiary colors Colors derived from mixing pigments or primary colors and the secondary colors that adjoin them on the color wheel.

Texture The surface character of materials as experienced by the sense of touch.

Texture gradient The relative roughness of nearby and distant objects in two-dimensional media; nearby objects are usually rendered with more detailed and rougher surfaces than distant objects.

Tholos In architecture, a beehive-shaped tomb.

Throwing (a pot) In ceramics, the process of shaping that takes place on the potter's wheel.

Tie-dyeing Making designs by sewing or tying folds in cloth to prevent a dye from reaching certain areas.

Tier A row or rank.

Tint The lightness of a color as determined by the extent of its mixture with white.

Transept The "arms" of a *Latin cross plan,* used by pilgrims and other visitors for access to the area behind the crossing square.

Transverse rib In architecture, a rib that connects the midpoints of a *groin vault.*

Tribune gallery In architecture, the space between the *nave* arcade and the *clerestory* that is used for traffic above the side aisles on the second stage of the elevation.

Triforium In a church, a gallery or arcade in the wall above the arches of the *nave, transept,* or *choir.*

Triglyph In architecture, a panel incised with vertical grooves (usually three; hence, *tri-glyph*) that serve to divide the scenes in a *Doric frieze.*

Trompe l'oeil A painting or other art form that creates such a realistic image that the viewer may wonder whether it is real or an illusion (from French for "fool the eye").

Truss A rigid, triangular frame used for supporting structures such as roofs and bridges.

Twill weave A weave with broken diagonal patterns.

Two-point perspective Linear perspective in which two vanishing points are placed on the horizon line.

Tympanum Semicircular space above the doors of a cathedral.

Typography The art of designing, arranging, and setting type for printing.

Umber A kind of earth that has a yellowish or reddish brown color.

Unity The oneness or wholeness of a work of art.

Upper Paleolithic The later years of the Old Stone (Paleolithic) Age.

Value The lightness or darkness of a color.

Value contrast The degrees of difference between shades of gray.

Vanishing point In linear perspective, a point on the horizon where parallel lines appear to converge.

Vantage point The actual or apparent spot from which a viewer observes an object or picture.

Vault In architecture, any series of arches other than an *arcade* used to create space. See *barrel vault* and *groin vault.*

Vehicle A liquid such as water or oil with which pigments are mixed for painting.

Veneer In architecture, a thin layer of high-quality material used to enhance the appearance of the facade of a structure.

Venus The Roman goddess of beauty; a prehistoric fertility figure, such as the Venus of Willendorf.

Venus pudica A Venus with her hand held over her genitals for modesty.

Vertical balance Balance in which the elements in the top and bottom of the composition are in balance.

Video A catch-all term for several arts that use a video screen or monitor, including, but not limited to, commercial and public television, *video art,* and *computer graphics.*

Video art Works that use a video screen or an assemblage of screens or monitors; images shown on video monitors.

Visible light That segment of the spectrum of electromagnetic energy that excites the eyes and produces visual sensations.

Visitation In Roman Catholicism, the visit of the Virgin Mary to Elizabeth; a church feast commemorating the visit.

Visual elements Elements, such as line, shape, color, and texture, that are used by artists to create imagery. Also termed *plastic elements.*

Visual texture Simulated texture in a work of art; the use of line, color, and other visual elements to create the illusion of various textures in flat drawings and paintings. Contrast with *abstract texture.*

Visual unity The unity in a work of art as created by use of visual elements. Contrast with *conceptual unity.*

Vitrify To become hard, glassy, and nonporous.

Volume The mass or bulk of a three-dimensional work; the amount of space such a work contains.

Volute In architecture, a spiral scroll ornamenting an Ionic or Corinthian capital.

Volute krater A wide-mouthed vessel (krater) with scroll-shaped handles.

Voussoir A wedge-shaped stone block used in the construction of an arch.

Ware Pottery or porcelain; a good to be sold by a merchant.

Warm color Colors—reds, oranges, and yellows—that appear to be warm and to advance toward the viewer. Contrast with *cool colors.*

Warp In weaving, the threads that run lengthwise in a loom and are crossed by the weft or woof.

Wash A thin, watery film of paint, especially watercolor, applied with even, sweeping movements of the brush.

Watercolor A paint with a water medium. Watercolors are usually made by mixing pigments with a gum binder and thinning the mixture with water.

Weaving The making of fabrics by the interlacing of threads or fibers, as on a loom.

Webbing In architecture, a netlike structure that composes that part of a ribbed vault that lies between the ribs.

Weft In weaving, the yarns that are carried back and forth across the warp. Also called *woof.*

Weight-shift principle The situating of the human figure so that the legs and hips are turned in one direction and the chest and arms in another. This shifting of weight results in a diagonal balancing of tension and relaxation. See *contrapposto.*

Wide-angle lens A lens that covers a wider angle of view than an ordinary lens.

Woodcut Relief printing in which the grain of a wooden matrix is carved with a knife.

Wood engraving A type of relief printing in which a hard, laminated, nondirectional wood surface is used as the matrix.

Woof See *weft.*

Wordwork A contemporary work of art whose imagery consists of words.

Zen a Buddhist sect that seeks inner harmony through introspection and meditation.

Ziggurat A temple tower in the form or a terraced pyramid, built by ancient Assyrians and Babylonians.

Zoogyroscope An early motion-picture projector.

Zoom To use a zoom lens, which can be adjusted to provide long shots or close-ups while keeping the image in focus.

INDEX